UNCERTAIN TERMS

Uncertain Terms

NEGOTIATING GENDER
IN AMERICAN CULTURE

EDITED BY FAYE GINSBURG
&
ANNA LOWENHAUPT TSING

BEACON PRESS · BOSTON

Beacon Press
25 Beacon Street
Boston, Massachusetts 02108-2800

Beacon Press books
are published under the auspices of
the Unitarian Universalist Association of Congregations.

97 96 95 94 93 92 91 90   8 7 6 5 4 3 2 1

Text design by Linda Koegel

Library of Congress Cataloging-in-Publication Data

Uncertain terms : negotiating gender in American culture / edited by
    Faye Ginsburg & Anna Lowenhaupt Tsing.
        p.   cm.
    Includes index.
    ISBN 0-8070-4612-4
    1. Feminism—United States.   2. Sex role—United States.
    3. Women—United States—Social conditions.   I. Ginsburg, Faye D.
    II. Tsing, Anna Lowenhaupt.
    HQ1426.U48   1990
    305.42'0973—dc20   90-52587
                                                            CIP

To Fred Myers and the late Michelle Rosaldo
for the inspiration and intellectual and emotional support
they have provided over the years

CONTENTS

INTRODUCTION

FAYE GINSBURG AND
ANNA LOWENHAUPT TSING

Are you an Asian woman with a serenely silky heart, 22–32? If so, please respond to balance the jade heart of a 6ft caucasian male, 36.

Spunky Bi Mom, 29, seeks relationship with caring person who values fun, family, community. No drug, alc, or rigid sex roles.

NO MORE POVERTY is yours if we click. I'm a successful SWM businessman. If you love a country lifestyle and a caring man, write me today. One child is fine.

Donor wanted. SJF, 39, wishes to have child but has no mate! Send medical history, photo, and note.

SWM 32, seeks dominant female who will train me to serve her properly. Wish only to please. Write with your list of demands.[1]

An exciting array of choices, or a litany of oppressive stereotypes? These personal ads—like so many gendered representations in the contemporary U.S.—offer us both. A seductive variety of "male" and "female" lifestyle options, political beliefs, and work and family roles—"alternative," "neo-traditional," "postfeminist"—appear available to the consumer as yet one more way to refashion the self, to be born again. Yet clearly the ideal of a free market of gender identities is an illusion. Each individual finds the way blocked at so many points; no choice escapes the daily injustices of poverty, racism, male dominance. Nonetheless, remarkable possibilities for reshaping gender do seem to have emerged in the last few decades. Do diversity and change disguise the stable contours of oppression? Or do they reveal the shapes of creative resistance and empowerment?

This volume takes up the challenge of such questions, central to under-standing gender in the United States. The contributors are American an-thropologists and feminist scholars who have turned their ethnographic gaze homeward to everyday life in our own society. Specifically, the essays explore how, in American culture, diverse understandings of gender, reproduction, and sexuality are constructed in a variety of settings.[2] Combining insights from both political economy and cultural and interpretive approaches in anthropology, we are interested in how meanings shape and are shaped by social processes and institutions.

The essays share the theoretical assumption that gender is not a unified category, but a many-faceted one, open to change and variation. Since gender's multiplicity is most clearly visible in moments of social and cultural discord,[3] many of the studies focus on situations in which the definitions and activities marked as female and male are in contention. The authors address these contested domains from an unapologetically engaged position. We are studying issues and conflicts that involve us as both analysts and actors. We are conscious of the political significance of research on both publicly debated topics such as abortion, teen pregnancy, and reproductive technologies, and on ongoing, local tensions in workplaces, communities, schools, and churches.

The theme of the collection is how gender is negotiated in the contemporary United States. By "gender" we mean the ways a society organizes people into male and female categories and the ways meanings are produced around those categories. In these essays, gender is seen not as fixed or "natural" but rather as a category subject to change, and specifically to *negotiation*. We concentrate on the idea of negotiation because it suggests a dynamic approach to understanding "difference," a concern that has preoccupied, in varied ways, much recent theory in anthropology, feminism, and post-structuralist philosophy.[4] This recent work has broken up monolithic categories such as "culture" and "society" by focusing on those people—particularly women and ethnic or racial minorities—who offer alternative perspectives and resistance to dominant institutions and ideas. As ethnographers, we pay attention to the ways in which people learn, accept, negotiate and resist the categories of "difference" that define and constrain them in everyday life.

Taken together, the articles in this collection articulate and combine two senses of "negotiating gender." They show how gendered terms and social relations are debated and redefined by people pursuing particular and often conflicting interests—as in negotiating a deal; and, they show women and men struggling with the ideas and institutions with which they live—as in negotiating a river.

The authors share another concern of much recent theory in exploring *how* gender gains definition and power in certain "discourses."[5] We understand discourses to involve both ways of speaking and clusters of nonverbal practices as these create and maintain social categories and identities. Thus, scientific language and institutions form a discourse; American debates regarding right-wing policy in the 1980s generated a discourse. Insofar as they shape relations among social actors and maintain patterns of dominance in institutions and social processes, discourses are always political. Indeed, political struggle comes about as the terms that create our ideas of what we want and deserve, and who we are, are challenged and redefined. Discourses can be displaced, or transformed. The concept of discourse thus can serve to break up the unity and homogeneity of classical anthropological understandings of "culture." The volume's contributors are also interested in the more literal sense of discourse. Anthropologists have always relied on what people say about themselves. The contributors here move beyond summaries and interpretations of this talk. They extend methods borrowed from literary criticism to look at its genres, its vocabulary, its narrative moves, its dialogic responses, and its social context.

The collection enters a discussion that has developed since the late 1960s with the growth of "second wave" feminism in the United States.[6] In the context of social transformations involving women in the late twentieth century—the growing number of women in the work force and in higher education, the rise in the divorce rate, the legalization and increased use of contraception and abortion, the decline in birthrate, and the increase in households headed by single mothers—second wave feminism has created a vocabulary that disrupts assumptions about men and women and offers new ways to speak of gender and power. Feminists have argued against older, sexist perspectives; they also have argued against each other. The complexities of how feminists, and women more generally, have responded to legal battles around surrogate motherhood or pornography are two recent examples of such disagreements. The arguments often reflect the unevenness of women's circumstances in daily negotiations of race, class, and sexuality. Because this volume reflects and addresses new feminist concerns with diversity, it is important to understand the evolution of these ideas especially as they pertain to anthropology.

FEMINISM, ANTHROPOLOGY, AND THE CHALLENGE OF DIVERSITY

American feminists concerned with the heterogeneity of women's interests have worked to enlarge an earlier feminist focus on male-female difference that assumed that all women's experiences were similar. This project has been best put forward by women of color. Writers such as bell hooks and Barbara Smith have criticized the racism and class bias that result when privileged white women universalize their culturally and historically specific agendas as if they were the goals of "all women." In writing about their experiences, women of color, particularly lesbians, have broadened feminist studies beyond issues important to white, middle-class, heterosexual women. Others have rediscovered a more inclusive history of women activists working for their communities—but not always on white feminists' terms.[7]

The revitalization of U.S. feminist theory by women of color has been especially welcome in a theoretical climate bogged down in generalizations removed from the dilemmas of social life that initially catalyzed second wave feminism. Many of the most visible strands of feminist theory in the last decade have assumed a homogeneous and pervasive framework of sexual difference. For example, in the 1970s, cultural feminists argued that gender differences underlie all other forms of inequality.[8] Many American psychological scholars have assumed a ubiquitous divide between male and female modes of self-definition, even when working from perspectives as different as socialization theory,[9] psychoanalysis,[10] or moral reasoning.[11] Many literary critics working with deconstruction and Lacanian psychoanalysis also take gender as a basic "signifier" of difference underlying all human communication.[12]

Such gender frameworks—ones that look for universal patterns—have an enduring appeal; for many feminist scholars, such theories have seemed the most satisfyingly "theoretical," as they battled to create academically legitimate theory against the backdrop of established intellectual traditions—the various Marxisms, structuralisms, psychoanalyses, etc. This is probably why feminist anthropology, which in the early 1970s focused on questions of women's universal subordination, was one of the most visible wings of women's studies at that time. Early second wave feminists posed questions for anthropologists regarding the world-wide origins and scope of gender inequality, male dominance, and patriarchy. In response, feminist anthropologists provided global answers. Some argued that women's childbearing and childrearing roles everywhere orient women to "domestic" concerns (in contrast to men's wider reaching "public" orientations),[13] or that these roles create symbolic associations in which "female" is more closely tied to the "natural" world and thus seems less fully "cultural" than "male."[14] Others suggested that women are everywhere subordinated as objects of male sexual and marital exchange.[15] Demanding more attention to history, those working in a Marxist framework rejected the idea of universal differences.[16] Yet in the 1970s some Marxists proposed rather global evolutionary schemes of their own. Gender inequalities, they argued, emerged with the rise of the state and private property,[17] while in more egalitarian pre-class societies, women and men enjoyed equal respect.[18]

All these explanations relied on an ethnographic record that itself had been shaped by the assumption that gender, despite cross-cultural differences, was everywhere constituted in the same way. However, as feminist researchers set out asking new questions about gender and male dominance, they found themselves describing a variety of cases that defied universalizing ethnocentric stereotypes, feminist and otherwise. For example, they described cultures without gender dichotomies of nature/culture or public/private.[19] They described lineage groups in which women as "sisters" have important public roles,[20] and matrimonial arrangements in which elder women often exercise as much influence as men.[21] Faced with contradictions between their training in recognizing cultural uniqueness and the generality of the currently popular frameworks of comparison, many researchers challenged the generalizations. By the 1980s, the theoretical challenge in feminist anthropology was to avoid global explanations in order to appreciate the diverse forms of gender cross-culturally and cross-historically.[22]

Many feminist anthropologists turned to the study of gender as one aspect of systems of inequality that might also include age, rank, ethnicity, class, etc. By investigating how different principles of inequality fit together, they created models of specific types of "gender systems" to replace the grand schemes of the 1970s.[23] For example, anthropologists studied the ways marriage conventions played an integral part in reproducing race and class hierarchies in colonial Cuba,[24] and the ways gender ideologies reproduced assymetries between elder and junior men in African tribal systems.[25]

Yet these models carried their own problems, particularly their insensitivity to issues of agency and the subjectivity of social actors. By the late 1980s there was again a call for more complex directions of analysis, this time to reveal the heterogeneity and instability of social and cultural processes even within societies.[26] Joining dialogue with scholars from other disciplines, feminist anthropologists developed new concerns with competing discourses, divergent forms of consciousness, and modes of resistance to oppressive circumstances.[27]

Rather than privileging a single arena, such as socialization or the structure of marriage, the essays in this volume show gender heterogeneously produced in a variety of social sites, including schools, clinics, churches, courtrooms, shopfloors, and social movements. By investigating these diverse locations, the essays suggest the complexity of gender formation in a single "culture." They undermine stereotypes in scholarship and popular culture that identify gender only with parenthood, sexuality, or the family; these stereotypes—looked at in their historical contexts—become objects of study rather than directives for study. Furthermore, gender is viewed as intertwined with other identities and forms of difference involving race, ethnicity, class, sexual preference, religion, and politics, to name a few.

In *Uncertain Terms,* women are recognized as active and self-conscious participants in constructing and contesting gender roles and other identities. The authors show gender refigured in social movements, strikes, and other forms of political activity. And while feminism's influence is central to these gender negotiations, the essays show that there is no single, static set of "women's interests," nor a monolithic debate between "feminist" and "nonfeminist" ideas.

In exploring women's subjective experience and the interplay of everyday consciousness with dominant ideology, a number of the contributors make use of the insights of feminist post-structuralist criticism. Such approaches stress that women's and men's identities are fragmented, multi-faceted, and shift in different contexts.[28] In this volume, however, such insights are extended beyond textual analysis to investigate how *social processes* produce, challenge, or confirm gender categories.

CONTRADICTIONS OF GENDER IN AMERICAN CULTURE

As the authors grapple with contemporary dilemmas in American culture, two themes in particular recur. First, many of the essays address the tensions between women's actual experience, on the one hand, and universalizing American ideals of women as selfless, nurturant mothers, on the other. Second (and not unrelated), many of the contributors explore the diversity of women's identities as workers, community members, and activists. The tensions between ideals and experience are a legacy of conditions that shaped the gender division of labor in the United States over two hundred years ago, and that have endured in varied forms since then.

Historically in the United States, "domestic" and "public" have been cast as separate but interrelated female and male spheres.[29] Since industrialization, the differentiation of "the home" as a woman's domain separate from "the workplace" was accompanied by the elaboration of the tasks and cultural meaning attached to housework, childrearing, and family care. Yet, despite its valorization, domestic labor remained unpaid in the household (or was underpaid and performed by women of disadvantaged class positions). In the discourses that evolved along with such arrangements, women were considered nurturers, exempt from the world of commerce and more interested in motherhood and the welfare of others than in their own needs. In contrast, the world of wage work was considered a male domain, a place of competitive, self-interested, individual achievement. Men's and women's social experience is clearly not congruent with such categories. African American wives and mothers, for example, have always had a very high rate of participation in the labor force. Yet the valorization of motherhood and the gendered separation of home and work continue to frame discussion, debate, and agendas for change involving the rights and roles of women and men.

Many of the essays in this volume document transformations in political, legal, and medical discourses on mothering that have rocked American culture in the last decade. However, as many of the authors point out, motherhood remains a contradictory status for women in the United States: it is both a constraint and a source of power. For example, in exploring reproduction as a contested domain, the volume shows why, despite the inroads of feminism, sanctions are imposed on those who differ from dominant norms of sexuality and parenting. The infertility of white middle aged professional women is regarded as their own failure; the fertility of teenage mothers is described as irresponsible. The very different circumstances that shape women's lives are often obscured by universalizing cultural assumptions. And these assumptions are extremely powerful as they are entrenched in the practices of institutions. Divorced mothers, for example, must conform to the legal system's rigid notions about "good mothers" in order to retain access to their children.

Without a clear vision of women's varied statuses, histories, and choices in relation to mothering, well-intentioned feminist projects can appear to be at cross-purposes. Attempts to make medical care more widely available to pregnant women are crucial but sometimes appear to ignore critiques that show patriarchal medicine holding questionable control over women's bodies. Feminist calls for respecting female nurturance of children can place feminists in an uneasy alliance with those who are contemptuous of women who do not have children, or who would limit women's rights to choose whether, when, and with whom to raise children. Questions regarding women's reproduction cannot be separated from social and economic inequalities in wage levels, parental benefits and leaves, daycare, health care, access to housing, equitable custody and support, discrimination against single and gay parents, and the like. In short, the volume's contributors underscore an appreciation for differences among women, within a continuing critique of inequality.

At the same time, many of the essays demonstrate how discourses on female nurturance are powerful and persuasive. They show how in recent years nurturance is no longer assumed to be natural to women but—as motherhood becomes socially recognized more as a matter of choice—is something to be *achieved*. Contemporary American women share with their foremothers an understanding of nurturance as a source of moral authority in their claims to political power. Yet, even as nurturance has been the basis for women's collective action to change society, it is also the source of their devaluation. Indeed, when women engage in efforts, small or large, to re-shape the social order, they always face a contradiction: they must work within their own culture's understandings of gender to establish the social power they need to transcend those categories that constrain them.

This contradiction is evident in how women are excluded from workplaces historically associated with men, as well as from discourses on work and social change. Until recently, class analyses ignored the work of women, who were too often acknowledged only as domestic support for men. A number of essays in this volume continue efforts of many feminists to show the importance of women's paid and unpaid labor.[30] Building on earlier work that stressed structures of gender and class exploitation, these authors explore stratification as well as agency and activism. They show the limitations of the cultural and analytic division between home and workplace as they demonstrate how family, community, and workplace relations mutually shape consciousness and action.

The authors' efforts to integrate gender into class analysis does not just create more sophisticated class analysis; it leads to entirely new models of social change. Many of the essays turn attention to the complex identities of the women and men who create change and the historical events that move them to challenge the assumptions of their workplaces and communities. This scholarship acknowledges families and communities as internally divided, contradictory sites. Kin and neighbors may provide a source of strength for women's activism in and out of the workplace, but their expectations may also undermine women's self-assertions. Indeed, in exploring the contradictions of these "ties that bind," the essays signal an important shift from an older search for a separatist solidarity—of class consciousness, community values, or female experience—to a new goal of collective action based on alliances that require a continual awareness of differences.[31]

Finally, the rejection of comfortable "home"-like solidarities becomes complete when the multifaceted nature of individual subjectivity is taken into account. Because each individual is situated in a complex relationship with the privileges and constraints of gender, class, race, ethnic, and sexual hierarchies, individual subjectivity—how the self is constituted and experienced—is also a site of contradictions. As feminist philosopher Teresa de Lauretis has argued, "differences among women are also differences within women"[32]—since all women hold multiple identities. An individual's position in a web of intersecting inequalities has too often been interpreted, and experienced, as paralyzing; yet an awareness of this complexity can also be politically empowering as it suggests new modes of self-respect and alliance.

ORGANIZATION OF THE VOLUME

The themes discussed above are the contemporary dilemmas with which the volume's essays are engaged. The book is divided into five parts, reflecting the themes of its theoretical as well as ethnographic contributions. Each part amplifies one aspect of contemporary scholarly conversations about gender in American culture.

The essays in the first part, "Backtalking Feminism and Femininity," challenge universal gender stereotypes; they show how race, class, and ethnicity give distinct shape to women's and men's gender identities. Katie Stewart introduces the term "backtalk" to refer to the contentious dialogue of Appalachian women through which they build community ties and differentiate themselves from men and from the dominant culture. Stewart shows how these women use talk to play with, expand, and undermine gender categories. Carol Stack similarly refers to "talking back," in her case talking back to feminist theories that universalize white middle-class agendas. Stack's study challenges Carol Gilligan's well-known theories of gendered moral reasoning. Among the African American return migrants to the South whom Stack studied, men and women are equally oriented to "caretaking" and "justice"; gender difference appears not in stated moral commitments, but in forms of action in the larger community. Rayna Rapp also speaks against overgeneralizations, feminist and otherwise, regarding the impact of new reproductive technologies. Rapp's study of pregnant women's responses to amniocentesis shows how ethnicity, race, and class affect their interpretations of medical language presented to them by genetic counselors.

The second part, "The Convention of Tradition: Feminism in Dialogue with the New Right," extends the first part's focus on differences among women, but this time concentrating on political and religious lines. The papers show how recent Christian and conservative formulations of gender have met the challenges of feminism. Faye Ginsburg demonstrates how right-to-life activists, influenced by the critiques of their pro-choice opponents, are reformulating ideas about unwanted pregnancies; no longer sources of shame, they now form the potential ground for the demonstration of heroic female nurturance. Discourses that explicitly denounce feminism may show feminist influence in the way issues are defined. Susan Harding explores the narrative strategies in a book by minister Jerry Falwell to look at the construction of fundamentalist Christian identities. Falwell refashions feminist discourse on women's reproductive rights to create a story of Christian paternal nurturance. Carole Vance shows how the 1986 Attorney General's Commission on Pornography borrowed from the feminist anti-pornography movement in calling pornography violence against women; at the same time, the Commission blamed feminism for causing sexual violence by advocating sexual freedoms. Yet, in contrast to conservative and Christian leaders who appropriate feminist discourse for their own agendas, some political and religious movements otherwise considered conservative have genuinely incorporated feminist insights into their practice. Judith Stacey and Elizabeth Gerard describe evangelical Christian women who pursue demands for equality with their husbands—but on Christian terms.

"Producing Gender in and out of the Workplace," the third part, returns to intertwined issues of gender, class, race, and ethnicity, as women negotiate these in relation to their identities as workers. The articles show that workplaces do not merely adopt already established standards of gender; these are created and contested on the job. Kath Weston shows how supposedly gender-neutral concepts such as "productivity" encode value-laden notions of male and female styles of work. Her study examines how women in blue collar work contend with male managers' and co-workers' assumptions that male styles are more productive. Cynthia Saltzman also explores how the gender terms that create the division of labor and the conditions of work may become targets of political debate. She tells an unusual success story in her analysis of how Yale University's clerical workers—a "pink collar" group expected to be internally divided and loyal only to their employers and families—formed a union and won a strike by rhetoric that carefully balanced class solidarity and women's empowerment. Sandra Morgen's study shows how understandings of gender can be an object of struggle even in a feminist workplace. When the middle-class white staff of the feminist health clinic she studied was integrated by including working-class women of color, the group was forced to come to terms with their race and class differences; a broader understanding of "women's interests" resulted, which led to a political revitalization of the clinic. M. Patricia Fernández Kelly's research stresses the relationship between wage work and family commitments. Ethnicity, class, and family organization shape the meaning

Hispanic women give to their wage labor: while Mexican American women work for independent survival as family heads, the Cuban American women she studied were striving to increase their male-headed families' class status. Through sensitivity to activist agendas as well as everyday tensions, the articles in this section offer new perspectives on how women workers interpret, contest, and transform their workplaces.

In the fourth section, "Stereotypes of Difference and Strategies of Identity," contributors examine the relationship between women's everyday practices and gender, race, and ethnic stereotypes. Two of the articles in this section show how women and men may inadvertently reproduce dominant gender stereotypes as they find personal strategies to deal with powerful institutions. Ellen Lewin examines the varied ways divorced mothers avoid child custody disputes. Both heterosexual and lesbian women, she argues, pursue similar strategies to prove they are good mothers. Some hold on to as many childcare responsibilities as they can, thus unexpectedly reproducing norms of mother-exclusive childcare. Joyce Canaan explores how young women and men internalize conventional gender models; the small rebellions of white middle-class teenagers against their teachers offer a dramatic moment when young people test and finally conform to established gender identities. Two other essays in this section ask how stereotypes are produced, and examine the strategies that exist around them and despite them. Suzanne Carothers describes how both racism and wage work give shape to African American mother-daughter relationships. She argues that African American women develop resourceful self-identities that contrast with the white middle-class images of devalued mothers and dependent daughters that have often been portrayed as universal. Riv-Ellen Prell demonstrates that negative ethnic stereotypes can be produced within a group itself, expressing gender-based tensions around issues of identity. Jokes about "Jewish American Princesses," she argues, are not reflections of Jewish American women's character traits so much as expressions of Jewish American men's anxieties about success and assimilation.

The final section, "Unbecoming Women: Tricksters, Monsters, and Unendurable Contradictions," examines the construction of women's marginality as well as women's sometimes unsettling responses to such situations. Sharon Thompson describes African American teenage mothers who turn around stereotypes that portray them as victims by presenting themselves as clever survivors who can "trick" the systems that work against them. Irma McClaurin-Allen presents a different kind of "borderlands" perspective in the life of a successful African American journalist, whose sense of the incongruities of her own race, class, and gender status fostered a creative and critical intelligence. McClaurin-Allen lets us hear this journalist's frustrations and discusses the ambiguous messages of her death. Emily Martin describes working-class women who express their pain during childbirth despite medical and middle-class admonitions to control themselves. Martin argues that women who are not party to middle-class requirements for control over the self more readily reject ideas of proper childbirth as self-regulated and composed. Anna Tsing retells "monster stories" developed in the criminal justice system that depict women who give birth without medical supervision, and whose newborns do not survive, as homicidal. She argues that these stories cast particular standards of motherhood as universal, while using them to differentiate between good and bad women, on the one hand, and between transgressors of varying race and class identities, on the other.

This volume demonstrates how gender is negotiated in diverse situations where struggles for power, however subtle, are always at issue. It is significant that we are studying our own society. The insights we offer are not seen as separate from our own social action, or from the experiences, consciousness, and agency of the other women and men described in these pages. By analyzing contested arenas in which we are often engaged as activists, we hope to contribute not only to scholarship but also to political awareness, whether we study dramatic controversies or everyday struggles for survival and respect.

NOTES

We are grateful to the many colleagues who discussed the issues involved in assembling this volume, and read and commented on drafts of the introduction. We are, of course, responsible for the ideas presented here. We particularly want to thank Carolyn Clark, Diane Gifford-Gonzales, Sandra Morgen, Fred Myers, Troels Petersen, Naomi Quinn, Rayna Rapp, Lisa Rofel, Carole Vance, Annette Weiner, and Joanne Wyckoff, as well as Lauren Bryant and Andy Hrycyna of Beacon Press. Thanks also go to Meg McLagan and Annette Wong for their assistance in preparation of the manuscript and research for the cover.

1. This list is based on personal ads that appeared in a local California newspaper in 1989.

2. The studies in this volume represent the confluence of two interrelated areas of innovative research in anthropology: the cultural and social meaning of gender, reproduction and sexuality; and arenas of conflict in contemporary American culture. Nearly half the papers in this collection were first presented at professional anthropology meetings in sessions addressing these trends. Papers by Susan Harding, Rayna Rapp, Anna Tsing and Carole Vance were first given at the American Ethnological Society (AES) meetings for invited panels on The Culture and Politics of Human Reproduction in April 1986. Related research was presented at the December 1986 meetings of the American Anthropological Association in a panel entitled "Speaking Women: Representations of Contemporary American Femininity" (Joyce Canaan) and in a session organized by Susan Harding entitled "Ethnographic America" (Kathleen Stewart). Papers by Faye Ginsburg, Carol Stack and Sandra Morgen were delivered at the 1987 AES meetings in sessions entitled "The Ascription and Achievement of Gender" and "State, Class and Changing Concepts of Gender."

3. Sally Falk Moore, in her essay, "Explaining the Present: Theoretical Dilemmas in Processual Ethnography," *American Ethnologist* 14, no. 4 (November

1987): 727–36, calls such moments "diagnostic events," which she defines as: ". . . one[s] that reveal ongoing contests and conflicts and competitions and the efforts to prevent, suppress, or repress these." (730) "An event is not necessarily best understood as the exemplification of an extant symbolic or social order. Events may equally be evidence of the ongoing dismantling of structure or attempts to create new ones. Events may show a multiplicity of social contestations and the voicing of competing cultural claims. Events may reveal substantial areas of normative indeterminacy." (729) In focusing on disruption and discontinuity, the authors develop the interest in social action, conflict and local events that distinguishes what has been called processual anthropology; and (with some differences), what Sherry Ortner, in her article "Theory in Anthropology Since the Sixties," in *Comparative Studies in Society and History* 26: 126–66, has called "practice" approaches, which focus on the relationships between a received cultural order, empirical event, and human action. Processual approaches, by contrast, stress continuous production and construction, whether transformative or not.

4. Most recent work on the question of "difference" shares with structuralism the position that the construction of difference is a fundamental process in the creation of meaning, and that subjectivities are constructed through language. However, poststructuralism is critical of the idea that categories (such as "male" or "female") are determined in every context. Rather identities are seen as shifting, multiple, and subject to change; meanings are not fixed in a culture's lexicon but are dynamic.

A summary of postmodern/poststructural positions shows different ways the instability of meaning is understood. For the French philosopher Jean Francois Lyotard in *Postmodern Condition: A Report on Knowledge* (Minneapolis: University of Minnesota Press, 1984), post-modernism is the end of "meta-narratives," through which fields of knowledge had been understood in modernism. Frederic Jameson, in his essay "Postmodernism and Consumer Society," in *The Anti-Aesthetic,* ed. Hal Foster (Port Townsend, WA: Bay Press, 1983), 111–25, associates post-modernism with responses to global transformations since the 1960s, characterized by "pastiche" or a hetereogeneous jumbling of elements, and a breakdown of normative relationships between signifiers and signifieds. While signifiers are transformed into images, they do not float free of referentiality; rather, as referents increasingly become other texts and other images, meaning is unstable and subject to different readings. According to the work of Jacques Derrida (for example, in *Of Grammatology* (Baltimore: Johns Hopkins Press, 1974), the fixed oppositions of structuralism conceal heterogeneity within categories. Positive definitions are understood as resting on the negation or repression of something represented as antithetical. Debates about meaning involve introducing new oppositions, reversing hierarchies, and attempting to expose the destabilizing effect of repressed terms. Adding to these insights, Michel Foucault in, for example, *L'Ordre du Discours* (Paris: Gallimard, 1971) challenged analytic separations between material conditions and the human thought and actions they are said to generate, since "interests" do not inhere in actors or their structural positions but are discursively produced. Those following Foucault's interest in "discourse" focus on power relations and the processes of conflict through which meaning is constructed and implemented in any society.

Of course, gender is deeply implicated in all of this as a central site for the organization of social difference as well as a site of conflict. While poststructuralist philosophers are seen as the originators of these ideas, in fact, they have appeared independently in many different locations. As feminist historian Lisa Duggan summed it up in her review/essay, "Vive la Difference: Joan Scott's Historical Imperatives" in the *Voice Literary Supplement* 71 (January–February 1989): 37: ". . . in arguing that the category woman is not unified and represses differences within it one might invoke equally Derrida or [feminist] Barbara Smith."

5. We use this term along the lines established by Richard Terdiman, in *Discourse/Counter-Discourse* (Ithaca, NY: Cornell University Press, 1985) in his illuminating elaboration of Michel Foucault's discourse theory.

6. "Second wave" feminism refers to the United States and European feminist movements that developed in the late 1960s. The "first wave" began in the late nineteenth century and was active through the 1920s.

7. For many of these writers, fiction and social criticism—rather than social science—have provided powerful ways to articulate their own experiences. Some important works are: Cherríe Moraga and Gloria Anzaldúa, eds., *This Bridge Called My Back: Writings By Radical Women of Color* (Latham, NY: Kitchen Table/Women of Color Press, 1983); Cherríe Moraga, *Loving in the War Years: lo que nunca pasó por sus labios* (Boston: South End Press, 1983); Angela Davis, *Women, Race and Class* (NY: Random House/Vintage Books, 1981); Gloria Hull, Patricia Bell-Scott, and Barbara Smith, eds. *All the Women Are White, All the Blacks Are Men, But Some of Us Are Brave: Black Women's Studies* (NY: Feminist Press, 1982); Audre Lorde, *Zami: A New Spelling of My Name* (Trumansberg, NY: The Crossing Press, 1982); Barbara Smith, ed. *Home Girls: A Black Feminist Anthology* (Latham, NY: Kitchen Table/Women of Color Press, 1983); bell hooks, *Feminist Theory, From Margin to Center* (Boston: South End Press, 1984); Paula Giddings, *When and Where I Enter* (NY: Bantam, 1984); Leslie Marmon Silko, *Storyteller* (NY: Seaver Books, 1981); Maxine Hong Kingston, *The Woman Warrior: Memoirs of A Girlhood Among Ghosts* (NY: Random House, 1977); Elly Bulkin, Minnie Bruce Pratt, and Barbara Smith, *Yours in Struggle: Three Feminist Perspectives on Anti-Semitism and Racism* (Brooklyn: Long Haul Press, 1985).

More recent writings on these themes include: Asian Women United of California, eds., *Making Waves: An Anthology of Writings By and About Asian American Women* (Boston: Beacon Press, 1989); Johnetta Cole, ed., *All American Women: Lines That Divide, Ties That Bind* (NY: The Free Press, 1986); Paula Gunn Allen, *The Sacred Hoop: Recovering the Feminine in American Indian Tradition* (Boston: Beacon Press, 1986); Gloria Anzaldúa, *Borderlands/La Frontera: The New Mestiza* (San Francisco: Spinsters/Aunt Lute, 1987); bell hooks, *Talking Back: Thinking Feminist, Thinking Black* (Boston: South End Press, 1989).

8. Some influential texts articulating the cultural feminist position include: Mary Daly, *Gyn/Ecology* (Boston: Beacon Press, 1978); Adrienne Rich, *Of Woman Born* (NY: Norton, 1976); Kathleen Barry, *Female Sexual Slavery* (Englewood Cliffs: Prentice-Hall, 1979); Andrea Dworkin, *Pornography: Men Possessing Women* (NY: Perigree/Putnam, 1979); Catherine MacKinnon, *Toward a Feminist Theory of the State* (Cambridge: Harvard University Press,

1989). For an interesting discussion of the debates in feminism around this position, see Alice Echols, "The Taming of the Id: Feminist Sexual Politics, 1968–83," in *Pleasure and Danger: Exploring Female Sexuality*, ed. C. Vance (Boston: Routledge & Kegan Paul, 1984).

9. See Nancy Chodorow, *The Reproduction of Mothering: Psychoanalysis and the Sociology of Gender* (Berkeley: University of California Press, 1978).

10. See Jessica Benjamin, *The Bonds of Love: Psychoanalysis, Feminism and the Problem of Domination* (NY: Pantheon, 1988).

11. See Carol Gilligan, *In a Different Voice: Psychological Theory and Women's Development* (Cambridge, Mass.: Harvard University Press, 1982).

12. For example, see Luce Irigiray, *Speculum de l'Autre Femme* (Paris: Les Editions de Minuit, 1974).

13. See Michelle Rosaldo, "Woman, Culture, and Society: A Theoretical Overview," in *Woman, Culture, and Society*, eds. Michelle Rosaldo and Louise Lamphere (Stanford, Ca.: Stanford University Press, 1974), 17–42.

14. See Sherry Ortner, "Is Female to Male as Nature is to Culture?" in *Woman Culture and Society*, 67–88.

15. See Gayle Rubin, "The Traffic in Women: Notes on the 'Political Economy' of Sex," in *Toward an Anthropology of Women*, ed. R. Rapp Reiter (NY: Monthly Review Press, 1975), 157–210.

16. See Rayna Rapp Reiter, "Introduction," in *Toward an Anthropology of Women*, 11–19.

17. See Eleanor Burke Leacock, "Introduction" to Frederick Engels, *The Origin of the Family, Private Property and the State* (NY: International Publishers, 1972), 7–69.

18. Karen Sacks, "State Bias and Women's Status," *American Anthropologist* 78 (1976): 565–69.

19. Marilyn Strathern, "No Nature, No Culture: The Hagen Case," in *Nature, Culture and Gender: A Critique*, eds. Carol MacCormack and Marilyn Strathern (NY: Cambridge University Press, 1980).

20. Annette Weiner, *Women of Value, Men of Renown* (Austin: University of Texas Press, 1976); Karen Sacks, *Sisters and Wives: The Past and Future of Sexual Equality* (Westport, Conn.: Greenwood Press, 1979).

21. Jane Goodale, *Tiwi Wives* (Seattle: University of Washington Press, 1971).

22. See, for example, Rayna Rapp, "Review: Anthropology" *Signs* 4 (1979): 497–513; Michelle Rosaldo, "The Use and Abuse of Anthropology: Reflections on Feminism and Cross-Cultural Understanding," *Signs* 5, no. 3 (1980): 389–417; Carol MacCormack, "Nature, Culture and Gender: A Critique" in *Nature, Culture and Gender*, eds. C. MacCormack and M. Strathern, 1–24; Sherry Ortner and Harriet Whitehead, "Introduction: Accounting for Sexual Meanings," in *Sexual Meanings: The Cultural Construction of Gender and Sexuality* (NY: Cambridge University Press, 1981); Patricia Caplan and Janet Bujra, *Women United, Women Divided* (Bloomington: Indiana University Press, 1979).

23. See, for example, Jane Collier and Michelle Rosaldo, "Politics and Gender in Simple Societies," in *Sexual Meanings*, eds. S. Ortner and H. Whitehead, 275–329; Jane Collier, *Marriage and Inequality in Classless Societies* (Stanford, Stanford University Press, 1988); Claude Meillasoux, *Maidens, Meal and Money: Capitalism and the Domestic Community* (NY: Cambridge University

Press, 1981); Karen Sacks, *Sisters and Wives;* Janet Siskind, *To Hunt in the Morning* (London: Oxford University Press, 1973).

24. Verena Martinez-Alier, *Marriage, Class and Colour in Nineteenth Century Cuba: A Study of Racial Attitudes and Sexual Values in a Slave Society* (London: Cambridge University Press, 1974).

25. Melissa Llewelyn-Davies, "Women, Warriors, and Patriarchs," in *Sexual Meanings,* eds. S. Ortner and H. Whitehead, 330–58.

26. For partial reviews of recent anthropological history see Sherry Ortner, "Theory in Anthropology Since the Sixties" in *Comparative Studies in Society and History* 26 (1984): 126–66; Arjun Appadurai, "Theory in Anthropology: Center and Periphery," *Comparative Studies in Society and History* 28 (1986): 356–61.

For other discussions of the transformations in the anthropological study of gender, see Jane Collier and Sylvia Yanagisako, "Introduction," and "Toward a Unified Analysis of Gender and Kinship" *Gender and Kinship: Essays Toward a Unified Analysis* (Stanford: Stanford University Press, 1987), 1–13, 14–50; Henrietta Moore, *Feminism and Anthropology* (Minneapolis: University of Minnesota, 1988); Louise Lamphere "Feminist Anthropology: The Legacy of Elsie Clews Parsons," *American Ethnologist* 16, no. 3 (August 1989): 518–33.

27. A few representative works, many of them interdisciplinary collections, include: Barrie Thorne and Marilyn Yalom, *Rethinking the Family: Some Feminist Questions* (NY: Longman, 1982); Ann Snitow, Christine Stansell, and Sharon Thompson, *Powers of Desire: The Politics of Sexuality* (New York: New Feminist Library/Monthly Review, 1983); Carole Vance, ed. *Pleasure and Danger: Exploring Female Sexuality* (Boston: Routledge & Kegan Paul, 1984); Karen Sacks and Dorothy Remy, *My Troubles Are Going to Have Trouble With Me* (New Brunswick, NJ: Rutgers University Press, 1984); Teresa de Lauretis, ed., *Feminist Studies/Critical Studies* (Bloomington: Indiana University Press, 1986); Emily Martin, *The Woman in the Body: A Cultural Analysis of Reproduction* (Boston: Beacon Press, 1987).

28. See, for example, Biddy Martin and Chandra Mohanty, "Feminist Politics: What's Home Got to Do With It?" in *Feminist Studies/Critical Studies,* ed. T. de Lauretis, 191–212; Teresa de Lauretis, *Technologies of Gender* (Bloomington: Indiana University Press, 1987); Denise Riley, *Am I That Name?* (Minneapolis: University of Minnesota Press, 1988); The Personal Narratives Group, *Interpreting Women's Lives: Feminist Theory and Personal Narratives* (Bloomington: Indiana University Press, 1989); Trinh T. Minh-ha, *Woman, Native, Other* (Bloomington: Indiana University Press, 1989).

29. The summary of the emergence of the gendered separation of home and work in the United States is based on the groundbreaking work in women's history by Barbara Welter, "The Cult of True Womanhood, 1820–1860," *American Quarterly* 18 (1966): 151–174; Nancy Cott, *The Bonds of Womanhood: Woman's Sphere in New England, 1780–1835* (New Haven: Yale University Press, 1977); Caroll Smith-Rosenberg, *Disorderly Conduct* (NY: Knopf, 1985); Mary Ryan, *Womanhood in America* (NY: Watts, 1983); and Carl Degler, *At Odds: Women and the Family in America from the Revolution to the Present* (NY: Oxford University Press, 1980) to name only a few of the excellent historians who have illuminated this process.

30. Feminist anthropologists have been particularly active in showing the

relationships among women's work, women's community ties, and histories of activism. Works include Carol Stack's *All Our Kin: Strategies for Survival in a Black Community* (NY: Harper, 1974); Ida Susser's *Norman Street: Poverty and Politics in an Urban Neighborhood* (NY: Oxford University Press, 1982); Ann Bookman and Sandra Morgen, *Women and the Politics of Empowerment* (Philadelphia: Temple University Press, 1988); Karen Sacks, *Caring by the Hour* (Urbana: University of Illinois Press, 1988); M. Patricia Fernández Kelly, *For We Are Sold, I and My People: Women and Industry in Mexico's Frontier* (Albany: SUNY Press, 1983); June Nash and M. Patricia Fernández Kelly, eds. *Women, Men and the International Division of Labor* (Albany: SUNY Press, 1984); Patricia Zavella, *Women's Work and Chicano Families: Cannery Workers of the Santa Clara Valley* (Ithaca: Cornell University Press, 1987); Louise Lamphere, *From Working Mothers to Working Daughters: Immigrant Women in a New England Industrial Community* (Ithaca: Cornell University Press, 1987). The recent history of Marxist feminist analyses of women's position under capitalism is discussed in an essay by Karen Sacks, "Toward a Unified Theory of Class, Race, and Gender," *American Ethnologist* 16, no. 3 (August 1989): 534–50.

31. In postmarxist theorist Chantelle Mouffe's terms, efforts to transform society based on singular group identities are "democratic antagonisms" that sometimes interfere with potential alliances with other disempowered groups. For further discussion of this idea, see her essay "Hegemony and New Political Subjects: Toward a New Concept of Democracy," trans. by Stanley Gray, in *Marxism and the Interpretation of Culture,* eds. Cary Nelson and Lawrence Grossberg (Urbana: University of Illinois Press, 1988), 89–104.

32. Teresa de Lauretis, "Feminist Studies/Critical Studies: Issues, Terms and Contexts," in *Feminist Studies/Critical Studies,* ed. Teresa de Lauretis, p. 14.

PART ONE

Backtalking Feminism and Femininity

CHAPTER ONE

Different Voices, Different Visions: Gender, Culture, and Moral Reasoning

CAROL B. STACK

Do women and men tend to see moral problems differently? According to some researchers, two moral visions shape our ways of assessing these questions. Carol Gilligan argues in her book, *In a Different Voice*, that "care reasoning," which compels us to respond to those in need, and "justice reasoning," which dictates that we treat others fairly, represent separate moral orientations.[1] In her view, these are not opposites, but are different ways of comprehending human dilemmas. Gilligan's subsequent research suggests that these moral perspectives originate in the dynamics of early childhood relationships, congeal in adolescence, and reappear in the resolution of moral conflicts throughout life.[2]

Feminist scholars are indebted to Gilligan and her colleagues, who have brought the voice of care to moral reasoning and to our understanding of the social construction of gender. Nevertheless, as Gilligan's own observations confirm, the cross-cultural construction of gender remains relatively unexplored. During the course of my study of African-American return migration to rural southern homeplaces,[3] moral voices of both justice and care emerged from my interviews with adults and 12- and 13-year-old boys and girls. However, their responses are strikingly different from the gender configurations in Gilligan's published findings.

In my research, I became interested in the vocabulary of gender and gendered discourse surrounding this return migration movement. Influenced by Gilligan's work on moral reasoning, and puzzled by the absence of reference to race and class, I chose to collect working-class adolescent and adult narratives on moral reasoning in addition to my own ethnographic research on return migration.[4] I asked these young people and adults about dilemmas similar to the difficult choices examined in Gilligan's studies. The people I interviewed were return migrants—men, women, and children who had moved back to rural southern homeplaces. The experiences of those I interviewed differed from those of African-Americans who never left the South, and from long-term and recent urban dwellers in many cities in the United States. Indeed, this work does not generalize from a specific group to all African-Americans.

This study argues that moral reasoning is negotiated with respect to individual or group location within the social structure. Gender is one, but only one of the social categories—including, among many, class, culture, race and ethnic structure, and region—which shape what we call morality. My goal is to discuss how gender differences contribute to a construction of morals. I hope to do this within the context of my current research on return migration, and thereby offer a modest challenge to explanations that fail to fully take into account gender differences.[5] In this paper I report the responses of 15 adults and 87 adolescents, borrowing the orientations of "care" and "justice". I merge two lines of research, bringing the issue of gendered strategies in moral reasoning into the realm of race, culture, and socio-economics.[6]

If we view the construction of gender across race, culture, and historical conditions, it transforms our thinking about moral reasoning. The creation of gender roles within specific historical and socio-economic circumstances is a creative process, one that is dynamic rather than static. Gender is negotiated among members of specific communities, for example, as they respond to situations of institutionalized oppression and/or racial stratification. As an anthropologist concerned with the construction of gender, it has been my hypothesis that gender relationships are improvised against local and global political and economic conditions and familial affiliations, all of which are always in transition. My perspective registers serious objections to frameworks built on polarities or fixed oppositions, especially notions that create an illusory sense of "universal" or "essential" gender differences.[7]

Historically, gender as an analytic category has unfolded from the early depictions of sex differences and the range of sex roles, to a full examination of how gender constructs politics and how politics, class, and race construct gender.[8] Anthropological studies of gender have moved from particular, to universal, and in this paper, to contextual. Feminist scholars emerge from analysis with a subtle category constructed from the concrete; deeply rooted in relationships of power, class, race, and historical circumstance.

Data from my earlier research in urban black communities in the 1970s[9] and from my recent studies of the return migration of African-Americans from the Northeast to the rural South[10] suggest new notions about the nexus of gender, race, and class relations. Class, racial formation,[11] and economic systems within rural southern communities create a context in which African-Americans—women and men, boys and girls—live in relation to production, employment, class, and material and economic rewards. They do so in strikingly similar ways, rather than the divergent ways predicted by theorists of moral reasoning. It is from the vantage point of over 20 years of research on the African-American family that I contribute to Carol Gilligan's discourse on moral voices.[12] I focus on gender as a social relation and suggest that gender is negotiated along lines of difference that are in a constant state of change.[13]

Although philosophers have debated Gilligan's distinction between care and justice reasoning, as well as her methods of interpreting and coding narratives of moral reasoning, in this paper I will not enter the debate. This present undertaking is narrower in scope. This research does not disentangle methodological issues surrounding Gilligan and her critics,[14] or debate on moral reasoning or moral stages of development. It does, however, question the validity of universal gender differences.

MORAL DILEMMAS

On separate occasions, several adults and adolescents who had returned home to rural southern communities worked with me on this research by constructing scenarios of difficult choices they face in their own lives. The way local community members construct dilemmas approximates Gilligan and colleagues' most current procedures, in which they ask people to talk about a situation where they weren't sure what the right thing to do was, and they had to make a choice.[15] I chose to elicit culturally relevant dilemmas, rather than employ the classic "Heinz dilemma" (whether Heinz should steal drugs for his dying wife) used by Gilligan. In Gilligan's current, more open-ended approach, people are then asked to respond to a dilemma of their own making. What is important in this style of research is not the specific nature of the dilemma, but what people say about it.

An intriguing aspect of my study of black return migration is the cyclical migration of children. Children accompany parents or extended kin, or journey alone along well-worn paths between their families' home bases in the North and in the South. Many of the parents of these children participated in cyclical migrations and occupied dual residences themselves. Today, dual patterns of residence are common for young black children whose kinship ties extend across state lines and regions of the country.[16] Their homes are wedged into both city and countryside; their schooling is divided between public schools in Harlem, Brooklyn, Washington, DC, and country schools in the South. Their cyclical changes of residence are common knowledge to school administrators, teachers, and social workers in their communities. I have been interested in how children experience their own migration, especially in light of the vivid descriptions they have given me of the tough choices they are asked to make. Straddling family ties in the North and South, and loyalties and attachments across the generations, children face real-life dilemmas over where to reside and with whom, and over what defines their responsibility to others. Their dilemmas dramatize cultural elements of migration.

Several 12- and 13-year-olds helped me construct a dilemma from the real-life situations they had described to me.[17] One child suggested that we put the dilemma in the form of a Dear Abby letter, since the Dear Abby column is popular reading in the local community. Eighty-seven children of the North-South return migration responded to the following dilemma:

Dear Abby:
I am 12 and my brother is 10. My mother wants us to go and stay with her in New York City, and my grandparents want us to stay here in New Jericho with them. What should we do?
Love, Sally

The way children resolved the "Dear Abby" dilemma and personalized their responses reflects children's experiences as participants in this migration trend. From what children "tell" Dear Abby, and from complementary life histories, we begin to understand how these boys and girls perceive their lives and construct their roles—gender, among others—as family members caught in the web of cultural, economic, and historical forces. Their responses are infused with both a sense of responsibility to those in need and an attempt to treat others fairly.

Here are a few examples.

Jimmy wrote:
I think I should stay with the one that needs my help the most. My grandmother is unable to do for herself and I should stay with her and let my mother come to see me.

Sarah wrote:
I should talk to my parents and try to get them to understand that my grandparents cannot get around like they used to. I want to make an agreement to let my brother go to New York and go to school, and I'll go to school down here. In the summer I will go and be with my parents and my brother can come down home.

And Helen wrote:
I should stay with my grandparents because, for one reason, there are many murderers up North, and my grandparents are old and need my help around the house.

A group of adults who had returned to southern homeplaces, women and men between the ages of 25 and 40, designed the "Clyde Dilemma":

Clyde is very torn over a decision he must make. His two sisters are putting pressure on him to leave Washington, DC and go back home to take care of his parents. His mother is bedridden and his father recently lost a leg from sugar. One of his sisters has a family and a good job up north, and the other just moved there recently to get married. Clyde's sisters see him as more able to pick up and go back home since he is unmarried and works part time—although he keeps trying to get a better job. What should Clyde do?

People deeply personalized their responses as they spoke of experiences within their own extended families. James Hopkins recalled, "Three of us rotated to keep my father at home," and he went on to remind me that "you must love a human being, not a dollar." Molly Henderson, who moved back in 1979, said, "Family should take care of family. It's a cycle. Someone has to do it, and it is Clyde's turn." Sam Henderson, Molly's uncle, told me, "You must take care of those who took care of you. Clyde's next in line, it's his turn." And Sam Hampton said, "He has no alternative." Others repeated, "It's not so hard if everybody helps," or "family is the most important sacrifice we can make."

FINDINGS

My findings pay particular attention to class differences, as well as ethnic and racial consciousness. They contrast dramatically with Gilligan's observations that while girls and women turn equally to rights and care reasoning, boys and men far less often turn to care reasoning, especially as they grow older.[18] All of the responses to the dilemmas were coded and analyzed for 15 adults and 87 adolescents (42 girls; 45 boys), according to the guidelines of Gilligan and Lyons, and recoded according to Gilligan and colleagues' new guidelines. Gilligan has a separate category termed "both," which I will call "mixed" (as in a mixture that cannot be separated into constituents). In the final analysis, my results do not differ, whether "mixed" is dropped or is counted as both justice and care. The presence of justice as a reason (with or without care) is not different for boys versus girls. Likewise, the presence of care as a reason (with or without justice) is not different for boys versus girls (Pearson Chi-square test). We come to the same conclusions for adult men versus women (Fisher exact test).

The patterns of percentages are virtually identical for boys and girls, with justice slightly higher than care in each group. The percentage was also nearly the same for boys and girls who used both.

	Boys ($n=45$)		Girls ($n=42$)	
Justice only	42%	(19)	43%	(18)
Care only	31%	(14)	31%	(13)
J & C	27%	(12)	26%	(11)

The adult women articulated both kinds of reasoning (care and justice) more than men did. There is no real difference between men and women in justice reasoning. Notice that only 1 (and that one a man) of 15 of the adults used care reasoning alone.

	Men ($n=7$)		Women ($n=8$)	
Justice only	43%	(3)	37.5%	(3)
Care only	14%	(1)	0	
J & C	43%	(3)	62.5%	(5)

The findings on moral reasoning in this study present a strikingly different configuration of gender differences and similarities from Gilligan's own results. Among African-American families returning South, adolescents and adults are close to identical when their responses are coded for care and justice reasoning. This suggests that situating gender difference in the context of class and race transforms our thinking about moral reasoning.

MORAL KNOWLEDGE, SOCIAL ACTION, AND GENDER

Two questions arise from these results. First, in contrast to Gilligan's findings, why the convergence between African-American male and female responses? How and why do these similarities exist? Second, what is the relationship between moral reasoning and the ways in which men and women carry out their lives and conduct social actions?

This research substantiates findings from my earlier studies of dependency relationships experienced by both African-American males and females. In many aspects of their work, and relationships to social institutions and political conditions, black women and other women of color affirm that their circumstances and experiences are very similar to those of men. In *Talking Back,* a recent essay on feminist thinking, bell hooks argues the over simplicity of viewing women as the victims and men as dominators; women can be agents of domination; men and women are both oppressed and dominated.[19] Such realities do not discount the role of sexism in public and private lives, or the participation of oppressed men in the domination of others. However, data from my study of return migration suggest that the shared experience informs both self-identity and group-identity among return migrants and these converge in the vocabulary of rights, morality, and the social good.

A collective social conscience manifests itself in several ways over the course of a person's life. From an early age girls and boys become aware of the tyranny of racial and economic injustice. By the age of 12 or 13, children are aware of the workplace experiences of their parents, of sexual favors rural women must offer to keep their jobs in southern mills and processing plants, of threats to the sanity and dignity of kin. Women and men who return south have a strong sense of both personal memory and community history. Those who return home confront their own pasts, and engage in a collective negotiation with social injustice. They carry back with them a mission or desire to fight for racial justice as they return to what they refer to as "my testing ground." They define themselves as "community" or as "race persons"—those who work for the good of the race.

These men and women also share a care orientation. Those who return to rural southern communities find refuge across the generations in their southern families. Both men and women are embedded in their extended families; they similarly experience tensions between their individual aspirations and the needs of kin. These tensions surface as a morality of responsibility; they are voiced loud and clear in the Clyde dilemma, and in life histories I collected during the course of my research.

Parallels in the way men and women experience external forces that shape their lives suggest that there is vast similarity between black men and women of all ages in their construction of themselves in relation to others. The way both men and women describe themselves indicates a sense of identity deeply connected to others, an "extended self"—to borrow Wade Nobles's language.[20] Individuals perceive their obligations within the context of a social order and anchored in others, rather than in an individualist focus on their own personal welfare.[21] In more than 1000 pages of self-narratives that I have collected during the course of the study of return migration, people affirm, with force and conviction, the strength of kinship ties to their rural southern families. Over and over they emphasize, "Family is the most important sacrifice." Family ties play out intricate dependencies for black men and women, especially for those on the edge of poverty.

Likewise, the interviews with children reveal a collective social conscience and a profound sensitivity among young people to the needs of their families. The children's voices tell a somber story of the fate, circumstances, and material conditions of their lives. Their expectations about where they will live in the coming year conform to the changing needs and demands of other family members, old and young, and family labor force participation.

The construction of gender, as black and other feminist researchers of color have emphasized, is shaped by the experience of sex, race, class, and consciousness.[22] Future research on the construction of gender must contribute another dimension to feminist theory. It should provide a critical framework for analysis of gender consciousness, and a cautionary reminder to those theorists who argue that gender is a pat and universal experience.

The coding of my data on care and justice reasoning among African-Americans returning South has shown startling results. Compared with Gilligan's early findings, it would appear that in contrast to the Harvard studies, gender configures fewer differences in ways of knowing among this specific group of African-Americans. But what is the relationship between ways of knowing and ways of acting?

My five-year study of African-American return migration to the rural south makes it clear that in any study we must examine multiple levels. Looking beyond the coding, the men and women who receive similar scores on Justice and Care reasoning have remarkably different gendered strategies for action. Men and women in these rural southern communities differ in their assumption of the work of kinship, in the roles they perceive as wage-earners and care-takers, and in their political actions.

Particularly striking are gendered strategies of political action. In their battle to subvert an oppressive social order, the men who return as adults to their southern homeplaces work principally within the local black power structure; they avoid confrontation with the close-at-hand white power structure. When they challenge existing mores, they confront the black male hierarchy within local land owning associations, or the Church. The social order women discover upon their return is a male symbolic order, both in dealings with the local black community and with the local white community. Women find themselves struggling between contradictory forces of the old south and their own political missions. They face a race and gender system in which they are drawn into dependencies created by male structures in the local black community. But these women, unlike the men who return, take action to circumvent this race/gender hierarchy, as well as the local patronage systems. They create public programs, such as Title XX Day Care and Head Start, by creating an extensive state-wide network of support in the public and private sectors. These women build community bases by carrying out their struggle in a public domain outside the jurisdiction of the local public power structure. Male preachers, politicians, and brokers also reproduce dependency relationships between blacks and whites. While men participate in public spheres within their local black communities, women bypass the local domination of both black and white male structures, moving within a more broadly defined public domain.

There is a division across race, culture, class, and gender between the study of moral voices—what people say—and observations of how people conduct themselves—what they do—in familiar places and public spaces. We must always study, side by side, both discourse, and course of action. This brings us face to face with the difference between interpretive studies of moral voices, and ethnographies of gender that regard moral reasoning in the context of everyday activity. Cross-disciplinary differences in feminist methodologies reinforce the importance within feminist scholarship of "talking back" to one another.

NOTES

I wish to thank the Rockefeller Foundation for a Gender Roles Fellowship and the Center for Advanced Study in the Behavioral Sciences for their support for this research. I am also indebted to Elizabeth Bates for her devotion to coding this material and her creative, challenging questions. I am also grateful to Marjorie Wolf and Brakette Williams who made valuable suggestions at early stages of this research, and to Jane Atanuchi, Nancy Chodorow, Jacqueline Hall, Krista Luker, Sandra Morgen, Laura Nader, Ruth Rosen, Nancy Scheper-Hughes, and Norma Wikler, who read and commented at length on earlier versions of this paper. My colleagues at the Center for Advanced Study in the Behavioral Sciences, Carla Peterson and Blanca Silvestrini, offered intellectual guidance and friendship throughout the year. Mary Ryan, director of Women's Studies at U.C. Berkeley, has been both a critical reader and a source of encouragement. The editors of this volume, Faye Ginsburg and Anna Tsing made important editorial comments, and Anna Tsing patiently prodded me to finish.

1. Carol Gilligan, *In a Different Voice: Psychological Theory and Women's Development* (Cambridge: Harvard University Press, 1982).

2. Carol Gilligan and Grant Wiggins, "The Origins of Morality in Early Childhood Relationships," in *The Emergence of Morality,* ed. J. Kagan and S. Lamb (Illinois: University of Chicago Press, 1987).

3. Carol B. Stack, *The Call to Home: African Americans Reclaim the Rural South* (forthcoming).

4. 326,000 black individuals returned to a ten-state region of the south between 1975–1980.

5. I am grateful to Nancy Chodorow for her view that this paper addresses gender differentiation and gender strategies rather than gender construction.

6. Carol B. Stack, "The Culture of Gender among Women of Color," *Signs* 12, no. 1 (Winter 1985): 321–324.

7. I am grateful to Laura Nader for helpful discussions of this topic.

8. Joan W. Scott, "Gender: A Useful Category of Historical Analysis," *American Historical Review* 91, no. 5 (December, 1986): 1070.

9. Carol B. Stack, *All Our Kin: Strategies for Survival in a Black Community* (New York: Harper and Row, 1974).

10. Carol B. Stack, *The Call to Home: African Americans Reclaim the Rural South* (forthcoming).

11. Michael Omi and Howard Winant, *Racial Formation in the United States* (New York: Routledge & Kegan Paul, 1986).

12. Carol Gilligan, *In a Different Voice: Psychological Theory and Women's Development* (Cambridge: Harvard University Press, 1982).

13. Teresa de Lauretis, "Eccentric Subjects: Feminist Theory and Historical Consciousness," unpub. ms., UC Santa Cruz.

14. Linda K. Kerber, Catherine G. Greeno and Eleanor E. Maccogy, Zella Luria, Carol B. Stack, and Carol Gilligan, "In a Different Voice: An Interdisciplinary Forum," *Signs* 12, no. 1 (Winter 1985): 304–333.

15. Jane Atanuchi, private communication.

16. Carol B. Stack and John Cromartie, "The Journeys of Children," ms.

17. All the names of people interviewed in this section have been changed.

18. Carol Gilligan, "Women's Place in Man's Life Cycle," Harvard Educational Review 49:4, 1979; *In a Different Voice: Psychological Theory and Women's Development* (Cambridge: Harvard University Press, 1982).

19. bell hooks (Gloria Watkins), *Talking Back: Thinking Feminist, Thinking Black* (Boston: South End Press, 1989). See, in particular, the discussion on page 20.

20. The concept of the "extended self" is a commonly used one in Afrocentric thinking.

21. Vernon Dixon, "World Views and Research Methodology," in L. M. King, V. Dixon, and W. W. Nobles, eds., *African Philosophy: Assumptions and Paradigms for Research on Black Persons* (Los Angeles: Fanon Center Publication, 1976).

22. Bonnie Dill, "The Dialectics of Black Womanhood," in *Feminism and Methodology,* ed. Sandra Harding (Bloomington and Indianapolis: Indiana University Press, 1987).

CHAPTER TWO

Constructing Amniocentesis: Maternal and Medical Discourses

RAYNA RAPP

When we walked into the doctor's office, both my husband and I were crying. He looked up and said, "What's wrong? Why are you in tears?" "It's the baby, the baby is going to die", I said. "That isn't a baby," he said firmly. "It's a collection of cells that made a mistake".
—Leah Rubinstein, white housewife, 39

The language of biomedical science is powerful. Its neutralizing vocabulary, explanatory syntax, and distancing pragmatics provide universal descriptions of human bodies and their life processes that appear to be pre-cultural or non-cultural. But as the field of medical anthropology constantly reminds us, bodies are also and always culturally constituted, and their aches, activities, and accomplishments are continuously assigned meanings. While the discourse of biomedicine speaks of the inevitable march of scientific and clinical progress, its practices are constantly open to interpretation. Its hegemonic definitions routinely require acceptance, transformation, or contestation from the embodied "objects" whose subjectivity it so powerfully affects.

The necessary contest over the meaning assigned embodied experiences is particularly clear in the field of reproductive health care, where consumer movements, women's health activism, and feminist scholars have sharply criticized biomedical practices. Public accusations against the demeaning and controlling nature of gynecological and obstetrical health care have led to dramatic results. Over the last 20 years, such criticisms have influenced the reform of medical services, occasionally encouraged the development of alternative health practices, and often inspired women to advocate for themselves and others. Contests over the means and meanings of women's reproductive health services are, thus, an ongoing part of American social and institutional life. These conflicts reflect the complex hierarchies of power, along which both providers and consumers of health care are organized. They cannot easily be resolved because the practices of biomedicine are at once emancipatory and socially controlling, essential for healthy survival yet essentializing of women's lives.

Reproductive medicine and its feminist critique thus share a central concern with the problem of female identity. In both discourses, as throughout much of American culture, motherhood stands as a condensed symbol of female identity. Changes in sexual practices, pregnancy, and birth are widely believed to be transforming the meaning of "womanhood" itself. This connection between women's reproductive patterns and a notion of female gender is longstanding: cries of alarm have been raised for over a century concerning the future of "the sex" as birth control practices spread, as abortion was criminalized and medicalized, as childbirth moved from the hands of female lay practitioners to male professionals, and as a discourse of explicitly female sexual pleasure became articulated. There is, of course, great diversity in women's experiences with medical care in general, and the medicalization of sexual activity and reproduction in particular. Yet, the image of "womanhood" as a central symbol in American culture has often been constructed as if motherhood were its stable, and uniform core, threatened by external changes in technology, education, labor force participation, medicine, and the like.

This shared and shifting object of embodied gender is revealed when we examine what have come to be called "the new reproductive technologies", dramatic and well-publicized interventions into fertility, conception, and pregnancy management and screening. Biomedical claims about the NRTs are usually framed in the available language of neutral management of female bodies to insure progress; feminist critiques are often enunciated as protection of women's core experiences against intrusion by "technodocs". Both discourses are fraught with old assumptions about the meaning of pregnancy, itself an archetypically liminal state. And both discourses are shot through with contradictions and possibilities for the health care providers, pregnant women, and feminist commentators who currently must make sense of the rapid routinization of new reproductive technologies.

This article presents an analysis of amniocentesis, one of the new reproductive technologies.[1] My examples are drawn from an ongoing field study of the social impact and cultural meaning of prenatal diagnosis in New York City, where I have observed more than 250 intake interviews, in which genetic counselors interact with pregnant patients; interviewed over 70 current users and refusers of amniocentesis; collected stories of 30 women who received what is so antiseptically referred to as a "positive diagnosis" (i.e., that something was wrong with their fetus), and participated and interviewed in a support group for parents of children with Down syndrome, the most commonly diagnosed chromosome abnormality, and the condition for which pregnant women are most likely to seek amniocentesis[2].

In New York City, unlike many other parts of the United States, prenatal diagnosis is funded by both medicaid and the City's Health Department, so it is available to a population of women whose ethnic, class, racial and religious backgrounds are as diverse as the City itself. The City's cytogenetic laboratory through which I work reaches a population of pregnant women who are approximately one-third Hispanic, one-third African-American, and one-third white, according to the racial/ethnic categories provided by both the City and State Health Departments. But these categories undoubtedly conceal as much as they reveal. At the present time, "Hispanic" includes Puerto Ricans and Dominicans long familiar with City services and the "new migrants" of Central America, many of whom are drawn from rural backgrounds, are desperately poor, and often undocumented, as well as middle-class, highly educated Colombians and Ecuadorians who may be experiencing downward mobility through migration. African-Americans include fourth-generation New Yorkers, women whose children circle back and forth between the City and rural Alabama, and Haitians who have lived in Brooklyn only a few months. "White" encompasses Ashkenazi and Sephardic Jews, Irish, Italian and Slavic Catholics, Episcopalian and Evangelical Protestants, as if being neither Black nor Brown placed them in a homogenized racial category. The categories themselves thus freeze a "racial map," which ignores the historic complexity of identity endemic to New York, and many other urban areas in contemporary America. Despite any understanding of the historic processes by which such a map has been created and promulgated, it is nearly impossible to escape its sociological boundaries when conducting and describing fieldwork in New York City.

My interviews and observations are tuned to the tension between the universal abstract language of reproductive medicine, and the personal experiences pregnant women articulate in telling their amniocentesis stories. Differences among women are revealed in their reasons for accepting or refusing the test; their images of fetuses and of disabled children; and the meaning of abortion in their lives. My working assumption is that a conflict of discourses necessarily characterizes the arena of reproductive technology, where nothing is stable: scientific "information", popular struggles both feminist and anti-feminist, and the shifting meaning of maternity and womanhood for individuals and communities with diverse ethnic, racial, religious, sexual, and migration histories are all currently under negotiation.

As one of the new reproductive technologies, prenatal diagnosis makes powerful claims to reveal and characterize biological bodies. Bypassing women's direct experiences of pregnancy, prenatal diagnosis uses sonography, an amniotic tap, and laboratory karyotyping to describe fetal health and illness to the woman (and her support network) within whose body the fetus grows[3]. Prenatal diagnosis focuses on pregnancy, first decontextualizing it and then inscribing it in a universal chronology, location, and ontology. Maternal serum alphafetoprotein blood screens (MSAFP), for example, may suggest a neural tube defect if readings are too high for a given pregnancy's dates, or a fetus with Down syndrome if values are too low. But the calibration of values is tricky, and potentially abnormal results must be recalibrated against a sonogram, whose measurement of cranial circumference and femur length is commonly considered the most accurate indicator of pregnancy dates. There is thus ample room for negotiating interpretations within the biomedical model. Many women already hold firm opinions about the dating of their pregnancies before they become acquainted with this highly technical process. Any woman may insist that she knows exactly when she became pregnant, or date her own growing pregnancy by signs phenomenologically available only to herself, contesting the narrative strategy of MSAFP, LMP (last menstrual period) and sono-dates. But when pregnancies are medically managed, most women learn to redescribe their bodily changes through the language of technology, rather than dating their pregnancies experientially. There is thus a continuous negotiation circling the description of any pregnancy in which a woman reveals and embeds herself and her perceptions of her fetus in a language shot through with medical, personal, and communal resources.

THE LANGUAGE OF TESTING

Women use very different language and reasons in describing their acceptance or refusal of the test. When I first began interviewing middle-class pregnant women about their amniocentesis decisions, it was hard for me to hear their cultural constructions, for, like my own, they mirrored the progressive message of science. Most (but not all) middle-class women, a disproportionately white group, accepted the test with some variant of this statement:

I always knew I'd have amnio. Science is there to make life better, so why not use its power? Bill and I really want a child, but we don't want a baby with Down's, if we can avoid it.
(Susan Klein, white accountant, 37)

But even white, middle-class women often express ambivalence and they do so in a language intricately intertwined with the language of medicine itself. Their fears and fantasies reflect thoughts that both question and sustain the dominant discourse itself, for example:

I cried for two days after I had the test. I guess I was identifying with universal motherhood, I felt like my image of my womb had been shattered. It still feels like it's in pieces, not like such a safe place as before. I guess technology gives us a certain kind of control, but we have to sacrifice something in return. I've lost my brash confidence that my body just produces healthy babies all by itself, naturally, and that if it doesn't, I can handle whatever comes along as a mother.
(Carola Mirsky, white school teacher, 39)

The low-income African-American women with whom I talked were far less likely to either accept, or be transformed by, the medical discourse of prenatal diagnosis. American black women who had grown up in the South, especially the rural South, often described alternate, non-medical agendas in their use of amniocentesis, invoking other systems for interpreting bodily states, including pregnancy. Dreams, visions, healing sessions, root work and herbal teas could be used to reveal the state of a specific pregnancy. One such woman, who at 27 became the mother of a Down syndrome baby, told me she had been refused amniocentesis in five city hospitals, always because of her young age. When I asked why she had wanted the test, she described a dream which recurred throughout the pregnancy:

So I am having this boy baby. It is definitely a boy baby. And something is wrong, I mean, it just is not right. Sometimes, he is missing an arm, and sometimes, it's a leg. Maybe it's a retarded baby. You can't really tell, it's all covered in hair. Once or twice, they give him to my husband and say, 'look at your son, take him the way he is'. As if the way he is isn't all right. I tried to get that test to make peace with that dream (Q: would you have had an abortion if you'd had the test?) Oh, no. The whole thing was going back to the dreams . . . just so's I could say, 'this baby is the baby in the dreams' and come to peace with it.
(May Norris, African-American hospital orderly, 27)

Another African-American woman, pregnant with a fourth, unexpected child at the age of 42, had this to say:

So I was three months pregnant before I knew I was pregnant, just figured it was change of life. The clinic kept saying no, and it's really the same signs, menopause and pregnancy, you just feel that lousy. So when they told me I was pregnant I thought about abortion, I mean, maybe I figured I was too old for this. But in my neighborhood a lot of Caribbean women have babies, a lot of them are late babies. So I got used to it. But the clinic doctor was freaked out. He sent me for genetic counseling. Counseling? I thought counseling meant giving reassurance, helping someone accept and find their way. Wisdom, help, guidance, you know what I mean. This lady was a smart lady, but right away she started pullin' out pictures of mongoloids. So I got huffy: 'I didn't come here to look at pictures of mongoloids', I says to her. So she got huffy and told me it was about mongoloids, this counseling. So we got more and more huffy between us, and finally, I left. Wasn't gonna sit and listen to that stuff. By the time I got myself to the appointment (for the test) I'd been to see my healing woman, a healer, who calmed me down, gave me the reassurance I needed. I knew everything was gonna be ok. Oh, I wouldn't have had an abortion that late in the game. I just got helped out by the healer woman, so I could wait out the results of that test without too much fussin'.
(Naiumah Foster, school teacher, 43)

And among women whose background includes no prior encounter with the scientific description of amniocentesis, the test may be accepted out of the desire to avoid the suffering of children; a respect for the authority of doctors (or the conflated image of genetic counselors in white coats); or simple curiosity. One recently arrived Salvadoran, now working as a domestic, told me, for example, that she wanted the test because science had such miraculous powers to show you what God had in store. This mixing of religious and secular discourses is no less awed (and awesome!) than that of the native-born professional woman who told me she wanted her test to be an advancement to science. She knew it was the only way geneticists could legally obtain amniotic fluid for their research, to which she ardently wished to make a contribution. Both women characterized amniocentesis as a path of enlightenment, but their motivations for its use differed sharply. The one characterized it in terms of God's grace; the other in light of scientific progress.

Even those rejecting the test often express amazement and interest in the powers of reproductive medicine. A Haitian Evangelist who said she would never accept amniocentesis wavered briefly when she learned it could tell her the sex of her baby: did such information cost more, she queried? (as the mother of four daughters, she had high hopes and great curiosity). Among those rejecting the test, reasons included anti-abortion attitudes often (but not always) articulated in religious terms[4]; fear of losing the baby after medical invasion[5]; anger and mistrust of the medical system; and fear of needles.

When I first began observing counseling sessions, it was easy for me to share the psychological lingo many counselors use privately, in evaluating patients' motives for accepting or rejecting the test. A discourse of fluent Freudian phrases is used by counselors trained in psychological-psychoanalytic thinking, as well as in human genetics. Women may easily be labelled "denying," "regressed," "passive," or "fatalistic" when their choices are seen as irrational to professionals trained to balance empathy against epidemiological statistics. Such labels, however, reduce social phenomena and cultural contexts to individual idiosyncrasies. I have often observed communication gaps, negotiated decisions, and situations of multiple meaning, which cannot be understood when reduced to a model of individual decision-making. When a Puerto Rican garment worker, aged 39, who is a Charismatic Catholic, replied to the offer of "the needle test," "No, I take this baby as God's love, just the way it is, Hallelujah," one genetics counselor felt hard pressed to understand what was going on. It was easier to fall back upon individualizing psycho-speak than to acknowledge the complexity of the patient's cultural life, which profoundly influenced her choices. When a Hungarian-born artist, 38, refused amniocentesis because "it wouldn't be done in my country until 40, and besides, we are all very healthy," I observed a genetics counselor probe extensively into genealogy, and finally discover one possibly Ashkenazi Jewish grandparent. Because of this, the counselor was able to recommend Tay-Sacks screening. Visibly shaken, the pregnant woman agreed. In instances such as these, the hegemonic discourse of science encounters cultural differences of nationality, ethnicity, or religion and often chooses to reduce them to the level of individual defensiveness. Yet what is being negotiated (or not negotiated, in the first example) is the power of scientific technology to intersect and rewrite the languages previously used for the description of pregnancies, fetuses, and family problems.

WHAT IS SEEN

Whether they accepted or refused amniocentesis, virtually all the women with whom I spoke had undergone a sonogram by the mid-trimester of pregnancy. My data on images of fetuses have been collected in light of the powerful restructuring of experience and understanding this piece of obstetrical technology has already accomplished. Several native Spanish-speaking women (both poor and middle-class) described their fetuses in nontechnological imagery: "it's a liquid baby, it won't become a solid baby until the seventh month"; "it's like a little lizard in there, I think it has a tail"; "it's a cauliflower, a bunch of lumps growing inside me". Their relative autonomy from technological imagery may be due as much to having recently emigrated from countries and regions where hospital-based prenatal care is both less common and less authoritative, as to anything inherently "Hispanic".

Most women were fascinated with the glimpses they received of the fetal beating heart; its imagery fits nicely into a range of Christian symbols. And several were also impressed by the fetal brain, which is measured during sonography. Heart and brain, feeling and intellect, are already subjects of prenatal speculation among women for whom fetal imaging has been objectified.

Most women born in the United States, whatever their ethnic and class background, invoked the visual language of sonography and its popular interpretation to answer my query, "Tell me what the pregnancy feels and looks like to you now?" For one it was "a little space creature, alone in space"[6], for another it was "a creature, a tiny formed baby creature, but because its eyes are closed, it is only a half baby". Another woman told me that as her pregnancy progessed, she felt the fetus' image becoming more finely tuned in, like a television picture coming into better focus. White middle-class women (especially those having a first baby) frequently spoke of following fetal development in books which included week-by-week sonograms. Thus, technological imagery is reproduced in text as well as image, available to be studied privately, at home, as well as in public, medical facilities. Learning about what the technology can do, and about what the baby appears to be, proceed simultaneously.

Poorer women were unlikely to have such primers, but they, too, had been bombarded by the visualization of fetuses (and amniocentesis, with its attendant moral dilemmas) in the popular media. When asked where they first learned about amniocentesis, many Hispanic and white working class women mentioned three episodes of "Dallas" in which prenatal diagnosis plays a large part, and one African-American woman said she knew about

Down syndrome "because the Kennedys had one" in a story she'd read in the *National Enquirer*. In the weeks following a Phil Donahue show devoted to Down syndrome children and their families, clinic patients spoke with great interest about that condition. Increasingly, health care providers must confront the popularization of their technologies, with all its attendant benefits and distortions, in their interviews with patients.

The widespread deployment of sonographic imagery is hardly innocent. Whatever its medical benefits, the cultural contests it enables are by now well known: anti-abortion propaganda is shot through with sonographic images, to which those who would defend abortion rights have had to respond.[7] Some people use this technology for political advantage in medical settings, as well as in popular culture. Several genetic counselors offered stories about Right-to-Life sonographers who aggressively insisted on delivering detailed verbal descriptions of fetuses and handing fetal images to women who were planning to have abortions after positive diagnoses. While this punitive behavior may seem excessive, even the seemingly neutral language of reproductive medicine affects pregnant women, who sometimes describe themselves as "maternal environments" in interviews. Until well after World War II, there were no medical technologies for the description of fetuses independent of the women in whose body a given pregnancy was growing. Now, sciences like "perinatology" focus on the fetus itself, bypassing the consciousness of the mother, and permitting her, as well as biomedical personnel, to image the fetus as a separate entity. I will return to the importance of this internal disconnection and reconnection to fetal imagery in the next section.

Because amniocentesis was explicitly developed to probe for chromosome-based disabilities and confront a woman with the choice to end or continue her pregnancy based on its diagnostic powers, my interview schedule includes questions about the images of disabled fetuses women carry and disabled children they might raise. Here, too, television and magazine representations of disability loom large. One Peruvian factory worker who had lived in New York for 14 years spoke of them as Jerry kids (a reference to Jerry Lewis' telethons—an image hotly contested by the disability rights movement). A white working-class woman who had adopted two disabled children told this story about arriving at her maternal choices watching the telethons:

Ever since I was a little girl, I always watched those telethons, I always knew it was a shame, a crying shame that no one loved those kids enough. So when I was a teenager, I got to be a candy-striper, and I worked with kids in wheelchairs, and I always knew I'd adopt them before I'd have them for myself. I'm not afraid of problems. I've got a daughter with spina bifida, and they said she'd be a vegetable. Fat chance! My other one's gonna be mentally retarded. I can handle it. I learned these kids need love on the telethon.
(Lisa Feldman, white home maker, 26)

Most women in my sample could recall someone in their own childhood or community who had a child with Down's syndrome. Their memories invoke mothers intensely involved and devoted. Many described positive relationships that women had with their mentally retarded children. And some even talked about the hidden benefits of having a "permanent child" as the mother herself grew older, and became widowed. Most middle-class women, however, drew a contrast between themselves and those Down syndrome mothers they had encountered:

It's too much work. There's a certain kind of relationship I want to have with my child, and it isn't like that one, that's so dependent, forever. I wouldn't be any good at it, I'd resent my child.
(Ilene Cooper, white college professor, 40)

Oh, I know I'd work really hard at it, I'd throw myself into it, but I'm afraid I'd lose myself in the process. I wouldn't be like her, she was a really great mother, so self-sacrificing.
(Laura Forman, white theatre producer, 35)

My aunt was terrific. But she stayed home. I know I'm going back to work after this baby is born, and I can't imagine what it would take to do it her way.
(Susan Klein, white accountant, 37)

What accompanied these she/me distinctions in the discourse of white, middle-class women was a running battle over the question of selfishness and self-actualization, a problem linked to the central importance of "choice" as a cultural value and strategy. This is a subject to which I will return below.

Working class and low-income African-American women were no less concerned about the possible diagnosis of Down syndrome, but they often saw their decision-making as taking place within networks of support. One low-income African-American single mother expressed strong anti-abortion sentiments, but requested the test. Had the results been positive, she intended to move home to Georgia, where her mother would help her to raise a baby with health problems. A black secretary married to a black plumber chose to end her third pregnancy after a prenatal diagnosis of Down Syndrome. When I asked her how she'd made the decision, and who had given her advice, support or criticism, she described the active involvement of clergy and community members in the church to which she belonged.

Among many Hispanic women, mostly working-class and low-income (both those choosing and refusing amniocentesis), the image of mothering a disabled child conjured less ambivalence than among white, middle-class women. Friends and relations with sickly children were recalled, and testimonies about the sacrificial qualities of maternity were offered. There was often a conflation of maternal and child suffering, including this madonna-like image:

When they told me what the baby would suffer, I decided to abort. But it was Easter, so I couldn't do it, I just couldn't do it until His suffering was ended. Then my child could cease to suffer as well.
(Lourdes Ramirez, Dominican house cleaner, 41)

THE MEANING OF ABORTION

The meaning of abortion loomed large in the consciousness of pregnant women discussing amniocentesis. All women could articulate reasons for and against late abortion after a prenatal diagnosis of a serious condition. These included the evaluation of the child's suffering; the imagined effects of a disabled baby on other siblings and on the parents themselves; the sense of responsibility for having brought a baby into the world who might never grow to "independence"; and, sometimes, the "selfishness" of wanting one's own life to be free of the burdens a disabled child is thought to impose. For Hispanic women, fear of the child's suffering was most salient, followed closely by the effects its birth would have on other children. They were, in principle, more accepting of the sacrifices they imagined disabled children to call forth from their mothers. It is hard to disentangle ethnicity, language, class and religion in these responses. As one Honduran domestic worker awaiting amniocentesis results told me:

Could I abort if the baby was going to have that problem? God would forgive me, surely, yes, I could abort. Latin Catholics, we are raised to fear God, and to believe in His love and forgiveness. Now, if I were Evangelical, that's another story. It's too much work, being Evangelical. My sisters are both Evangelicals, they go to Church all the time. There's no time for abortion for them.
(Maria Acosta, 41)

Many Hispanic women reported having had early, multiple abortions and did not discuss the procedure as morally problematic. Yet many also identified *late* abortion as a sin, because quickening has occurred. In this case, a set of subtle and differentiated female experiences is being developed as popular theology.

Low-income African-American women weighed nonmedical agendas in deciding to accept amniocentesis and possibly consider abortion: confirmation of dreams, prior omens and use of healers all figured in the stories they told about why the test might be of use to them. Many low-income Hispanic women appear wrapped up in intertwined images of maternal and child suffering. White middle-class women seem most vulnerable to the abortion controversy currently raging in our national, political culture. Virtually all of the women I interviewed from this group, whether Catholic, Jewish, or Protestant, provided critical exegeses on the tension between "selfishness" and "self-actualization". Again and again, in assessing the possibility or the reality of aborting a disabled fetus, women questioned whether that decision would be selfish. Their concerns revealed something of the limits of self-sacrifice that mothers are alleged to embody.

I share a lot of the feelings of the Right-to-Life Movement, I've always been shocked by the number of abortion clinics, the number of abortions, in this city. But when it was *my* turn, I was grateful to find the right doctor. He helped me to protect my own life, and that's a life, too.
(Mary Fruticci, white home maker, 44)

This reflection over selfishness and self-actualization is mirrored in two counter-discourses, one particularly "male", one more classically "female". Several middle-class, white husbands went to some length to point out that a decision to bring a disabled child into the world knowingly was, in their view, "selfish":

If you have a child that has severe defects, the natural thing I think that would happen would be that it would die at a very early age and what you're doing is you're prolonging, artificially, the child. And I think that most of the people that do that, do it for themselves, they don't really do it for the child, and it tends to be a very selfish thing for people to do.
(Jim Norton, white lawyer, 42)

Their inversion of selfishness neatly reverses the vector of blame, which Right-to-Life imagery would pin on their wives.

Several white, middle-class women articulated a different discourse, one which confronted selfishness with an implicit critique of medical technology, and nostalgia for a lost and imagined maternity:

The whole time they were doing more sonograms, checking the chromosomes, confirming their diagnosis, that whole time I kept thinking, "I'll keep the baby, I'll go to the hospital, I'll nurse right there. Who knows, in a year, two years, this baby might get better". I just kept romancing that, wanting to believe that I could be that kind of mother.
(Jamie Steiner, white health educator, 33)

If only I could have become supermom, given that baby everything she needed. But I can't even bake an apple pie, so how could I do it all? Meanwhile, I kept going for more tests, more consultations. (Q: why did you take a month to make the decision to abort?) The technology was so interesting. And you know what, I became an interesting case. I know this sounds sick, but I've got to be honest and tell you that this technology replaced the baby in what was making me special.
(Sybil Wootenberg, white artist, 41)

For some, the critique of technological reasoning is more explicit:

You know, I kept thinking after the genetic counseling, the amniocentesis, they just keep upping the ante on you, they really do. Now, I'm not even allowed to pet my cat, or have a glass of wine after a hard day's work. I'm supposed to think that three cigarettes a day is what caused my first miscarriage. They

can see a lot of patterns, but they sure can't explain them. But they talk as if they could explain them. I mean, they want you to have a baby by the statistics, not from your own lifestyle.
(Laura Forman, white theatre producer, 35)

I was hoping I'd never have to make this choice, to become responsible for choosing the kind of baby I'd get, the kind of baby we'd accept. But everyone, my doctor, my parents, my friends, everyone urged me to come for genetic counseling and have amniocentesis. Now, I guess I'm having a modern baby. And they all told me I'd feel more in control. But I guess I feel less in control. It's still my baby, but only if it's good enough to be our baby, if you see what I mean.
(Nancy Smithers, white lawyer, 36)

Why are white middle-class women so self-critical and ambivalently technological? Three themes contextualize their concerns.

The first is that the material conditions of motherhood really are changing, dramatically so, within these women's lifetimes. White women who "have careers" and postpone babies are directing their lives differently than the women in the communities from whom they learned to mother. Unlike African-American women, for whom working mothers are longstanding community figures, and motherhood is a culturally public role, and unlike many Hispanic respondents, who painted images of sacrificial motherhood, for white middle-class women, individual self-development looms large as a cultural goal.

While *all* Americans prize "choice" as a political and cultural value, large scale changes in education, labor-force participation, postponed marriage and childbirth have enabled many white middle-class women to maintain at least an illusion of control over their lives to a degree unprecedented for other groups. Their relative freedom from unwanted pregnancies and child illness and death is easily ascribed to advances in medical science. Medical technology transforms their "choices" on an individual level, allowing them, like their male partners, to imagine voluntary limits to their commitments to children.

But it does not transform the world of work, social services, media, and the like on which a different sense of maternity and the "private" sphere would depend. Moreover, that "private" sphere and its commitment to child bearing is now being enlarged to include men. Fathers, too, can now be socially created during the pregnancy, through birth-coaching, and early bonding. These new fathers may also claim the right to comment on women's motives for pregnancy and abortion in powerful ways.

Individually, white middle-class women may be "becoming more like men", freer than ever before to enter hegemonic realms of the culture from which they were formerly barred, but at the price of questioning and altering their traditional gender identity.[8] Modern, high-technological maternity is part of the gender relations now under negotiation, and may belong to new, emergent traditions. But it presently lies in an ambivalent terrain, a kind of "no man's land" between the technological claims to liberation through science, and the feminist recovery and romance with nurturance as a valuable activity.

A second reason for white middle-class women's ambivalence about pre-natal diagnosis and abortion may well be, paradoxically, their close con-nection with the benefits and burdens of the increasing medicalization of pregnancy. While "everybody" now undergoes pregnancy sonograms, not everybody is as committed as this group to the medical discourse, and its images in pregnancy primers. For them, a paradoxical separation and re-connection to fetuses appears to be underway. On the one hand, they can "see" their fetuses in pictures and on medical screens. This allows for the "early bonding" which runs rampant through the parenting and obstetrical literature. But a seen fetus is also a separate fetus, one to whom one connects as a "maternal environment", in obstetrical language, and as a "sanctuary" in the words of The Silent Scream.[9] Paradoxically, white middle-class women are both better served by reproductive medicine, and also more controlled by it, than women of less privileged groups. They are likely to be educated in the same institutions in which doctors are produced, and their own language closely mirrors medical speech and its critique in both the Right-to-Life's discourse of "selfishness" and mainstream feminism's "self-actualization".

A third reason for complex and contradictory feelings about abortion is not confined to white middle-class women, although the cultural and med-ical importance of individualism may make them particularly vulnerable to its effects. This reason concerns the shifting historical ground on which abortion practices rest. That point was dramatically made to me in one amniocentesis story:

For three weeks, we tried to develop further information on oomphaloceles and satellites on the chromosomes, and the whole time, my mother kept saying, "why are you torturing yourselves, why don't you just end it now, why do you need to know more"? She'd had an abortion between her two pregnancies. And my mother-in-law had even had a late abortion when she first got to this country, and she kept saying the same thing: "I put away one, just do it, and get it over with". And I was so conflicted, and also so angry. So finally I turned on my mother and asked her, "How can you be so insensitive, it's such a hard decision for us, you can't just dismiss this". And as we talked, I realized how different their abortions were from mine. They were illegal. You've got to remember that, they were illegal. They were done when you worried about the stigma of getting caught, and maybe, getting sick. But you didn't think about the fetus, you thought about saving your own life.
(Jamie Steiner, white health educator, 33)

Illegal abortions were dangerous and expensive. They were performed under the shadow of death—maternal, not fetal. Morbidity and mortality from the complications of abortion dropped sharply after 1973, in the wake of Roe V. Wade. Indeed, "Abortion related deaths have decreased by 73 percent" within a decade of abortion decriminalization.[10] Criminal prosecution, morbidity and mortality, were the fears attached to illegal abortions but not "selfishness." A variety of social forces, including medical reform and feminist political organization, led to abortion law reform. On the heels of its success, the Right-to-Life movement was quickly organized. We cannot really understand the talk of "selfishness" articulated by middle-class women, and used against all women, until we locate the meaning of abortion at the intersection of culture, politics, technology, and social change.[11]

Science speaks a universal language of progress. But women express their diverse consciousness and practices in polyglot, multicultural languages. When women speak about the medicalization of reproduction, what they tell us must be placed in its historical, social context. Amniocentesis and other new reproductive technologies open a Pandora's box of powerful knowledge, constructed through scientific and medical practices. But messages sent are not necessarily messages received. New technologies fall onto older cultural terrains, where women interpret their options in light of prior and contradictory meanings of pregnancy and childbearing. Any serious understanding of how "motherhood" is changing under the influence of the New Reproductive Technologies depends on realizing women's stratified diversity. Otherwise, it will reproduce the vexing problem of the false universalization of gender which feminism itself initially promised to transcend.

NOTES

Earlier drafts of this article were read by Faye Ginsburg, Evelyn Fox Keller, Shirley Lindenbaum, and Anna Tsing. I thank them for their criticisms and suggestions. Faye Ginsburg deserves my greatest gratitude: without her support and direction, this paper would never have been completed.

1. Support for the field research on which this article is based was provided by the National Science Foundation, the National Endowment for the Humanities, the Rockefeller Foundation's "Program in Changing Gender Roles", and the Institute for Advanced Study. I thank them all. I am especially grateful to the many health care providers who shared their experiences with me, and allowed me to observe them at work, and to the hundreds of pregnant women and their supporters who shared their amniocentesis stories with me. Where individual illustrations are provided in the text, all names have been changed to protect confidentiality.

2. Additional reports on the fieldwork from which this article is drawn can be found in "Moral Pioneers: Women, Men and Fetuses on a Frontier of Reproductive Technology," *Women & Health* 13 (1987): 101–116; "The Powers of Positive Diagnosis: Medical and Maternal Discourses on Amniocentesis," in Karen Michaelson, ed. *Childbirth in America: Anthropological Perspectives* (South Hadley, Mass.: Bergin & Garvey, 1988); "Chromosomes and Communication: The Discourse of Genetic Counseling," *Medical Anthropology Quarterly* 2 (1988): 121–142; and "Accounting for Amniocentesis," in Shirley

Lindenbaum and Margaret Lock, eds., *Analysis in Medical Anthropology* (New York: Cambridge University Press, forthcoming).

3. See Ann Oakley, *The Captured Womb* (Oxford, England: Blackwell, 1984), ch. 7, for an interesting discussion of how medical technology bypasses and reconstructs knowledge of fetuses, which excludes the perceptions of pregnant women.

4. Religiously framed anti-abortion sentiments were expressed more often among Evangelicals than Catholics, at least among Hispanics and Caribbean Blacks. At the same time, many Hispanic Pentecostals and Charismatic Catholics, and Black Seventh Day Adventists accept amniocentesis in City clinics. It is important to distinguish official Church theology from local practices, including the discursive resources, social networks, and strategies particular church membership may provide.

5. Amniocentesis adds an increase of one-third of one percent to the miscarriage rate. This is considered statistically insignificant, but as genetic counselors are quick to point out, no risk is insignificant when assessing a given pregnancy, rather than simply constructing statistics. And prior reproductive history powerfully shapes how this statistic is interpreted.

6. Barbara Katz Rothman, *The Tentative Pregnancy* (New York: Viking Penguin, 1986), 114, provides an excellent discussion of the implications of sonography for maternal/fetal separation. Rosalind Petchesky has written a powerful critique of the history and hegemony of fetal images in "Fetal Images: the Power of Visual Culture in the Politics of Reproduction", *Feminist Studies* 13 (1987): 263–292. See Oakley, *The Captured Womb,* for a history of sonography.

7. My understanding of the importance of fetal imagery in political struggles is deeply indebted to Rosalind Petchesky, "Fetal Images . . ." Most activists have viewed "The Silent Scream" and Planned Parenthood's video "Response to the Silent Scream" and clips from both were widely available on television in 1984 and 1985, the years of their release.

8. Faye Ginsburg, "Dissonance and Harmony: The Symbolic Function of Abortion in Activists' Life Stories," in The Personal Narratives Group, ed., *Interpreting Women's Lives* (Bloomington, Ind.: Indiana University Press, 1989).

9. Again, see Rosalind Petchesky, "Fetal Images . . ."

10. Rosalind Petchesky, *Abortion and Woman's Choice* (Boston: Northeastern University Press, 1984), 157.

11. See Faye Ginsburg, *Contested Lives: The Abortion Debate in an American Community* (Berkeley & Los Angeles, Calif: University of California Press, 1989) for an excellent analysis of these historical intersections.

CHAPTER THREE

Backtalking the Wilderness: "Appalachian" En-genderings

KATHLEEN CLAIRE STEWART

In the no-man's-land between American and French feminism, talk has turned to the question of women speaking from the wilderness. "Civilization," it is said, is an ideology that constructs itself by banishing the woman, the primitive, and the body to the margins; civilization inflates itself against the constant deflations of the back talk, looks, silences, inefficiencies, irrationalities, ironies, confusions, contradictions, excesses, and laughter inscribed in everyday life. A disembodied "female" voice drifts and hovers at the margins, a silent but knowing "exile," a "madwoman in the attic," a "successful woman" who "passes" as a man, or the back-talking resistance of a woman who "speaks for herself."

The question of "woman's voice" has been the subject of wide debate and a focus of theoretical differences between Anglo-American and French feminism.[1] At issue have been the nature and origins of "a woman's voice",[2] its multiple and intertwined elements,[3] its power as cultural resistance or deconstruction,[4] and the place of the very concept of a unitary "woman's voice" in dominant first world ideologies.[5] De Lauretis or Kristeva would argue that the "female" voice is decentered because of its "doubleness"[6] for it simultaneously constructs gender and deconstructs it as it represents itself to itself. Spivak suggests that "gender" is "... networks of power/desire/interest" and these "are so heterogeneous that their reduction to a coherent narrative is counterproductive—a persistent critique is needed ..."[7] "Women's voice," then, need not be treated as having a particular content or as being a predictable "female" response to a fixed "male" view. Instead, it can be historically traced in its movements in and against the networks of power. The question becomes not "what is woman" or what is a "woman's voice" but how in cultural discourses—"our own" and "the Other's"—does "the feminine" find itself determined[8]—as madwoman, exile, or the woman with a tent of her own ...

Of course the very claim that there is a "woman's voice" that "back talks" the dominant culture sometimes reproduces structures it criticizes. Willis identifies this process as an ironic, unintended consequence of cultures of resistance.[9] Yet if this process is socially and historically contingent, we should be able to trace the interpretive practices that transform contentious, dialogic speech into fixed concepts of male and female and back again. Here I will look at particular practices in a prolifically discursive and marginalized culture—the "Appalachian" coal camps of southwestern West Virginia where "speaking as a woman" is not an expression of a female essence but a matter of "speaking for yourself" in the conventional genre of women's *back-talk*. This case is itself a kind of back-talk to a gender analysis of an earlier feminist theory which explained gender assymmetry in universal gendered dichotomies (i.e. domestic/public, nature/culture, reproduction/production). The task of analysis is to track the complex, contested domains of gendered discourses.

In this century everyday forms of speech such as storytelling, banter, and rhetoric have been progressively devalued, regulated, marginalized, or otherwise bounded. A psychological discourse of self-expression and its constraints is replacing, increasingly, the kind of talk that uses shared, conventional genres and styles. Such styles of speech are more and more the distinctive features of America's Others from "ethnic cultures" to the "eccentric" or "local" cultures that crowd the margins surrounding the domains of privacy, respectability, and polite speechlessness. But these voices from West Virginia propose yet an Other form of cultural resistance—one which specifically undermines and fragments the reification of categories such as Civilization with socially situated talk. Their "wilderness" is no place of silence but a cultural territory stuffed with talk and back-talk. Ask a person there what something "means" and they will say "Well I don't have no ideal (i.e. idea). It's just talk is all it is. Honey, this place ain't nothing *but* talk. Write that down in your book."

BACK-TALKING THE WILDERNESS

The West Virginia coalfields are an industrial wasteland: a place that has been bought, used up, and abandoned after a century of internal colonization that began with the deforestation of the hills and the loss of the old family farms. It continued in the company camps, the violent labor wars, the waves of unemployment that sent whole generations of unassimilated migrants back and forth between *these here hills* and *the cities of Hell*. There was the strip mining of the hills in the 1960s and 1970s, and the final closing of the mines between 1982 and 1985. A local culture is cut adrift and thrown back on the wild and shifting patterns of daily social interaction, and the proliferation of stories and named "ways" of talking that pile up like the junked appliances and trucks that spread out from a person's *place* into the hills, blurring the boundaries between "culture" and "nature."

They say *thangs is got down* and *a body has to stand up and speak for yourself.* The present is constructed in stories that elicit back talk. There are stories of old people done bad by insurance companies or greedy doctors, poor people treated like dogs at the welfare office, women and men done wrong by each other. But whatever the subject, the stories position the speaker to talk back. "Now, that man makes me mad. I cain't see that, can you? I'd tell him there's the door honey and don't come back and see me . . ." . . . "I told that doctor, I said, don't you do him that a way, cain't you see he's nothin but an old man ain't got nobody? . . ." The talk goes on all day with the relentless repetition that builds an insistent sense of right and the almost constant urge to talk back. Ironically, eccentricity and *orneriness* become the "hillbilly" identity, the means and meanings of relationships in the camps. They say "you cain't take nothin' from em"—not from the company, the doctors, the lawyers, the police, the schools, the welfare office, the nosy neighbors, the men, the women, the utility companies. . . .

A day in the camp is a twisting, discursive construct in which words and events mingle inextricably. Nothing that happens is left bald; multiple stories converge on every event as its possibilities and differing social values. The "meaning" of what is said depends on who says what to whom, on known genres of story, on the time of day and the place, and so on. Ways of talking such as *runnin your mouth, braggin, lyin,* and *talkin trash* set up social relations as confrontations. Social identities are taken up as certain ways of speaking; "speaking as a woman," or "speaking as a man" or as a Christian or a sinner, a Milam or a Smith, is a matter of literally "speaking for yourself." In short, ways of talking, including back talk, comments, and asides *produce* a social reality rather than merely "express" an inner reality or "describe" an outer reality.

Spouses, for instance, use a variety of stylized speech positions. At first, marriage is taken to be a potentially dangerous displacement; it takes two people out of their families and sets them adrift in a potentially *crazy love* that may turn violent and is likely to be *shameless* (i.e. socially ignorant and unplaced). Over time spouses "get used to" one another and "settle" into a rhythm of often contentious talk and comment; talk between spouses is talk between a McKinney and a Graham, a woman and a man, a waitress and a miner, a big mouth and a big heart, a drinkin' man and a fat woman, an animal and a mother . . . So central is the rhythm of talk and comment to the "meaning" of the talk between spouses that the speaker will pause and wait if the ordinary onslaught of running comment from the other is not forthcoming. If necessary they will explicitly request or demand comment before moving on. From time to time couples blow off steam with dramatic fights in the middle of the night that are loud enough for the rest of the camp to hear. The next day the fighting couple will have visits (she in the house, he in the alley next to his truck) from neighbors who will not press them for the story but wait to see if they "say anything" and listen intently for disjunctures, contradictions, and hidden messages if they *do* "say anything."

When a group of unrelated women and men somehow find themselves together—at the doctor's office or at a "community" meeting—they will "place" themselves in relation to each other by making a spectacle of sexual difference with highly stylized and excessive sexual banter. It is usually the oldest man and the oldest woman who do the talking, while the others form a quiet but "tickled" audience. They watch intently as the words fly back and forth in idioms of "cacklin' hens" and "roamin', good-for-nothin' roosters", of smothering (female) houses and wrecked broken down (male) trucks with their parts hanging out or put together wrong, of pots of gold buried in an old woman's back yard ("you know you cain't take it with you") and the old man's threat to dig them up in the night ("with what, that broke down old shovel a yours?"). The spectators may offer comment as if the speakers were not there at all, calling attention to the talk itself: "She really can put her words together, can't she," "Well now there's one I've never heard." When the display is over the talk will move quietly into conversation among people related along the specific social lines of gender or age or workplace or neighborhood or church. Even with mixed crowds of people who already know each other, there is the same display of sexual banter as everyone crowds into the kitchen; then, after a little bit, one sex will take a walk or step outside on the porch "so we can talk."

Gendered social "places" are interpretive spaces established through encounters with an Other. Otherness is inscribed in them like a ghostly apparition or felt possibility just outside the boundary of the established domain. The borders between male and female places are charged. The houses belong to the women and the men have their trucks, the mines, and the bars. Dangerous maleness clusters at the entrance to the house when mothers threaten their children toward the end of the day—"daddy's gonna whup the fire out of you when he gets home . . . B'lieve that's him comin now." A man never enters the house of a woman he is not related to because that would fill the house with illicit sexuality (both in the experience of the woman and man inside and in the interpretation of the ever observing neighbors); but in banter a man may threaten such a visit. Dangerous femaleness clusters around the *mouth* of a mine and apparitions of a ghostly widow or maiden floating (displaced) through the dark passages of the mine signal a roof fall or explosion (i.e. the collapse of the male social place).

Gender "ways" are so conventionalized and so dramatically performed that they tend to be clearly externalized as discourses rather than internalized as identities. In fact any move to internalize gender as an identity or to treat gendered domains as God-given is repelled with the same force that polarizes gender to begin with. Ask about gender differences and there will be loud and universal claims that men work in the mines and women keep the house, that men bring in the money and women get up and fix the breakfast, etc. But because such claims are made with such certainty they, like any other *braggin* talk, will also elicit an immediate counter claim that begins with the words "still yet." "Still yet" there is nothing more ridiculous than a woman who will not split wood or haul coal or shoot off the head of a thief in the night just because she is a woman. Nothing is so ridiculous as a man so "babified" he cannot cook himself a meal if he has to. Anyone "fool enough" to *take anything from* a spouse will draw condemning back-talk from a collective righteous voice of "the order of things"—"Way she takes it, she acts like she's an animal, or a robot or somethin'. Like that show we watched, 'Stepford Wives.' You cain't blame them women for getting mad and what they done (i.e. killed the men, blew up the town). Cause that's aggra*va*tin', I mean it honey." The only way to "set him (her) straight" is to "turn it back on him" (or her) and this they do with such polemical excess that talk moves into the ridiculous and ridiculing, decon-structing any possible claims to "natural" orders in a flourish of obvious constructions of *talk*. The social process involved is graphically referenced in Sissy Miller's description of what she said and did when her husband, Buddy, suggested that she could be more sexual and she "got mad and turned it back on him."[10]

> I don't have to take that from him.
> So I said 'Okay honey'
> and me and Joyce got to talkin
> and we went down Hoovers and got us a bucket a red paint
> the bright red
> and we painted that bedroom from the floor to the ceilin', we
> like to *died* laughin!
> an he come in and I told him 'Honey, come in here a minute.'
> an his eyes come up *out* of his head like a fish.
> an I said, 'Well, what's wrong, *honey*? You want me to act like
> a whore, now I got me a nice red room for it.'
> Well we like to *died*.

Here "speaking as a woman" directly contests an interpretation that would claim this as an "expression" of an essential female identity. Rather, such "back-talk" fragments and externalizes any assumed feminine char-acter, exposing the multivocal, contested social meanings that bring the categories of gender to attention in the first place. In their stories, women and men create engendered places and figures that—whether taken seriously or in jest, contentiously or harmoniously, or for whatever purpose—are in any case left open to response and elaboration.

Even the institutional sanctioning of gendered domains only functions to call attention to the policed borders and licenses the others' "outside" com-ment. For instance, only men are supposed to debate scripture in the (fun-damentalist) churches but this also means that the women keep up a commentary from their pews. (They also interrupt debates with an Other ungendered speech of spontaneous ecstatic trances, weeping, and testifying.) If a preacher dares to overstep his own bounds by suggesting, for instance, that women should not "imitate man" by wearing pants, he will only elicit back-talk from the women—a back talk that begins by setting the limits for his domain of authority: "Well, now, I b'lieve women shouldn't wear pants to church but no one is going to tell me I cain't wear my own pants in my own house." If he does not back down, their counter-attack will imitate to excess his own inappropriate speech; their *talk* will turn to his personal failures and dramatize the figure of "the greedy preacher" who is "in it" for the money, the hypocrite, two-faced, snake tongued preacher, and the womanizing fast talking preacher. Chances are good that he will be found out and expelled or that the "confusion" in the church (i.e. the free wheeling conflict of unplaced, polemical discourses) will lead to a schism. No matter what the ending, the moral of the story will be that a preacher, like everyone else, ought to "speak for his own self."

The two sexes become associated with places and objects but the associations are scrutinized, parodied, and unpacked in the very process of proposing them. Each sex becomes the object of the other's jokes; men elaborate on a link between women and their chicken houses that ends in wild imitations of women's "cackling" voices and women joke about men and their (liquor) bottles—"They aren't *like* babies, they *are* babies." So conventionalized and ridiculous are the jokes that they are reframed not as real gendered identities but as fantastic storied figures. And finally, each gender turns the same fragmenting, externalizing gaze on gender itself. Ask a generalizing or abstract question and you will only elicit "answers" that reopen the question, reintroduce multiplicity into the unitary gender category, and call for back talk, as in the following response to the question: "Why did women have so many children 30 years ago?"

"Well I don't have no ideal.
Go ask Maude Miller, she had 15.
Well, I'll tell you *what,*
it's just like *animals* is what it is.
Go ask Maude, come back tell me what she said."

Gender is not constructed as a closed identity but enacted as a shifting position that has to be continually reconstructed in encounters with the unnatural and other. Far from being a given set of attributes, it is read as an achievement requiring heroic (or foolish) self-assertion. So, for instance, far from assuming that women are "naturally" good mothers or house-keepers, every woman claims that she, for one, is "not the type." Mothers recount childbirth as a dangerous and bloody accident in the truck racing over the hills to get to the hospital on time. They complain that their children "hang on them" grotesquely, like animals, and then the mother-child relationship is enacted as a dramatic, contentious encounter. Children, they say with pride, are *mean* (i.e. independent, back-talking, clever, self-assertive). Mothers play out vacillating extremes of intimacy and threats of "violence" with them; the children, even when they are very young, respond with conventionalized, socially astute postures of indifference, fearlessness, back talk, or placid, unwavering "innocence." Wives say marriage makes women "spread and get fat" and they launch radical diets, abandon them, and relaunch them in a battle with nature and with "jealous" husbands who, they claim, would just as soon keep them fat so they can't "do anything" (with another man). Housework is storied as a battle with *the nasty* and with the excess things that pile up in the corners or closets; one day a woman will *take to the bed with the dizzy, smothered* with the stuff that has taken on a life of its own; but then, having set the stage for action, she may get up the next day (or perhaps it will take days or weeks) and launch a campaign to paint every room in the house, working ecstatically at an incredible pace. They prefer to "get out" and work in the garden and there is talk of snakes that could sneak up on them. The dramatic action response is to organize women's snake hunting parties that go up into the hills armed with garden hoes to find the snakes in their infamous snakey places and chop off their heads.

Men, like women, are not "naturally" suited to gender roles; but quite the contrary. They are not "naturally" good husbands or good providers but just "by nature" given to drinking and fighting and running the roads. Then they "turn around" suddenly in dramatic conversions to "borned again" Christianity—"I put that bottle down and I never touch it again. Never wanted to." Mining, they say, "gets in the blood" and is "passed on" from father to son. It is not "natural" but rather a dramatic encounter with danger produced by the *unnatural* act of entering the mouth of a mine and crawling on one's belly into the belly of the mountain. Mining is constructed in stories of explosions and roof falls and wild encounters with bosses and scabs; "the miner" is storied as a series of possible failures and successes. There are figures of the *experienced miner* who can *hear* the one crack in the ceiling that signals a roof fall, and the *ignorant* miner who smokes or drinks in the mines and wouldn't see the danger that killed him, and the miner whose uncontrolled (or unencountered) fear is a danger to himself and to his buddies. The space inside the mines (like the inside of the house for women) is en-gendered by the repeated encounters with the unnatural and dangerous. Where women dramatize encounters with *the nasty,* the piled up smothering houses, *the dizzy,* the snakes, spreading bodies, and clinging children, the men encounter *the nerves,* alcohol, violence, restlessness, and melancholia. The worst anyone can be is shameless (i.e. ignorant of socially situated ways of talking and acting) and hard hearted (i.e. unresponsive to people, politics, and poetics).

In short, gender in the coal camps is constructed in talk that reflects back on itself. When people speak "as a woman" or "as a man" they are claiming social and cultural "places". These enable them to collectively fashion a subjectivity by inscribing daily life and its structures and relations with a particular fiction or system of representations. These fictions do not appear to arise out of Nature (or out of the nature of the Self or Society) because they are voiced in elaborate story and contentious back-talk to an Other. They are exaggerated and parodied so that their engenderings are made obvious. Gender "identities" are not left as inert "internalized" essences but constantly questioned and their meanings set in motion when people insist on "speaking for themselves."

This is not to say that gendered practices in the camps are "ideal" but rather to argue that what we have thought of as fixed, "gender ideologies" with readable "meanings" have to be understood, not only in this case but in every case, as the effects of interpretive practices. The "meaning" of engendering practices shifts with social, historical, political, and storied situations. The metaphors of "inside" and "outside," or "centered" and "marginal" voices are themselves storytelling operations that enclose contested practices in the skins of one "thing" and another. But in the camps "things" are not taken for granted in this way, because in speaking as a woman every claim to gender identity elicits its counter claim. Every "center" of social and cultural constructions is made up of chinks and crannies. "Reality" remains contradictory, multiple, and open to comment and contest.

A VOICE IN THE WILDERNESS

Consider the figure of Eva Mae. Old, black, poor, and crazy, she spends her days walking back and forth along the road between the two coal camps called Amigo and Odd. She is the very figure of marginality and wildness in a region that is itself already marginal to "America" and given to wild proliferations of junk-filled yards, wild talk, and passionate extremes of heartbreak, violence, poverty, and religious ecstasy. Eva Mae is certainly further "off center" than most, but people develop eccentrically here and the others watch the development carefully, tracing the eccentric lines with an artistic attention to form.

Like everyone else, she makes a story of herself and other people and she "sees" herself both through the act of narrating and as the object of others' stories of her. She acts "the wild mountain woman" when she roams the road mumbling to herself. and she openly *talks trash* when she pauses at the house of "some snake" to proclaim the *talk* going around about him. Other women threaten to go crazy but Eva Mae fulfills the threat with action, making herself a walking allegory: as she walks she carries a gun, a butcher knife, or an axe and from time to time she stops to pose on the side of the road and wave the deadly weapon at a passing car.

Her words are her weapons, and she aims them carefully at the particular fictions of social order being bantered about in these camps at this point in their history. They say women walking on the side of the road are either in need of help or looking for sex. Yet the women *do* walk, in pairs and for exercise, and as they walk they dare the others to talk. Eva Mae only pushes it beyond the already challenged limits of the ordinary when she dresses in her outfit of a shimmering red dress, huge rhinestone necklace and earrings, and a red wig sitting askew on her head.

That'll give em somethin' to talk *about.*
They say I prostitute! Hah! I don't want no old man sweatin' over *me,* honey. You know they talks, but I sees em out there layin' out of a night, they ain't foolin' nobody.
Now these people, they'll try an mess with you, but they don' mess with me, honey, 'cause they knows I knows.

The other women "get a kick out of her" just as they "get a kick out of" the occasional scandalous woman who carries rebelliousness to extremes, like Dreama's neighbor who blared her music all over the holler day and night and who drank and danced with strange men in her living room and shot at the utility man who came to shut off her lights, and who bared her breasts against her window in the face of a nosy neighbor woman. Or the young woman on drugs who walked through the camp one day without a shirt and embarrassed all the men—"An' you should a seen the look on his face when he saw her a comin'! I thought I'd die! That tickled me, it really did." They say:

You might think Eva Mae's crazy, way she acts, but now you stop and *talk* to her, well really, she's *good* to *talk* to.
There ain't nothin' wrong with her *mind,* she's just *crazy.*
She don't *care,* buddy. She'll say anything, and right to their face, you have to give it to her.

Like other women, she speaks for herself; *runnin' her mouth,* she carries women's complaint against (male) *hypocrisy* and blacks' complaint against (white) *viciousness* beyond ordinary limits. Her power to fascinate lies in her power to transform her own Otherness into the disruptive power of excess, and her marginality into the exciting possibility of emotional abandon. When she comes to rest on her rock on the outskirts of town, the stories of her life flood out of her, washing away what are to her nothing but the infuriating hypocrisies of order and truth plastered onto the surface of a world sunk as low as low can go. The others, too, tell stories of how things have got down and tragic stories of victims treated mean, but for her there is no line between heartfelt excesses of meaning and the outlines of history . . . She says she had a father but they worked him to death in the mines until one day his heart burst and the blood came up in his lungs and smothered him and got in his eyes and blinded him and he died. She says she had a mother but they raped and murdered her in her bed, split her face with an axe. She says she had a son but he laid down on the railroad tracks and kicked his feet raw until they took him away to an institution and she has never seen him since (someone else remembers the day they took him away). Her daughter, she says, went crazy and left years ago, roaming from man to man and state to state and a few times she has come through town—bare footed, dazed, and you can't talk to her. She has a sister in the area but Illa drinks awful bad and when she drinks she gets mean and she'll kill you. Eva Mae says Illa has killed three men and sometimes when I would give her a ride to her sister's she would hesitate on the side of the road and then start back to Amigo—"b'lieve she's drunk up there." The others do not step outside the stories to wonder what parts are true; to their minds, too, such things can happen and the social world of the camps depends on *making somethin' of thangs*. So they say Eva Mae may be "crazy" but there's nothing wrong with her mind.

EN-GENDERING THE WILDERNESS

The gendered self who moves through the decentered "wilderness" is a bricoleur, constructing meaning from odds and ends of everyday life. S/he keeps up a constant excavation with borrowed shovels and garden hoes, endlessly dismembering and remembering, violating, discarding, and reinscribing. The most significant stories begin when "somethin' happens." And so it was one night in January, shortly after I had moved to Amigo, when the camp's water main burst in the alley in front of my house. When I heard the water rushing under the house and went out to see, the yard was already covered in two or three inches of water. The neighbor women—Sissy, Kitty, Dreama, Miss Lavender, Krystal, and CoraJane—were standing in the alley admiring the small geyser and telling apparently hilarious stories of other Amigo disasters. They yelled "Well welcome to 'migo, honey. Now you know you're *really* here. How do you like West Virginia?"

They decided to dig a trench in the frozen ground to divert the water into a culvert (which had itself been pieced together, from scraps, in another "situation" two years earlier, which involved a territorial dispute between neighbors). They went off and came back with their garden hoes, laughing about how they did not know where the men kept the shovels or if they even had any, and how ridiculous they all looked trying to dig a trench with garden hoes and housecoats. Other women leaned out windows to comment on the "pitiful lookin' road crew they sent down this time." Although it was very cold I was the only one who seemed to feel it. We worked slowly, stopping every few minutes to lean on the hoes and talk. Sissy went in several times to call the water company and then came back to tell us what had been said. Her claims grew more and more dramatic in stories of flooding and suits if they did not make it down tonight to fix the rupture.

I told em, I said,
 'Honey, there's *water* down here, and its a comin' *up*.'
 He said, 'Well where is this *at*.'
 said 'Well you know 'migo, doncha?'

said, 'Oh *yeah,* we know *'migo'*
'Well then,' said, 'You know something might happen.'
These people is mad and you cain't do nothin' with 'em if you make 'em mad
and when you git drownded people and you got water in your house an' your
livin' room's floatin' down the creek people git mad.
Said 'You better git on down here 'fore somethin' happens.'
He said *'Where* you say you're a callin' from?'
Well, that tickled me, it did.

When the trench was finally dug we stood around for another hour talking
over the fence and watching the water flow into the culvert. A red headed
woman living in the next county had murdered her husband and there were
grotesque stories of blood all over the walls and soaking the carpet. "They
said she blowed his brains out and they had a time of it cleanin' it up."
"Now which one was he? Was he one a them McKinney's up Basin Mountain?" "Basin Mountain! There ain't no McKinney's up on Basin Mountain." "Oh yeah, because Jimmy worked with one of 'em and one of 'em—
and now he had red hair—he was up at Doctor Roberts' last week where
Bobby and them seen him. Said he was all cut up." "Well, I don't know,
it might a been him but now I don't b'lieve I've ever *seen* him." Finally
when they went home they said: "well, welcome to 'Migo. How do you
like it?"

A HAUNTED WILDERNESS

The life of the local place hinges on dramatized efforts in the face of life's
constant trouble and the more pressing threat that things here are coming
to an end. Remember that "thangs is got down." The younger generation
is migrating unsuccessfully and painfully back and forth between the hills
and the city or to the R. J. Reynolds Company tobacco fields in North
Carolina in the summer and home to live with relatives, "all piled up like
cats and dogs" when the migrant labor is done. The pressure produces
failure as well as success, meanness as well as heroics. A broken water main
fills the place with engendered talk and action, but when someone fails to
stand up and speak for themselves, the wilderness of silence hunkers in and
haunts the others. So it was with Ivory and Kitty when a new neighbor
deposited herself in the field like an inert object, refusing to speak for herself.

4/30/82. Ivory says she believes she's seen everything now. Her sister-in-
law Kitty came over and told her to come see the "new neighbors." So she
went to see and what she saw haunted her so bad she couldn't sleep all
night. Al said "Ive, go to sleep" but she could *not* get it out of her head.

Well, we went down the holler and I said, 'Kitty
what in the world are *you talkin'* about?
There *ain't* nobody stays down there!'
She says, says 'Well you jes look *here.'*
And here is this woman, and her retarded boy, he's about 14,

and they are a livin' out *in* the field.

Honey, I mean *out of doors.*

Girl, I mean to *tell you.*

And here she is, got her a refrigerator and a stove,

and she's got her bed, and she's set up just like she's settin' in the couch readin' the damn paper!

shit! the lamp ain't got no lights!

I said, '*Girl,* somebody got you turned around.' Said, 'What are you a *doin* out here like this? You cain't *stay* like this.'

She's talkin at me about the *mosquitoes* botherin' her.

'Mosquitoes!' I said, said 'what are you *talkin* about mosquitoes? Honey you won't have to worry 'bout *them* long, because the *snakes* gonna come get *you* in your *bed.*'

Well she says she cain't hep it.

Says her old man come after her with a gun,

and he tells you 'You can take some furniture but git out.'

And they loaded her stuff up on the pickup and dumped her off, side the road. Hah! I said, 'Say *what?* You cain't let no old man run you off like 'at!' He's got a gun! *Huh!* Buddy I'd get *my* gun and shoot *his* damn *head* off. I told her, 'Honey you need to git yourself somebody *hep* you.'

Run her off!

I said Lord have Mercy, I'm a *tellin' you.*

Well I went on home but I cain't sleep with all that a goin' on up there.

Haunted by the image, and captured by a sleepless, unbreakable attention to a story with no storyteller, Ive told and retold the story herself. Her own story filled with dialogues between herself, Kitty, Al, the woman in the snakey field, the boy, and the man who dumped them out. Figured were the woman's ridiculous speechlessness and Kitty and Ive's back talk. But without a storyteller of its own the dramatic pathos of the story kept building. Ive saw "that po' little ole mental boy" go past with his radio and a few hours later he passed again carrying a little bag of groceries and no radio. "He sold his radio, the only thing he had." Still the woman in the snakey field said nothing and did nothing. She could have narrated herself as "a woman dumped in a snakey field by a no good man." Or her story could have resonated with the others of "how things are anymore," resonating, in particular, with the story of the strikers who were put out of their company houses in the 30s and sat outside in the alley "like they was in their own living room and the snow comin' down." Instead her silence flattened the possibility of a cultural world made up of interpretations into the literal, emptied enclosure of a "real world." This is the kind of world that is figured in the women's nightmarish stories of their lives as migrants in the cities up north; they say "there was nothing" and recount the deadened contents of a single room where they would sit with nothing and no one to talk to all day waiting for "him" to get back from work. They are not stories, really, but litanies and inventories of things representing an unspoken world: "It was one room and four walls and me. Well we had a bed and a chair to set by the window. Two burners, two pots, two plates, no garden and nowhere to go. Nothing. It was nothing."

Well, the woman in the snakey field left Ive and Kitty so haunted they finally had to do something. So they went and told her she could move into the deserted shack that had been Ive's mother's place; Ive got some windows for it and made the men put them in and Kitty took her to town to get on welfare and had a fight with the welfare worker: "She looked at me like I'm crazy or somethin' and I said 'Honey, this ain't *my* problem, I'm just tellin' you what it is and *here* it is.' I said 'go on now, tell her what that man done to you, tell her your own self, you got a tongue like anybody else.' "

CONCLUSION

The "wilderness" here is no silenced exile but a space filled to excess; the desire for a "women's voice" is less that of a Virginia Woolf longing for a room of one's own or a Charlotte Perkins Gilman wrapped in the madness of the wallpapered tent and more that of Bell Hooks' account of growing up in a southern black community where talking was not first an expression from within but a "back-talk" filled with layers of poetic resonance and the significances of talk itself.

. . . (in) the home where the everyday rules of how to live and how to act were established it was black women who preached. There, black women spoke in a language so rich, so poetic, that it felt to me like being shut off from life, smothered to death if one was not allowed to participate.[11]

To a self who participates in the constructions of known discourses, the problem is not to fragment surroundings or to emerge from silence into speech, as if these were ends in themselves, but to piece together what is daily fragmented by the Other, to place yourself somewhere in the chinks and margins of things; to speak for yourself.

The difference is not a difference in the "nature" of two "systems" but a difference in the position of the interpreting subject. On the one hand, the child of a traditional humanism, still centered, if only in fantasy, around a seamlessly unified self sees given individuals or given collectivities such as Society or Gender Systems: "Gloriously autonomous, it banishes from itself all conflict, contradiction and ambiguity."[12] On the other hand, the un-named, multiple Other leaves its traces in the rememberings, discardings, and reinscriptions of a self that is heterogeneous and contested. In this latter positioning, in the elsewhere within, gendered discourses will have to be interpreted in terms of the social and political contexts of their use and the circumstances of their production, circulation, and reception. And the question remembered will be not "what is woman" but rather how, in a discourse, does a woman "speak for herself"—as back-talking outsider, shifting object, big mouth, wildwoman, the mother of *mean* children, the spreading body of the married woman, the neighbor woman who notices things and *makes something of them,* or the woman who wakes up to find herself in a snakey field and must *make somethin' of* even that.

NOTES

I thank Faye Ginsburg and Anna Tsing for what was a laborious and brilliant (and gracious) editing of many drafts of this paper. And I thank Susan Harding, Elizabeth Taylor and John Hartigan for the long wonderful talks that inspired me to write it and the careful readings and comments that told me what it was about. I thank my neighbor women in West Virginia who know much more than I do about these things and who would never write them in the way that I have. And then there is my mother and my sister who are the source of uninterrupted dialogue in my life.

1. Moi, Toril, *Sexual/Textual Politics: Feminist Literary Theory* (London and New York: Methuen, 1985); Flax, Jane, "Postmodernism and Gender Relations in Feminist Theory," *Signs* 12, no. 4 (Summer 1987): 621–643; Nye, Andrea, "Woman Clothed with the Sun: Julia Kristeva and the Escape From/To Language," *Signs* 12, no. 4 (Summer 1987): 664–686.

2. Irigaray, Luce, "Women's Exile," interview in *Ideology and Consciousness* (May, 1977): 62–76; Gilligan, Carol, *In a Different Voice* (Cambridge: Harvard University Press, 1982).

3. Kristeva, Julia, *Desire in Language: A Semiotic Approach to Literature* (Oxford: Blackwell, 1980).

4. Showalter, Elaine, "Feminist Criticism in the Wilderness," *Critical Inquiry* 8, no. 2 (Winter 1981): 179–206; Spivak, Gayatri, "Can the Subaltern Speak?" in *Marxism and the Interpretation of Culture,* eds. Cary Nelson and Lawrence Grossberg (Urbana: University of Illinois Press, 1988), 271–315.

5. Spivak.

6. De Lauretis, Teresa, *Alice Doesn't: Feminism, Semiotics, Cinema* (Bloomington, Indiana: Indiana University Press, 1984); Kristeva.

7. Spivak, 272.

8. De Lauretis.

9. Willis, Paul, *Learning to Labour* (New York: Columbia University Press, 1977).

10. The names of people interviewed and the names of some places have been changed.

11. Hooks, Bell. "Talking Back" *Discourse* 8 (Fall-Winter 1976–1977): 123–128.

12. Moi, 8.

PART TWO

The Convention of Tradition:
Feminism in Dialogue with the New Right

CHAPTER FOUR

The "Word-Made" Flesh: The Disembodiment of Gender in the Abortion Debate

FAYE GINSBURG

During the course of my prayer vigil, I asked God to tell me how he wanted me to pray. After this, the Lord showed me the house—the Abortion Clinic—wrapped in barbed wire. I meditated on the meaning of this, how impossible it would be to enter it if it were bound in this way. Then the wire turned into a crown of thorns, some red with the blood of Jesus. The words came to mind: "My love can close those doors." The prayers of the faithful can bring love to bear.
—*"Thoughts About Prayer,"* LIFE Newsletter, *December 1981*

These words were the thoughts of a right-to-life activist as she prayed in front of the first and only abortion clinic in the state of North Dakota, the Fargo Women's Health Organization.[1] Through such rhetoric, she and others like her have been attempting to resignify not only the physical site of abortion—the clinic—but also the pregnant bodies that enter its doors. For many other women in the region, the clinic's opening in 1981 signalled a long-awaited blessing: it greatly increased their access to safe, sympathetic, and reasonably priced abortions.

In the 1980s, right-to-life protests centered more and more on abortion clinics,[2] which still are unevenly available in their delivery of services nearly two decades after abortion's legalization.[3] The battles taking place over clinics are both more intense and more local than those that were waged during the first wave of right-to-life activism in the 1970s.[4] Abortion activists—pro-life or pro-choice, as they define themselves—are primarily white, middle-class, and female. Clearly, women—even with similar class and cultural backgrounds—do not experience themselves and act as a homogeneous social group with a universal set of interests.[5] It is more the case, in the

abortion controversy that competing definitions of gender are being negotiated in terms of cultural understandings and practices of procreation,
sexuality, and nurturance in America.

This essay is based on the research I carried out with grassroots activists
on each side of the ongoing battle over Fargo's abortion clinic.[6] The focus
here is on right-to-life activism in particular, concentrating on the period
in the 1980s when both local and national right-to-life strategies shifted to
direct efforts to win over the members of the population most likely to have
abortions: young women with unwanted pregnancies. A close examination
of this activity reveals how notions of gender are being reformulated in
relation to the conditions and discourse created by legal abortion. As reproduction has become more a matter of choice, one sees a steady transformation away from essentialism, in which gender is assumed to be
determined *by* the body. In the abortion debates, as each side takes a different position on "women's interests," neither can claim that there is an
essential femininity. Instead, it is a woman's *stance toward* her body, and
pregnancy in particular, that becomes a kind of crucible of female identity,
and the focus of gender discourse.

The developments in the Fargo case presented here illuminate how the
struggle over the interpretation and cultural status of reproduction is taking
place. This struggle does not play out as a static demonstration of two fixed
positions. Rather, one sees a dialectical process in which each side's position
evolves over time in response to the other and to internal dynamics of the
movements.

STIGMATIZING THE CLINIC

Broadly sketched, the public controversy over abortion in Fargo has mirrored the course of events and sentiments fueling the conflict at the national
level. The first wave of activism occurred between 1967 and 1972, over
efforts to liberalize abortion laws. When the clinic opened in 1981, many
Fargo residents opposed it.[7] Confronted with this symbol of undesirable
social change, pro-life forces dramatized their resistance to what they saw
as alternative cultural values and formed a group called LIFE Coalition.
During the first year of the Fargo clinic's existence, the Coalition organized
popular support to close the clinic through legal and political processes.
While the initial battle made the clinic and its opponents into a local *cause
célèbre* and polarized many of Fargo's citizens, the pro-life efforts to shut
the clinic down through such means were unsuccessful.[8] Having tried and
failed in the political arena, the Coalition members shifted their goals. LIFE
Coalition activists, recognizing they were unlikely to get rid of the unwanted
clinic, decided to express their concerns through public protests.

Their protests were held right outside the clinic. These pro-life activists
hoped to use a variety of tactics to reframe the clinic, literally and figura-
tively, and attempted to stigmatize it by maintaining an oppositional pres-

ence on the edge of the building's property. This, in turn, focused attention on the clinic's actual or potential clientele, who must encounter protestors in order to have access to abortion.

Like any political controversy, the abortion debate transforms quickly as both the local and national situations change. The activities I am describing occurred while I was in the field, between 1981 and 1984. They were carried out by what I am calling "moderate" pro-life activists who were the key players at that time. Mostly, these were women born in the 1950s, many of them college-educated young mothers who were in or had recently left the work force, with modest or declining middle-class household incomes. To generalize, they are active in both civic organizations and Catholic, Lutheran, or other mainline Protestant congregations. While they and people like them are still important and active players in the movement, other pro-life groups, such as Operation Rescue, which endorse more violent activity, have become more prominent both nationally and locally since 1983. By contrast, members of the latter groups are predominantly male, often marginal to other parts of the community, and are associated mainly with Fundamentalist, Evangelical, and Charismatic churches.[9]

The staple of LIFE Coalition's activities against the clinic in its first year was what they called the Prayer Vigil. Pro-life volunteers dedicated at least two hours a week to this action, which entailed walking back and forth along the sidewalk in front of the clinic, engaged in silent prayer, often with a Bible in hand. Those who participated call themselves "Prayer Vigilantes." Their stated intention is to draw attention to the clinic and offer an alternative interpretation of its activities to passersby. They describe their actions as "a sacrifice on our part to show the outcry of concern we have over the death chamber in Fargo." Despite its obvious public aspects, the Prayer Vigil drew little general attention; the clinic is on a side street that gets little traffic and the protestors were quickly accepted as a regular and unremarkable feature by most Fargo citizens. However, LIFE Coalition members, rather than becoming *more* disruptive in order to attract attention, emphasized their larger goal of developing a reputation for moderation. This was evident, for example, in the following list of instructions given for the "Peaceful Prayer Walk."

1. This is a two-person Vigil of prayer only, not a demonstration.
2. Pray silently and unobtrusively.
3. Stay on sidewalk; keep moving; do not get in anyone's way.
4. DO NOT: Argue, explain, discuss, answer questions with [sic] anyone, including press. (If the press comes say only that you'll talk to them at another location when you are finished.)
5. Do nothing demonstrative except walk and pray—no signs or gestures.
6. Do not congregate —two cars for two people.
7. Do not cross the boulevard, grass, etc. Stay on sidewalk.

WE ARE CALLED TO LOVE

Almost every issue of LIFE Coalition's monthly newsletter has a short piece on the subjective experience of the Vigil, in which the prominent themes are critical life choices for women, and women's responsibilities for each other's actions. Such writing reveals how actions like the Vigil generate internal conviction and support among activists. The symbolic construction of the stories, and the fact of their reiteration in newsletters and meetings are essential to the process by which collective meaning is constituted from action. In the following selection, the speaker links the experiences of "the girls" seeking abortions and the counselors who advise them at the clinic in terms of her own sister's difficult life and death.

About 4 weeks to the day before Christmas, I was walking my usual time (from 10 a.m. to 11 a.m.) on the Prayer Vigil. I was alone as I usually am on the walk. I had been reading my prayer book and had been reflecting on life as a whole and the importance of each person's life—the hard things we go through, the joys—and all the help we need from each other. My oldest sister had just died on November 7. She had just dropped dead. I was missing her and thinking of her life, which included tragedy and much suffering on her part. In spite of her hardships, I thought of her faith in God, her strengths and also her failings and guilt that resulted from these weaknesses.

I then thought about the girls and families where mistakes had been made and these girls were being counseled and having abortions as I was walking there in front of the place where this was going on. I thought about the counselors. I prayed for all concerned and prayed especially that counselors were doing just that—a thorough job—and my, what a disservice to the girls if life is treated lightly. Each girl's life is so important that decisions made are of utter importance. She has to live her life the day, or month, or year after the counselor has sat across from a desk and said "whatever". Anyhow, these were my thoughts that morning. ("A Walk In November," *LIFE Coalition Newsletter,* January 1982)

Like Christian conversion testimonies, such stories provide a vehicle for each participant to infuse prayer with personal meaning by constructing a narrative that links her life and immediate situation to the goals of the movement. Clearly, the Prayer Vigil is not just an activity that sustains interest and activist support. The prayers are effective in and of themselves. For those who utter and hear them, the very *act* transforms the area around the clinic from a sidewalk, lawn, and entryway into a highly charged battle zone for "prayer warriors." A Fargo pro-life leader explained her view of the power of prayer in political action:

Prayer is one method of attack and the others—whether legislation, rallies, counseling, personal opinion offered at a crucial time, are all made more effective if prefaced by prayer.

REINTERPRETING THE UNWED MOTHER

On the first year anniversary of the clinic's opening, LIFE Coalition members decided to escalate their activities. They were responding to internal criticism that they were not doing enough to fight the clinic, and to external accusations that they showed no compassion for the women seeking abortions. The latter pro-choice critique pushed LIFE leaders to address more directly and personally the pregnant women who came to the clinic. The Coalition hired a "problem pregnancy counselor" and organized what they call a "sidewalk counseling program." Sidewalk counselors behave very much like the prayer vigilantes; they walk quietly, usually in twos, back and forth in front of the clinic. In addition, they approach people entering the clinic and give them literature and suggest they think about alternatives to abortion. By handing out business cards with LIFE Coalition's phone number, counselors convey that the organization offers sources of emotional and material support for carrying an unwanted pregnancy to term. The counselors attempt to engage clinic clientele in conversation and take them to a nearby coffee shop—named, coincidentally, "Mom's"—to talk over the decision. Generally, encounters in which the woman changes her mind about abortion are unusual. Indeed, in 1983, when a pro-life counselor succeeded in winning over a women who, unbeknownst to LIFE members, the clinic had turned away *because* of her ambivalence, it was a local media item for a week.

Despite the difficulties in reaching women who were using the clinic, LIFE nonetheless put considerable time and effort into the counseling endeavor. LIFE's coordinator described the work involved:

The prayer vigil only requires one or two workshops a year. The counselors have a much more involved process of training. They need workshops, meetings, phone calls, baby-sitting services. . . .

At the training workshops that I attended, at least half of those present were new volunteers. The meetings usually had about ten people, two of whom were LIFE staff or board people. Almost all the trainees were women, usually in their mid to late twenties, and generally friends of those already engaged in pro-life work who had urged them to come. The very form of LIFE's recruitment and activism tends to generate a more moderate membership, made up (usually) of women who are pro-life but not inclined toward confrontation—a conscious choice on the part of the coordinator:

The kind of person who works best is someone who is pro-life but really feels for the women. Someone who is super anti-abortion can't do it.

Most of the talk at meetings centered on depicting and assigning meaning to the "other," the woman having the abortion. For example, at one gathering, the following typology was offered by LIFE's problem pregnancy counselor.

There are three types you encounter going to get abortions:
1. Women's Libber: She needs a lot of education. She's hostile and cold.
2. Ambivalent Type: She is conflicted and let's others make up her mind for her.

3. Ignorant: The kind that is really pro-life but doesn't know there is another way.

She then offered a broader interpretation of the meaning of abortion:

With Christianity came the acceptance of the child without it having to bear its father's sins. Abortion is a sign of a decline in the culture. I view it [abortion] as the rape of motherhood, of the gender, of the uterus, of the womb. If you think sex is natural, birth is even more natural. The first love you feel is for your mother. What is the furthest reach of the devil? Not murder, not sex, not rape. It's abortion.

In such discourse—a staple of these frequent, small, face-to-face meetings, which maintain and generate pro-life membership—abortion is fused with the imagery of destructive, decadent, and usually male sexuality. In this case, "the rape of motherhood" is fused with "the decline of the culture." Abortion is contrasted to pregnancy, birth, and maternity. The latter are cast as the domain of female experience, creation, childhood innocence, pure motive, and nurturance: "the first love you feel is for your mother." Unable to make the termination of pregnancy illegal, abortion activists are attempting at least to redefine it: women who advocate or have abortions are not only misguided or immoral; they are not properly female. Sidewalk counseling thus promoted not only an interpretation of abortion but also a particular construction of (appropriate) female gender as nurturant, peaceful, and loving. Ironically, the activists were constrained in their own actions by that very construction.

In their political performances in front of the clinic, demonstrators felt obliged to display themselves according to this view of feminine identity in which nurturant love was prominent. One of the pro-life leaders explained the dilemma to me:

In the East, they have sit-ins. I doubt that we'd get women here to do that. The community would turn against us. The women have to deal with their family and friends. Their husbands have to be supportive.

I don't want to picket out there cause we'll scare them. It's the most we can do. If we picket we can't reach them. We've worked so hard to prove we're loving and caring.

For LIFE Coalition members, conforming to their formulated image of compassion and nurturance was at least equal to, if not more important than, the more immediate objective of stopping women from using the clinic.

THE PROBLEM PREGNANCY INDUSTRY

As part of their agenda to persuade people of their compassion, in the spring of 1983, LIFE Coalition activists decided to open a "Problem Pregnancy Center" to back up its sidewalk counseling campaign. That decision was also part of a new emphasis in national pro-life strategy to promote "alternatives to abortion".[10] It indicated, as well, the shifting understandings of the young unwed mother since the legalization of abortion in 1973. She was no longer the guilty social outcast to be shunned, but the catalyst for community efforts to develop sex education and, most notably, the target for what I am calling the "Problem Pregnancy Industry", a new focus of attention in the Fargo area. The struggle to redefine and claim women with an unwanted pregnancy was not just taking place between pro-life and pro-choice activists. It extended to social service, voluntary and governmental agencies, and divided constituents within the pro-life ranks, as well. Each group has a different understanding of the "problem" and the "solution." This is all part of a political economy of gender in which power and resources are being renegotiated constantly in relation to changing attitudes toward pregnant women, especially teenagers.

In the United States, the combination of the rise in teen pregnancy and the legalization of abortion (teenagers comprise approximately one-third of all abortion clients) has contributed to the creation of this new category of "problematic women." Because such definitions are a crucial determinant of governmental, legal, and political actions and public and private allocation of benefits and services, control over their meaning is the focus of conflict. Unwed mothers are defined and redefined as possible abortion clients, potential mothers needing prenatal care, children needing protection from parents, or students unable to complete their education, to name a few possible understandings.

A short overview of a decade of changes in Fargo regarding problematic pregnancies should make clear the impact of such redefinitions in the institutions that structure daily life there. In 1973, the main home for unwed mothers in town was closed down due to disuse. That same year, a handful of pro-life veterans established a chapter of Birthright, a pro-life group that seeks to help women with unwanted pregnancies to carry, deliver, and place their babies for adoption. At that time the only professionally-trained counselor for problem pregnancies in Fargo was a woman named Mary Mintz. Ten years later, in addition to Mary, three other professionally-trained "problem pregnancy counselors" were hired at Lutheran and Catholic agencies. By 1982, two state-sponsored programs offering nutritional, medical and social support to pregnant single women had been organized by the N.D. State Council on Problem Pregnancy. A daycare center for single and poor mothers was, for the first time, receiving support from the United Way (although it had to redefine its purpose as "preventing juvenile delinquency" to receive funding). In 1983, several support groups for single mothers sponsored by social service agencies were in place and the local Junior League began a community advocacy group for "school-age parents." A North Dakota chapter of WEBA (Women Exploited by Abortion) started in 1984, a group "for women who have had an abortion, now realize it was the wrong decision, and want to educate other women on the trauma of abortion." At the end of that year, in addition to the Catholic social work agency, three other pro-life groups *each* had "problem pregnancy centers." They were Birthright, LIFE Coalition, and a new group called Save-A-Baby. By September 1985, a pro-life home for unwed mothers opened in a former boarding house. In short, over one decade during which the number of pregnant adolescents in North Dakota tripled,[11] new groups, including the abortion clinic, were formed in Fargo to deal with and compete for these teenagers, bringing the total number of groups to fourteen.

The competition is readily apparent to those involved in problem pregnancy groups in Fargo. When the plan for starting a problem pregnancy center was first discussed at a LIFE board meeting, members spoke of an "expanding market." In the words of one activist:

It's like a business. If they [the abortion clinic personnel] don't get enough clients, they'll have to close the doors.

The struggle to win both the actual clientele and the power to determine the outcome of unwanted pregnancies is not merely between pro-life and pro-choice activists. As one social worker expressed it to me:

There really is competition between agencies. They don't admit it. Nobody says we're competing but we are. The bread and butter of this agency is adoption. 65 percent of unwed girls opt to have abortions. And nearly 95 percent of the rest keep their babies who can. Very few release their babies for adoption. I want our agency to be the best and first so of course I'm competitive.

The increasing competition divided constituents within the pro-life ranks as well. In its initial stages, LIFE had worked together with Birthright, which had been helping pregnant teens find "alternatives to abortion." Birthright, begun in 1973, had been the project of the first wave of local pro-life activists, mostly older women, many newly widowed. By 1983, most of them were in their mid to late sixties or older. New pro-life activists, primarily younger women more politically involved in the national right-to-life movement than their predecessors, became increasingly impatient with Birthright. In their view, it was too low key, unprofessional, and insufficiently public. As LIFE focused its efforts more and more on "reaching the woman," which is also Birthright's agenda, the conflict intensified. Under pressure from LIFE, Birthright hired a new director who was instructed to be more aggressive. She began active fundraising and advertised in the local paper and on radio stations.

Despite Birthright's efforts, LIFE decided to go ahead with its own plans for a Problem Pregnancy Center, which opened in August 1984. This competition for sources of local support for pro-life work intensified a few months later when an Evangelical Christian man rumored to have links with Jerry Falwell opened yet another pro-life pregnancy support center with his wife. Backed by a group called Save-A-Baby, the Board of Directors was made up primarily of congregants from the Assemblies of God. Insult was added to injury when they named their center Life Clinic. This was a rather obvious attempt to benefit from the carefully cultivated reputation of LIFE Coalition. The LIFE Board tried but was unable to stop this new effort, although they did persuade the "clinic" to change its name. The new name, The Women's Help Clinic of Fargo, got them into a lawsuit with the Fargo Women's Health Organization: the abortion clinic claimed that the pro-life group selected a name similar to their own to deceive women into thinking that the Women's Help Clinic offered abortions.

With the other competing pro-life group embroiled in legal problems, LIFE was determined to "control the market" and gain legitimacy as the pro-life alternative to abortion. LIFE Coalition's Problem Pregnancy Center had only a few clients in its first year.[12] Most were women who had mistaken it for the abortion clinic. Yet the Coalition's investment of time, energy, and money in their center indicated that they thought ignorance led many women to abortion. Phrased in terms of individual motivation, the woman who seeks an abortion is, to use one counselor's words, "confused, kind of weak, and uneducated" about the fetus. Therefore, pro-lifers are convinced that, if she received adequate emotional and material support, and if she had knowledge of fetal life as they see it, she would not choose to abort.

FETAL IMAGERY AND FEMALE IDENTITY

The idea that knowledge of fetal life, especially confrontation with the visual image of the fetus, will "convert" a woman to the pro-life position has been a central and increasingly dominant theme in both local and national right-to-life activism. The relationship between knowledge (seeing), belief, and action, draws on more general constructs regarding witnessing and conversion in American culture. It is this cultural logic that resulted in the introduction of the fetal image into pro-life political activities in the 1970s, and its persistent presence in current pro-life propaganda. A popular quip summarizes this position: "If there were a window on a pregnant woman's stomach, there would be no more abortions."

This view, that a pro-choice position is due to ignorance of fetal life, is constructed and reinforced in two of the main pro-life media pieces—the 52-minute film "Assignment Life" and the videotapes, "The Silent Scream" and "The Eclipse of Reason," released in 1984 and 1987 respectively. During the time I was in Fargo, "Assignment Life" was shown not less than once a month at some pro-life gathering. To judge by audience response, it had a lot of shock value for new recruits and solidified conviction among the converted.[13] "The Silent Scream" shows an abortion "from the point of view of the unborn child" using sonogram imagery. Sonograms, part of the high-tech experience of pregnancy since the 1980s, are generally associated with confirmation of a desired pregnancy and, according to some, provide a new site for the formation of the initial maternal-fetal bond.[14] By provocatively juxtaposing this imagery with abortion, "The Silent Scream" relies on the notion of the power of the fetus to convert.

The idea that once the fetus is "seen" one has no choice but to become pro-life underscored the 1985 North Dakota Right-to-Life Convention, entitled "Rescue and Restore." The theme was explicit in the Biblical verse from Proverbs that welcomed conventioneers:

Rescue those who are being taken to their death; and from those staggering toward slaughter will you withhold yourself? If you say, 'See we did not know this,' does not the One who weighs hearts perceive it? And He who watches over the soul, does He not know and shall He not repay each man for his deeds? Proverbs 24: 11–12

As is the case in conversion, the assumption conveyed in the chosen quote is that once a potential convert witnesses a certain "truth" and comes "under conviction," there is only one path to follow.[15]

The right-to-life belief that conversion will take place after seeing the "truth" about abortion relies on the root metaphor of the fetus as "the unborn child."[16] Right-to-life visual material offers two representations that are frequently shown together. The principal one is the magnified image of the fetus—for example, floating intact inside the womb, or with its tiny perfectly formed feet held between the thumb and forefinger of an adult. These pictures are usually in warm amber tones, suffused with soft light, rendered more mysterious by their separation from the mother's body. Juxtaposed to these photographs are gruesome, harshly lit, clinical shots of mutilated and bloody fetal remains "killed by abortions." These are what pro-lifers refer to as "the war pictures." Thus, the qualities evoked by the representations of the fetus—the mystery of conception, warmth, unconditional nurturance, radical innocence and maternity—are continually contrasted with visions of its possible violent destruction.

In the 1983 version of a popular slide show produced by National Right-to-Life Committee President Jack Willke, the associations to these images were expanded to take on more explicit political meaning. The "war pictures" of fetuses were intercut with old news photos of Southeast Asian civilians burnt by napalm. These slides are accompanied by the following narration:

Do you remember Cambodia?
We ignored the genocide then until our nation saw the horror through our media. These horrible pictures woke people up. There is another war going on today. This nation should also see the horror of that reality. Every citizen of this country should see what we call "the war pictures."
[The slide on at this point shows dead fetuses from late abortions piled in garbage cans; it then switches to a shot of a 21-week fetus aborted by a saline injection which turns the skin a shiny red color.]
We call this the candy-apple baby. The saline must feel like napalm. Neither the abortionist nor the bombardier saw their victim.

Through such symbolic constructions, those who would participate in abortion are associated with genocidal practice.

Moreover, in drawing analogies to war, the aborted fetus becomes a sacrifice offered for the redemption of America. This is demonstrated not only in verbal and visual media, but in other forms of symbolic action. At the 1985 North Dakota Right-to-Life Convention, a permanent memorial for "All of our nation's children who have died by abortion" was erected next to the War Veteran's Memorial. As a local pro-life leader observed:

The symbolism was clear. More babies have died through abortion than in all the wars our country has fought. Abortion on demand is clearly the war on our unborn children. The veterans died to protect freedom everywhere, yet for the unborn there are no rights. A few yards from the gravesite also stands the flagpole with the American flag overhead.

Similarly, the redemptive power of the aborted fetus informed the following comments made to me by a sidewalk counselor on the fourth of July:

Ask yourself this question: On the fourth of July we celebrate all the people who died that we might have freedom. And I'm wondering if some of these children aren't dying so that we will appreciate life, marriage, and relationships more fully. To keep a sixteen-year-old from getting pregnant, she needs a good self-concept. If she has that, she won't get pregnant. If it makes us go back and think of that, it may not be in vain.

While the associations of the fetus with life and death are charged with historically specific meanings, these polarities are also often taken out of time and place by the analogy to Christian religious imagery. Explicitly or implicitly, the fetus is linked frequently to Jesus and the woman with the unwanted pregnancy is likened to Mary, as in a December 1986 article in the AAA Problem Pregnancy Center Newsletter entitled "Jesus Became A Fetus."

Luke's Gospel tells us that an angel named Gabriel visited a virgin named Mary and said, "Rejoice, O highly favored daughter. The Lord is with you . . ." (Luke 1:28) . . .
How does Jesus feel about an abortion? Might Jesus have said, "For I was unborn and you killed me. I became a fetus, a little one, and you turned me into property." . . . (Michael Gaworski, Pro-Life Action Ministries)

Thus, the battle over abortion is cast as one in which the sacrifices entailed in bearing an unwanted child will redeem the woman caught in the unfortunate circumstance of unwanted pregnancy. More generally, these associations give larger meaning to the struggles and everyday difficulties of life.

Given the increasing focus on "abortion-prone" teenagers and women as objects of political struggle and social redefinition, the relatively small number of images of pregnant women in pro-life visual material is striking. This absence, I believe, indicates the shifting status of pregnancy in the abortion debate, which must be understood within the broader context of an ever fluctuating cultural construction of gender.

In American culture, as in most other cultures, pregnancy (especially first conception) places women in a liminal status, a temporary condition in which the subject is in transition between two structural states. In Arnold Van Gennep's classic formulation of rites of passage,[17] the liminal subject or initiate is usually secluded from public view and only regains visibility when he or she reenters the social system with a new status—one that is ascribed, more or less culturally predetermined. Reincorporation of the liminal person into the appropriate role serves to legitimate, for the subject and observers, a particular interpretation of social reality as not only necessary but "natural". Deviation from the prescribed outcome is not only a serious violation of social rules; it also exposes the possibility that there could be alternative interpretations of a particular situation. Thus, sanctions are often severe because such "deviance," by presenting the possibility that categories and social arrangements could be different, threatens the whole cultural order.

When abortion was illegal, the assumption for a pregnant woman was that her liminality would end when she gave birth and was given the ascribed status of motherhood. Because deviations from that script were either hidden or punished, they confirmed the dominant discourse. With abortion legal and available, the liminality of pregnancy carries a new and contested semantic load. The state into which the pregnant woman can pivot is no longer predetermined; rather than become a mother, she *may* choose to end the pregnancy and return to her former state. Thus, legal abortion subverts the prior associational chain that pregnancy "must" result in childbirth and motherhood.

In other words, with the acceptance of abortion, the dominant and oppositional discourses regarding the place of pregnancy and abortion in women's lives were suddenly reversed. Although abortion is now legal, right-to-lifers clearly do not consider termination of pregnancy an option. Yet, their view now exists within the new social and discursive context created by abortion's legalization. To succeed, right-to-lifers cannot simply defend past arrangements, as stereotypes would have it, but must construct their own position in positive terms that address the current situation. In pro-life action and discourse—particularly in the focus on women with problem pregnancies—one can see how this accommodation has been made in a particular and telling way: the decision to keep the pregnancy *despite* adverse circumstances becomes an achievement, rather than the inexorable if begrudging fulfillment of an ascribed role. The woman who decides to carry an unwanted pregnancy signifies an assertion of a particular construction of female identity—now experienced as oppositional by pro-lifers—in which nurturance, achieved through accepting pregnancy and birth, despite hardships, is of paramount value.

Now, the once dominant narrative of pregnancy in American culture is only one of several acceptable scenarios associated with the image of the pregnant women. Thus, that absence in pro-life visual imagery is less of a paradox. Otherwise, the fetal image would have to compete with the other possible associations that a representation of a pregnant woman might evoke, and which are compelling conditions justifying most abortions—poverty, age, other children, lack of a partner, etc. Instead, the right-to-life visual focus on the fetus denies the varied circumstances of women's lives that shape reproductive decisions.

Some have argued from this data that pro-life materials simply repress all consideration of the circumstances of the mother.[18] I think such a reading inappropriately decontextualizes the image from right-to-life rhetoric, in which a choice of motherhood over abortion as the outcome of problem pregnancy is reframed as a heroic achievement of nurturance over adversity. The construction of this image is clear, for example, in the following statement of a Fargo pro-life activist:

I think we've accepted abortion because we're a very materialist society and there is less time for caring. To me it's all related. Housewives don't mean much because we do the caring and the mothering kinds of things which are not as important as a nice house or a new car. I think it's a basic attitude we've had for some time now.

Thus, abortion is generalized to signify a withdrawal of unconditional, self-sacrificing nurturance, the devaluation of human life, and a denial of the reproduction of the culture.

ABORTION AND METAPHORS OF SOCIAL REPRODUCTION

In their vigils, sidewalk counseling, prayers, and meetings, female right-to-life activists reframe abortion as undermining the gendered bases of nurturance and compassion in our culture. In the words of a pro-life activist:

Abortion is of crucial importance because it negates the one irrefutable difference between men and women. It symbolically destroys the precious essence of womanliness—nurturance . . .

In the pro-life view, women who choose in the face of problematic circumstances to keep an unwanted pregnancy when abortion is a choice, are "truly" female. A woman's decision to carry a pregnancy to term under these conditions is understood simultaneously as a decision not to abort, and as a heroic act in which a woman's capacity for nurturance has been tested.

This chain of associations from sex to reproduction to nurturance is central to the organization of meaning in pro-life discourse. Within that discourse, abortion undermines not only the reproductive potential of sex but also the differentiation of male and female character. As one leader phrased it:

Pro-abortion feminists open themselves to charges of crass hypocrisy by indulging in the very same behavior for which they condemn men: the unethical use of power to usurp the rights of the less powerful.

In this view, then, abortion represents the possibility of women moving into structurally male positions and links it with the corruption of the cultural order. A woman who endorses abortion denies the links between female reproduction and nurturant character and thus becomes culturally male. Thus, the interpretation of gender that has developed in pro-life arguments in the 1980s is based not on a woman's possession of her reproductive capacities but in her responses to them. Thus, contrary to those who claim that for right-to-lifers, the category "woman" is determined by the female body, I would argue that women are distinguished ultimately *not* by their bodily differences from men, but by *acceptance* of their reproductive capacities and the attributes seen to follow from them.

The development of pro-life ideology and action in the abortion debate in the 1980s was clearly more than a static political debate over reproductive and fetal rights. In it one saw a renegotiation of the meaning of female gender in relation to women's reproductive capacities. As pro-choice activists set new terms in which pregnancy is seen increasingly as a *choice,* right-to-life rhetoric regarding gender has also been transformed. As motherhood is being reframed as an achievement (rather than an ascribed status change) in the construction of female identity in American culture, so a general understanding of gender is shifting as well as the players themselves recognize (and make use of) its mutability.

More generally, the changing views of women over time in this controversy shows how our own society's views of gender are altered through social action. Through the debate, then, we are increasingly made aware of a larger cultural process: the disembodiment of gender from the bodies that ultimately bear the consequences and contradictions entailed in its shifting cultural and social formulations.

NOTES

Portions of the material presented in this paper also appear in my book Contested Lives: The Abortion Debate in an American Community *(Berkeley: University of California Press, 1989). For the fieldwork on which this work is based, I gratefully acknowledge research support from the following sources: American Association for University Women Dissertation Fellowship, a Newcombe Fellowship for Studies in Ethics and Values; the David Spitz Distinguished Dissertation Award, CUNY; and a Sigma Xi research grant. I would also like to thank the women in Fargo with whom I worked, who were so generous with their time and insights. Their identities are disguised and they shall remain anonymous, as was agreed. For invaluable emotional and intellectual support, I am grateful to Fred Myers.*

1. Run by a local abortion rights activist, the clinic is one of 10 such facilities set up in small metropolitan areas by the National Women's Health Organization. This business seeks to bring abortion to those parts of the country where services have not been readily available, usually due to the conservatism of the local medical community. Since the 1973 Roe v. Wade decision legalizing abortion, over 1000 such freestanding clinics providing first-trimester abortions have been established throughout America.

2. Struggles over local delivery of abortion services have dominated the conflict in the 1980s, while legislative right-to-life efforts have been relatively unsuccessful. The judiciary is another arena for action, since the possibility remains that the Roe v. Wade decision might be reversed by the Supreme Court, particularly with the appointment of more conservative Justices, Antonin Scalia and Anthony Kennedy by former President Ronald Reagan. The concern of people on either side is, of course, whether they will join like-minded colleagues on the Court—Rehnquist, O'Connor, and White—and thus constitute a new working majority in the Court that might overturn or erode Roe v. Wade, particularly in the wake of the 1989 Webster v. Reproductive Health Services ruling which essentially allows states to place limitations on abortion services. One effect of this decision has been a renewed mobilization of pro-choice activists, most significantly young women not involved in earlier reproductive rights battles, and Republican women who are dissenting from their party's official position.

3. Frederic Jaffe, Barbara Lindheim and Philip R. Lee, *Abortion Politics: Private Morality and Public Policy* (NY: McGraw-Hill, 1981).

4. Raymond Tatalovich and Byron W. Daynes, *The Politics of Abortion* (NY: Praeger, 1981).

5. For arguments regarding the rather homogeneous sociological profiles of activists on each side see Faye Ginsburg, *Contested Lives* (Berkeley: University of California Press, 1989); Daniel Granberg, "The Abortion Activists," *Family Planning Perspectives* 13, no. 4: 158–61; and Kristin Luker, *The Politics of Motherhood* (Berkeley: University of California Press, 1984).

6. I went to Fargo in order to see this critical "backstage" setting for the national abortion drama, to get a sense of the specific shape and impact it has at the local level. The conflict, which I have been following since 1981, including two six-month periods of fieldwork, illuminates larger cultural processes. During the first stint of fieldwork in 1982, I was also working as a producer for a documentary on the clinic controversy. During the second six months I spent in Fargo in 1983, I identified myself as an anthropologist. In addition to following the development of the organizations that formed for and against the clinic and participating in community life in general, I also collected life histories from 35 people involved in the conflict, in order to see how their activism and personal and historical experiences were intertwined.

7. Like Muncie, Indiana, described in the classic *Middletown* studies (Lynd and Lynd), Fargo is small enough to provide a coherent social universe, yet sufficiently large and diverse to encompass farmers and professionals, a working class and a university community; Catholics, Lutherans, Evangelicals, a small Jewish population and some native Americans. While many people in Fargo view themselves as politically conservative, they also value a tradition of populism and defense of the individual rights.

8. For a full discussion of that conflict, see "The Body Politic: The Defense of Sexual Restriction by Anti-Abortion Activists" in *Pleasure and Danger: Exploring Female Sexuality,* ed. Carole Vance (Boston: Routledge and Kegan Paul, 1984), 173–188.

9. See Faye Ginsburg, "And the Lord is On Our Side: Violence in the Anti-Abortion Movement" in *Remaking the World: Fundamentalist Impact,* Martin Marty, ed. (forthcoming).

10. *National Right to Life News,* 12, no. 1 (1984). Since the early 1980s, the number of pro-life "problem pregnancy centers" has mushroomed from almost none to over 2000. Over a dozen have been the subject of litigation, including the one in Fargo. Women seeking abortion services contend the centers misled them through false advertising.

11. See North Dakota Department of Human Services, *Children Born Out of Wedlock* (Bismarck, 1982), Table 1.

12. According to the Problem Pregnancy Center's Report in its February 1987 Newsletter, in 1986 an average of 15 clients per month came into the office and "1200 contacts were made by phone." The Center's report in the December 1986 Newsletter is instructive as to how to understand these figures: "Each girl who comes into the Center, both positive and negative tests [sic], view [sic] our educational presentation and receives individual counseling. Six of the fifteen girls had positive tests. Four girls decided to carry their babies; one girl, though still not certain, is leaning toward carrying her baby; and one was lost to abortion . . . five of the six girls came into the Center considering abortion, and changed their minds." The Center advertises in the newspaper and Yellow Pages under "Pregnancy Counseling", through public service announcements on local television and radio, posters at area colleges, and an installation of a large street sign outside the Center bearing its name.

13. "Assignment Life" is essentially a conversion tale. The main character, a young female journalist, reluctantly takes an assignment from her older male editor to cover the abortion issue. She proceeds with her investigation, conducting interviews with almost all the key leaders in the right-to-life movement, as well as "average women," such as a reformed prostitute, and a child who announces, "If abortion had been legal, I wouldn't be here." The reporter also visits a California gynecologist who allows her to film a suction abortion. At the end, she comes to the conclusion that abortion is murder. The structure of the film is a narrative model for the pro-life conviction that if a woman had knowledge of fetal life she would not choose to abort.

14. See John Fletcher and Mark Evans, "Maternal Bonding in Early Fetal Ultrasound Examinations," in *The New England Journal of Medicine* 308 (1983): 392–3.

15. See Susan Harding, "Convicted by the Holy Spirit: The Rhetoric of Fundamental Baptist Conversion," *American Ethnologist* 14, no. 1 (February 1987): 167–81.   •

16. In his book *Dramas, Fields, and Metaphors* (NY: Cornell University Press, 1974) (p. 51), Victor Turner argued that such paradigms produce "a certain kind of polarization of meaning in which the subsidiary subject is really a depth world of prophetic, half-glimpsed images, and the principal subject, the visible, fully-known . . . at the opposite pole to it, acquires new and surprising contours

and valences from its dark companion . . . because the poles are 'active together' the unknown is brought just a little more into the light by the known."

17. Arnold Van Gennep, *Rites of Passage* (Chicago: University of Chicago Press, 1960 [1908]).

18. See for example Rosalind Petchesky's excellent essay, "Fetal Images: The Power of Visual Culture in the Politics of Reproduction," *Feminist Studies* 13 no. 2 (Summer 1987): 263–92.

CHAPTER FIVE

If I Should Die Before I Wake: Jerry Falwell's Pro-Life Gospel

SUSAN HARDING

The bedroom scene on the dustcover of *If I Should Die Before I Wake* . . . evokes a sense of innocent remembrance, a wistfulness, "a moment you'll never forget," a moment laced with haunting, foreboding feelings.[1] The room is bare. The bassinet is empty. Something's missing. The ellipsis in the book's title bespeaks incompleteness as well. More literally, the title evokes the nearness of death, appropriating an old, familiar Protestant prayer (Now I lay me down to sleep/ I pray the Lord my soul to keep/ If I should die before I wake/ I pray the Lord my soul to take), and converting it into an eerie allusion to abortion. The empty cradle flashes back and forth between womb and coffin, a spooky place that mingles sleep and terror, birth and death, safety and danger, innocence and error.

Jesus Christ, "the Lord" of the prayer, silently brackets the title. He is imaged in the light, accompanied by the Holy Spirit in the gentle wind, coming through the window, bringing hope and the possibility of overcoming evil. He merges with the visible sense that "something's missing"—a phrase that appears frequently in conversion stories. Christ is the "something" that is missing. Christ and the missing baby coalesce. The bassinet intimates the manger and the empty tomb. Abortion echoes crucifixion, the slaughter of innocents. Saving babies partakes of Bethlehem, the resurrection, salvation and the Blessed Hope.

The dustjacket blurb reveals that *If I Should Die Before I Wake* . . . is

the story of Falwell's dedication to creating an alternative to abortion—but with an unusual twist. Jennifer Simpson, one of the first young women to join the Liberty Godparent Homes program (providing homes for pregnant teen-agers) tells the story of the decision she made. With chapters alternating between Falwell and Jennifer, *If I Should Die Before I Wake* . . . breaks down the barriers of misunderstanding by offering a hopeful alternative to this overwhelming issue.

The two voices, Jerry's and Jennifer's, and their stories unfold and intertwine across 12 chapters. Their narrative moves are interdependent. She must choose, twice, whether to sacrifice her unborn child. He is called, twice, and must choose how to sacrifice himself on behalf of the unborn. The fetus is passed back and forth between them, now dead, later alive. Her stories prepare the ground for his action; she participates, speaks upon, jointly produces, becomes the landscape for his heroic response, his sacrificial action. His action then opens the way for her narrative to move on, indeed, changes the world around her so that her story may have, through her reciprocal sacrificial action, a new ending, a new beginning. She bears her baby; he bears the world in which her baby may be born.

If I Should Die Before I Wake . . . is a masterfully seductive and intimate missive of almost love-letter intensity from its preacher-author to his people-readers. Jerry Falwell's born-again readers know they are handling a gospel text (a life-changing text of love, death, and redemption), if not from his name alone, then from the dustcover murmerings of "something missing." If they read *If I Should Die* as they read the Bible, "literally," its juxtaposed and laminated stories will pile up, talk to each other, and narrate a multi-dimensional world that "speaks to" them, pulls them into its inner spaces, and becomes "truth." The text will prepare a place for its readers, a kind of gospel passage, through a series of sacrifice stories, which are perpetually incomplete. They mark a loss, an absence, something given and not returned—an empty cradle— and engender a desire, a longing, for wholeness, completion, return—(re)birth. Readers may fill in what is "missing" by contributing substantially to the gospel at hand and, more meaningfully, they may be themselves "infilled" with the Holy Spirit, that is, they may undergo subtle and much sought-after changes of habit and of "heart."[2]

These born-again cries and whispers would likely be lost on unborn-again readers, who might be more inclined to read through the name Jerry Falwell (founder of the Moral Majority, leading spokesman for the Christian Right), the book's title, the dustjacket and all the stories to a polemical subtext about abortion, sexuality, gender, family, feminism and patriarchy. The sentimental language of *If I Should Die* would become translucent—like a veil thinly disguising what the book is "really" about—re-essentializing gender differences, vilifying abortion and feminism, and revitalizing patriarchy. Jerry and Jennifer's enticing, yawning labyrinth of little stories of sacrifice, redemption, and unearthly love would give way to someting more sinister, monolithic, authoritarian, conspiratorial and hateful.

Ironically, this hypothetical reading, by fixing a singular, "real" meaning of Falwell's book, matches the unborn-again stereotype of a "literal interpretation" a good deal more than does the way in which born-again readers interpret the text, in their own terms, "literally." And what it—the hypothetical reading—yields, of course, is some sort of feminist, not fundamentalist, subjectivity.[3]

Gender meanings are contested in *If I Should Die*, but not as something segregated from discursive practice, not as a subtext or ideology or even encultured bodies, but as discourse itself. Falwell's book is an instance of born-again Christian discourse whose principal interlocutor is feminism. The text (and Liberty Godparent gospel and ministry more generally) appropriates a central feminist narrative ("women are sexual victims of men and patriarchy, and abortion liberates them") and renarrates it from a born-again point of view, thereby constituting that point of view and reproducing it in its cooperative readers. The language of *If I Should Die* does not "express" or "reflect," say, male domination, as if it were a code "underlying" the text. Rather, the text is more like a workshop producing born-again Christian subjectivity (with a fundamentalist accent) out of raw materials provided by the feminist, and particularly the pro-choice, movement. That is, the book effects a domination of feminist discourse by born-again discourse.

The fact that *If I Should Die* is written as a collection of stories, rather than, say, a polemic, is what makes it generative, subjectively speaking, for born-again readers. Born-again Christian discourse, as a whole and in its parts, is transferred narratively. Being born-again means figuring oneself and one's world in terms of Biblically framed stories. These stories create a narrative landscape, which simultaneously "speaks" Biblical and contemporary discourses, submitting the latter to the terms of the former (which is also, strictly speaking, a contemporary discourse). *If I Should Die's* Biblically framed stories of transformation (Jerry's, Jennifer's, and the Liberty Godparent Home girls') fashion a "rite of passage," which, as readers undergo it, transfers narrative authority to them: the right, the ability, and the desire to speak the pro-life gospel.

The born-again transfer of narrative authority is constituted in gender terms in two interrelated ways: It is a movement across the gender boundary, from a "male" (saved, speaker, author) to a "female" (lost, listener, reader) position; and it is a moment of "rebirth," a second (spiritual, Fathered) birth that overtakes the first (fleshly, mothered) birth, converting the lost into the saved; "female" into "male." Modern feminism challenges these fundamental asymmetries, hence the very mechanism by which born-again Christian subjectivity is reproduced.

This essay explores the ways the feminist challenge is being contested in the "narrative rituals" of *If I Should Die*: first, through its reiterated enactments of gendered asymmetries, both in and across male and female bodies; second, by inventing a born-again, that is, Biblically framed, "tradition" of opposition to abortion; and third, by reconfiguring and occupying the cultural turf claimed by feminism, the space of women's reproduction, before and after birth.

IN THE BEGINNING, THERE WAS "MALE" AND "FEMALE"

If the dustcover scene intimated that gender and Christian discourses would intersect in *If I Should Die,* its prologue ("Who Will Answer the

Challenge?") carries the whole project in miniature form. The opening scene, an encounter between Falwell and a secular female reporter, transforms (converts) Falwell and launches him on his journey across the landscape of women's bodies, authorizing both his mission and his book.

Cornered by reporters in an anonymous airport, flashbulbs popping, microphones thrust into his face, Jerry Falwell endures another impromptu press conference. Just as he breaks away, a "young newswoman," also nameless, tags him with one last question, "You say you are against abortion . . . but what practical alternative do pregnant girls have when they are facing an unwanted pregnancy?" "They can have the baby," Falwell replies. The reporter persists, "Do you really think it's that simple?" Falwell is taken aback.

I looked at her for a moment in silence. This was not just a reporter's question, asked to fill space in a paper or on the evening news. The look in the eyes of that reporter made me feel that her question came from deep and private places down inside her . . .

"Most of the girls in this country facing an unwanted pregnancy are young and poor and helpless," she said, taking advantage of my silence . . . "Is it enough to take a stand against abortion," the woman concluded, "when you aren't doing anything to help the pregnant girls who have no other way?" . . .

Out of that confrontation a dream was born. I decided that the reporter was right. It wasn't enough to be against abortion. Millions of babies were being killed, and I would go on fighting to save their lives, but what about the other victims of abortion, the mothers of those babies who desperately need help to save their babies? (10–11)

The story of the encounter contains not one Biblical reference, but it is saturated with Biblical innuendos and pretexts. Falwell's appropriation of women's reproductive issue (both senses) echoes Christian conversion, in which natural, female birth is subverted, overcome, by a spiritual birth mediated by the Father. As a story of his election to "answer the challenge," it recalls Biblical tales of God's calling prophets and apostles. In these stories, unwitting moral inferiors figure as messengers, momentarily occupying the "male" position of superior speech as they deliver God's word to a man of God. "Out of that confrontation a dream was born" implies an annunciation of sorts and reinforces the figuring of Falwell in the "female" (listening) position.

Born-again readers come to a gospel text prepared to place themselves in its stories in the "female" position and to undergo its transformations. This understanding between Falwell and his readers is made explicit at the end of the prologue, where he begins to fashion the sacrificial passage and to prepare a reciprocal place for his readers—his sacrifice will soon enough call forth theirs—and makes it plainer still that the place may be occupied by both men and women:

This book is my answer to that reporter's question. I've asked Jennifer Simpson . . . to tell her dramatic true story in chapters that alternate with mine. You may know a young lady like her. Or you may be facing this problem now, just as she did. Or you may be simply watching the abortion battle from the sidelines, as I once did, trying to decide what you believe and whether or not to become involved.

"Is there no other way but abortion?" I believe we have found an answer to that reporter's question. Read on and see if you agree. (11)

"What's missing?" The incompleteness of the book cover scene is opened up by the reporters's question; the space of reproduction, women's bodies, will become the ground for redemptive speech and action. As Falwell ("man") publicly acknowledges the right of the reporter ("woman") to speak for herself and other women, he acquires the right to enter her body with his speech, appropriates her concern, in effect, her power, and with it strikes out to fashion a "new" pro-family discourse. The reporter—a working woman, assertive and articulate, representing women's point of view— stands for feminism (a feminism "Christianized" before it is spoken—she calls him "Dr. Falwell"). Her words do not close off but rather open up the subject—women, and their reproductive power and problems—to him, his gaze, his speech. It is she who portrays women who need abortions as young, helpless, poor victims. It is she, not he, who places them under him and, like the babies they carry, in need of his help.

She, in effect, delivers him the feminist storyline. The feminist image of "a woman gaining control over her body and her life through abortion rights" is reinscribed as "a victim, a helpless woman [girl] who is driven to abortion because she has no other way." The feminist line that men oppose abortion rights to deprive women of elemental, bodily, equality and liberty is displaced by the image of a born-again male hero rising up in the country of reproducing women, a man-father-Father figure who will save mothers as well as babies from the capacious maw of death.

The strange gender moves in the encounter suggest that the occupation of born-again narrative figures and frames on the discursive territory claimed by feminism will be complicated: a secular female reporter asks Jerry Falwell a question he cannot answer, and Falwell, silenced, opens up, listens to this brassy young woman who throws him off guard in public. Their exchange is intimate: she holds him with her speech at some length, and he looks into her eyes, into "deep and private places down inside her." As her words enter him, his gaze enters her, and he is infilled with a dream. Together they become, in a way, the first Liberty Godparents. The strangeness, of course, is the role reversal in the reproductive metaphor: She takes on a "male" privilege, public speech, and, as it were, fertilizes him. He is feminized in the encounter, by submitting (listening) to a woman and giving birth to a dream—the Liberty Godparent gospel and ministry.

Men may occupy the "female" position and women the "male" position in dialogic encounters, but the point is not that men and women are equal, any more than the "male" speaking position being marked "superior" means that men necessarily dominate women. The gender reversals in the encounter between Falwell and the female reporter are not "really" about bodily men and women; instead, the reversals regenerate the essential subject positions in born-again discourse. The point is that gender differences are deployed to constitute born-again Christian subjectivity, not the reverse. Gender differences are, of course, fashioned in the process of being deployed, but as a side effect or, rather, an "a priori" supplement of born-again discourse. Gender is both the rib and the "without which not" of orthodox Christian identity formation.

To the extent that feminism "brought up" gender publicly and then declared war on its asymmetries, the movement was liable to provoke a reaction from born-again Christians who, as it were, speak themselves through a submerged display of asymmetical gender meanings. How abortion rights came to be such an incandescent issue for born-again Christians is somewhat less straight foward.

PREFIGURING ABORTION

Catholics drew on a long tradition of speech and action to promptly protest the 1973 Supreme Court decision, Roe v. Wade, which repealed state bans on abortion. Evangelical Protestants did not respond immediately, but by the early 1980s they had become formidable abortion foes, contributing much materially, organizationally and rhetorically to what had become known as the pro-life movement. Social movements often seem to arise abruptly, but a little "archaeology" usually reveals precedents and roots, including a network of pre-movement organizations and ideas that anticipated and gave form and content to the movement. No such prior history exists in the case of the born-again movement against abortion. The mid-19th century campaigns that banned abortion were led by physicians, not Protestant preachers, and there is only one iota of evidence that Jerry Falwell, in particular, ever mentioned abortion before 1973, and little evidence that he said much more until 1978.[4] For all intents and purposes, the "tradition" of opposition to abortion among Falwell's following was invented during the late 1970s and early 1980s.[5]

Opposition to abortion became the linchpin of the Christian Right coalition that formed at the end of the 1970s, as born-again Protestants simply appropriated Catholic right-to-life rhetoric, stripped of its distinctly Catholic markers. But what made abortion into a volcanic issue for born-agains— the only issue that spun them in large numbers into political organizations, support groups, public hearings, demonstrations and, most recently, jail— was the "Biblicalization" of anti-abortion rhetoric, carried out mostly by preachers.[6] Since 1979, with what seems in retrospect remarkable speed, they have piled up ways of figuring and framing the abortion issue in Biblical terms, which pushed opposition to abortion into the very heart of what it means to be a born-again Christian.[7]

Early in the evolution of his own rhetoric, Jerry Falwell demonstrated God's opposition to abortion in the conventional fundamentalist manner: citing dozens of Biblical verses that "prove" it.[8] He also embedded the "sin of abortion" in the pre-millennial vision of the End Times, a period of rampant immorality and social decay that precedes the rapture, the Great Tribulation, the Battle of Armageddon and the Second Coming of Christ. Although resistance to "loosening" sexual practices and gender relations is audible here, Falwell and his co-pastors did not directly elaborate the "sin of abortion" as an attack on "the family" or "family values." Rather, from the beginning, they figured it as an ultimate violation of the relationship between person and God, on a par—a slippery slope—with murder, the holocaust, the slaughter of innocents, and, ultimately, the crucifixion of Christ.

Falwell's Liberty Godparent campaign intensified and expanded on this process of Biblicalizing opposition to abortion. The campaign's major breakthrough was to emerge from the womb and generate the female bodies, lives and experiences surrounding the endangered fetus. In *If I Should Die*, this ground, the embodied landscape upon which Falwell acts, is, as we shall see shortly, most fully fashioned by Jennifer; in other words, by a woman-in-need-of-abortion elaborated as "helpless victim."

One of the principal innovations of Falwell's early chapters, on the other hand, is to narrate an inside story of Falwell's conversion to pro-life activism (before he met the reporter; before he formed the Moral Majority), thus creating some history for born-again opposition to abortion for the period between 1973 and 1979. Given the agreement of born-again readers (listeners) to undergo the transformations of anointed authors (speakers), Falwell's story becomes his readers', and the history becomes experience, as well as "fact." The other innovation in Falwell's chapters is one Jennifer will carry out more explicitly. Falwell's story is only lightly marked by Biblical cues, yet manages to nest abortion and anti-abortion activism fully in the central narrative frames that transfer authority in born-again culture.

One of the "credentials" of hard-core pro-life activists is that they can remember where they were and what they were doing the day Roe v. Wade came down.[9] So, in his first chapter in *If I Should Die*, Falwell remembers reading about the decision in the newspaper as his eggs, bacon, raisin toast and coffee grew cold—and, behold, anti-abortion rhetoric came fully formed into his head. Indeed, it had been there a long time:

I will never forget the morning of January 23, 1973. . . . The Supreme Court had just made a seven to two decision that would legalize the killing of a generation of unborn children. I couldn't believe that seven justices on that Court could be so callous about the dignity of human life. Were they misinformed? Had they been misled? Were they plunging the nation into a time of darkness and shame without even knowing what they were doing? . . . I had preached on abortion and its meaning to my people and had used abortion as an example in several sermons over the past ten years. But, as I read the paper that day, I knew something more had to be done, and I felt a growing conviction that I would have to take my stand among the people who were doing it. (31–32)

There were other signs, small moments of "growing conviction". For example, when Jerry "saw a full-color picture of an unborn child. . . . a tiny, trusting child whom God had created"—but he "still hesitated to take a public stand" (36).

It was his children who officially mediated his actual conversion to political action. During family devotions, when Jerry laments "the legal murder of millions of America's unborn children," his children (in gendered voices) call him to task:

"Why don't you do something about it, Dad?" my spunky red-headed son finally interrupted, rising up on one elbow and looking me in the eye.

"Yeah," chimed in my daughter. "Do something for the babies." (37)

His children "hounded" him for weeks. He prayed and argued, his "convictions began to grow," and he finally overcame his fundamentalist scruples about activism and "jumped into the political arena feet first." If God later would use a woman to deliver Falwell access to the discourse of women's bodies, He first used children to open the discursive door to the womb.

Still, there were years to pass between this moment and the formation of the Moral Majority, Falwell's actual debut as a political leader. Falwell occupied the time, it turns out, educating himself, reading everything he "could get [his] hands on concerning the issues," voraciously consuming all manner of texts: academic and popular, legal, medical, scientific, and political. When, in his second chapter, Falwell takes us through what he learned, we find ourselves caught up in a welter of stories of fetal life and death.

Jerry tells us about the dumpster in L.A. stuffed with remains of 1700 human babies, mutilated, little bitty bodies all torn to pieces, hands chopped off, and the incinerator of burning bags of dead babies from a hospital in Wichita. He lifts the terror briefly to envision how Jennifer's first baby would have developed had she (yes "she") lived, only to recount, in graphic detail, how she was torn from her "liquid nursery," her "secret sanctuary," and disposed of by medical personnel. "There would be no monument for the courageous struggle for life the baby mounted until she died" (67). Lengthy, detailed, vivid descriptions of abortion methods follow. "Picture it." Cutting the body into pieces, crushing the head, extracting, sucking the pieces into a container.

Falwell's recounting here is uncustomarily free of Biblical citations that would prove that the fetus is "life" and abortion "murder." He refrains from overtly sacralizing the first birth, and, instead, renders it in palpable secular terms and deploys "scientific facts" to construct abortion as murder.

The account's relentless detail squares with the tradition of "common sense empiricism" in fundamentalism, and also with Falwell's personal narrative, by generating the "worldly" ground upon which he will take his public stand—and enjoin his readers to take theirs.[10]

Still, there is a way in which Falwell's figuring of fetal life and death in *If I Should Die* worms its way into the core of born-again discourse. Any narrative reiteration of life versus death would do so (Billy Graham defined Christianity as "the conquest of death"), but the fetal struggle also opens the possibility of commenting on Christian discourse itself, which Falwell fully realizes. In effect, he figures abortion as the death of the first ("female,") birth, a death which precludes the second ("male") birth and thus disrupts the narrative transfer of spiritual authority.

All that chopping and cutting, the excessively vivid, repeated dismembering of little unborn babies resonates (not automatically, but as an outcome of preacherly discourse) as sinful sacrifice; ritual action that defiles and destroys the relationship between person and God; an act that abolishes the very context in which the relationship might be restored. Among fundamental Christians, the first birth prefigures the second birth in the same way that Abraham's willingness to sacrifice Isaac prefigured Christ's death and resurrection. The first story frames, enables, anticipates the second story; it marks an incompleteness which the second story fills, fulfills; the second story depends on, cannot happen without, the first story. What if Abraham had disobeyed God in the end and killed his son? No Isaac, no Christ. That is what, in Falwell's language, abortion does. It destroys the first story/birth ("female," flesh) which prefigures the second story/birth ("male," spirit), thus cutting and chopping the narrative channel that transfers born-again authority. Constituted in these terms, the right to abortion puts the very heart of born-again Christianity at stake.

THE PROMISED LAND

Jennifer's chapters weave in and out of Falwell's, unfolding the intimate, vulnerable, embodied landscape upon which Falwell, and other born-again preachers and believers, must act. He invites his readers to look at abortion from "the woman's point of view." He does this implicitly in his long review of "the physical and psychological damage" (ranging from uterine perforations to drug addiction; from bad marriages to suicide) inflicted on women who have abortions, and explicitly just before Jennifer begins her abortion story ("try to feel how she felt that awful day her baby died" [47]). But it is she who takes up where the secular reporter left off and constitutes the born-again version of the woman's point of view, filling the feminist space of "adult women exercising control over their bodies" with the image of "a teenage girl who needs help."

Whereas Falwell was inventing born-again tradition in fashioning a history and new Biblically-based narrative grounds for anti-abortion activism,

Jennifer works against the grain of a born-again interpretive legacy regarding "unwed (teenage) mothers." That legacy would cast girls like Jennifer in a "war against sin," vilifying them as sexual transgressors, framing the maternity homes, or "homes for unwed mothers," as places to hide in shame, and posing childbirth and childrearing as the "price that must be paid" for sin. With Falwell's help, Jennifer reinscribes the girls as innocent (in the sense of naive or abused) victims, the maternity home as a place where teenage lives are restored, childbirth as God's will, and childrearing as ill-advised in this instance. It turns out that "the better way," which Falwell conceives in his prophet-making scene with the reporter includes giving up for adoption the babies "saved from abortion." Accordingly, the Liberty Godparent Home is at once a (pleasant) maternity home and an adoption agency for married born-again Christian couples.

It seems that Falwell and his collaborators are not simply responding to feminism but adjusting their language and practice to certain facts of born-again life in the 1980s. Even in their communities, more teenagers are having sex, girls are getting pregnant and having abortions, and couples who wish to adopt are finding babies scarce.[11] The adjustment is not an easy one, however. By what narrative logic may girls be led to give up their babies for adoption after so much ink has been spilled convincing them to "save" them from abortion? Several chapters of *If I Should Die* are devoted directly to "making the difficult decision," and Jennifer's and the other LGH girls' stories seem to work overtime on behalf of "adopting out." Their stories pitch toward adoption most notably in their portrayal of the girls as innocent and dependent victims whose lives need to be restored, in the ongoing sacralization of the fetus-child, and in the radical marginalization of the biological father. Ultimately, and utterly without precedent, "adopting out" is constituted as the second birth anticipated by the first birth, at least in the lives of unwed teenage girls.

While Falwell's story is one of steady, if slow progress toward the pro-life right, Jennifer goes down before she goes up. As she moves through her moment of maximum descent, the abortion, through the turning point when she decides to "save" her second baby, to her triumphant arrival at the Liberty Godparent Home in Lynchburg, Jennifer's story accumulates Biblical figures of speech, which exculpate her, demonize abortion and sanctify giving birth . . . all without essentializing the relationship between (biological) mother and child (preborn or postborn).

Details of time and space frame Jennifer's abortion as an anti-worship service, as sacrilegious sacrifice: Jennifer and her parents drive past their church on their way to the abortion appointment at 11:00 one Sunday morning. "Nobody noticed us drive by." The sky is overcast, storm clouds are piling up, the wind is blowing dirty paper plates and empty beer cans across the highway, and by the time they arrive at the Planned Parenthood clinic (anti-church), they are "irritable and grumpy" and "scared". The waiting room is full of naive girls, frightened and listless, many of whom had been there before. The nurse (anti-Sunday School teacher) lectures them on abortion procedures. "I suppose we didn't really listen to the nurse for the same reason passengers on an airplane don't really listen to the warnings of the stewardess. Who wants to hear the bad news [anti-good news]?" (55).

"I'll always remember how embarrassed I felt that day when the young male doctor [anti-pastor] entered the room to find my two bare legs sticking almost straight up into the air and my hands gripping the [anti-communion] table for dear life." (56) Jennifer glimpses the suction tube in the doctor's hand just before he injects the anesthesia:

I don't know what he did to me after that. I woke up on a bed. A nurse was removing a bloody pad from between my legs. It was gross. . . . I lay there thinking I was going to die when the receptionist entered the room and placed a glass of milk and a plate of Oreo cookies beside me. . . . I felt terribly foolish. It didn't look anything like a last supper. The abortion was over. The little intruder was gone forever. I felt weak and dizzy and high. (57)

The "last supper" [anti-bread and wine] spins an even more explicit thread between the abortion and Christ's sacrifice than do the situating details. It also evokes the last meal of a convicted murderer and intimates "the wages of sin is death." At the same time, Jennifer's naive narrative voice and the image of milk and cookies deflect those connotations from her and suggest "I am innocent."

Abortion is evil—it carries the full weight of sin—and Jennifer emerges scathed but untainted. She is the girl next door, a sixteen-year-old middle-class Baptist Georgia city girl whose father is a deacon; her mother, the church secretary. Neither she nor those who counseled her to get an abortion (her parents, the health teacher, a Baptist pastor) denies the "personhood" of the fetus. They are oblivious to it. "Nobody thought about the baby. Not even me" (29). Jennifer laments in retrospect. "Ignorance" not sin was the culprit as far as these otherwise good Christians are concerned.

If Jennifer's abortion is an anti-worship service, the moment she decides to "save" her second baby is a cross between an annunciation and a salvation experience. Her parents had "just seen a special on TV about a place in Virginia" and thus knew about "a better way" when Jennifer told them she was pregnant again. She balks at the idea of going there to have her baby, but then, while driving alone about midnight on a highway, she runs out of gas, pulls into a filling station that was closed for the night (liminal time, place, and circumstance, with innuendos of sexual danger and a sign of spiritual hope: the filling station), and has a revelation. Having called a friend to come get her, she curls up in the backseat of her car to wait and watches a moth fly into a hot light and sizzle to death.

I pictured myself fluttering and dancing about the light. I determined that this time I would be smart enough to fly away to safety. That awful night was one of the best things that ever happened to me. There beside the filling station in the middle of nowhere, something changed within me. I grew up. "Dear Lord, please help me." I hadn't prayed for a long time, not a real prayer, not like this one. "I'm in real trouble again, Lord, and I don't know what to do about it." I stared out into the darkness trying to find God out there. (95)

The echoes of Mary's annunciation (an unmarried girl visited by a messenger; a male birth foreshadowed) are mixed with innuendoes of Christ's death (a meaningful death: He died so that we might live), and "something changed" within Jennifer. That night, she submits to God ("Dear Lord, please help me"), and the next day she tells her parents she wants to go to that "place in Virginia." Jennifer chooses life over death, joins God's plan, and the hidden meaning of things and events will begin now to "infill" her.

The Biblical innuendos break the textual surface when Jennifer arrives at the Liberty Godparent Home. As the director, Jim Savley (his real name), ushers Jennifer and her parents into his office, she notices the pictures of his wife and family, a framed telegram from President Reagan, certificates and diplomas, and "an impressive painting of Mary riding on a donkey carrying the baby Jesus in her arms. Joseph walked close by." Jennifer tries to remember the story, "but all I could see was the look in Mary's eyes as she stared lovingly into her baby's face." Mr. Savley, answering her unasked question, tells her that Mary and Joseph were fleeing to Egypt "to save the life of their baby" (125).

I understood why the painting was chosen for his office. My family and I had traveled to Lynchburg for a similar reason—to save my baby. There was an unborn child growing inside me and this time the baby would not die. (126)

Jennifer becomes Mary; her parents, Joseph; LGH, Egypt; and, by narrative implication, the abortionists, King Herod bent on slaughtering the innocents. Falwell, the absent author of it all, casts a decidedly supermundane shadow. This time, the baby-Christ will be spared.[12]

Jennifer's arrival scene at LGH foreshadows, as did the moth scene, a male birth and clinches the equation, first murmured on the dustcover, between Christ and the baby-saved-from-abortion. It also cleanses Jennifer, wrapping her in Mary's mantle, "virginalizing" the unwed pregnant teenage girl threatened by the specter of abortion—Herod. At the same time, it locates her reproductive issue squarely in God's plan, not in her hands, much less in the hands of the biological father. These threads are spun out in the rest of Jennifer's story and in Jerry's, which begins to merge topically with Jennifer's once she enters LGH.

When her parents first told Jennifer about the LGH, she imagined "a haunted house with army nurses and big needles behind locked doors and barred windows" (91). In effect, she envisioned a place where she would be punished, drilled, and terrorized. In an intervening chapter, Falwell assures his readers that nothing could be further from the truth and rewrites the maternity home from darkness to light, from shame to self-confidence:

We now know that an unwanted pregnancy makes a teenage girl feel ugly, embarrassed, and unwanted. . . . The young woman feels like hiding her shame from the world. . . . That's why it becomes so easy to kill the baby, to end the nightmare, and to try to begin again. That's why Liberty Godparent maternity homes provide a sense of permanence, safety and beauty to restore the self-confidence and self-worth in the pregnant girls it exists to serve. (110)

And, of course, Jennifer is greeted by the warm, intuitive Mr. Savley, not an "army nurse," and the place is surrounded by oak trees and blue jays, green lawns and bright yellow flowers, and inside there were bay windows overlooking the garden, Early American maple tables and chairs, and a "chef," her arms brimming with grocery bags.[13]

Jennifer and Jerry collaborate here in reinscribing the maternity home, converting a 19th and early 20th century figment of anti-sex discourse into a 1980s anti-abortion sanctuary. Accordingly, the stories of how Jennifer and the other girls at LGH "got pregnant" portray them as passively, not actively, sexually transgressive; not as sinners but as victims. When she was sixteen, surrounded by the tempting music, visual images and banter of teen culture, Jennifer feels her body changing and stirring ("just brushing past a boy going through a classroom doorway made me feel excited and curious and a little afraid" [14]), and vulnerable to any boy's attention ("I felt ugly and rejected and alone most of the time" [15]). She spends a weekend unchaperoned at a summer cottage with some other girls. Boys arrive one night, she finds herself alone on the dunes with a strange boy, and . . . "the romantic dream became a nightmare" (23). After her abortion, she is "miserable and angry most of the time" and "desperately needed someone or something" to make her "feel good again" (85). That "someone" is Jeff, that "something," sex, and she gets in trouble again.

The other LGH girls fall into two camps, sexually speaking. There are girls like Jennifer, victims of physical urges, low self-esteem, teen culture, and lack of supervision, who "made mistakes," implying that "these things happen, even in (middle-class) Christian families." And there are other girls to whom unthinkable things happen (lower class, not Christian). They are victims of incest, rape, pornography, poverty, negligence. Missy, thirteen, was abused by her father and impregnated by a stranger. JoAnn's alcoholic father beat his four daughters, sexually abused three of them, and got JoAnn pregnant at fourteen. An unnamed fourteen-year-old girl called the LGH hotline operator from Baltimore and said her father sexually abused her, made pornographic movies with her and her two-year-old brother, and had just killed their mother. Either way, whether victims of bad boys or evil men, the girls are let off sin's hook lightly, as the causes of their pregnancies are narratively dispersed in circumstances rather than lodged in the girls, in their sinfulness or their "sin nature."

The victimizers lurk on the margins of the girls' stories. They are misguided boyfriends who mislead girls who make mistakes and cruel fathers/strangers who rape defenseless girls. Just once, in a few lines, Falwell casts a light on the boys, pointing out that some of them try to change, some try to help the girls they have hurt, and not all of them are "irresponsible and uncaring" (191–192), though, by implication, the rest of the boys, and all the adult men who impregnate teenage girls, are. Their narrative banishment—the erasure of the natural father—combines with the Mariological insinuations surrounding the girls to intensify the sense of fetal divinity and de-essentialize the relationship of fetus-child to both its parents. Biological fathers are given no say in the fate of the babies, before or after birth, and, while the girls must make the "difficult decisions," it is absolutely clear, given that fetuses belong to and are essentially of God, that the first birth ought not be aborted.[14] It is not so clear what the girls ought to do with God's issue after birth.

THE EMPTY CRADLE

Alongside tales of personal and spiritual growth and restoration at LGH, Jennifer narrates her painful search for "the right thing to do for the baby" as she listens to other girls make up their minds and talks over her qualms with the women who work at LGH. Falwell, in his parallel chapters, is likewise much preoccupied by the choice the girls must make between keeping their babies and giving them up for adoption. Its importance, delicacy, and complexity is forcefully indicated by the narrative space it occupies. Jennifer and Jerry slow down the pace of their storytelling, expand the details, and fill the margins of their thoughts with inset tales that explore other options and outcomes. Although other choices are permitted fairly good endings, the girls are under unequivocal narrative pressure to "adopt out," sacrificing their children, for their own good, to Christian couples.

Andrea kept her son and started a new life in Lynchburg, but working full-time meant long hours in daycare for little Brian and the abrupt end of her own adolescence. The failure to make a timely sacrifice called for other sacrifices with uncertain, open-ended consequences. Tammy, on the other hand, kept her baby even though she, at age fourteen, had been counseled that adoption was "the preferred option," and later we find her happily married to a "tall, blond seminary student from Chicago" who told Falwell, "I don't agree with all your politics . . . but you saved my son and I'll always love you for that" (211).

JoAnn did not, as did Tammy, have a middle-class home to return to, and her story, drawn out over several pages, accentuates the costs of keeping the baby. A fourteen-year-old victim of incest, poverty, and neglect, JoAnn took her baby back home to the perils of her father's house. Falwell said,

I selected JoAnn's story because struggling with her kind of complex and confounding reality is the responsibility of any person who takes a serious stand against abortion . . . JoAnn's story isn't over yet. We don't know what God has in mind for her little girl. Whatever it is, we are glad and grateful that God will have His chance in her life. It is risky business reaching out to people in despair. It is risky business helping babies be born into our world. (158–159)

The echoes of a second birth deferred are strong in this passage. "JoAnn's story isn't over yet," "we don't know what God has in mind . . . ," "it is risky business reaching out to people in despair"—these are phrases out of in-house metagospel talk, forms of speech used among soulwinners consoling themselves over "the ones that got away," the lost souls who seemed to say "no" when they heard the message of Christ's saving grace. Though the timing is always ultimately given back to God, no born-again Christian has any doubt that "the better way," if not necessarily the only route to narrative completion, is to choose Christ ("adopt out" to a born-again couple) now.

Jennifer decides to give her child up for adoption shortly after witnessing a conversation between thirteen-year-old Missy and Rosemary, an LGH volunteer who herself had given her baby up for adoption a few years before. Rosemary tells Missy,

You love your baby too much to keep her. You don't have a home or a family or a husband to offer your baby. You can't provide anything you want her to have . . . There is a young couple right this minute who cannot have a baby of their own. They have a good income. They have a beautiful home with a nursery and toys and baby clothes and an empty cradle. They are praying for a baby, Missy. They can take care of the baby. They can give the baby what you want to give her . . . (139)

There is that empty cradle again, that sense of "something missing." It is no longer the consequence of abortion (the death of the first birth) but is now the space awaiting adoption (the second birth made possible by the first). Jennifer, like Missy and several other girls, decides to (ful)fill it, but their decisions are labored, even belabored.

Jennifer agonizes over "adopting out" for months, worrying if she will have the courage to stick to it, dwelling on the moment when she will have to give the baby up. The sense that she is engaged in making a rightful (just short of ultimate) sacrifice is clinched when she receives word of her baby's sex and name from Falwell: "I had chosen Stephen for my baby's name. I was convinced I was going to have a boy after Dr. Falwell had preached on Stephen, the first Christian martyr" (194–195). Just before he is born, Jennifer wrote Stephen a letter he will never receive:

You were not unwanted . . . I want the very best for you, and if I could give it to you, don't think for a moment that I wouldn't. God has a very special plan for you and right now it's for you to have both a mother and a father . . . I love you. (202)

Some thoughts are being precluded through all this self-denial, most especially any suggestion that giving Stephen up for adoption was "convenient" for Jennifer.

Jennifer, the other girls, and Falwell—the LGH gospel—must sanction adoption for teenage girls without resorting to language that born-again

Christians impute to feminism. They must suppress any innuendos that babies are "unwanted" or "inconvenient," that they get in the way with girls resuming their adolescence, going to college, having a career, or getting properly married. Hence, the sacrificial excess:

"Do you know that I love you, son?" I whispered into his tiny ear. "Will you remember? We have to trust God now. He'll take care of you. Will you forgive me? Will you love me anyway?" Words poured out of me. Stephen looked as if he was trying to understand . . . When they took him back to the nursery, I pulled the thin yellow blanket up so that the nylon edge was touching my face. The heavy drapes covered the huge windows. It was twilight outside. The room was almost dark. I was alone again. (202–203)

This bedroom scene completes, fulfills, the one on the dustcover. Jennifer has sacrificed herself so that Stephen might live, but her "death" marks a new beginning, not an end, as she walks boldly back into a middle-class adolescence, restored and brimming with possibilities. By the time she reappears in Falwell's final chapter, which jumps ahead a few years and narrates a Memorial Day celebration on the grounds of LGH in memory of "the unborn children who have died from abortion," Jennifer has become a communications major at his Liberty University and is emerging as a national spokesperson for Liberty Godparent Homes. Clearly, God blesses those who seek and follow his will.

When Falwell finally makes his pitch, in the penultimate chapter, for readers to assume their place in the sacrificial landscape unfolded for them, it is relatively soft and pro forma. It concludes with a vague entreaty, "Will you seriously consider joining us in helping save the unborn babies of our nation?" (191). Although the book rehearses all the moves of gospel speech, marking out a multitude of "lacknesses" for readers to complete, *If I Should Die* appears in the end to be less a gospel text designed for the unconverted and more a metagospel text for the converted—a training manual, comparable to a collection of sermons, for the elaboration and refinement of gospel speech. Instead of building toward a "moment of salvation" in which pro-life discourse is acquired, the stories assume "saved" readers and effect a continuous transfer of narrative authority.[15]

WORKING OUT GOD'S WILL IN HISTORY

The stories of Jerry Falwell's pro-life campaign appropriate and displace feminist discourse in ways that are at once crude and complex. On the one hand, much is simply blotted out: feminism and the feminist movement are never named in *If I Should Die,* and adult women and married teenage girls who choose abortion make no textual appearances. In effect, the feminist storyline is shamelessly caricatured. All of the "women who need abortions" are unmarried teenage girls, all of them were sexual victims, and all of them "need help." Jennifer, by dint of dependency, age, name (Falwell's childrens' names begin with "J") resonates daughter to Falwell's father/Father. Such moves plainly rig the narrative campaign in favor of Falwell's authority.

On the other hand, the campaign deploys the most powerful and sophisticated narrative resources of born-again Christian culture, resources that have countless times proven themselves capable of reconfiguring the subjective springs of action. The campaign, in figuring abortion as the death of the first birth, saving babies as the first birth, and "adopting out" and the second birth, lodges the pro-life movement in the discursive heart of born-again culture, in the supple and irresistable play of reciprocal sacrificial action across stories, written, spoken, and lived.

The stories of *If I Should Die* do not represent "preexisting" asymmetries as fixed eternal truths that must be swallowed whole, but (re)constitute them. They transfer these new configurations from author to reader, with tremendous force and tenderness, through the narrative logic of prefiguration and fulfillment. Repeatedly, superior persons (Falwell), terms ("male," spiritual, second birth, saved), stories (Jennifer's arrival at LGH, Falwell's listening to her Memorial Day speech), and discourses (born-again) incorporate and arise out of the transcendence of inferior persons (the reporter, Jennifer), terms ("female," flesh, first birth, lost), stories (Jennifer's abortion, Falwell's encounter with the reporter), and discourses (worldly). The logic binding inferior and superior is neither literary nor causal, but divine; foreordained and indelibly written by God. If Isaac, then Christ. If first birth, then second birth. If "female," then "male." If Jennifer, then Falwell-cum-maternity-home-maker.

Born-again preachers and pro-life leaders have been able to engage their communities in an escalating movement against abortion by embedding the movement in "the greatest story ever told." What they achieve, in collaboration with their followers, as they trace out alterations of character, motif, motive, action, and circumstance across sequences of stories and events, is nothing less than the further working out of "God's will in history."

If I Should Die ends with Jennifer Simpson making her debut as a public speaker at the Memorial Day celebration. As he sits on the platform and listens to her, Jerry Falwell ponders what would have happened "if people hadn't cared enough to save" the babies of the girls at LGH.

I imagined their children sliced into pieces and suctioned from their mother's womb or burned and blackened by salt poisoning and born dead . . . "You are alive, little Brian," I said quietly to myself. "Thank God, Stephen, you are alive." (216)

In the book's opening scene, the secular female reporter handed Jerry Falwell the feminist storyline and "the woman's point of view." Jennifer and Jerry renarrated them in born-again terms across their intertwining chapters. Together they converted the cradle emptied through abortion into the cradle (ful)filled through adoption. In the book's closing scene, once again, a woman speaks in public while Falwell listens, but this time it is he who created the grounds upon which she speaks, even as she embodied the landscape upon which he acted. Although Jennifer has a public voice, she acquired it through Falwell's sacrificial action. The hint of feminism carried by the female reporter has finally been erased.

NOTES

I would like to thank the editors, Faye Ginsburg and Anna Tsing, and John Hartigan, Mary Lou Roberts, Joan Scott, Mary Steedly and Kathleen Stewart for their comments on this essay.

1. Jerry Falwell, *If I Should Die Before I Wake . . .* (Nashville, Tennessee: Thomas Nelson Publishers, 1986).

2. See Susan Harding, "Convicted by the Holy Spirit: The Rhetoric of Fundamental Baptist Conversion," *American Ethnologist* 14 (1987): 167–181.

3. *If I Should Die* also presents certain conundrums of authorship which might elude unborn-again readers but not believers. Although Falwell appears on the book's dustcover and in the credits as sole author, the chapters are clearly co-authored with Jennifer Simpson, a subsuming which neatly implies that he is her author. Falwell doubled the book's authorship again, at least for his church and TV audiences, when he introduced from the pulpit its ghostwriter, Mel White, furnished for the purpose by the publisher.

Such authorial ambiguities, rather than casting doubt on the text's veracity, enhance it by recalling debates over the authorship of Biblical books and thus nesting *If I Should Die* in a corpus whose authority (authorship) is accepted as a testament of faith. It is the responsibility of faithful readers to "unify" the authorial and narrative voices in their interpretation and to "harmonize" the text with other texts, spoken and written, so that it comes "true." Falwell's speech and writing are always already double-voiced, in any case, in the sense that it is never entirely clear whether he or God is the author of his words.

4. Jerry Falwell, *Capturing a Town for Christ* (Old Tappan, New Jersey: Fleming H. Revell Company, 1973): "Some come [to Falwell's church] seeking forgiveness, as a young father who was guilty of pressuring his wife to get an abortion; he wondered if God would forgive him for murdering an unborn child" (53). This quote, which is the earliest reference to abortion I have found under Falwell's name, establishes that Elmer Towns, who actually wrote *Capturing a Town*, was folding right-to-life phrases into born-again gospel rhetoric at least by 1973, possibly in 1972.

In 1976, abortion appeared on Falwell's list of "America's sins" in his bicentennial "I Love America" crusade sermons and tracts. But it was just one among many others, not the *cause célèbre* it was to become. Elmer Towns told me in an interview that it was he who finally convinced Falwell, in spring of 1978, to speak out at length against abortion. Towns knew because he wrote Falwell's first pro-life sermon. Still, it was a while before the issue took off; two books on the moral state of the nation published later under Falwell's name do not mention abortion—*America Can Be Saved* (Murfreesboro, Tennessee: Sword of the Lord Publishers, 1979) and *How to Clean Up America* (Lynchburg, Virginia: Old-Time Gospel Hour Publications, 1981).

The chapter on abortion in *Listen America!* (New York: Bantam, 1981), is Falwell's first extended treatment in print; it relies heavily on right-to-life rhetoric, on the work of Bernard Nathanson, an "abortionist" who converted to the pro-life movement, and on Francis Schafer and Dr. C. Everett Koop's *What Ever Happened to the Human Race* (Old Tappan, New Jersey: Fleming H. Revell, 1979), the first highly successful born-again polemic against abortion.

5. Opposition to abortion among more moderate born-again Christians emerged dialogically out of debates over the issue in the 1960s and 1970s and did not begin to crystallize as the prevailing view on abortion until the late 1970s; see Paul Fowler, *Abortion: Toward an Evangelical Consensus* (Portland: Multnomah Press, 1987). The pro-life position was not an "inevitable" or "logical" consequence of born-again faith or morality, nor is it even now uncontested within orthodox Protestant communities.

A symposium of evangelical physicians and theologians organized by *Christianity Today* in 1968 affirmed the principle that, "The Christian physician will advise induced abortion only to safeguard greater values sanctioned by Scripture. These values should include individual health, *family welfare, and social responsibility*" (emphasis added); in *Birth Control and the Christian*, eds. Walter O. Spitzer and Carlyle L. Saylor (Wheaton, Illinois: Tyndale House, 1969), xxvi. A special issue of *Eternity* magazine on abortion in 1971 (February) still presented a range of opinions on the circumstances under which abortion might be advised. Even in 1984, an attempt by Wheaton College's student government to adopt a strong anti-abortion resolution produced a heated public debate among the faculty (Fowler, 83).

This evidence argues against the notion that pro-life mobilization emerged, as if inevitably, out of a preexisting "worldview," a position most fully developed by Kristin Luker in *Abortion and the Politics of Motherhood* (Berkeley: University of California Press, 1984) and which I once defended, in "Family Reform Movements: Recent Feminism and Its Opposition," *Feminist Studies* 7 (1981): 57–75.

6. By "Biblical," I do not refer to what is "in" the Bible, but to born-again interpretation of what is "in" the Bible. Note also that there are distinct understandings among born-again Protestants regarding the Bible and distinct idioms of opposition to abortion. In his LGH campaign, Jerry Falwell seems to be "crossing over" between two dialects, blending his own Baptist fundamentalism into a more mainstream (non-charismatic) evangelical tongue.

7. There was a similar rhetorical rupture among evangelical Protestants in the 1830s, when activism against slavery rather suddenly intensified, shifting from a commitment to gradual abolition to a call for immediate abolition. Pastors reinscribed slavery as the ultimate expression of sinful self-gratification, and the committment to immediate abolition became a kind of "rebirth," hence a sign of whether or not someone was truly saved. Abolition, in effect, became a form of evangelism, a sacred vocation. See Donald M. Scott, "Abolition as a Sacred Vocation," in *Anti-Slavery Reconsidered*, eds. Lewis Perry and Michael Fellman (Baton Rouge: Louisiana State University Press, 1979).

8. "Scriptures for Life" invariably accompanies pro-life literature put out by the LGH campaign. It lists 23 Bible passages (there are others) as "proof-texts" against abortion; that is, they prove that God opposes it. For example, and often cited, Jeremiah 1:5, "Before I formed thee in the belly I knew thee: and

before thou camest forth out of the womb I sanctified thee." Inscribed on the Monument to the Unborn, a huge gravestone placed on Falwell's Liberty University campus, is Matthew 18:6, "But whoso shall offend one of these little ones which believe in me, it were better for him that a millstone were hung around his neck and to be drowned in the sea."

9. Faye Ginsburg, *Contested Lives: The Abortion Debate in an American Community* (Berkeley: University of California Press, 1989).

If I Should Die presents itself as "true stories," and we may ask, "true" in what sense? "Truth" in born-again culture is authenticated by its author; everything in the Bible is "true" because God wrote it, and everything Jerry Falwell (a man anointed by God) says is "true" because he said it. Discrepancies in parallel stories are not unsettling (because stories do not represent a fixed natural reality) but, rather, revealing (because the alterations constitute the working out of God's will).

10. See George Marsden, *Fundamentalism and American Culture* (New York: Oxford University Press, 1980), 16–19. Note here Falwell's discursive interlocutors on the matter of abortion as such, those whose authority he would appropriate, seem to be scientists, doctors, lawyers, justices, politicians, not just feminists.

11. Teenage sexuality (once an unthinkable juxtaposition of terms for born-again Christians, especially fundamentalists) became a frequent topic of sermons, books, and seminars in the mid-1980s. Josh McDowell, perhaps the "leading expert" on the subject, reported that "between 55% and 60% of evangelical Christian youth are involved in sexual activity" (*"What I Wish My Parents Knew About My Sexuality"* (San Bernadino: Here's Life Publications, 1987), 15; also see his *Why Wait?* (San Bernadino: Here's Life Publications, 1987).

I was told in Lynchburg that the waiting list of Christian couples who wish to adopt LGH babies is a long one and that they pay substantial "fees" for the privilege, conditions which suggest the success of Falwell's Liberty Godparent campaign may be as much due to its adoption as its anti-abortion aspect.

12. Note here Jennifer's discursive interlocutors, whose authority she is displacing, include Catholics and Jews as well as feminists.

13. The images evoked in Jennifer's arrival at LGH reverse the connotations of her trip to the abortion clinic. Aggressively cheery and nostalgic, strikingly flat and drenched in primary colors, the images seem like a cartoon (not to say caricature) of a born-again middle-class heaven-on-earth: "As we neared the historic little town, we drove through gentle hills of iron-red clay, blanketed by deep green forests. The sky was azure blue and great white clouds piled up over the Blue Ridge mountains. We followed the road past a new shopping center and an historic old red brick church, and then wound our way on a tree-lined street through a gentle neighborhood of old but tidy homes, with neat lawns and front porches with swings. Dad drove our car into the long circular driveway at 520 Eldon Street and we sat looking at my temporary new home. . . . I noticed two squirrels playing at the base of a giant oak tree and a noisy bluejay scolding them from a branch overhead. Two very pregnant girls were sitting on a bench nearby feeding bread crumbs to a flock of sparrows that darted about them. There were green lawns and bright yellow flowers. It was Friday the thirteenth but nothing seemed quite so ominous as it had before" (124–125).

14. *If I Should Die* establishes the primacy of the fetal-God relationship (and the *in*dependence of the fetus from the mother) through largely narrative means, but its readers bring other arguments to that effect to the text. Perhaps the strongest among them is the argument that the fetus is a "person," which lodges opposition to abortion in the founding premise of Protestantism, "the priesthood of the believer"—the relationship between person and God is mediated by no man . . . or woman. ("The personhood of the fetus" is, of course, originally a Catholic doctrine, yet in the mouths of these Protestants it acquires a slight anti-Catholic spin.)

15. Pointed demands for money, "a sacrificial gift of $400 to save the life of a baby," came in televised and direct mail fundraising pitches. *If I Should Die* figured in these pitches as a persuasive force after the fact, that is, as a "free gift" given in return to those who sacrificed themselves by sending in $400 to become "Liberty Godparents."

CHAPTER SIX

"We Are Not Doormats": The Influence of Feminism on Contemporary Evangelicals in the United States

JUDITH STACEY AND SUSAN ELIZABETH GERARD

We begin this essay by asking readers to indulge us by participating in a silent multiple-choice quiz. Please select the answer that best describes the author of the book from which the following excerpt is drawn:

Feminism is a response to structural questions which will not go away. There is widespread injustice to women in our society. The same issue crops up in family life, education, the law, the Church and marriage: women are not re-spected as men's equals. They are frequently used and abused. Many women in fact experience not only frustration and discrimination but also real oppres-sion at the hands of some men . . . the patriarchal emphasis of our society means that the unjust way many men behave towards women is legitimated in legal and economic structures. It is embedded in attitudes and stereotypes. Those women who object to all of this are frequently pilloried; their womanliness is challenged because they will not have it defined for them by a male-dominated culture. An individual response then can only work away at small areas. The problem is also an overall structural one, and as such needs a coherent structural response.

The author of this statement is: a) a feminist sociologist; b) an evangelical Christian; c) a married, heterosexual mother; d) an anti-abortion philoso-pher; e) none of the above; f) all of the above.

The best answer, as suspicious readers may have guessed, is (f) all of the above. The statement appears in *What's Right with Feminism*,[1] a book in which Elaine Storkey, a feminist sociologist and theologian, proposes and theorizes "a biblically rooted Christian feminism."

We imagine that most readers of this article will be as surprised as we were to discover the existence of the growing body of literature to which Storkey's book belongs, or to learn of the extensive diffusion of feminist ideas within contemporary evangelical discourse that it represents. Most secular feminists (and most feminists are secular), consider contemporary feminism and Christian evangelicalism to represent incompatible world views and social movements, and they interpret the gender ideology of the latter largely as a reactionary backlash response to the former. Certainly Phyllis Schlafly, Jerry Falwell, Beverly La Haye and other leaders of the most visible, politically organized segments of the Christian right wing have given feminists ample provocation for such a reading. But, as our introductory quiz implies, and the remainder of this paper demonstrates, the gender ideology and politics of born-again Christians in the United States today are far more diverse, complex and contradictory than widely held stereotypes allow.

We examine the diffusion of feminist ideas within Christian evangelicalism in order to contribute to assessments of the nature and status of feminism in the conservative 1980s and 1990s. Is feminism progressing, in retreat, or in a new mode of phase? In earlier articles, one of us argued that "postfeminism" was an apt term to capture the enormous influence of feminism on American culture in a period when overt feminist activism is less evident.[2] By postfeminism we mean the simultaneous incorporation, revision and depoliticization of some of the central goals of Second Wave feminism. Feminists who object to the term believe it sounds a premature death knell for the feminist movement.[3] We agree that feminist activism survives in the Reagan-Bush era, but believe it coexists with postfeminism, a consciousness that accepts many feminist convictions, while rejecting both the feminist label and feminist political engagement.

This essay depicts the presence of both feminism and postfeminist consciousness among contemporary Christian evangelicals. Like most feminists, we regard evangelicals as the vanguard of the anti-feminist backlash. If feminist ideology has permeated there, it suggests the magnitude of feminist influence upon American culture. Drawing upon national evangelical literature and media materials and from fieldwork conducted in a small evangelical Christian ministry in California's Silicon Valley, we show that contemporary evangelicalism in the United States is not a monolithic, patriarchal restorationist movement. Instead, evangelical theology and institutions are serving as remarkably flexible resources for renegotiating gender and family relationships, and not exclusively in reactionary or masculinist directions.[4]

CONTEMPORARY EVANGELICAL GENDER IDEOLOGY

Evangelical religions have flourished, while mainstream churches have declined during recent postindustrial decades; and women have swelled the burgeoning ranks of the former in proportions even greater than they out-number men in the latter. Estimates of evangelicals range from 18% to 40% of the adult population, and more than 60% of the participants in this fastest growing variety of religious orientation in the United States today are women.[5] The growth in the numbers, visibility and respectability of evangelicals has alarmed feminists and other progressives, who have as-sumed that evangelicals are a politically cohesive, well-organized, conser-vative and anti-feminist constituency. But, as few besides those who study American religion recognize, evangelicals are remarkably diverse.

Evangelicals believe in the full truth and authority of the bible and in its usefulness as a practical guide to the conduct of everyday life. They have differing views, however, on the nature of biblical truth. While strict con-structionists attempt to interpret the scriptures literally, many evangelicals incorporate metaphorical and contextual readings of the book that they all consider to be the inspired word of God. The most definitive characteristic of contemporary evangelicals is their conviction that a deeply personal re-lationship with Jesus Christ is the only path to a meaningful life and to salvation after death. Most have had a "born-again" or conversion expe-rience, which led to an emotionally intimate relationship with Jesus, whom they view as a friend who intervenes personally in their lives. As his evan-gelicals, they commit themselves, in turn, to spread the "Good News" by bearing public witness to their faith.[6]

Born-again Christians do not share a unified political perspective. They hold views on most political issues almost as diverse as those affirmed by once-born Americans.[7] Most analysts characterize fundamentalism as the right wing of evangelicalism. Fundamentalism is a separatist movement that formed at the turn of the century in reaction to the adoption of the social gospel by mainstream Protestantism; in this separatist spirit many funda-mentalists think of themselves as the only true evangelicals. Partly in re-sponse to fundamentalist insularity, a less separatist movement called neo-evangelicalism arose in the 1940s. It shares the conservative theology of fundamentalism, but is more ecumenical in spirit and more "in the world". Billy Graham, the most prominent neo-evangelist, brought the evangelical message to the ears of presidents and to the living rooms of middle-Amer-icans. The respectability Graham brought to this movement paved the way for its explosive growth during the late 1960s and 1970s. A number of right wing televangelists built large ministries in this period, but evangelicalism also achieved an appeal to members of the urban middle-classes with middle-of-the-road and even liberal politics. In 1976 the United States elected its first evangelical president, Jimmy Carter.[8]

The secular new left that emerged in the same period inspired parallel political developments, not only within mainstream Christianity, but among evangelical Christians as well. A small, but vocal minority of leftwing evan-gelical Christians have formed communal living and working groups that publish an evangelical brand of liberation theology in such periodicals as

Sojourners, Radix, and *The Other Side.* The March 1988 issue of *Sojourners,* the most prominent of these journals, featured articles on the religious beliefs and pretensions of presidential candidates, peace protests at the Reagan-Gorbachev summit, a Lutheran bishop's work in El Salvador, and a sermon on healing in the community and nation, as well as in personal lives. In addition, there was a short item on the Women's Budget of the Women's International League for Peace and Freedom, a column analyzing the puerile, male-fantasy content of newspaper comics, and an announcement of two job openings at the magazine, for which "women and minorities are encouraged to apply."[9]

In a similar fashion and period, the rise of evangelical feminism paralleled that of secular feminism. It had early ties with the evangelical left but soon developed as an autonomous movement. Evangelical women published critical feminist articles in Christian magazines as early as 1966.[10] In 1973 a meeting of the leftwing Evangelicals for Social Action was convened to discuss social issues; women struggled successfully to include in the meeting's final declaration: "We acknowledge that we have encouraged men to prideful domination and women to irresponsible passivity. So we call both men and women to mutual submission and active discipleship."[11] The organizational base that feminists established at this meeting enabled them the following year to found a feminist evangelical monthly, *Daughters of Sarah.* One year later, an evangelical feminist conference in Washington, D.C., attended by 360, endorsed the ERA and formed a lasting organization, the Evangelical Women's Caucus.[12]

Evangelical feminists are serious about both their evangelicalism and their feminism, and each belief system modifies the other. They bring feminist criticism to their Christian communities and theology; and their deeply-felt Christian commitment shapes their feminist ideology. "Biblical feminists" or simply "Christian feminists," as many often identify themselves, contend that the inspiration for the notion that women are the equals of men is not the affairs of the world, but the teachings of the New Testament. They devote most of their attention to dialogue with evangelicals in their confrontation with patriarchal church leaders, or toward efforts to win evangelical women and men to feminism. Consequently they scrupulously seek, and find, scriptural justification for their feminist beliefs. Evangelical feminists have focused most of their energies on three issues: claiming women's right to leadership roles in the church, including ordination; demonstrating the need for the Bible and its interpreters to employ "inclusive language" that presents God, not as male, but androgynous;[13] and challenging the scriptural basis for the subordinate role of women in marriage.

The third issue has been the arena in which biblical feminists have made their greatest impact on evangelical theology and gender ideology. To counter evangelicals' standard patriarchalist reading of the scriptural foundation for women's subordination to their husbands, Christian feminists have developed an ingenious, and perhaps somewhat forced, doctrine of mutual submission. Biblical feminists argue that the essence of Christ's message and practice was a radically egalitarian challenge to prevailing patriarchal society, a society so profoundly patriarchal that Jesus was compelled to couch his subversive and implicitly feminist teachings in terms comprehensible and tolerable to his compatriots. When read in this context, those troubling passages in the bible that direct wives to submit to their husbands, such as Paul's notorious message to the Ephesians, can be understood to mean instead mutual submission:

It is in the context of mutual submission that we must read the famous passages about the submission of Christian wives to their husbands, in particular Ephesians 5:22 and following . . . Therefore, when Paul speaks of wives' submitting themselves to their husbands, he is building upon the concept that every Christian is intended to submit to every other Christian, to serve every other Christian, to defer lovingly to every other Christian . . . The Christlike husband takes upon himself the form of a servant, humbles himself, and dies to himself by living for the best interests of his family. He loves his wife as he loves his own body, because he and his wife are one flesh.[14]

A doctrine of mutual submission leaves little room for feminist anger. Biblical feminists challenge unequal marriages as unChristian, and they take feminist positions on many issues unpopular with most fundamentalists, like their support for the ERA, for singlehood as a worthy option for women, and their (far from unanimous) acceptance of homosexuality and abortion as matters of personal conscience.[15] However, their writings lack the righteous anger that characterizes much of secular feminist literature. Instead, evangelical feminists believe that the key to women's liberation is not anger, but love. Women must learn to love themselves, and women and men must learn to love each other in a Christlike way:

According to the New Testament, the Christlike person exhibits the best in human qualities: love, joy, peace, patience, kindness, goodness, faithfulness, gentleness, self-control, humility, integrity, meekness, sensitivity, empathy, purity, submissiveness, confidence, courage, strength, zeal, determination, compassion, common sense, generosity, and self-sacrifice.[16]

Although only a minority of evangelicals are feminists,[17] the impact of feminism on evangelical discourse is profound and diffuse. Some prominent male theologians have absorbed and now teach feminist ideas,[18] and the feminist impact on evangelicalism goes well beyond this selfconscious engagement by evangelical leaders. According to a 1980 Gallup Poll, although the political views of evangelicals on "social issues" were predictably more conservative than those of non-evangelicals, the majority of the former (53%, compared with 66% of the latter) still favored the Equal Rights Amendment.[19] Moreover, there is considerable evidence that a pervasive postfeminist ideology has infused evangelical culture. James Hunter's study of students in evangelical colleges and seminaries finds them affirming a curious amalgam of conservative and feminist attitudes towards gender and family relationships.[20] Although a majority of these students claim that the husband should have the final say in a family's decision making, a majority also find sensitive, gentle men and assertive, self-reliant women as appealing as more stereotypical men and women. Most students agree that a woman should put her husband and children ahead of her career (although some commented that a man should also put his family ahead of his career). However, they do not agree with the statement, "a married woman should not work if she has a husband capable of supporting her." In these respects, their views are only slightly more conservative than those of the U.S. population as a whole.[21] The strong emphasis evangelicals place on family life, however, leads them to value male participation in early child care, albeit not equal participation, even more than do their less religious counterparts. The overwhelming majority (about 98%) of Hunter's respondents believe that both father and mother have the responsibility to care for small children.[22]

Popular Christian evangelical literature displays this same pervasive post-feminist ideology, revealing feminist influence on Christian ideals of family life as its most prominent feature. *Today's Christian Woman (TCW)* and *Virtue,* for example, portray women working outside the home as a taken-for-granted arrangement; in fact, the subscription pitch for *TCW* says it offers "practical ideas for coping with the challenges of marriage, family, and career." Concrete advice to women for building satisfactory Christian marriages dominates the pages of Christian women's magazines, and much of this advice suggests feminist influence. A fairly typical statement by one advice columnist echoes the biblical feminists' view of Christian marriage:

A healthy marriage allows both partners to be themselves. Balancing personal needs with the needs of the relationship requires compromise and negotiation. But if one mate continually subordinates her or his needs in order to please the other, the relationship suffers.[23]

Christian journalists offer readers strategies for improving the emotional quality of their marriages, and few of these advocate the mixture of submission and saran wrap Marabel Morgan once peddled.[24] A fairly representative article in *Virtue* contends that women's frustrations about lack of intimacy in their marriages spring from the fact that women and men see relationships differently. The authors blame men and their difficulties with self-disclosure for this lack of intimacy and conclude: "It's not up to the woman to be the one responsible for the level of intimacy in the marriage relationship."[25]

Even James C. Dobson, a right wing evangelical who founded Focus on the Family, a multimedia ministry committed to combatting feminism's pernicious influence on American family life, shows postfeminist influences on his own family views. He advises women in troubled marriages that the Bible does not demand that they tolerate disrespect or abuse from their husbands:

Please understand that I believe firmly in the biblical concept of submission, as described in the book of Ephesians and elsewhere in scripture. But there is a vast difference between being a confident, spiritually submissive woman and being a doormat. People wipe their feet on doormats, as we know.[26]

While popular evangelical literature decidedly privileges heterosexual marriage, it also offers a surprising amount of support for singlehood. Even Dobson views being "single by design" as "a legitimate choice, which should be respected by friends and family alike." "Believe me," he remarks, "a bad marriage is far worse than the most lonely instance of singleness."[27] A record review in *Virtue* also gives the stamp of approval to singleness:

This new release also presents a song called "The Gift," encouraging Christians to give special honor and support to those who are called to a life of celibacy, serving God as single adults rather than as married couples.[28]

And, within evangelical churches and communities, singles ministries and groups designed both to support and, perhaps, to reduce the ranks of the uncoupled, flourish.

As Barbara Ehrenreich, Elizabeth Hess, and Gloria Jacobs have pointed out, even elements of the sexual revolution have "penetrated" the Bible Belt,[29] but sexuality remains, we believe, the most conservative aspect of evangelical gender ideology. Even most biblical feminists find it difficult to overcome scriptural and personal antipathy to homosexuality and abortion, and the popular evangelical literature is almost uniformly reactionary on these issues. We personally believe that this is the political arena in which the new Christian right has scored its most disturbing and significant ideological victory.[30] Nonetheless, the Metropolitan Community Church, one of the largest gay religious churches in the country, is evangelical, and Christian women's magazines show modest signs of recognizing moral complexities to anti-abortion politics.[31]

Secular feminists can find numerous other surprises in Christian women's magazines, including information on rape self-defense, a criticism of social pressures for thinness and youth, and reviews for books celebrating friendships between women. Such literature lends support to Hunter's provocative claim that despite the small numbers of evangelical feminists, "feminist sensibilities are, nevertheless, ingrained within substantial sectors of Evangelicalism."[32] In our view, however, postfeminism better characterizes the dominant gender ideology of contemporary evangelicals.

GLOBAL MINISTRIES OF LOVE

Fieldwork conducted between 1984 and 1987 among participants in a small, evangelical Christian ministry in the Silicon Valley illustrates some of the creative uses to which evangelical women apply postfeminist evangelical doctrines and institutions.[33] Global Ministries of Love[34] is a nondenominational, grassroots ministry that operates its own small church and evangelizes among youth, derelicts, the infirm, and the institutionalized in the Silicon Valley and in two other states, where it has established mission branches. Global Ministries was founded in the early 1970s, during the height of Second Wave feminism, by Eleanor Morrison, a divorced, white, single mother who supported her children by working as an electronics employee. Eleanor, and the male pastors whom she attracted to her ministry and continues to guide, advocate a marital doctrine of male headship and wifely submission. At the same time, however, they offer their female constituents considerable support for creative adaptations of Christian gender ideology towards more egalitarian family reform projects. Global's director and many of her followers selectively employ and revise Christian theology in order to reform and strengthen heterosexual marriages, as well as to forge a variety of viable alternatives to nuclear family life.

The *tabula rasa* premise of born-again theology, that one's life before conversion is morally irrelevant, may be its most seductive feature to new recruits. Global Ministries applies this second chance cosmology to marital relationships with some unexpected consequences. Those who regard evangelical Christians as the last bastion of stable marriages in an era of family turmoil should be as surprised as we were to note the prevalence of divorced and remarried individuals in Global Ministries. "I don't care what a person's done outside of Christ—rape, murder, the most awful things don't change it, if people completely repent," Bill Jensen, the senior pastor of the ministry explained when one of us expressed amazement at the number of divorced people she had encountered in this Christian community. This can be a deeply appealing message to those suffering the rejection, bitterness, or anxieties of marital rupture. Like its founder, many members of the ministry have found the Global community to be a supportive environment for recovering from a failed marriage.

Global Ministries does celebrate marital commitment, however, and it seems to provide a fruitful milieu for helping previously unsuccessful spouses to achieve it the second time around. Ministerial staff often assist cupid's labors towards this end. For example, after 15 years as a single mother, Eleanor fell in love with a new recruit to her ministry, Paul Garrett, a recently divorced man 13 years her junior. Pastor Jensen encouraged Eleanor to express her love to Paul and, when Paul responded with trepidation, the pastor spent a day helping him pray for release from his fears and for the ability to decide to commit himself to loving Eleanor. His prayers were answered, and delighted to have secured the male "covering" deemed proper by most evangelical Christians, Eleanor appointed her self-selected head-of-household to co-direct the ministry. Still blissful newlyweds nearly four years later, the couple conduct seminars on love, sex, and marriage where they present themselves as a model of committed, Christian union.

Global ministers perceive no inconsistency in such advocacy of conjugal permanence, because they draw a sharp distinction between Christian and secular marriages. Pastor Jensen articulated the contrast while officiating over an unusual wedding ceremony. A secular marriage, he informed the bride, the groom, and gathered well-wishers, is based on a contract which, in turn, is based on a lack of trust. Secular marriages, as a result, do not last. Christian marriage, by contrast, "involves a covenant which is much deeper than a contract, a covenant based on trust in each other and in Jesus, and," he concluded, "that is why Christian marriage is permanent." These were reassuring words to the bride and groom, Pamela and Albert Gama, who both had divorced previous spouses, cohabited intermittently for five years, been legally married for four years and then separated and reunited before deciding to fortify their commitment with Christian nuptial vows. Three years later, Pam judged the pastor's analysis perceptive. Christian conversion enabled Al to make a deepened level of commitment to their marriage, and Pam identifies the security she derives from this as the most valuable outcome of the Christian nuptial ceremony.

Pam had been a feminist for more than a decade when her estranged second husband had the religious conversion experience that led him, through Pam's born-again daughter Katie, to the Global Ministries community. Like most feminists, Pam had deep reservations about the patriarchal character of Christian marital doctrine. Nonetheless, Pam was so impressed with profound emotional changes in Al that his conversion appeared to have inspired, that she had decided to suspend these reservations and to resume their marriage with the assistance of Christian marital counseling. Pastor Jensen had served as marriage counselor for the new recruits, guiding them to renew their conjugal commitment with a Christian gender ideology sufficiently revisionist to temper most of Pam's residual feminist objections.

"A ring is not a shackle, and marriage is not a relationship of domination, but of equality," Pastor Jensen gently reminded Al during the wedding ring ceremony, as he proceeded to lecture him on the responsibilities of a Christian husband. "You are the head of the household, Al," he continued, "and therefore, you have the larger responsibility, but that has nothing to do with dominating a wife." The pastor did advise Pam to submit to her "husband in all things as we all submit to Jesus," but, employing terms strikingly reminiscent of those found in Christian feminist literature, he attempted to rid the directive of its authoritarian connotations. Submitting to a husband is actually submitting to Jesus, Jensen explained, and thus a wife "does so with love and trust, knowing that the husband must love his wife as his own body and as Jesus loves us."

During an interview several months later, the pastor elaborated his revisionist understanding of the doctrine of submission. Feminists and other critics of evangelical marriage principles misunderstand this Christian concept, Jensen argued. They fail to recognize the "big difference between obedience and submission," or that authority is a burden and submission a privilege. "Rebellious humanity" resists humility, but "to be humbled is good." Just as Bill's role as pastor is to serve his congregation, "the person in authority should actually be the servant." Thus, "the husband's job is not to dominate, but to serve his wife." Although Pastor Jensen enjoyed defending the doctrine of submission, he thought it beside the point entirely to scrutinize Christian marriage through a judicial lens. He tried to teach the couples like Pam and Al whom he counseled that Christian marriage is "a total giving relationship," and thus,

you don't look at fairness and unfairness, at what you get for yourself. In fact, it's ridiculous to apply standards of justice to marriage, because it's amazing how little we know about justice. Christian marriage is no fifty-fifty, give-and-take affair; in marriage it's one hundred percent.

Pam found herself quite receptive to Jensen's views and impressed with their salutary effect on her marriage. Having failed in her past efforts to establish a committed, egalitarian, intimate relationship guided by democratic, feminist principles, she was willing to modify these in exchange for a marriage reform strategy she found more effective. Because the doctrine of love and marriage preached by Global Ministries seemed to demand and exact greater changes from Al than from her, Pam judged it "not so bad a deal" to accept nominal patriarchal authority in exchange for greater intimacy and security.

By all accounts, including his own, Al's religious conversion had profoundly transformed his approach to love and marriage. A rather taciturn, noncommittal man by disposition, Al had become much more committed to Pam, more open, loving, and expressive since joining the Global fold. He credited his Christian rebirth with releasing his previously truncated capacity for love, and the Christian marriage counseling with teaching him the means for expressing it.

Although Al was predictably more enthusiastic than Pam about the patriarchal principles of Christian marriage, he interpreted these, like Pastor Jensen, to mean he had the greater responsibility to make his marriage work:

I'm not really an open person, and to be a truly loving person is not something you just get into being because somehow you get converted. I take most of the responsibility for our problems because it's up to me to make the difference, because I can't make her do anything, but I can make a change in myself . . . I don't consider myself an honest person. I don't always say anything. I don't always have that need to be talking like she does. But you know one thing good about being a Christian is that, I tell you, sometimes you can just open up like you never did before. There's a certain amount of love that comes into your heart that was not there before.

Few contemporary feminists would be likely to find fault with Al's description of his goals for his relationship with Pam:

I just hope that we can come closer together and be more honest with each other. Try to use God as a guideline. The goals are more openness, a closer relationship, be more loving both verbally and physically, have more concern for the other person's feelings.

The concept of male authority Global Ministries appears to disseminate might best be described as "patriarchy in the last instance."[35] Eleanor and her disciples, like Pastor Jensen, urge couples to talk over everything and to resolve their differences through mutual discussion. Only if a conflict proves to be irreconcilable should a wife submit to her husband's will. Such a circumstance is so rare, in fact, that neither Eleanor, Pam, nor Pam's young, married daughter Katie could provide a single illustration of it. "We never let the sun set on our anger," Katie explained. Eleanor's husband conceded that he was more likely to yield to his loquacious wife than the other way around: "I have the responsibility to listen to her, too, because she may just be the one with the answer." "That's really true," Eleanor affirmed. And Pam employed the principle only when she wished to enlist Al's assistance in resolving her ambivalence about decisions she found difficult to make on her own.

In Global Ministries' version of born-again theology, women find powerful resources for efforts to remake their husbands in their own images. The dominant discourse on desirable heterosexual relationships that the ministry propagates is a Christian version of what Francesca Cancian has aptly termed the "feminization of love."[36] Ironically, feminist Cancian is critical of the woman-centered ideology of love that evangelical Global Ministries celebrates. She criticizes current love ideals for celebrating emotional expressiveness and ignoring "the more instrumental and physical aspects of love that men prefer."[37] Pastor Jensen, however, urges men to develop their capacity for expressive love:

One of the greatest failures in marriage is communication. The husband is afraid to reveal his emotions. Women are generally much better at this. A man needs to learn to open up emotionally, to cry on his wife's shoulders. Now I realize how this might sound chauvinist, but most women, not all, but most still want a strong leader in a husband. But it's not weak to reveal your emotions. A lot of men have the wrong idea about how being emotional is being weak. . . . And sex has so much more meaning than just the physical act. It's an ultimate expression of a spiritual and emotional relationship. Often men abuse this. Men often just want sex for its own sake. Women want more from sex emotionally. Sex is a sacred thing; it's not just physical. It's holy. But a lot of men expect their wives to make love to them without even communicating or regardless of what's going on between them emotionally. And they don't realize how abusive that is to a woman, because a woman integrates the sexual and emotional more.

Although Global Ministries offers women effective resources for securing marital commitments and fostering emotional transformations of men, it exhibits far less nostalgia for the 1950s nuclear family ideal than feminists might expect. Perhaps Eleanor's personally traumatic experience with nuclear family life in that decade bred the more creative and pluralist pro-family strategies she encourages in her ministry. Having spent 15 years as a single, working mother, Eleanor has learned to appreciate the benefits of extended households. She treats her own domestic sites as accordion constructions whose membership regularly expands and contracts. Blood and marital ties determine some of the participants in Eleanor's matrilocal domiciles. Her divorced mother lived with her for several years, and later when her daughter married a young Chicano who joined the ministry, not only did Eleanor welcome her new son-in-law into her household, but she ordained him as well. Not all who have shared Eleanor's living quarters are formal relatives, however. Friends have lived with Eleanor, and she has been foster mother to 15 adolescents, a few of whom made her a foster grandmother also.

Indeed, Eleanor has achieved much more socio-spatial integration in her life than most feminists or other progressives who decry the modern schisms between public and private worlds, between work and family life. Wherever she lives also becomes Global's organizational and social hub, the site of its staff meetings, its recording studio, and its public relations office. Global's matriarchal leader encourages her "sheepies" to form joint households also. The ministry purchased and leased several adjacent houses, which it subleases to Global staff and recruits so that they too can derive the benefits of "living in community." These Christian communes serve as a laboratory for Eleanor's attempts at social engineering, the experimental terrain for her activist approach to family reform. Eleanor points out the economic advantages of communal households. The ministry provides full support to four pastors and their families, all of whom live "in community" with others, like Katie and her husband, who subsidize the pastors' rent and food expenses at the same time that they reduce their own.

Eleanor is even more enthusiastic about the social benefits of cooperative living. The communes provide a means to integrate single people into Global family and community life. The long years Eleanor spent as a divorcee have made her unusually reflective about the social needs of single women and probably fueled her quite activist responses to the single woman "crisis." Eleanor herself and other Global women have reaped matrimonial benefits from the ministry's not-always-casual matchmaking services. But Eleanor does not rely on romantic attachments alone to extend kin ties and familial arrangements to the unmarried. She consciously seeks to maintain a balance of married and single members in the community and regards the communes as an opportunity to bridge the social gulf that might divide them. "In fact," Eleanor explains:

there's a scripture that I love, that the single belongs in the family. And we feel, Paul and I both agree on this, that singles in the family of God are there to serve the family. And the families are also to serve the singles by providing that that they need. I think single people need to see married people, they need to be around them, because they need to see something good and positive in that kind of a relationship. So that's why we have singles living with all of our marrieds.

Since marrying Paul, Eleanor has made it Global policy to "yoke" singles to married couple-headed households. This, she believes, prevents social isolation for the singles and anti-social withdrawal by the marrieds.

Single women "yoked" to married couples who are to model the benefits of conjugal relationships to them might legitimately resent the implied denigration of their own single status. The delight Eleanor takes in her second-chance romance with Paul probably has inclined her to privilege conjugal over single life. However, not all the forms of support or the messages that Global directs towards women celebrate coupledom. Pastor Bill explains that the ministry does not offer legalistic opposition to divorce or support to marriage. It celebrates a particular vision of Christian marriage against which many earthly representations might well be found lacking. When the deficiencies are severe, Global officials encourage women to trade in their abusive husbands and lovers for a more rewarding marriage to Jesus. "You will find Jesus the most interested and responsive Lover ever," Eleanor and Paul promise readers of a column they titled "Romancing Jesus" in one of Global's monthly newsletters. Emulate brave "*Ms.* Loveless," suggests a cartoon in another, depicting a working mother of two who receives the Lord and ousts the man who exploited and beat her: "Jim, I'm afraid you will have to leave. I have decided to live *for* Jesus so I can't live *with* you anymore. Now I have someone that I don't have to take care of Him, *He* takes care of me and the kids!"[38]

Global Ministries gives more than rhetorical support to unwed mothers. It established a shelter for "girls in crisis" to help pregnant adolescents; and unlike other Christian homes for unwed mothers that offer adoption as the only alternative, the Global shelter supports teenage mothers who wish to keep and raise their children without husbands. Eleanor has always taken an activist approach to supporting pregnant teenagers. Perhaps it is her long years of experience in this work that makes her opposition to abortion less strident or rigid than we had anticipated. "It makes me sick to see people signing petitions about abortion and not doing anything for those pregnant girls," she volunteered. Eleanor regards abortion as tragic and sinful, but, unlike most born-again opponents of women's reproductive freedom, she concedes that, "In certain situations, I can't say in my heart it wouldn't be right."

Global Ministries, unlike Elaine Storkey and other biblical feminists, rejects feminism, but like the Christian women's magazines, it propagates a gender ideology that has been deeply informed by it. Although Eleanor and her followers accept the nominal patriarchal authority principles of the Bible, they read the scriptures as selectively as do other religious faithfuls, and their reading preferences have been influenced by personal and political events that challenge traditional patriarchal values. Eleanor is an impressive "mover and shaker", easy to envision as a grassroots feminist activist. Feminists might legitimately regret the vagaries of biography and history that prompted Eleanor instead to employ her considerable proto-feminist impulses in a direction that so effectively absorbs and depoliticizes feminist challenges to male institutional authority. We would be mistaken, however, to dismiss her as antifeminist, or to fail to appreciate the attractiveness of her "feminine-ist" family reform strategies to women suffering the personal costs of the dramatic family and economic instabilities of postindustrial society.

CONCLUSIONS

It has been challenging and painful for feminists to explain why many women who have been exposed to feminist ideas and values voluntarily embrace a Christian ideology of male headship and female submission, often attempting to convert their more secular husbands. For in postindustrial America, although male supremacy is alive and well, participation in a formally patriarchal marriage is a woman's choice. The social and material conditions that underwrote the Victorian family, the family many evangelicals portray erroneously as the biblical family, are long gone. Thus, as a recent ethnography of a fundamentalist community notes, no fundamentalist husband can dominate a wife who doesn't choose to submit today.[39] Julie Cabrera, coordinator of women's Bible study at Crossroads Bible Church in San Jose, California, asserts this more directly. Told that an evangelical feminist interprets submissive Christian women as fearful of divorce, Cabrera replies, "Nonsense. I am in submission to my husband by choice. I do this in order to please God. He has put our husbands in the head of us. We choose to be in this position. We are not doormats."[40]

We agree partially both with that evangelical feminist and with Cabrera. Women remain structurally disadvantaged in postindustrial society, but from that position they make their own choices and develop their own strategies (including patriarchal Christian marriage). Women's gender strategies are creative, resourceful, and often contradictory, and these in turn are always revising received institutional and cultural forms. The surprising emergence of postfeminist evangelicalism is just such a strategic and cultural phenomenon. A decidedly postmodern excrescence, it is difficult for secular feminists to appraise. Generated partly as a backlash against feminism, postfeminist evangelical gender ideology also selectively incorporates and adapts many feminist family reforms. Secular and biblical feminists alike, we believe, can take credit for the extraordinary diffusion of our ideological influence on even this most unlikely of constituencies.

Women's turn to evangelicalism represents a search not just for spirituality, but for stability and security in turbulent, contested times; but it is a strategy that refuses to forfeit, and even builds upon, the feminist critique of men and the "traditional" family. Acute "pro-family" and spiritual longings in this period comingle with an uncompleted, but far from repudiated feminist revolution. Part of the genius of the postfeminist evangelical strategy is its ability to straddle both sides of this ambivalent divide. To heterosexual women like Eleanor and Pam, more exhausted than outraged by the insecurities of contemporary family and work conditions, joining a community that promises love and affirmation can be deeply appealing, particularly when it provides effective strategies for reshaping husbands in their own image. And, ironically, one of the main places where the commune movement of the sixties still survives is in the evangelical world.[41]

Postfeminist evangelicalism poses thorny challenges for feminists. Accompanying the impressive diffusion of feminist ideals within evangelicalism, as we have seen, is a defusion of them, as well. The struggle for evangelical feminism is constrained by the conservative institutional context in which it occurs, and, as the new Christian Right has demonstrated, contemporary evangelicalism appears more susceptible to political mobilization by reactionary than by progressive forces. Especially troubling has been the success of the conservative politics of sexuality they have fostered.

Nonetheless, feminists make a mistake, we believe, to dismiss evangelical postfeminism as a monolithically reactionary phenomenon. Thus, we differ with many feminist assessments of the gender politics of Christian evangelicals. Ehrenreich, Hess, and Joseph, for example, in their entertaining and insightful discussion of the sexual revolution in the Bible Belt, draw a sharp contrast between what they view as its significant but politically irrelevant impact on fundamentalists and the absence of feminist influence on their gender ideology.[42] In contrast, we judge the effect on born-again Christians of feminist gender and family views to be profound, and we are less certain that these will prove so easy to contain. While we neither deny nor discount the significance of actively mobilized and politically effective, anti-feminist evangelical women, we consider it crucial, and reassuring, to recognize that they represent only a minority of evangelical women. Most evangelical women, like most women, including many secular feminists, are far more ambivalent, contradictory, and complex.

The gender views and strategies of contemporary evangelical women indicate the fluid and contradictory character of feminist politics in this period. Although feminist activism is far less visible or confrontational than it was in the militant late 1960s and early 1970s, it continues in new and often surprising guises. Such activism, however, coexists with postfeminism, the extraordinary diffusion of feminist principles in American culture discernible in even the most unlikely places and among people who shun the feminist label and avoid political engagement. Feminism appears to be advancing, retreating, and assuming new forms, all at once.

NOTES

We wish to thank Linda Collins, Gary Hamilton, Sherry Katz, Deborah Rosenfelt, Ellen Ross, and Herb Schreier for their responses to an earlier version of this article. Portions of this essay appear in Judith Stacey, Brave New Families: Stories of Domestic Upheaval in Late Twentieth Century America *(NY: Basic Books, 1990).*

1. Elaine Storkey, *What's Right with Feminism* (Grand Rapids: Eerdmans Publishing Company, 1985). Quotation is from p. 160.

2. Judith Stacey, "Sexism By a Subtler Name: Postindustrial Conditions and Postfeminist Consciousness in the Silicon Valley," *Socialist Review* 96 (November-December 1987): 7–28; Deborah Rosenfelt and Judith Stacey, "Second Thoughts on the Second Wave," *Feminist Studies* 13, no. 2 (Summer 1987): 341–61.

3. See Rayna Rapp, "Is the Legacy of Second Wave Feminism Postfeminism?" *Socialist Review* 97 (January-March 1988); Myra Marx Ferree, personal communication to author.

4. An important early exception to feminist treatment of evangelicals as monolithically submissive, antifeminist, and reactionary was Carol Virginia Pohli, "Church Closets and Back Doors: A Feminist View of Moral Majority Women," *Feminist Studies* 9, no. 3 (Fall 1983): 529–58. Pohli argued that there were inherent tensions in evangelical world views and organizational structure that limited evangelical participation in reactionary politics and allowed limited opportunities for feminist dialogue with evangelical women. More recently, Susan D. Rose portrayed deeper conflicts about gender norms and power relationships among women in a charismatic Christian community; see her "Women Warriors: The Negotiation of Gender in a Charismatic Community," *Sociological Analysis* 48, no. 3 (Fall 1987): 245–58. The most dissident feminist interpretation of evangelicalism we have seen is Elizabeth Brusco's provocative analysis of the progressive and womanist effects of Protestant evangelicalism in Colombia, "Colombian Evangelicalism as a Strategic Form of Women's Collective Action," *Feminist Issues* 6, no. 2 (Fall 1986): 3–13. Brusco argues that growing numbers of Colombian women are using Protestant evangelicalism to combat machismo, reform their husbands, and improve their lives. She goes so far as to interpret Colombian evangelicalism as a radical challenge to gender inequality that "may have more practical results for women in terms of improving their condition (and surely for some men) than any feminist reform movements I know of." (p. 10). Brusco attributes the progressive effects of evangelicalism in Colombia to particular historical and cultural conditions. But in societies, "where there is less sex segregation, less female dependency, and a more individualistic orientation for both men and women," Brusco speculates, "such a movement would not be viable in terms of improving women's status but it would also probably never get off the ground anyway." (p. 11). As the rest of this article demonstrates, however, just such a movement is thriving in the highly individualistic United States today.

5. James Davison Hunter, *American Evangelicalism* (New Brunswick, NJ: Rutgers University Press, 1983), see esp. p. 50. Since 1965, evangelical denominations are reported to have increased their memberships at an average five-year rate of 8% while membership in liberal denominations declined at an

average five-year rate of 4.6%. James Davison Hunter, *Evangelicalism: The Coming Generation* (Chicago: University of Chicago Press, 1987), 6. For estimates of numbers of evangelicals, see also Richard Quebedeaux, *The Worldly Evangelicals* (San Francisco: Harper & Row, 1978); R. Stephen Warner, *New Wine in Old Wineskins* (Berkeley: University of California Press, 1988); and Pohli.

6. For discussion of the characteristics of contemporary evangelicals, see Hunter, *American Evangelicalism*; Quebedeaux; and Warner.

7. For discussions of the political beliefs of evangelicals, see Richard Quebedeaux, *The Young Evangelicals* (New York: Harper & Row, 1974) and Quebedeaux, *The Worldly Evangelicals*; Hunter, *Evangelicalism* and *American Evangelicalism*; Nancy Tatom Ammerman, *Bible Believers: Fundamentalists in the Modern World* (New Brunswick, NJ: Rutgers University Press, 1987); and Warner.

8. For historical treatments of fundamentalism and evangelicalism, see George W. Dollar, *A History of Fundamentalism in America* (Greenville, SC: Bob Jones Univ. Press, 1973); George Marsden, ed., *Evangelicalism and Modern America* (Grand Rapids: Eerdmans Publishing Company, 1984); Richard Quebedeaux, *By What Authority: The Rise of Personality Cults in American Christianity* (San Francisco: Harper & Row, 1982); Quebedeaux, *Young Evangelicals*; and Quebedeaux, *Worldly Evangelicals*.

9. *Sojourners: An Independent Christian Monthly* 17, no. 3 (March 1988).

10. Quebedeaux identifies Letha Scanzoni's "Women's Place: Silence or Service?" in the February 1966 issue of *Eternity* as one of the earliest of these feminist essays. *The Worldly Evangelicals*, 121.

11. Chicago Declaration, cited in Letha Dawson Scanzoni and Nancy A. Hardesty, *All We're Meant to Be: Biblical Feminism for Today*, rev. ed. (Nashville, Abingdon Press, 1986), 18–19.

12. For histories of evangelical feminism, see Quebedeaux, *Worldly Evangelicals*; Scanzoni and Hardesty; and Margaret Bendroth, "The Search for 'Women's Role' in American Evangelicalism, 1930–1980," in Marsden, 122–34. The first edition of the Scanzoni and Hardesty book is described in *Christian History* magazine as "the 1973 classic that set in motion a substantial biblical feminism." *Christian History* VII, no. 1, issue 17 (1988): 36.

13. Virginia Mollenkott, a prominent biblical feminist, devotes one of her books to an androgynous reading of divine imagery, with such chapter titles as "God as Nursing Mother," "God as Midwife," "God as Mother Bear," "God as Female Homemaker," "God as Female Beloved," and "God as Dame Wisdom." In the chapter on God as homemaker, she argues that "Psalm 123:2 gives us permission to see in Proverbs 31 a full-scale description of Yahweh as the perfect female homemaker, the perfect wife to a humanity which is cast by this image into a masculine role." Virginia Ramey Mollenkott, *The Divine Feminine: The Biblical Imagery of God as Female* (New York: Crossroad, 1983), 62.

14. Virginia Ramey Mollenkott, *Women, Men and the Bible* (Nashville, TN: Abingdon Press, 1977), 23–24. For other examples of this form of interpreting scripture, see Evelyn Stagg and Frank Stagg, "Jesus and Women," *Christian History* VII, no. 1, issue 17 (1988): 29–31; Alvera Mickelsen, *Women, Authority*

& the Bible (Downers Grove, Illinois: InterVarsity Press, 1986); Scanzoni and Hardesty; Storkey.

15. Responding to feminist criticism of the first edition of *All We're Meant to Be,* Scanzoni and Hardesty revised the second edition of their book to take a more sympathetic stand on homosexuality. The Evangelical Women's Caucus International was split in July 1986 by approval of a resolution that recognized "the presence of the lesbian minority in EWCI" and called for "a firm stand in favor of civil-rights protection for homosexual persons." Beth Spring, "Gay Rights Resolution Divides Membership of Evangelical Women's Caucus," *Christianity Today* 30, no. 14 (Oct. 3, 1986): 40–43.

16. Scanzoni and Hardesty, *All We're Meant to Be,* 108.

17. About 2000–3000 women are active in chapters or on the mailing list of the Evangelical Women's Caucus, according to Quebedeaux, *The Worldly Evangelicals,* 122. The evangelical feminist journal *Daughters of Sarah* has 3,400 paid subscribers, and a study of contemporary evangelical college students identifies 9% of them as "strongly committed and politically oriented feminists." Hunter, *Evangelicalism,* 105.

18. For example, Gilbert Bilezikian, a professor of biblical studies at evangelical Wheaton College, calls for "deliberate programs of depatriarchalization" to overcome sex role socialization. See his *Beyond Sex Roles* (Grand Rapids, MI: Baker Book House, 1985), 10–11. A conference on Evangelical Christianity and Modern America held at Billy Graham Center at Wheaton College in 1983 included a talk on "The Search for 'Women's Role' in American Evangelicalism." *Women, Authority & the Bible* is a collection of papers from the Evangelical Colloquium on Women and the Bible held in 1984 in Oak Brook, Illinois. In 1988 *Christian History* magazine published a special issue on "Women in the Early Church."

19. The Gallup Poll data are reported by Hunter as evidence of the more socially conservative views of evangelicals. Hunter, *Evangelicalism,* 126. We, however, were more surprised by the evidence of significant resistance to such conservatism.

20. Hunter, *Evangelicalism,* esp. chap. 4.

21. An analysis of national survey data on female and male attitudes toward women's familial and work roles finds not a backlash, but a continuing trend toward support for more egalitarian roles among all cohorts and sectors of the population in the U.S. Not surprisingly, support is greater for female equality in paid work than for equal male responsibility for unpaid domestic and child care work. See Karen Oppenheim Mason and Yu-Hsia Lu, "Attitudes Toward Women's Familial Roles: Changes in the United States, 1977–1985," *Gender & Society* 2, no. 1 (March 1988): 39–57.

22. Pointing out that these students' beliefs stand in sharp contrast to those espoused by many evangelical leaders, Hunter concludes that, "the Evangelical family specialists (including many ministers) advocate and defend a model of the family that is said to be traditional . . . in the name of a constituency that has largely abandoned it in favor of an androgynous/quasi-androgynous model." See his *Evangelicalism,* p. 114. Just as Mason and Lu find more egalitarian views on family issues among women than men, Hunter found women evangelical students to hold more feminist views than their male counterparts.

23. Jan Kiemel Ream. "Help!" *Today's Christian Woman* 10, no. 1 (March/April 1988): 70.

24. Marabel Morgan, *The Total Woman* (Old Tappan, NJ: F. H. Revell, 1973).

25. Bill Carmichael, Nancie Carmichael, and Timothy Boyd. "Paving the Way to Intimacy." *Virtue* 10, no. 6 (1988): 16–19.

26. James C. Dobson, *Love Must Be Tough* (Waco, TX: Word Books, 1983), 25.

27. Dobson, 191–192.

28. Lee Zanon, "What's New." *Virtue*, 8.

29. *Re-Making Love: The Feminization of Sex* (Garden City, New York: Anchor Press, 1986), chapter 5.

30. The 1980 Gallup Poll data reported by Hunter found 41% of evangelicals, compared with 29% of non-evangelicals, claiming to support a ban on abortion. Hunter, *Evangelicalism*, 126. Perhaps because of the wording of the poll, this seriously understates the sexual conservatism of evangelicals and their impact on the broader American populace. Confusingly, Wuthnow cites an essay by Hunter as his source for a 1978 Gallup Poll which found 97% of evangelicals opposed to premarital sex, 95% expressing "opposition to abortion," and 89% opposed to homosexuality. Wuthnow interprets these data as evidence that while evangelicals "remained deeply divided in many other ways . . . on questions of morality they were unified." Robert Wuthnow, "The Political Rebirth of American Evangelicals," in Robert C. Liebman & Robert Wuthnow, eds., *The New Christian Right: Mobilization and Legitimation* (New York: Aldine, 1983), 178. Although Wuthnow, we believe, slightly overstates the case, we share his view that this is the most distinctive feature of contemporary evangelical beliefs.

31. A recent *TCW* editorial, for example, concludes: "Aborting a baby is wrong, but simply stopping an abortion is not enough . . . And I pray that the next time someone needs help, God will give me the strength to go beyond my idealistic theology and live with the realities of commitment." Dale Hanson Bourke, "The Cost of Commitment," *Today's Christian Woman*, 7.

32. Hunter, *Evangelicalism*, 106.

33. Between 1984 and 1987, Judith Stacey conducted oral histories and participant observation fieldwork in this evangelical group as part of her study of changing family life in the Silicon Valley. For a full description of that study, see her *Brave New Families: Stories of Domestic Upheaval in Late Twentieth Century America* (New York: Basic Books, 1990).

34. We employ pseudonyms to refer to the ministry and to all participants in the field study.

35. Barbara Epstein first coined this apt descriptive phrase. (personal communication to author)

36. "The Feminization of Love," *Signs* 11, no. 4 (Summer 1986): 692. See also Francesca M. Cancian, *Love in America* (New York: Cambridge University Press, 1987).

37. "The Feminization of Love," 692.

38. The cartoon strip is titled "Christian" and its creator identified as "Betty Lorde" in the monthly newsletter.

39. See Ammerman, 141.

40. Quoted in David Early, "Equal Before God," *San Jose Mercury News,* March 1986.

41. Quebedeaux, *Worldly Evangelicals* describes the communes of left wing evangelicals. Warner's study of a Methodist church in Mendocino, California recounts the wholesale conversion of The Land, a libertarian sixties commune, into The Holy Land, an ascetic evangelical Christian community. Brusco emphasizes the collective ethos of Colombian evangelicalism and stresses as most revolutionary its capacity to transform intimate relationships.

42. Ehrenreich, Hess and Joseph, *Re-making Love.*

CHAPTER SEVEN

Negotiating Sex and Gender in the Attorney General's Commission on Pornography

CAROLE S. VANCE

Larry Madigan began his testimony in the Miami federal courthouse. Dark-haired, slight, and dressed in his best suit, he fingered his testimony nervously before he was recognized by the chair. The podium and microphone at which he stood were placed at the front of the auditorium, so when the thirty-eight-year-old looked up from his typed statement, he saw only the members of the Attorney General's Commission on Pornography. They sat on the raised dais, surrounded by staff aides, federal marshals, the court stenographer, and flags of Florida and the United States. Behind him sat the audience, respectfully arrayed on dark and immovable wood benches that matched the wood paneling which enveloped the room.

"At age 12," he began earnestly, "I was a typical, normal, healthy boy and my life was filled with normal activities and hobbies." But "all the trouble began a few months later," when he found a deck of "hard core" pornographic playing cards, depicting penetration, fellatio, and cunnilingus. "These porno cards highly aroused me and gave me a desire I never had before," he said. Soon after finding these cards, his behavior changed: he began masturbating, attempted to catch glimpses of partially dressed neighbor women, and surreptitiously tried to steal *Playboy* magazines from the local newsstand. His chronicle went on for several minutes.

"By the age of 16, after a steady diet of *Playboy, Penthouse, Scandinavian Children,* perverted paperback books and sexology magazines, I had to see a doctor for neuralgia of the prostate." His addiction worsened in his twenties, when he began watching pornographic videos. He went on to "promiscuous sex" with "two different women," but eventually found Christ. He concluded, "I strongly believe that all that has happened to me can be traced back to the finding of those porno cards. If it weren't for my faith in God and the forgiveness in Jesus Christ, I would now possibly be a pervert, an alcoholic, or dead. I am a victim of pornography."[1]

The audience sat in attentive silence. No one laughed. Only a few cynical reporters sitting next to me quietly elbowed each other and rolled their eyes, although their stories in the next day's papers would contain respectful accounts of Mr. Madigan's remarks and those of his therapist, Dr. Simon Miranda, who testified as an expert witness that many of his patients were being treated for mental problems brought on by pornography.

The Attorney General's Commission on Pornography, a federal investigatory commission appointed in May 1985 by then-Attorney General Edwin Meese III, orchestrated an imaginative attack on pornography and obscenity. The chief targets of its campaign appeared to be sexually explicit images. These were dangerous, according to the logic of the commission, because they might encourage sexual desires or acts. The commission's public hearings in six U.S. cities during 1985 and 1986, lengthy executive sessions, and an almost 2000 page report[2] constitute an extended rumination on pornography and the power of visual imagery. Its ninety-two recommendations for strict legislation and law enforcement, backed by a substantial federal, state, and local apparatus already in place, pose a serious threat to free expression. Read at another level, however, the commission's agenda on pornography stands as a proxy for a more comprehensive program about gender and sexuality, both actively contested domains where diverse constituencies struggle over definitions, law, policy, and cultural meanings.

To enter a Meese Commission hearing was to enter a public theater of sexuality and gender, where cultural symbols—many dating from the late nineteenth century—were manipulated with uncanny intuition: the specter of uncontrolled lust, social disintegration, male desire, and female sexual vulnerability shadowed the hearings. The commission's goal was to implement a traditional conservative agenda on sexually explicit images and texts: vigorous enforcement of existing obscenity laws coupled with the passage of draconian new legislation.[3] To that end, the commission, dominated by a conservative majority, effectively controlled the witness list, evidence, and fact-finding procedures in obvious ways that were widely criticized for their bias.[4] But the true genius of the Meese Commission lay in its ability to appropriate terms and rhetoric, to deploy visual images and create a compelling interpretive frame, and to intensify a climate of sexual shame that made dissent from the commission's viewpoint almost impossible. The power of the commission's symbolic politics is shown by the response of both spectators and journalists to Larry Madigan's testimony, as well as by the inability of dissenting commission witnesses who opposed further restriction to unpack and thus counter the panel's subterranean linguistic and visual ploys.

Convened during Ronald Reagan's second term, the commission paid a political debt to conservatives and fundamentalists who had been clamoring for action on social issues, particularly pornography, throughout his term of office. Pornographic images were symbols of what moral conservatives wanted to control: sex for pleasure, sex outside the regulated boundaries of marriage and procreation. Sexually explicit images are dangerous, conservatives believe, because they have the power to spark fantasy, incite lust, and provoke action. What more effective way to stop sexual immorality and excess, they reasoned, than to curtail sexual desire and pleasure at its source—in the imagination. However, the widespread liberalization in sexual behavior and attitudes in the last century coupled with the increased availability of sexually explicit material since the 1970s made the conservative mission a difficult, though not impossible, task.[5] The commission utilized all available tools, both symbolic and procedural.

PROCEDURES AND BIAS

Appointed to find "new ways to control the problem of pornography," the panel was chaired by Henry Hudson, a vigorous anti-vice prosecutor from Arlington, Virginia, who had been commended by President Reagan for closing down every adult bookstore in his district. Hudson was assisted by his staff of vice cops and attorneys and by executive director Alan Sears, who had a reputation in the U.S. Attorney's Office in Kentucky as a tough opponent of obscenity.[6] Prior to convening, seven of the 11 commissioners had taken public stands opposing pornography and supporting obscenity law as a means to control it. These seven included a fundamentalist broadcaster, several public officials, a priest, and a law professor who had argued that sexually explicit expression was undeserving of First Amendment protection because it was less like speech and more like dildos.[7] The smaller number of moderates sometimes tempered the staff's conservative zeal, but their efforts were modest and not always effective.

The conservative bias continued for 14 months, throughout the panel's more than 300 hours of public hearings in six U.S. cities and lengthy executive sessions, which I observed.[8] The list of witnesses was tightly controlled: 77% supported greater control, if not elimination, of sexually explicit material. Heavily represented were law-enforcement officers and members of vice squads (68 of 208 witnesses), politicians, and spokespersons for conservative anti-pornography groups like Citizens for Decency through Law and the National Federation for Decency. Great efforts were made to find "victims of pornography" to testify,[9] but those reporting positive experiences were largely absent. Witnesses were treated unevenly, depending on whether the point of view they expressed facilitated the commission's ends. There were several glaring procedural irregularities, including the panel's attempt to withhold drafts and working documents from the public and its effort to name major corporations such as Time, Inc., Southland, CBS, Coca-Cola, and K-Mart as "distributors of pornography" in the final report, repeating unsubstantiated allegations made by Rev. Donald Wildmon, executive director of the National Federation for Decency. These irregularities led to several lawsuits against the commission.

The barest notions of fair play were routinely ignored in gathering evidence. Any negative statement about pornographic images, no matter how outlandish, was accepted as true. Anecdotal testimony that pornography was responsible for divorce, extramarital sex, child abuse, homosexuality, and excessive masturbation was entered as "evidence" and appears as supporting documentation in the final report's footnotes.

GENDER NEGOTIATIONS

The commission's unswerving support for aggressive obscenity law enforcement bore the indelible stamp of the right wing constituency that brought the panel into existence. Its influence was also evident in the belief of many commissioners and witnesses that pornography leads to immorality, lust, and sin. But the commission's staff and the Justice Department correctly perceived that an unabashedly conservative position would not be persuasive outside the right wing. For the commission's agenda to succeed, the attack on sexually explicit material had to be modernized by couching it in more contemporary arguments, arguments drawn chiefly from anti-pornography feminism and social science. So the preeminent harm that pornography was said to cause was not sin and immorality, but violence and the degradation of women.

To the extent that the world views and underlying ideologies of anti-pornography feminism and social science are deeply different from those of fundamentalism, the commission's experiment at merging or overlaying these discourses was far from simple. In general, the commission fared much better in its attempt to incorporate the language and testimony of anti-pornography feminists than that of social scientists. The cooptation of anti-pornography feminism was both implausible and brilliantly executed.

Implausible, because the panel's chair, Henry Hudson, and its executive director, Alan Sears, along with the other conservative members, were no feminists. Hudson usually addressed the four female commissioners as "ladies." He transmuted the term used by feminist anti-pornography groups, "the degradation of women," into the "degradation of femininity," which conjured up visions of Victorian womanhood dragged from the pedestal into a muddy gutter. Beyond language, conservative panelists consistently opposed proposals that feminists universally support—for sex education or school-based programs to inform children about sexual abuse, for example. Conservative members objected to sex abuse programs for children, contending that such instruction prompted children to make hysterical and unwarranted accusations against male relatives. In addition, panelists rejected the recommendations of feminist prostitutes' rights groups like COYOTE and the U.S. Prostitutes Collective,[10] preferring increased arrests and punishment for women (though not their male customers) to decriminalization and better regulation of abusive working conditions. More comically, conservative panelists tried to push through a "vibrator bill," a model statute that would ban as obscene "any device designed or marketed as useful primarily for the stimulation of human genital organs." The three moderate female commission members became incredulous and upset, when they realized that such a law would ban vibrators.

During the course of the public hearings, conservative and fundamentalist witnesses made clear that they regarded the feminist movement as a major cause of the family breakdown and social disruption which they observed during the past twenty years. Feminists advocated divorce, abortion, access to birth control, day care, single motherhood, sexual permissiveness, lesbian and gay rights, working mothers—all undesirable developments that diminished the importance of family and marriage. Conservatives and fundamentalists were clear in their allegiance to a traditional moral agenda: sex belonged in marriage and nowhere else. Pornography was damaging because it promoted and advertised lust, sex "with no consequences," and "irresponsible" sex.

Anti-pornography feminists, in their writing and activism dating from approximately 1977, saw the damage of pornography in different terms, though other feminists (and I include myself in this group) objected to their analysis for uncritically incorporating many conservative elements of late nineteenth-century sexual culture.[11] Nevertheless, the anti-pornography feminist critique made several points which differed sharply from those made by conservatives. They argued that most, if not all, pornography was sexist (rather than immoral). It socialized men to be dominating and women to be victimized. Moreover, pornographic imagery lead to actual sexual violence against women, and it constituted a particularly effective form of anti-woman propaganda. At various times, anti-pornography feminists have proposed different remedial strategies ranging from educational programs and consciousness-raising to restriction and censorship of sexually explicit material through so-called civil rights anti-pornography legislation first drafted in 1983. But a consistent theme throughout anti-pornography feminism, as in most feminism, was intense opposition to and fervent critique of gender inequality, male domination, and patriarchal institutions, including the family, marriage, and heterosexuality.

The conflict between basic premises of conservative and anti-pornography feminist analyses is obvious. Nevertheless, the commission cleverly used anti-pornography feminist terms and concepts as well as witnesses to their own advantage in selective ways, helped not infrequently by anti-pornography leaders and groups themselves. Anti-pornography feminist witnesses eagerly testified before the commission and cast their personal experiences of incest, childhood sexual abuse, rape and sexual coercion in terms of the "harms" and "degradation" caused by pornography. Anti-pornography feminist witnesses, of course, did not voice complaints about divorce, masturbation, or homosexuality, which ideologically give feminists no cause for protest, but they failed to comment on the great divide that separated their complaints from those of fundamentalists, a divide dwarfed only by the even larger distance between their respective political programs. Indeed, some prominent anti-pornography feminists were willing to understate and most to avoid mentioning in their testimony their support for those cranky feminist demands so offensive to conservative ears: abortion, birth control, and lesbian and gay rights. Only one feminist anti-pornography group, Feminists Against Pornography from Washington, D.C., refused to tailor its testimony to please conservative members and attacked the Reagan administration for its savage cutbacks on programs and services for women.[12] Their testimony was soon cut off on the grounds of inadequate time, though other anti-pornography groups and spokespersons, including Andrea Dworkin, Catharine MacKinnon, and Women Against Pornography (New York) would be permitted to testify at great length.

In the context of the hearing, the notion that pornography "degrades" women proved to be a particularly helpful unifying term, floating in and out of fundamentalist as well as anti-pornography feminist testimony. By the second public hearing, "degrading" had become a true crossover term— used by moral majoritarians, vice cops, and aggressive prosecutors, as well as anti-pornography feminists. Speakers didn't notice, or chose not to, that the term "degradation" had very different meanings in each community. For anti-pornography feminists, pornography degrades women when it depicts or glorifies sexist sex: images that put men's pleasure first or suggest that women's lot in life is to serve men. For fundamentalists, "degrading" was freely applied to all images of sexual behavior that might be considered immoral, since in the conservative world view immorality degraded the individual and society. "Degrading" was freely applied to visual images that portrayed homosexuality, masturbation, and even consensual heterosexual sex. Even images of morally approved marital sexuality were judged "degrading," since public viewing of what should be a private experience degraded the couple and the sanctity of marriage. These terms provided by anti-pornography feminists—"degrading," "violence against women," and "offensive to women" (though conservatives couldn't resist adding the phrase "and children")—were eagerly adopted by the panel and proved particularly useful in giving it and its findings the gloss of modernity and some semblance of concern with human rights.

Although the commission happily assimilated the rhetoric of anti-pornography feminists, it decisively rejected their remedies. Conservative men pronounced the testimony of Andrea Dworkin "eloquent" and "moving" and insisted on including her statement in the final report, special treatment given no other witness. But anti-pornography feminists had argued against obscenity laws, saying they reflected a moralistic and anti-sexual tradition which could only harm women. Instead, they favored ordinances, such as those developed for Minneapolis and Indianapolis by Dworkin and

MacKinnon,[13] which would outlaw pornography as a violation of women's civil rights. The commission never seriously entertained the idea that obscenity laws should be repealed; given its conservative constituency and agenda, it couldn't have.

The commission's report summarily rejected Minneapolis-style ordinances. These had been "properly held unconstitutional" by a recent Supreme Court decision, the panel agreed, because they infringed on speech protected under the First Amendment. But the panel cleverly, if disingenuously, argued that traditional obscenity law could be used against violent and degrading material in a manner "largely consistent with what this ordinance attempts to do," ignoring anti-pornography feminists' vociferous rejection of obscenity laws. The panel recommended that obscenity laws be further strengthened by adding civil damages to the existing criminal penalties. This constitutes a major defeat for anti-pornography feminists. But unlike social scientists who protested loudly over the commission's misuse of their testimony, the anti-pornography feminists have not acknowledged the panel's distortion. Instead, they commended the panel for recognizing the harm of pornography and continued to denounce obscenity law,[14] without coming to grips with the panel's commitment to that approach.

Even more startling were MacKinnon's and Dworkin's statements to the press that the commission "has recommended to Congress the civil rights legislation women have sought,"[15] and this comment by Dorchen Leidholdt, founder of Women Against Pornography: "I'm not embarrassed at being in agreement with Ed Meese."[16] Over the course of the hearings, it seems that each group strategized how best to use the other. However, the vast power and resources of the federal government, backed by a strong fundamentalist movement, made it almost inevitable that the Meese commission would benefit far more in this exchange than anti-pornography feminists.

The commission attempted another major appropriation of feminist issues by recasting the problem of violence against women. Since the backlash against feminism began in the mid-1970s, conservative groups most decisively rejected feminist critiques of violence in the family, particularly assertions about the prevalence of marital rape, incest, and child sexual abuse. Such sexual violence was rare, they countered, and only exaggerated by feminists because they were "man-haters" and "lesbians" who wanted to destroy the family. Accordingly, conservatives consistently opposed public funding for social services directed at these problems: rape hotlines, shelters for abused wives, programs to identify and counsel child victims of incest. Such programs would destroy the integrity of the family, particularly the authority of the father, conservatives believed.

The commission hearings document a startling reversal in the conservative discourse on sexual violence. Conservative witnesses now claimed there is an epidemic of sexual violence directed at women and children, even in the family. Unlike the feminist analysis, which points to inequality, patriarchy, and women's powerlessness as root causes, the conservative analysis singles out pornography and its attendant sexual liberalization as the responsible agents. Men are, in a sense, victims as well, since once their lust is aroused, they are increasingly unable to refrain from sexual aggression. It is clear that the conservative about-face seeks to respond to a rising tide of concern among even right wing women about the issues of violence and abuse, while at the same time seeking to contain it by providing an alternative narrative: the appropriate solution lies in controlling pornography, not challenging male domination; pornography victimizes men, not just women. In that regard, it is striking that the victim witnesses provided by anti-pornography feminist groups were all female, whereas those provided by conservatives included many men.

Ironically, the conservative analysis ultimately blames feminism for violence against women. To the extent that feminists supported a more permissive sexual climate, including freer sexual expression, and undermined marriage as the only appropriate place for sex and procreation, they promoted an atmosphere favorable to violence against women. The commission's symbolic and rhetorical transformations were skillful. The panel not only appropriated anti-pornography feminist language to modernize a conservative agenda and make it more palatable to the mainstream public, but it also used issues of male violence successfully raised by feminists to argue that the only reliable protection for women was to be found in returning to the family and patriarchal protection.

THE PLEASURES OF LOOKING

The commission's campaign against sexually explicit images was filled with paradox. Professing belief in the most naive and literalist theories of representation, the commissioners nevertheless shrewdly used visual images during the hearings to establish "truth" and manipulate the feelings of the audience. Arguing that pornography had a singular and universal meaning that was evident to any viewer, the commission staff worked hard to exclude any perspective but its own. Insisting that sexually explicit images had great authority, the commissioners framed pornography so that it had more power in the hearing than it could ever have in the real world. Denying that subjectivity and context matter in the interpretation of any image, they created a well-crafted context that denied there was a context.

The foremost goal of the commission was to establish "the truth" about pornography, that is, to characterize and describe the sexually explicit material that was said to be in need of regulation. Pornographic images were shown during all public hearings, as witnesses and staff members alike illustrated their remarks with explicit, fleshy, often full-color images of sex. The reticence to view this material that one might have anticipated on the part of fundamentalists and conservatives was nowhere to be seen. The commission capitalized on the realistic representational form of still photos and movie and video clips, stating that the purpose of viewing these images was to inform the public and themselves about "what pornography was really like." Viewing was carefully orchestrated, and a great deal of staff time went toward organizing the logistics and technologies of viewing. Far from being a casual or minor enterprise, the selection and showing of sexually explicit images constituted one of the commission's major interventions.

The structure of viewing was an inversion of the typical context for viewing pornography. Normally private, this was public, with slides presented in federal courthouse chambers before hundreds of spectators in the light of day. The viewing of pornography, usually an individualistic and libidinally anarchic practice, was here organized by the state—the Department of Justice, to be exact. The ordinary purpose in viewing, sexual pleasure and masturbation, was ostensibly absent, replaced instead by dutiful scrutiny and the pleasures of condemnation.

These pleasures were intense. The atmosphere throughout the hearings was one of excited repression: witnesses alternated between chronicling the negative effects of pornography and making sensationalized presentations of "it." Taking a lead from feminist anti-pornography groups, everyone had a slide show: the F.B.I., the U.S. Customs Service, the U.S. Postal Service and sundry vice squads. At every "lights out," spectators would rush to one side of the room to see the screen, which was angled toward the commissioners. Were the hearing room a ship, we would have capsized many times.

Alan Sears, the executive director, told the commissioners with a grin that he hoped to include some "good stuff" in their final report, and its two volumes and 1,960 pages faithfully reflect the censors' fascination with the thing they love to hate. It lists in alphabetical order the titles of material found in sixteen adult bookstores in six cities: 2,370 films, 725 books and 2,325 magazines, beginning with *A Cock Between Friends* and ending with *69 Lesbians Munching*. A detailed plot summary is given for the book, *The Tying Up of Rebecca,* along with descriptions of sex aids advertised in the books, their cost, and how to order them.

The commission viewed a disproportionate amount of atypical material, which even moderate commissioners criticized as "extremely violent and degrading."[17] To make themselves sound contemporary and secular, conservatives needed to establish that pornography was violent rather than immoral and, contradicting social science evidence, that this violence was increasing.[18] It was important for the panel to insist that the images presented were "typical" and "average" pornography, but typical pornography—glossy, mainstream porn magazines directed at heterosexual men—does not feature much violence, as the commission's own research (soon quickly suppressed) confirmed.[19] The slide shows, however, did not present many carefully airbrushed photos of perfect females or the largely heterosexual gyrations (typically depicting intercourse and oral sex) found even in the most hard-core adult bookstores. The commission concentrated on atypical material, produced for private use or for small, special interest segments of the market or confiscated in the course of prosecutions. The slides featured behavior which the staff believed to be especially shocking: homosexuality, excrement, urination, child pornography, bestiality (with over 20 different types of animals, including chickens and elephants), and especially sadomasochism (SM).

The commission relied on the realism of photography to amplify the notion that the body of material shown was accurate, and, therefore, they implied, representative. The staff also skillfully mixed atypical and marginal material with pictorials from *Playboy* and *Penthouse*, rarely making a distinction between types of publications or types of markets. The desired fiction was that all pornography was the same. Many have commented on the way all photographic images are read as fact or truth, because the images are realistic. This general phenomenon is true for pornographic images as well, but it is intensified when the viewer is confronted by images of sexually explicit acts which he or she has little experience viewing (or doing) in real life. Shock, discomfort, fascination, repulsion, and arousal all operate to make the image have an enormous impact and seem undeniably real.

The action depicted was understood as realistic, not fantastic or staged for the purposes of producing an erotic picture. Thus, images that played with themes of surrender or domination were read as actually coerced. A nude woman holding a machine gun was clearly dangerous, a panelist noted, because the gun could go off (an interpretation not, perhaps, inaccurate for the psychoanalytically inclined reader). Images of obviously adult men and women dressed in exaggerated fashions of high school students were called child pornography.

Sadomasochistic pornography had an especially strategic use in establishing that sexually explicit imagery was "violent." The intervention was effective, since few (even liberal critics) have been willing to examine the construction of SM in the panel's argument. Commissioners saw a great deal of SM pornography and found it deeply upsetting, as did the audience. Photographs included images of women tied up, gagged, or being "disciplined." Viewers were unfamiliar with the conventions of SM sexual behavior and had no access to the codes participants use to read these images. The panel provided the frame: SM was non-consensual sex that inflicted force and violence on unwilling victims. Virtually any claim could be made against SM pornography, and, by extension, SM behavior, which remains a highly stigmatized and relatively invisible sexuality. As was the case with homosexuality until recently, invisibility reinforces stigma, and stigma reinforces invisibility in a circular manner.

The redundant viewing and narration of SM images reinforced several points useful to the commission—pornography depicted violence against women and promoted male domination. An active editorial hand was at work, however, to remove reverse images of female domination and male submission; these images never appeared, though they constitute a significant portion of SM imagery. Amusingly, SM pornography elicited hearty condemnation of "male dominance," the only sphere in which conservative men were moved to critique it throughout the course of the hearing.

The commission called no witnesses to discuss the nature of SM, either professional experts or typical participants.[20] Given the atmosphere, it was not surprising that no one defended it. Indeed, producers of more soft-core pornography joined in the condemnation, perhaps hoping to direct the commission's ire to groups and acts more stigmatized than themselves.[21] The commission ignored a small but increasing body of literature that documents important features of SM sexual behavior, namely consent and safety. Typically, the conventions we use to decipher ordinary images are suspended when it comes to SM images. When we see science fiction movies, for example, we do not leave the theater believing that the special effects were real or that the performers were injured making the films. But the commissioners assumed that images of domination and submission were both real and coerced.

In addition, such literalist interpretations were evident in the repeated assertions that all types of sexual images had a direct effect on behavior. The idea that sexual images could be used and remain on a fantasy level was foreign to the commission, as was the possibility that individuals might use fantasy to engage with dangerous or frightening feelings without wanting to experience them in real life. This lack of recognition is consistent with fundamentalist distrust and puzzlement about the imagination and the symbolic realm, which seem to have no autonomous existence; for fundamentalists, imagination and behavior are closely linked. If good thoughts lead to good behavior, a sure way to eliminate bad behavior was to police bad thoughts.

The voice-over for the visual segments was singular and uniform, which served to obliterate the actual diversity of people's response to pornography. But sexually explicit material is a contested ground precisely *because* subjectivity matters. An image that is erotic to one individual is revolting to a second and ridiculous to a third. The object of contestation *is* meaning. Age, gender, race, class, sexual preference, erotic experience, and personal history all form the grid through which sexual images are received and interpreted. The commission worked hard to eliminate diversity from its hearings and to substitute instead its own authoritative, often uncontested, frequently male monologue.

It is startling to realize how many of the Meese Commission's techniques were pioneered by anti-pornography feminists between 1977–1984. Claiming that pornography was sexist and promoted violence against women, anti-pornography feminists had an authoritative voice-over, too, though for theorists Andrea Dworkin and Catharine MacKinnon and groups like Women Against Pornography, the monologic voice was, of course, female. Although anti-pornography feminists disagreed with fundamentalist moral assumptions and contested, rather than approved, male authority, they carved out new territory with slide shows depicting allegedly horrific sexual images, a technique the commission heartily adopted. Anti-pornography feminists relied on victim testimony and preferred anecdotes to data. They, too, shared a literalist interpretive frame and used SM images to prove that pornography was violent.

The Meese Commission was skilled in its ability to use photographic images to establish the so-called truth and to provide an almost invisible interpretive frame that compelled agreement with its agenda. The commission's true gift, however, lay in its ability to create an emotional atmosphere in the hearings that facilitated acceptance of the commission's world view. Its strategic use of images was a crucial component of this emotional management. Because the power of this emotional climate fades in the published text, it is not obvious to most readers of the commission's report. Yet it was and is a force to be reckoned with, both in the commission and, more broadly, in all public debates about sexuality, especially those that involve the right wing.

RITUALS OF SEXUAL SHAME

An important aspect of the commission's work was the ritual airing and affirmation of sexual shame in a public setting. The panel relentlessly created an atmosphere of unacknowledged sexual arousal and fear. The large amount of pornography shown, ostensibly to educate and repel, was nevertheless arousing. The range and diversity of images provided something for virtually everyone, and the concentration on taboo, kinky, and harder-to-obtain material added to the charge. Part of the audience's discomfort may have come from the unfamiliarity of seeing sexually explicit images in public, not private, settings, and in the company of others not there for the express purpose of sexual arousal. But a larger part must have come from the problem of experiencing sexual arousal in an atmosphere where it is condemned. The commission's lesson was a complex one, but it taught the importance of managing and hiding sexual arousal and pleasure in public, while it reinforced secrecy, hypocrisy, and shame. Unacknowledged sexual feelings, though, did not disappear but developed into a whirlwind of mute, repressed emotion that the Meese Commission channeled toward its own purpose.

Sexual shaming was also embedded in the interrogatory practices of the chair. Witnesses appearing before the commission were treated in a highly uneven manner. Commissioners accepted virtually any claim made by anti-pornography witnesses as true, while those who opposed restriction of sexually explicit speech were often met with rudeness and hostility. The panelists asked social scientist Edward Donnerstein if pornographers had tried to influence his research findings or threatened his life. They asked actress Colleen Dewhurst, testifying for Actor's Equity about the dangers of censorship in the theater, if persons convicted of obscenity belonged to the union, and if the union was influenced by organized crime. They questioned her at length about the group's position on child pornography.

Sexual shame was also ritualized in how witnesses spoke about their personal experiences with images. "Victims of pornography" told in lurid detail of their use of pornography and eventual decline into masturbation, sexual addiction, and incest. Some testified anonymously, shadowy apparitions behind translucent screens. Their first-person accounts, sometimes written by the commission's staff,[22] featured a great elaboration of the sexual damage caused by visual images. To counter these accounts there was nothing but silence: descriptions of visual and sexual pleasure were absent. The commission's chair even noted the lack and was fond of asking journalists if they had ever come across individuals with positive experiences with pornography. The investigatory staff had tried to identify such people to testify, he said, but had been unable to find any. Hudson importuned reporters to please send such individuals his way. A female commissioner helpfully suggested that she knew of acquaintances, "normal married couples living in suburban New Jersey," who occasionally looked at magazines or rented X-rated videos with no apparent ill effects. But she doubted they would be willing to testify about their sexual pleasure in a federal courthouse, with their remarks transcribed by the court stenographer and their photos probably published in the next day's paper as "porn-users."

Though few witnesses chose to expose themselves to the commission's intimidation through visual images, the tactics used are illustrated in the differential treatment of two female witnesses, former *Playboy* Playmate Micki Garcia and former *Penthouse* Pet of the Year Dottie Meyer. Garcia accused Playboy Enterprises and Hugh Hefner of encouraging drug use, murder, and rape (as well as abortion, bisexuality, and cosmetic surgery) in the Playboy mansion. Her life was endangered by her testimony, she claimed. Despite the serious nature of some of these charges and the lack of any supporting evidence, her testimony was received without question.[23] Meyer, on the other hand, testified that her association with *Penthouse* had been professionally and personally beneficial. At the conclusion of her testimony, the lights dramatically dimmed and large blowups of several *Penthouse* pictorials were flashed on the screen; with rapid-fire questions the chair demanded that she explain sexual images he found particularly objectionable. Another male commissioner, prepared by the staff with copies of Meyer's nine-year-old centerfold, began to pepper her with hectoring questions about her sexual life: Was it true she was preoccupied with sex? Liked sex in cars and alleyways? Had a collection of vibrators? Liked rough-and-tumble sex?[24] The female commissioners were silent. His sexist cross-examination was reminiscent of that directed at a rape victim, discredited and made vulnerable by any admission or image of her own sexuality. Suddenly, Dottie Meyer was on trial, publicly humiliated because she dared to present herself as unrepentantly sexual, not a victimized woman.

The ferocious attack on Dottie Meyer—and by extension on any display of women's sexual pleasure in the public sphere—is emblematic of the agenda of conservatives and fundamentalists on women's sexuality. Although they presented their program under the guise of feminist language and concerns, their abiding goal was to reestablish control by restricting women—and their desires—within ever-shrinking boundaries of the private and the domestic. The falsity of the panel's seemingly feminist rhetoric was highlighted by the moment when a lone woman speaking of her own sexual pleasure was seen as a greater threat than all the male "victims" of pornography who had assaulted and abused women. The conspicuous absence of any discourse that addressed women's definitions of their own sexual pleasures, that enlarged rather than constricted the domain of their public speech or action, unmasked this agenda. Unmasked, too, was the commission's primary aim: not to increase the safe space for women, but to narrow what can be seen, spoken about, imagined, and—they hope—done. The invisibility and subordination of female sexual pleasure in the commission's hearings is a straight-jacket which conservatives and fundamentalists would like to extend to the entire culture. Feminist language, disembodied from feminist principles and programs, was used to advance the idea that men, women, and society could be protected only through the suppression of female desire. In the face of false patriarchal protections embedded in shame and silence, feminists need to assert their entitlement to public speech, variety, safety, and bodily and visual pleasures.

NOTES

I am grateful to Frances Doughty, Lisa Duggan, Ann Snitow and Sharon Thompson for reading early drafts and for helpful comments, criticisms, and encouragement. Thanks also to editors Faye Ginsburg and Anna Tsing for thoughtful suggestions and patience.

Thanks to the Rockefeller Foundation for a Humanist-in-Residence Fellowship (1987–88) at the Center for Research on Women, Douglass College, Rutgers, the State University, New Brunswick, New Jersey, which supported my research and writing.

Parts of this analysis have appeared in "The Meese Commission on the Road," The Nation, *243, no. 3 (August 2–9, 1986), 65, 76–82 and "The Pleasures of Looking: The Attorney General's Commission on Pornography versus Visual Images," in* The Critical Image: Essays on Contemporary Photography, *Carol Squiers, ed. (Seattle: Bay Press, 1990), 38–58. Earlier versions of this paper were presented at the annual meeting of the Society for Photographic Education, Rochester, New York, March 17, 1989; at the panel "Gender Rituals and the Sexual Self," American Anthropological Association, November 21, 1987; and at the panel "Contested Domains of Reproduction, Sexuality, Family and Gender in America," American Ethnological Society, Wrightsville Beach, North Carolina, April 24, 1986. Thanks to panelists and members of the audience for helpful comments.*

1. Attorney General's Commission on Pornography, Miami transcript, public hearing, November 21, 1985.

2. Attorney General's Commission on Pornography, *Final Report*, 2 vols. (Washington, D.C.: U.S. Government Printing Office, July 1986).

3. See *Final Report*, pp. 433–458, for a complete list of the panel's recommendations. These include mandating high fines and long jail sentences for obscenity convictions, appointing a federal task force to coordinate prosecutions nationwide, developing a computer data bank to collect information on individuals suspected of producing pornography, and using punitive RICO legislation (the Racketeer Influenced and Corrupt Organizations Act, originally developed to fight organized crime) to confiscate the personal property of anyone convicted of the "conspiracy" of producing pornography. For sexually explicit material outside the range of legal prosecution, the commission recommended that citizen activist groups target and remove material in their communities which they find "dangerous or offensive or immoral."

4. For a detailed critique of procedural irregularities, see Barry Lynn, *Polluting the Censorship Debate: A Summary and Critique of the Attorney General's Commission on Pornography* (Washington, D.C.: American Civil Liberties Union, 1986).

5. For changes in sexual patterns in the last century, see (for England) Jeffrey Weeks, *Sex, Politics and Society: The Regulation of Sexuality Since 1800* (New York: Longman, 1981) and (for America) John D'Emilio and Estelle B. Freedman, *Intimate Matters* (New York: Harper and Row, 1988). For a history of pornography, see Walter Kendrick, *The Secret Museum* (New York: Viking, 1987).

6. Sears went on to become the executive director of Citizens for Decency through Law, a major conservative antipornography group. (The group has since changed its name to the Children's Legal Foundation.)

7. Attorney Frederick Schauer argued that sexually explicit expression which was arousing was less like speech and more like "rubber, plastic, or leather sex aids." See "Speech and 'Speech'—Obscenity and 'Obscenity': An Exercise in the Interpretation of Constitutional Language," *Georgetown Law Journal* 67(1979), 899–923, especially pp. 922–923.

8. My analysis is based on direct observation of the commission's public hearings and executive sessions, supplemented by interviews with participants. All the commission's executive sessions were open to the public, following the provision of sunshine laws governing federal advisory commissions. Commissioners were specifically prohibited from discussing commission business or engaging in any informal deliberations outside of public view.

Public hearings were organized around preselected topics in six cities: Washington, D.C. (general), Chicago (law enforcement), Houston (social science), Los Angeles (production and distribution), Miami (child pornography), and New York (organized crime). Each public hearing typically lasted two full days. Commission executive sessions were held in each city in conjunction with the public hearings, usually for two extra days. Additional work sessions occurred in Washington, D.C. and Scottsdale, Arizona.

9. Victims of pornography, as described in the *Final Report*, included "Sharon, formerly married to a medical professional who is an avid consumer of pornography," "Bill, convicted of the sexual molestation of two adolescent females," "Dan, former Consumer of Pornography (sic)," "Evelyn, Mother and

homemaker, Wisconsin, formerly married to an avid consumer of pornography," and "Mary Steinman, sexual abuse victim."

10. Los Angeles transcript, public hearing, October 17, 1985.

11. Major works of antipornography feminism include Andrea Dworkin, *Pornography: Men Possessing Women* (New York: G. P. Putnam, 1979); Susan Griffin, *Pornography and Silence: Culture's Revenge Against Nature* (New York: Harper and Row, 1981); Laura Lederer, ed., *Take Back the Night* (New York: William Morrow, 1980); Catharine A. MacKinnon, "Pornography, Civil Rights, and Speech," *Harvard Civil Rights-Civil Liberties Law Review*, vol. 20 (Cambridge: Harvard University, 1985), 1–70.

Opinion within feminism about pornography was, in fact, quite diverse, and it soon became apparent that the antipornography view was not hegemonic. For other views, see Carole S. Vance, ed., *Pleasure and Danger: Exploring Female Sexuality* (New York: Routledge & Kegan Paul, 1984); Varda Burstyn, ed., *Women Against Censorship*, (Vancouver: Douglas & McIntyre, 1985) and Kate Ellis et al., eds., *Caught Looking: Feminism, Pornography, and Censorship* (New York: Caught Looking, Inc., 1986).

12. Washington, D.C. transcript, public hearing, June 20, 1985.

13. For the version passed in Indianapolis, see Indianapolis, Ind., code section 16–3 (q) (1984); and Andrea Dworkin, "Against the Male Flood: Censorship, Pornography, and Equality," *Harvard Women's Law Journal* 9(1985): 1–19. For a critique, see Lisa Duggan, Nan Hunter, and Carole S. Vance, "False Promises: Feminist Antipornography Legislation in the U.S.," in *Women Against Censorship*, ed. Varda Burstyn (Toronto: Douglas & McIntyre, 1985), 130–151.

14. Women Against Pornography press conference, July 9, 1986, New York.

15. Statement of Catharine A. MacKinnon and Andrea Dworkin, July 9, 1986, New York, distributed at a press conference organized by Women Against Pornography following the release of the Meese commission's *Final Report*.

16. David Firestone, "Battle Joined by Reluctant Allies," *Newsday*, July 10, 1986, p. 5.

17. Statement of commissioners Judith Becker and Ellen Levine, *Final Report*, p. 199. In addition, they wrote: "We do not even know whether or not what the Commission viewed during the course of the year reflected the nature of most of the pornographic and obscene material in the market; nor do we know if the materials shown us mirror the taste of the majority of consumers of pornography."

18. Recent empirical evidence does not support the often-repeated assertion that violence in pornography is increasing. In their review of the literature, social scientists Edward Donnerstein, Daniel Linz, and Steven Penrod conclude, "at least for now, we cannot legitimately conclude that pornography has become more violent since the time of the 1970 obscenity and pornography commission" (in *The Question of Pornography: Research Findings and Policy Implications* [New York: The Free Press, 1987], 91).

19. The only original research conducted by the commission examined images found in the April 1986 issues of best-selling men's magazines (*Cheri, Chic, Club, Gallery, Genesis, High Society, Hustler, Oui, Penthouse, Playboy, Swank*). The study found that "images of force, violence, or weapons" consti-

tuted less than 1 percent of all images (0.6%), hardly substantiating the commission's claim that violent imagery in pornography was common. Although the results of this study are reported in the draft, they were excised from the final report.

20. For recent work on SM, see Michael A. Rosen, *Sexual Magic: The S/M Photographs* (San Francisco: Shaynew Press, 1986); Geoff Mains, *Urban Aboriginals* (San Francisco: Gay Sunshine Press, 1984); Samois, ed., *Coming to Power*, 2nd ed. (Boston: Alyson Press, 1982); Gini Graham Scott, *Dominant Women, Submissive Men* (New York: Praeger, 1983); Thomas Weinberg and G. P. Levi Kamel, *S and M: Studies in Sadomasochism* (Buffalo: Prometheus Books, 1983); Gerald and Caroline Greene, *S-M: The Last Taboo* (New York: Grove Press, 1974).

21. The proclivity of mildly stigmatized groups to join in the scapegoating of more stigmatized groups is explained by Gayle Rubin in her discussion of sexual hierarchy (Gayle Rubin, "Thinking Sex: Notes for a Radical Theory of the Politics of Sexuality" in *Pleasure and Danger: Exploring Female Sexuality,* ed. Carole S. Vance [Boston: Routledge & Kegan Paul, 1984], 267–319.)

22. Statement of Alan Sears, executive director (Washington, D.C. transcript, June 18, 1985).

23. Los Angeles transcript, public hearing, October 17, 1985.

24. New York City transcript, public hearing, January 22, 1986.

PART THREE

Producing Gender In and Out of the Workplace

CHAPTER EIGHT

Production as Means, Production as Metaphor: Women's Struggle to Enter the Trades

KATH WESTON

The foreman and I had been talking for over 20 minutes. He had reviewed my resumé, noted the training classes in mechanics, verified my three years' experience working on cars, and shown me around the shop. "Just one question," said the man. "How do you check a U-joint?" Easy, I thought. "You put one hand on each side of the joint and twist. If you feel any play, the joint's bad." "Hey," he said, looking me in the eye for the first time, "you really *do* know your stuff!"

The foreman's surprise was genuine, and as he spoke I recalled similar stories told by other women who had applied for jobs in the trades. In the face of a weight of evidence indicating that a woman has the knowledge, skill, and experience to do a job, employers and coworkers still have difficulty believing that she will be *able* to produce. To me, the look on that foreman's face suggested that there was something about the situation which would be glossed rather than explained by concepts like discrimination or lack of gender parity. Gender parity, which describes the numerical ratio of men to women in a given occupational category, cannot explain the persistent references to productive capacity and gendered traits when managers allocate tasks or evaluate performance. Discrimination, for its part, cannot differentiate between blind resistance and shock or disbelief.

The potential for high earnings in the trades has been a major factor motivating women to seek access to so-called nontraditional occupations in a highly sex-segregated job market. But as women have attempted to enter skilled blue-collar jobs, they have come face to face with intertwined notions of gender and production that shape the opposition to their presence on the job site. Production is a cultural category infused with notions about gender, race, age, and class. To make a place for themselves in the trades, women have had to do more than fight for a well-paying job: they have struggled to reconfigure prevailing interpretations of productivity, capability, and competence.[1]

Many feminist scholars have argued that the sexual division of labor lies at the root of sexual inequality, expecting its amelioration to redress inequities and improve women's position in society.[2] But experience teaches that the sexual division of labor does not simply disappear in the face of exhortations for women to take up carpentry or men to assume their share of child care responsibilities. No more successful is the practice of simply juggling individual men and women from one job category to another, since occupations historically have tended to resegregate along gender lines.[3]

In industrial societies the persistence of a sexual division of labor has been variously attributed to technological innovation, historical circumstance, or self-serving calculation. While many theories of occupational sex segregation invoke culture to explain the form of the sexual division of labor—which particular jobs are allocated to women, which to men—they seldom implicate cultural factors in the perpetuation of that division as a whole. Segregated labor markets are held to be maintained by interests and economic variables predicated on the wider framework of capitalism and the profit motive,[4] or by patriarchy and men's desire to preserve male dominance.[5] Culture enters as a nebulous influence on employer and worker behavior, a residual factor that comes into play only after other motivations have been credited.

Some theories of occupational sex segregation cast gender typing of occupations as a "sexual idiom" that management and workers endorse in pursuit of their (presumably objective) interests. Others present gender typing as an example of static "beliefs" or "norms," seen as elements of a mythical tradition handed down through generations of male employers and employees. Although the tradition admittedly may change, it does so in an enigmatic manner, identifiable only in retrospect and hardly susceptible to intervention by women who wish to lay claim to "male jobs."

Ideology appears in these arguments as mere rationale or after-the-fact mystification, the icing on the cake of perceived interest.[6] But if this is all that ideology represents, why do male supervisors and workers alike so often invoke gendered traits *in particular* to explain women's historical exclusion from the trades?[7] Surely, it is significant that, when challenged about their resistance to hiring women, the answers male employers most often give to job developers and women applicants are variations of "women can't do the job" and "women don't have what it takes."[8] This focus on gendered traits and productive potential suggests that there is far more to the creation of segmented labor markets than the straightforward pursuit of interests, or "divide and conquer" tactics devised by management to maintain control over the labor force.[9]

To treat ideology as a masking idiom or an amalgam of beliefs and norms offers a classic example of what I call "the Culture moves in mysterious ways" approach to social analysis. More challenging is to develop an analysis that grants insight into how the process works. How do individuals bring beliefs into play in social arenas like the workplace, and how do these understandings change? Building better theory will require accounts of workers and employers actively engaged in social give-and-take, rather than patriarchal versions of an ideal-typical "economic man," or a patchwork of explanatory variables whose whole seems to yield less than the sum of its parts.[10]

Much has been made in anthropology in recent years of how ideology and symbolism are always and already integral to practice.[11] Within the Marxist tradition, Raymond Williams has formulated a similar critique of the analytic division between structure and superstructure—between economics and culture, if you will.[12] What has proved more elusive than mounting a theoretical critique has been the challenge of tracing this integration of ideology and action in the ethnographic material provided by everyday life. The "real-world" stakes are enormous: for women in the trades, it can mean the difference between being hired or being terminated, between a substantial or a poverty-level paycheck, between continuous harassment or the establishment of positive relationships with male coworkers.

"Doing your work is not enough," claimed Jessica, a construction worker.

You do twice as much work. You do twice as well . . . Dealing with [men on the job] is dealing with their ego, and dealing with their ego is like trying to hold a raw egg in your hand without the shell, and still do your work at the same time. But I've got a way with words (laughs). I do it.

The tactics women have developed to gain entry to blue-collar occupations and the criteria men invoke to keep women out are part of a process in which actors contest, defend, and transform the cultural meanings that organize work. Understanding why some techniques intended to disrupt the sexual division of labor fall short while others prove effective demands a reexamination of the ways people link notions of gender to productive capacity and articulate gender through activity on the shop floor. What women who cross gender lines in their search for employment discover is nothing so simple as a sexual division of labor, in which men and women merely occupy discrete categories of jobs, but rather *gendered divisions* of labor, in which gender permeates not only the bodies and identities of workers, but production itself.

BACKGROUND

In the 1970s and early 1980s, California witnessed the emergence of numerous training programs and advocacy groups intended to facilitate women's entry into skilled trades. Over the past decades, these programs have achieved a remarkable degree of success at placing women from a broad range of racial and class backgrounds in "traditionally" male blue-collar jobs and apprenticeships. In focusing here on community-based initiatives I do not mean to detract from the importance of governmental and institutional support for implementing affirmative action during the same period.[13] Even with federal rulings and regulations in place, however, the overwhelming number of companies and unions that dragged their feet on affirmative action encouraged activists to develop tactics they could deploy effectively at the local level. The challenge was to develop strategic responses that worked to get women in the door and, once hired, to retain their hard-won employment.

From 1978 to 1979 I helped to organize a series of conferences that brought together Department of Labor personnel, high school counselors, joint apprenticeship committee members, and representatives of community organizations, to coordinate efforts to bring women into the trades. As a writer/consultant for the California State Department of Vocational Education in 1980, I interviewed staff from community-based advocacy groups across the state working to place women in apprenticeships. The information collected became the basis for a procedures manual that outlined paths of entry into skilled blue-collar jobs, offered suggestions for networking with local agencies, and presented strategies for overcoming particular obstacles that women entering the trades can expect to face. Several years later I participated in a vocational training program dedicated to placing women and minorities in skilled blue-collar jobs, while simultaneously completing a community college course in auto mechanics where I sometimes felt lost in a sea of male classmates. During this period I went out on job interviews, talked at length with other students, visited job sites, and listened to innumerable stories from women already employed in "nontraditional" jobs. Although this essay primarily draws on participant observation, I also have incorporated material from open-ended interviews conducted with job developers, agency directors, clients of advocacy groups, and women I met during my year in trade school.

GENDER AND PRODUCTION

Managers are concerned with production in the broad sense of "getting the job done." Of course, related objectives like profit, efficiency, and control of the labor force also figure in managerial discourse, but in the context of blue-collar work, productivity remains the concept most frequently invoked when managers evaluate workers and assign them to jobs. In skilled trades, production can be measured in cars serviced, sprinklers installed, and buildings framed—or, alternatively, in the time taken to accomplish any one of these tasks. From this perspective, labor appears as just one of many material resources channeled into the production process. But hiring practices and job structures cannot be so easily quantified. Production is organized not only in terms of labor actually performed (concrete labor), but also in terms of the human qualities managers and coworkers *believe* will contribute to the accomplishment of job tasks.

According to Marx, it is *labor power* (the capacity to perform labor), not the activity of *concrete labor,* that a worker hires out for a period of time in return for a 'wage. From the worker's point of view, her labor power constitutes a commodity that must be exchanged in order to survive in a capitalist society. From the point of view of the employer, that labor power represents just another element in the means of production, one of many resources required to produce a particular product. Because the labor power purchased by the capitalist must be translated into concrete labor, or labor actually performed, management devises control strategies to extract labor from the worker. If an employer perceives—for whatever reason—that a worker lacks the productive capacity to accomplish certain tasks he will likely refuse to hire her, judging that she will prove of little use to him.[14] In setting up and periodically transforming the production process, what management creates is not a concrete division of labor but a division of labor power, in which jobs and the capacities believed necessary to perform them become reciprocally defined.

What Marx does not explore is the possibility that labor power, in the sense of capacity and capability, is not a neutral term. Our society describes people in general and job applicants in particular as possessors of inherent "traits" of character and competence—traits that incorporate cultural notions of gender, race, class, age, and what it means to be "able-bodied." In popular discussions of working-class employment, women are often supposed to possess greater "manual dexterity" and "patience" than men, while men are favored with superior "physical strength," "mechanical aptitude," and "aggressiveness." Jobs, in turn, are described in terms of qualities considered necessary to perform them, "requirements" believed intrinsic to the work itself. The hiring process becomes a method of pairing jobs with applicants on the basis of traits "possessed" and traits "required". The gender-typed qualifications sought in job applicants then appear to be a direct outgrowth of occupational demands. All an employer has to do is perform the "impartial" task of matching one to the other.

Consider the cultural opposition between "heavy" and "light" work, terms that carry gendered meanings affecting perceptions of who will be the best candidate for a given job. In a phone conversation, a counselor affiliated with my automotive mechanics program advised me, as a woman, to choose "light-duty" work in a brakes class over a course that would involve handling "heavy" engines. Never having met me, he had no way to assess my physical capabilities; intent on characterizing engines as heavy objects, he ignored the fact that auto engines, which indeed weigh too much for a man or a woman working alone to lift, are removed and replaced with the aid of a hoist. In another case, a supervisor assigned women to do all the tungsten (TIG) welding aboard a ship, despite significant health hazards, because the thin sheets of metal being welded led him to view it as "delicate" work.

Most men who do the hiring in the trades seem convinced that traits do inhere in potential employees, traits they anticipate will translate into successful completion of job tasks. When male managers and workers object to women in skilled blue-collar work, they often appeal to traits grounded in cultural notions of biology and anatomy, along with mental attitudes like "toughness." Women are not as "strong" as men, the most common argument goes, so they don't belong in the trades because they can't do the work.[15] Even for the occasional employer with some concealed motive for denying women jobs, the voiced objection that gender will limit a woman worker's productivity remains the opening gambit that women must counter to negotiate employment successfully. Such statements define the arena of discourse in which women engage with those who oppose their presence on the job site.

Women themselves are not immune from the cultural equation between male "strength" and "heavy" labor. Knowing this, a counselor for an advocacy group pointedly avoided describing a job as involving the operation of heavy equipment when she announced the opening of operating engineer apprenticeships. Instead, she depicted the work as learning to run "big yellow Tonka toys"—bulldozers, backhoes, and the like. During a similar session, a classified ad that called for "ability to lift 50 pounds" lost much of its power to intimidate after counselors reminded women to look to their own experience rather than to preconceived ideas of their abilities, observing for good measure that several women present had carried "heavy" children into the meeting that day.

GETTING IN THE DOOR

Persons do not possess gender-typed qualities so much as they use symbols to fashion presentations of self that incorporate gender.[16] During the application and interviewing process, women work to convince managerial gatekeepers of their capacity to be productive workers. Since applicants rarely receive an opportunity to demonstrate abilities by actually executing tasks, they have learned to deal in indexical relations. Qualities such as courage, aggressiveness, or strength, which describe the type of labor power considered desirable for skilled blue-collar work, represent intangibles that cannot be observed directly. Using the cultural knowledge that traits can be displayed in appearance, women have found it advantageous to assemble "outward" indicators that point to the secrets of qualities presumed to be locked within the body's musculature and psyche, "in there" where most people in the United States believe the "true self" resides.

Realizing that many women are accustomed to applying for clerical and other "pink-collar" jobs, advocacy groups began to offer a sort of blue-collar dress for success program. When going on an interview, they recommend long-sleeved shirts and bulky sweaters to convey an impression of upper body strength. Women are told to wear work shoes or boots to job sites, intentionally scuffed, sandpapered, or spattered with paint if necessary.

They are advised to take along a toolbox even if they don't expect to need it and to make tools look used and dirty, not like they just came off the shelf. Pre-interview roleplaying gives clients an opportunity to develop a firm handshake and a "no-nonsense" attitude. Because "let me see your hands" is not an uncommon request during an interview, some groups encourage women to plunge into manual labor of any sort, even if unrelated to their particular trades.

Each of these nonverbal indicators is intended to signify that the applicant is ready and *able* to work in a blue-collar environment. Implicit is the recognition that employers will base hiring decisions at least in part on their evaluation of productive potential. This evaluation weighs *signs* of ability to do the job, rather than observations of concrete achievements. The point of coaching women in such symbolic presentations is not to get candidates who lack appropriate technical skills or experience past employers. Advocacy groups assess women's work histories, train them in tool use, and may encourage regular workouts at a gym. But the counselors and job developers who staff the organizations understand that it is often a symbolically constituted impression of productive capacity that gets a person the job. Because competence in the trades is so closely identified with traits such as physical strength or mechanical aptitude that are commonly attributed to men, creating an impression of capability remains an uphill battle for women.

To shift attention away from questions of capacity, advocacy groups do everything possible to get women onto a job site where they will have the opportunity to complete actual assignments. In their contact with foremen and managers, job developers from these groups counter objections by throwing the burden of proof back on the employer: "She can't do the work? How do you know? Have you ever tried hiring a woman? Give me the specifics of what you *think* she can't do. Give her a chance and let her show you!" In the course of challenging the congruence between gender and jobs, these women have effectively redrawn the lines of confrontation, shifting discourse away from metaphorical depictions of productive capacity or labor power, toward an emphasis on the concrete labor necessary to accomplish whatever task is at hand.

ON THE JOB

Given the opportunity to work, women commonly find that managers and coworkers are reassured by demonstrated accomplishment of job tasks. Many men in the trades harbor a sincere concern that women really cannot do the work and will not be able to "pull their own weight." They fear that hiring women will only increase their own workload. Barbara Shaman, an outside machinist, tells the story of how her supervisor assigned one of the biggest guys on the job to help her move something. After her coworker failed to budge the object, Shaman successfully moved it, and he never again questioned her abilities.[17] Some of the women I met made a point of reminding supervisors and coworkers that they were "just here to do a job," crediting this emphasis on production with stopping harassment in its tracks. Tabling questions of ability while giving center stage to demonstrated accomplishments or time taken to complete a task can resolve doubts about women's capacity to handle "nontraditional" occupations. This tactic attempts to disrupt preconceived links between work and gender by bringing observation and measurement into play. Concrete labor replaces labor power at the heart of discourse on job performance.

The appeal of this strategic separation of ability to work from work performed rests on the expectation that on-the-job achievements will prove sufficient to refute stereotypes of women's incompetence. The gradual realization that the means of production carry their own metaphors proves disconcerting to women who enter the trades expecting "good work" to be self-evident.[18] Men may ignore successfully completed job tasks, focusing instead on work yet undone or expectations that are less clearly defined. One woman at the auto school complained of a male tow truck driver on her night job who knew very little about cars. In the field, he repeatedly had to call on her for assistance through the dispatcher. When she arrived he would ask her to analyze the problem, and stand by while she got the industrial jack down from the truck—acknowledged among drivers as the "heaviest" part of the job. Rather than crediting her efforts, he maligned her driving ability, playing on the old saw that women make lousy drivers. Without a wider audience, she found it difficult to make her accomplishments count.

The conceptual links between gendered traits and job requirements are so powerful that they can influence what men on the job see when they watch a woman work. In the context of an occupation like automotive repair, where deadlines are constant, the female-typed trait of patience is considered no virtue. Time and again women mechanics described the experience of having tools literally taken out of their hands by male coworkers who proceeded to try this and try that, when a more systematic approach would likely have saved time in the long run. What these women conceived as a calculated troubleshooting procedure could equally well be interpreted as a failure to aggressively tackle the job, an absence of male style, or a patient ineffectiveness. In this way, ideologies about women's inability to do the work can become self-confirming.

Perception may defer to meanings that link gender and job performance. After several weeks in an auto electrical course, I noticed that the individual labeled the best student by teacher and students alike took longer than many of his classmates to get cars up and running. Little distinguished his results from those obtained by his peers: he traced the same kinds of shorts, using identical equipment and equal amounts of connectors and electrical tape. Why was he singled out as a better student? As far as I could ascertain, this judgment rested on three factors. First, he proceeded without recourse to wiring diagrams, a method that took much longer but which gave him an air of independent initiative and "natural aptitude" for the job. He also shunned customary safety precautions, taking electrical shocks rather than disconnecting the negative battery cable or using the insulated tools available. Finally, he made great shows of physical strength by, for instance, supporting a component with one hand while examining wires located behind it with the other. I must give him credit for a certain ingenuity in this regard, since it is much more difficult to create opportunities for flexing the muscles when working with wires than, say, when removing a transmission.

Many workers in the trades present displays that reference gendered traits in order to affirm their work competence before peers or supervisors. Working without safety gear is supposed to demonstrate courage and toughness, just as exhibitions of force assert a worker's physical strength. Yet these displays are not universally taken as signs of proficiency. One morning the instructor in my auto mechanics class chased a male student out from under a car that was resting on a hydraulic floor jack without safety stands, yelling, "Do you want to die?" The student walked away muttering, "So what if it falls, I'm not afraid. I don't need those things." Similarly, the vocational training class I attended included a number of men who, whenever they encountered a particularly frustrating obstacle to finishing a job, would force bolts until the metal snapped, creating much more time-consuming problems than the ones they were originally attempting to fix. They tended to attribute such occurrences to bad luck or a stubborn fastener, rather than faulty technique and a misplaced emphasis on displays of physical strength. The derogatory term "hammer mechanic" was coined by some men to deride just such attempts to indicate possession of strength through unreflective recourse to force.

Despite occasional disparities in readings of gendered displays, however, the degree to which gendered traits and job descriptions are reflexively defined often leads workers to feel that they must conform stylistically to the notions of gender embedded in their work. In the trades male workers do many things to look more productive on the floor. I have seen electrician apprentices working on live circuits when they could easily have thrown a circuit breaker, plumbers knowingly sawing through asbestos insulation without so much as a dust mask, tool crib attendants with back trouble lifting great weights when dollies or hand trucks were available.[19] In each case, the procedures followed did not significantly affect the time it took to complete the task. However, the women who witnessed these incidents (some of whom followed suit) believed that a certain disregard for safety and flexing of the muscles were linked to the men's reputation as "hard" workers.

Workers cannot always easily drop the gendered displays they take up at work when they put away their tools and head for home. Many women report changes in behavior and self-perception after being placed in blue-collar jobs, from "rough" talk and transformed body posture to the newly acquired habit of making a mess and leaving it behind for someone else to clean. "I am a lot more shut down at work than I would even ever dream of wanting to be anywhere else in my life," said a woman doing metal fabrication. "I would never want to be that stone cold type of a person that I am at work." There is general agreement among women in the trades that a woman has to be "tough" to handle the work, not necessarily because job tasks are so demanding, but because they feel they must be able to present male typed traits in order to satisfy management or head off criticism from coworkers.

After noticing such effects, many tradeswomen resist the pressure to conduct work as a gendered activity. They may question the assertion that the installation of sheet metal ductwork requires strength by arguing that an understanding of leverage will serve to get the job done. They may protest the symbolism of assigning women to small drill presses and men to larger versions of the same machines, though the operations performed on each are identical. They may stage small but creative rebellions, like the woman who riveted wheels to the bottom of her toolbox and pulled it along behind her on a rope, rather than lugging it from place to place in the shop like her male peers. "What's the matter, too much for you?" jeered coworkers when the rolling work station made its debut. She considered it a personal triumph when wheels appeared under the toolboxes of several men in the months that followed.

Some women ridicule the gendered displays that are intended to show competence. Dolores was a mechanic who had learned her trade as one of the few women in a training program:

When I took a brake maintenance class . . . years ago, the guys started lifting my tires for me and carrying them across the room. I had to go take them to the tire thing [tire buster], you know. And they came over and picked up the tires (laughs). I did not care. They *were* heavy. But you could have just rolled them over there. I didn't tell them that. They were real stupid. You just turn them on the edge and roll them across! You don't have to think about it. They'd pick them up and *carry* them over!

Pointing to the products of their labor rather than incorporating gendered displays into work routines also allows women to reject the backhanded compliment: "You're as good as/smart as/strong as/fast as a man."

Oh, sure, you get customers who come in and treat you like you're doing this wonderful thing. And then I feel bad, because I'm doing exactly what I want to be doing in my life . . . and I'm not struggling to be a mechanic . . . So it's kind of embarrassing when people start giving you all these strokes for 'doing a man's job,' and, 'Gee, it must be real hard for you.'

As they encounter resistance to the dissociation of demonstrated accomplishment from gendered display, many women come to expect that the struggle will be ongoing.

Attempts to take the gender out of work will inevitably fall short of the utopian goal of establishing objective standards for job performance. It is a testimony to the beauty and the bother of human symbolic capacity that notions of work and ability remain subject to interpretation. Yet strategies that stress accomplishment over display have helped open the trades to women to the extent that such tactics disrupt the presumed correspondence between gendered traits and job requirements, the mesh of gendered meanings which does so much to perpetuate the feeling that women do not "belong" in the skilled blue-collar workplace.

CONCLUSION

Occupational settings, no less than households and families, are loci for the production and reproduction of gender in the United States. Not surprisingly, then, the dialectical relations linking style to accomplishment and ideology to practice become especially apparent to workers who cross gender lines in their search for employment. Women may struggle to change the workplace, but many have found that if they allow men to define the terms of that struggle by centering discourse on gendered attributes, the workplace will in turn shape them.

Of course, the reasons for women's historical exclusion from skilled trades in the United States are more complex than they may appear from this brief discussion. As individuals, women and men on the job site do not inevitably develop adversarial relationships. Not all women adopt the activist approach of contesting correspondences between gendered traits and job requirements. Some men believe that gendered displays do little to improve speed or productivity, and subscribe to the adage, "Work smart, not hard." The male instructor who chased the student from under the car did not promote hazardous risks to index bravery. Shifting alliances may form along lines of race or ethnicity in addition to gender. Age differences can also become a factor: some older men, too weary or too wise to carry tires across the room, become as critical of gendered displays as their female coworkers.

Extremely significant in this context are nascent class differences that divide men from one another. To "work smart," to pause for a moment to don safety equipment, to think through a problem before running to the parts shelf or tool chest, all represent work styles that implicitly reconstitute a mental/manual division of labor. In my experience, these styles are more likely to be promoted by supervisors than male workers, suggesting that resistance of male workers to women in the trades may be different in kind than that of their male employers. "Just develop your skills and get your speed up," one foreman advised me. "We can always find an Arnold Schwarzenegger for $3.50 an hour to do the grunt work." The particular types of gendered displays discussed here would therefore more accurately be described as an assertion of working-class male styles, rather than male style per se. It is possible that when working-class men incorporate gendered displays into work routines, they affirm a sort of class solidarity, which women unwittingly threaten to disrupt when they appear to take the side of management by enlisting brains rather than brawn in their approach to job tasks.

These caveats aside, women's efforts to break into the trades over the past twenty years have demonstrated that their power to strategize and to act can indeed have an impact on occupational sex segregation, especially when coordinated with the efforts of community-based advocacy groups. Ultimately, the preconceptions and preferences of men on the job cannot determine women's presence or absence in "non-traditional" occupations. No relationship and no struggle is that one-sided. It has always struck me as curious that men, of whatever class, do most of the acting in neoclassical and even socialist feminist accounts of occupational sex segregation. Depending upon the theory, any shifts in a given pattern of segregation will be dictated by the preferences of male employers and/or employees, whether those preferences are considered a matter of "taste" or motivated by socioeconomic factors. Women must wait for male employees to search for greener pastures elsewhere, or for the introduction of new technologies like the typewriter, or for wartime to bring about the extenuating circumstances that will allow them to assume "traditionally" male roles.[20] This tendency to underplay women's power to act makes sense only to the extent that the structural explanations for job segregation developed by feminists and Marxists address human capital theories which attribute women's economic troubles to women's "voluntary" choices.

Nevertheless, by viewing actors in isolation and by focusing on male resistance to women's presence, most theories of job segregation have rendered invisible the struggle that has accompanied women's movement into skilled blue-collar occupations. After relying initially on skill and determination to make a place for themselves in "non-traditional" employment, tradeswomen have gradually discovered that ability and achievement cannot speak for themselves. Over time they have developed strategies to disrupt the impression of superior competence and productivity fostered when workers "show" gendered traits that correspond to gendered job descriptions.

Fighting occupational sex segregation begins by disentangling gendered displays and notions of gendered capacity from labor performed. Far from representing some rhetorical flourish on the outskirts of culture, meaning and metaphor lie at the heart of hiring decisions and production processes.[21] Rather than arguing that women too are strong, that women are tough, that women have been prepared by typing and macrame to be technically inclined, advocacy groups have done their best to get away from discussions of gendered traits. Work can then be redefined to encompass any mode, any style, of accomplishing a given task. Ignore the significance of gendered meanings in the rush to place women in "men's jobs," and shopfloor relations will continue to transform production into a metaphor for maleness.

NOTES

My thanks to Celeste Morin, Kathy Phillips, Lisa Rofel, and Sylvia Yanagisako for their suggestions and support.

1. Contrast, for example, the approach of Myra H. Strober and Carolyn L. Arnold, "The Dynamics of Occupational Segregation among Bank Tellers," in *Gender in the Workplace*, ed. Clair Brown and Joseph A. Pechman (Washington, D.C.: The Brookings Institution, 1987), 107–157. This study of women's movement into bank telling treats competence as something related to intrinsic job requirements, without considering that requirements and notions of competence can themselves be questioned and meaningfully interpreted.

2. Michèle Barrett, *Women's Oppression Today: Problems in Marxist-Feminist Analysis* (London: Verso, 1980); Nancy Chodorow, *The Reproduction of Mothering: Psychoanalysis and the Sociology of Gender* (Berkeley: University of California Press, 1978); Zillah Eisenstein, ed., *Capitalist Patriarchy and the Case for Socialist Feminism* (New York: Monthly Review Press, 1979).

3. For discussions of a shift in composition from male to female in particular occupations, see Joan M. Greenbaum, *In the Name of Efficiency: Management Theory and Shopfloor Practice in Data-Processing Work* (Philadelphia: Temple University Press, 1979), and Myra H. Strober, "Toward a General Theory of Occupational Sex Segregation: The Case of Public School Teaching," in *Sex Segregation in the Workplace: Trends, Explanations, Remedies*, ed. Barbara F. Reskin (Washington, D.C.: National Academy Press, 1984), 144–156.

4. Margery Davies, "Woman's Place Is at the Typewriter: The Feminization of the Clerical Labor Force," in *Labor Market Segmentation*, ed. Richard Edwards et al. (New York: D.C. Heath, 1975), 279–294; Richard Edwards, *Contested Terrain: The Transformation of the Workplace in the Twentieth Century* (New York: Basic Books, 1979); Ruth Milkman, "Redefining 'Women's Work': The Sexual Division of Labor in the Auto Industry during World War II," *Feminist Studies* 8 (Summer 1982): 337–372; Ruth Milkman, *Gender at Work: The Dynamics of Job Segregation by Sex during World War II* (Berkeley: University of California Press, 1988).

5. Heidi Hartmann, "Capitalism, Patriarchy, and Job Segregation by Sex," in *Women and the Workplace: The Implications of Occupational Segregation*, ed. Martha Blaxall and Barbara Reagan (Chicago: University of Chicago Press, 1976), 137–169; see also Strober.

6. Cf. Graeme Salaman, "The Sociology of Work: Some Themes and Issues," in *The Politics of Work and Occupations*, ed. Geoff Esland and Graeme Salaman (Milton Keynes, England: Open University Press, 1980), 1. Salaman's call for more attention to the role of ideology in "mystifying and buttressing work hierarchies and inequalities" reflects the degree to which the view of ideology as an overlay obscuring more fundamental socioeconomic factors permeates the sociology of work.

7. To reduce discourse on gendered traits to a rationalization for paying women lower wages cannot account for persistent references to gendered traits when employers justify their use of *higher*-paid male labor in skilled trades. Cf. Lourdes Benería, "Gender and the Dynamics of Subcontracting in Mexico City," in *Gender in the Workplace*, ed. Clair Brown and Joseph A. Pechman (Washington, D.C.: The Brookings Institution, 1987), 159–188.

8. Kathleen M. Weston, *The Apprenticeship and Blue Collar System: Putting Women on the Right Track* (Sacramento: California State Department of Education, 1982).

9. On labor market segmentation theory, see Edwards; and David M. Gordon et al., *Segmented Work, Divided Workers: The Historical Transformation of Labor in the United States* (New York: Cambridge University Press, 1982). Theo Nichols' "Management, Ideology and Practice," in Esland and Salaman, 279–302, correctly notes that scholars have studied management more through pronouncements of industry journals and business school texts than through observation of action and decision-making processes. To his list of neglected subjects, I would add the less codified ideologies that affect management practices.

10. Cf. Karen Oppenheim Mason, "Commentary: Strober's Theory of Occupational Sex Segregation," in Reskin, 157–170.

11. Pierre Bourdieu, *Outline of a Theory of Practice* (New York: Cambridge University Press, 1977); John L. Comaroff, *Rules and Processes: The Cultural Logic of Dispute in an African Context* (Chicago: University of Chicago Press, 1981); Marshall Sahlins, *Culture and Practical Reason* (Chicago: University of Chicago Press, 1976). I speak here of ideology in its widest sense, as the culturally constituted symbols, meanings, and everyday "common sense" understandings that allow us to reason and perceive, to persuade, implicate, and struggle.

12. Raymond Williams, *Marxism and Literature* (New York: Oxford University Press, 1977).

13. On the uncelebrated success of such small local programs, see Barbara F. Reskin and Heidi I. Hartmann, eds., *Women's Work, Men's Work: Sex Segregation on the Job* (Washington, D.C.: National Academy Press, 1986). The same authors note that when the OFCCP (Office of Federal Contract Compliance Programs) targeted the mining industry in 1978, the number of women working as underground miners rose from 1 in 10,000 to 1 in 12 within two years.

14. Karl Marx, *Capital* (New York: International Publishers, 1967). See also John Storey, *Managerial Prerogative and the Question of Control* (Boston: Routledge & Kegan Paul, 1983).

15. Less common objections include "men won't work with women around" and "we had one once but she didn't work out," both of which touch on employer concern with production. Also mentioned were "women aren't dependable," "women belong in the home," "women have children and quit," "women can't handle swearing," "we only have one bathroom," and "my wife won't let me hire a woman" (Weston, 139–145).

16. Suzanne J. Kessler and Wendy McKenna, *Gender: An Ethnomethodological Approach* (Chicago: University of Chicago Press, 1978).

17. In Jean Reith Schroedel, *Alone in a Crowd: Women in the Trades Tell Their Stories* (Philadelphia: Temple University Press, 1985), 171.

18. In his labor theory of value, Marx pays relatively little attention to the mode of expending labor power, since it contributes nothing in and of itself to the exchange value of a product. See Isidor Walliman, *Estrangement: Marx's Conception of Human Nature and the Division of Labor* (Westport, Conn.: Greenwood Press, 1981).

19. Sometimes, of course, employers fail to issue required safety equipment to discourage workers from using it, often in the belief that its use will slow down production. This type of overt negligence should not be confused with subtler pressures that associate competence and productivity with displays intended to "show" gendered traits.

20. See Davies; Strober; Strober and Arnold; Milkman 1982, 1988.

21. Cf. James W. Fernandez, *Persuasions and Performances: The Play of Tropes in Culture* (Bloomington: Indiana University Press, 1986).

CHAPTER NINE

Unseen Women at the Academy

CYNTHIA SALTZMAN

On September 26, 1984, 1,600 mostly female clerical and technical employees went on strike against Yale University, the largest employer in the city of New Haven, to protest low wages and lack of promotional opportunities. Striking secretaries, typists, research assistants, and laboratory technicians, members of Local 34 of the Hotel and Restaurant Workers Union, were supported by 950 blue-collar service and maintenance workers, who had already organized in Local 35, the brother local of Local 34.

When picket lines appeared, many students and faculty members refused to cross them and moved 400 classes off campus to churches, private homes, and community centers. Twenty-two dining halls were closed. During the strike, 625 union members and their supporters were arrested in demonstrations. The Yale strike gained national media attention for the issue of comparable worth, of paying equivalent wages for jobs of comparable economic value. It also highlighted the economic plight of women in the United States that has come to be called the feminization of poverty.

It took four consecutive years of organizing, fifteen months of negotiating, and a bitter ten week strike for members of Yale's clerical and technical workers' union to get their first contract. According to one newspaper account, the National Director of Organizing for the Hotel and Restaurant Workers Union estimated that the international union had spent more than $4 million since 1980 in organizing the Yale clerical and technical workers. The newspaper quoted him as saying that "the result was worth it. 'When you consider the anti-union climate in this country—with companies demanding give-backs and unions not organizing—it's one of the great victories in the past 25 years.' "

Supported by a viable organization waging an effective grassroots campaign, women at Yale bucked a growing anti-union sentiment in the country and successfully formed a union. As clerical and technical workers across the United States become involved in union organizing struggles, particularly on university campuses, it becomes clear that working class women, whom scholars and many feminist activists have often considered to be at the fringes of the women's movement in this country, are in fact not only in the vanguard of fighting for women's equality on the job, but are winning some of the biggest victories for organized labor in this country. Clerical employees, who represent over one-third of all women in the paid labor force, are, in the name of women's equality, spearheading workplace efforts to organize unions precisely at a time when the American labor movement is otherwise on the decline.

My research on this trend is one of an increasing number of anthropological attempts to study American women's workplace culture and resistance, a subject area hitherto the domain of feminist social historians and sociologists.[1] This essay, in keeping with the anthropological accounts in this volume, looks at the way in which women at Yale came to understand concepts of gender through social action.

The union struggle at Yale helped women to clarify their interests, define their rights, and broaden their own understanding of their sphere and influence. First, it made clear that work on the job is a salient realm for women and that "women's work," including clerical work, is as valuable as "men's work." Second, it made clear that women ought to be paid adequately for the work they do. Third, it stressed that the path to secure adequate pay was through collective organization. By pressing these points, the union drive provided a context in which women saw the workplace as their domain, as much as the home and the community, and saw the fight for rights in the workplace as a fight for women's rights. During the union struggle at Yale, women created new definitions of themselves as women, workers, members of the working-class, and disadvantaged. But ultimately the focus of their self-perception shifted from a sense of disadvantage to a commitment to activism. Through active involvement in organizing, women who had previously viewed unions as a male domain claimed the union as their own vehicle for achieving workplace equality.

NATIONAL CONTEXT AND LOCAL CONDITIONS

The events at Yale—the May 18, 1983 Local 34 close election victory (1,267 to 1,228 in favor of a union), the subsequent strike less than one year later, and the successful negotiation of a first clerical and technical workers' contract at the university—were especially noteworthy when placed in the general context of labor organizing. These events occurred as the American labor movement was confronting its greatest crisis since the 1930s. Major industrial unions in the country were struggling during a period of lay-offs and concessions. The approximately 2,700 office workers at Yale, nearly 80% of whom are women, successfully organized a union at the university in the wake of an event that was nationally disastrous to unions, the national air traffic controllers' strike. President Reagan insisted that the strike was illegal, and subsequently fired workers who walked off their jobs, sending an implicit message to all workers that active organizing would not always be to their benefit.

In 1980, although the gap had narrowed, only 15.9% of women in the United States work force were in labor unions, compared to 28.4% of men, and union membership had fallen to an all time postwar low of 20.9% of the labor force. Over one-third of all employed women in this country were working in clerical jobs, and they remained the largest category of wage workers who were nonunionized. Yet, these figures gloss an important trend, which suggests that female clerical workers are playing a critical role in shaping the future of organized American labor. Statistics indicate a gradual increase in the percentage of white-collar workers in unions. In fact, the fastest growing unions throughout the seventies were those with a high percentage of office workers.[2]

The increased unionization of female clerical workers in the United States has many causes. As women work for an increasing number of their adult years they become more and more concerned with higher wages and promotional opportunities. Moreover, the organization of work itself is changing. As it becomes more mechanized and impersonal over time, worker dissatisfaction grows. For these reasons, unions interested in expanding their ranks are focusing upon office workers as appropriate targets of unionization. Finally, a feminist sensibility, or what Milkman calls "trade union feminism," has begun to pervade clerical workers' orientation towards work and lead to changed attitudes about unionization.[3] Women faced with the prospects of low-paying or dead-end jobs, have a new consciousness or heightened expectations of work. Union organizing at Yale, I discovered, represented employees' growing realization that they need to work, that they are in the work force to stay, and that, unless they protest through collective action, the university will continue to pay them with low wages in dead-end jobs.

Employees at Yale during the time of my research came from diverse social backgrounds. There was a relatively transient population: young graduate students' wives, many of whom were highly educated; young single women who were geographically mobile; young men and women who were technical employees and used their jobs as stepping stones to graduate school or better paid positions elsewhere. The more permanent population was mostly represented by persons living in the greater urban area: divorced, widowed, and single heads of household and married women working to maintain their family's standard of living. Women in nearly every category were becoming increasingly aware of the value of their work and troubled by their low wages and lack of job mobility. During the course of organizing, all these categories of women began to define themselves in terms of their shared experience as women in the workplace.

Women clerical and technical workers at Yale who voted for a union saw themselves as permanent members of the American work force and realized that their income was critical to their own support and the well-being of their households; they felt that only if they organized to represent their interests could they improve their pay and chances for promotions. As their identity became strongly linked to the work they did on the job, their collective organization and identification with other women workers became the path to ensuring individual household economic security. Women began to define themselves in gendered terms, as women with collective needs, rather than as individuals with conflicting needs from disparate class and familial backgrounds. Moreover, women began to see how the workplace defined their economic position, regardless of background and family position, and became aware of the devaluation of female gender-typed work at the university.

EARLY ORGANIZING EFFORTS

Clerical workers in this country have suffered a steady decline in their salaries relative to other occupations. As Braverman first noted, in 1959 the earnings for clerical and sales jobs were almost equivalent to blue-collar manual jobs but by 1970, only a decade later, the salaries for clerical workers were below all forms of blue-collar jobs.[4] Women from working-class backgrounds in white-collar clerical jobs can no longer claim any real economic advantage over manual laborers. Women from working-class backgrounds at Yale who received college educations have become frustrated that their new credentials buy them no more than the same secretarial job that their mothers had with only a high school diploma.

At Yale, the problem of relatively declining wages was exacerbated by another phenomenon. The increased bureaucratization of university management and the greater mechanization of work in the 1960s (continuing throughout the next decade into the 1980s) gradually led employees to shift their view of the university as benevolently paternalistic. They began to see it as a powerful institution with little concern for their needs.

One woman who came to work at Yale in 1958 described the intimacy of the workplace at that time:

The University treated its employees in a very paternalistic fashion then, as if we were one big family. That was both good and bad. There were no standard rules governing salary, vacations, etc., but if an individual employee needed a raise or was getting married and wanted time off or a loan, that was generally granted. You felt you would be taken care of in an emergency . . ."[5].

By the late sixties, however, the women's movement began to influence women's understanding of their working conditions, especially their low status and low wages. One militant woman, writing in 1969, reflected a changed attitude:

A lot of anger is building up. Yale is an institution, run by underpaid females—women work in the kitchens, at the brooms, at the typewriters, in the library stacks, and in the homes. Women work at one-third men's wages. Yale is a male dominated institution whose primary function is to produce the future male leaders of the male society.[6]

In 1965 after almost a 20 year lull in white-collar union activity at Yale, clerical and technical workers began a series of organizing attempts that persisted over an eighteen year period and eventually culminated in the election victory of Local 34 of the Hotel and Restaurant Workers Union on May 18, 1983. Attempts to organize office workers at Yale in the sixties were coincident with a wave of popular protest in New Haven against racial discrimination, substandard housing for the poor, American involvement in the Vietnam War, and later, concern with the rights of women. Some of the key union activists at Yale in the 1960s saw themselves as involved in a broad social protest against a host of issues that plagued America. The fact that New Haven was home to well-organized groups of liberal and leftist political activists who were vocal in their support of civil rights and later their opposition to the War in Vietnam made the social climate in the city a hospitable one in which to engage in union activity. Left-leaning union activists attempted to build grassroots participation in creating a more re-sponsive, egalitarian, and democratic society. By the late 1960s, union or-ganizing at the university spearheaded by community activists took on the character of a social movement, an all-encompassing vision of social change.

But young single women, highly-educated, products of the sixties, often voiced their protest in harsh terms that estranged the ranks of older, long-time employees at Yale. Paradoxically, despite the employees' fervor, the centrality of work in women's lives seemed to become subordinated during the course of unionizing to a broader political agenda. One local newspaper reported that the union movement "lost the support of the married, working women at Yale early in the campaign when its dungaree-clad organizers began talking to employees about the 'oppression of the bosses' and the 'fat cats' on the Yale Corporation who were indifferent to the needs of the workers. The socialist rhetoric was distasteful to many employees . . ." Fur-thermore, the language of protest that encouraged women to fight against male authoritarianism in the workplace, as well as in the home was partic-ularly threatening to a large group of married workers who relied upon their husbands for emotional and financial support.

Moreover, throughout the 1960s and well into the 1970s, unions that addressed the needs of clerical workers still seemed to buy the idea that women worked largely for pin money or that they were incapable of or-ganizing. At Yale, the union campaigns throughout the sixties and into the seventies received only scanty financial resources and few organizers. Unions gave more lip service than concrete support to clerical and technical em-ployees' efforts to form a union on campus. Moreover, there were (and still are) many aspects of university employment that workers enjoyed and wished to preserve, and they feared that a union's presence would destroy those very qualities: the informality, intimacy, and the flexibility of work conditions that existed in many Yale departments.

Despite the feminist rhetoric of some union supporters, the pro-union activists at Yale in the 1960s had to contend, as did their counterparts during earlier and later efforts, with images of union membership as a largely male blue-collar phenomenon. They had to deal with employees' suspicions that unions were uninterested in the real concerns of a mostly female clerical and technical work force and that even if unions appreciated employees' true needs, they were too weak to defend them against a powerful Yale administration. Only later at Yale, in the 1980s, with the backing of an effective union organization, did women clerical and technical workers wholeheartedly embrace unionization as a vehicle for social change. As women assumed critical positions in the union movement on campus, they also began to reconceptualize unions and to see them, not as narrowly gender linked, but as means for women to seek real change.

TWO COMPETING UNIONS AT YALE

Two unions, each eager to form the new collective bargaining unit on campus, bitterly contested control over office workers' attempts to organize at Yale. The United Auto Workers had been trying for nearly two years to organize all the office workers on campus when, on a cold windy evening in November 1980, the Hotel and Restaurant workers announced their decision to enter the competition.

As a small group of UAW supporters, mostly women, passed out fliers crying for a 'call to unity' between the two unions, the dynamics for a union battle were set into motion. With the entry of a second union, workers not only opposed management, but were pitted against each other. That competition continued until January 1982, when the UAW withdrew from the effort and cleared the path for Local 34. As an anthropologist studying the increased movement towards the unionization of female clerical workers, I was in the delicate position of maneuvering among factions that supported either one of the two unions or the university in the dispute.

The United Auto Workers was hampered in its efforts by the fact that the affiliated international union was confronting its greatest crisis since the 1930s and its organizers were outnumbered by over three to one. But also damaging were the union's assumptions about gender, which shaped its organizing tactics. The UAW acted on the premise that women's socialization limited organizing activity and that with the proper education women would become more confident about their own self worth and more assertive about fighting for their rights. It placed the source of women's problems partially in their own training and background. The organizers adhered to what sociologists call an "individual model" of behavior and change. By assuming that "factors producing inequities at work are somehow carried inside the individual," the union's strategy had the effect of reinforcing the view that women's problems resided in their own psychology.[7] This approach became an excuse for a slow moving campaign. As one employee told me, "I don't think we need so much education. It's demeaning."

Although the UAW did not adequately emphasize learning by doing and the organizers failed to translate their ideology into action, they did stimulate interest in a union and laid the groundwork among employees for acceptance of a clerical and technical workers' union at Yale. Local 34 had the distinct advantage of being able to build upon this union's initial efforts, not least of which was the forging of friendships between "townies" and Yale graduate student wives.

One graduate student wife, Sue Ellen (a pseudonym), who worked in the medical school, told me that she felt "rejected and scorned" by her co-workers because of her status as graduate student wife and in turn viewed the townspeople as "creeps, unintelligent and unimpressive individuals with low ambition." She continued to feel this way until she began organizing for the UAW and met Dorothy (another pseudonym), a clerical worker in the medical school at Yale, and a woman who defied Sue Ellen's stereotyped image of the "ignorant New Haven townie." Dorothy was bright, cunning, and politically astute. Sue Ellen viewed her own decision to support the UAW drive as a dramatic turning point in her education, politics, and understanding of the workplace. Once Sue Ellen turned to me wearing an expression of some amazement and said, "You know I really am a *laborer*." Through her discussions with the UAW organizers and other employees, she had completely transformed her point of view about the need for a union at Yale, and her own identity as a woman and as a worker.

THE SUCCESS OF LOCAL 34

Local 34 was successful in organizing clerical and technical workers at the university because it stressed the centrality of work in women's lives and built upon the premise that women's employment was both individually and socially advantageous. The union at Yale gave credence—political support and eloquent verbal expression—to an idea that was already gaining widespread societal acceptance: that paid employment was an appropriate sphere of adult women's labor and lives, desirous to women as individuals and to society at large. For millions of women of the working-class and middle-class, paid employment had long been an economic reality of their adult years, but now on the brink of the 1980s and into that decade, women's paid employment in the United States had come to be socially sanctioned as salient, respectable, and critical to women's individual economic independence and to the support of women's households and families. The union effectively and powerfully articulated a pervasive and changing attitude towards women's work into the related notion that it was in women's collective and self-interest, both as individuals and as family members, to strive for decent wages. Women's paid work had in fact long been a critical necessity for adult women of the working class, but in the 1980's, women's adult employment gained middle-class respectability.

As women work outside the home for more years of their lives and assume financial responsibilities for themselves and their families, they no longer see their jobs as temporary. Women have become increasingly concerned with promotional opportunities, adequate salaries, and job security. Moreover, women are increasingly concerned with the status derived from their job. Clerical and technical workers at Yale who voted for a union saw themselves—regardless of their background—as permanent members of the American work force and realized that their income was critical to their own support and the well-being of their households. Collective action became the vehicle for improving their pay and chances for promotions.

Local 34 used a number of highly effective tactics to organize women at Yale and to attract women to the union from diverse social backgrounds. (1) It emphasized grassroots democracy and individual self-empowerment. (2) It reinforced women's ties to their husbands and built solidarity between the mostly female clerical and technical work force and the mostly male blue-collar workers in Local 35. (3) It transformed union activism into a social struggle concerned with issues of comparable worth. (4) Finally, it turned organizing into a broad-based community movement.

The union proclaimed that all clerical and technical workers at Yale were discriminated against by virtue of their gender and in so doing united women from different backgrounds. By the time of the Local 34 strike, the rhetoric had shifted again, from an emphasis upon the need for power, respect, and dignity, to the particular discrimination women workers confront in the workplace, the feminization of poverty, and the issues of comparable worth. It was with such shifts in rhetoric, a conscious highlighting of a trade union feminism, and the testing of democracy in action by promoting women in leadership roles during the negotiating process, that women who had been shy and timid emerged as dynamic speakers and leaders as they spoke before large audiences of several hundred persons. The major flaw in all this, which deserves separate treatment, was that the union's use of high pressure tactics frequently alienated employees who came to view the union as an intrusive and coercive force.

GRASS-ROOTS DEMOCRACY

The thrust of organizing focused upon female solidarity and women's leadership, but the union campaign also began to articulate the relationship between issues of class and gender. Local 34's political strategy was to form a loose coalition with other constituent groups at the university and isolate the administration. The union, by stressing the centrality of work in women's lives and highlighting the issue of comparable worth, dramatized the bread and butter issues of the union conflict and translated them into a contemporary issue of economic justice with broad appeal.

From the very beginning, Local 34 decided to wage a "positive campaign and to stress the advantages of union organization rather than the disadvantages of working at Yale. In this way, Local 34 began to project the union as a vehicle through which clerical and technical workers could gain respect and recognition for their work, as opposed to simply a mechanism for obtaining higher wages or better benefits."[8]

Employees were aware that their income was critical to their self-support, as well as the support of their households, and through the union, they began to fight for "respect and dignity," key issues of the strike that relate to an egalitarian conception of power, the right to make decisions that determine one's own work situation.[9] These ideas certainly had ramifications for women's lives, in their kitchens and in their bedrooms. Nevertheless, by focusing its rhetoric unambiguously on the workplace, the union never suffered the fate of ERA and pro-choice campaigns that ended up being labelled anti-family because they broached issues that threatened women's domesticity or the social cohesion of the family. The union's strength was that its campaign upheld the values of a two-paycheck family that had become an economic necessity for so many clerical and technical workers at Yale.

The union meetings were very effective in getting women to confront the seriousness of their economic situation head-on. One full-time organizer said, "Most of these people are blue-collar people with hopes and dreams for middle-class status. The union's organizing effort forced a lot of women to sit down and take a look at reality. They had to give up their hopes and dreams a little".[10]

Ruth Sidel in her book on the plight of poor women in affluent America describes how union organizers at Yale talked individually with many women who had a basic lack of self-confidence, and encouraged them to talk about their opinions. The union attempted to recognize indigenous leaders among groups of Yale employees and then scheduled successive meetings in which women were encouraged to discuss, "What are we worth." Sidel examines how the process was understood from the union's perspective.

As Kim [McLoughlin, a full-time Local 34 organizer,] describes it, this process was reminiscent both of consciousness raising among women's groups in this country and of 'Speak Bitterness' meetings in the liberated areas of China during the late 1930s and 1940s. Once leaders were identified in a Chinese village, the women of the village were brought together to hear one or two women speak about their bitter lives. The others would identify so intensely with the experience of other women that their own anger was mobilized and they could then perceive their own oppression all the more clearly.[11]

The union's strategy of providing a forum for women to talk among themselves led to women recognizing and identifying with the power of their mutual anger. One sixty-two-year-old woman who had worked at Yale for almost ten years opposed the idea of a union. After talking with Local 34 organizers, she became convinced that low wages were a sign of economic discrimination against women. Fighting for a union she said, was not just a fight for clerical and technical workers at Yale, but a fight for women all across the country.

Local 34 was successful in tapping into and reinforcing women's new expectations of work, of politicizing consciousness, and channeling it into a union protest. However, no ideological commitment could adequately compensate for a weak political campaign. Women wanted to be able to exercise their political clout. Employees were most concerned about siding with a winning team and wanted to join a union that would ultimately be strong in negotiating with a powerful administration. Local 34 allowed the greatest possibility for workers' participation in the formation of a union. The focus upon women, democratic action, and power transformed the union at Yale during the negotiating process and the events of the strike, into a union *for* women, not just *of* women.

Ruth Milkman has pointed out in a recent study of two feminist organizational efforts within the labor movement what happens when labor unions organize without paying close attention to issues of gender. Milkman says that when unions focus on women as members of occupational groups that just happen to be largely female, rather than show a special commitment to organizing women as women, the result is that "women are squarely *in* the labor movement, but are generally still not of the labor movement".[12] Local 34 of the Hotel and Restaurant Workers Union chose to emphasize Yale's pattern of discrimination against female clerical workers, not because union leaders necessarily adhered to a feminist ideology, but because this emphasis proved to be a strategy that worked.

Although most of the people in the leadership of the international union and the chief negotiator for Local 34 were male, female clerical and technical workers played the central role in determining the terms of the contract to be negotiated and they formed the union's negotiating team. At an institution which places a hallmark on an intelligentsia, articulate clerical and technical workers became the new teachers on campus and the most eloquent and effective spokespersons for the union. For the first time, employees were on an equal status with the administration, sitting across from representatives at the negotiating table.

INVOLVING MEN

By involving husbands and blue-collar workers on campus, Local 34 established a union that gave credence to the importance of the two-paycheck family in Yale workers' lives. By rallying the support of women and men, it also united female clerical, and male blue-collar workers in the cause of forming a clerical/technical union on campus.

At Yale, many husbands supported their wives in the task of organizing, demonstrating both the husbands' and wives' conscious awareness that two incomes were needed to support the family's standard of living. By enlisting office workers husbands' support for the drive, Local 34's strategy buttressed organizing as a cooperative family endeavor and in so doing, intensified women's commitment to organizing. Of particular interest is that women married to blue-collar workers at the university were invariably pro-union, although their loyalties to the two competing unions on campus were divided. Local 34's characterization of itself as a sister local to the blue-collar union on campus, and its emphasis upon the ways in which the two unions would be able to strengthen and support one another eventually had considerable appeal to this group of women.

Local 34 relied upon the support of the blue-collar workers in Local 35 who also walked out in sympathy. The cooperative efforts between the two groups refutes one of the explanations social scientists have offered to explain the low level of office workers' union affiliation. This argument states that women identify union membership with low status blue-collar labor and that being in marginal positions, office workers are particularly status conscious. They therefore set up artificial barriers between themselves and manual workers and prefer to identify with management. In fact, office workers were aware that by joining with Local 35 they would become a more powerful bargaining unit with considerable leverage in negotiations with the university.

Local 34 organizers encouraged male blue-collar workers on campus to help organize their wives, relatives, friends, and other office workers they knew on campus. To show their support for the union drive, blue-collar workers in Local 35 agreed to contribute a small amount of their union dues each month toward the union organizing drive. Over time these dues amounted to a considerable sum. June Nash writes about how working-class women's husbands often oppose or interfere with women's efforts to organize and that gaining husbands' support may be a critical strategy in women's organization.[13] Local 34, rather than regarding the family household or women's husbands as a hindrance to organizing, strengthened the family unit, by turning organizing into a family concern.

Local 34 exploited an effective strategy that previous unions attempting to organize at Yale had not tapped. They paid home visits to employees and in the process broke down the barriers between home and the workplace. Husbands became involved in discussions about the union and participated in strategy sessions. Children were taught to sing union songs. Union organizing became a family enterprise. (It must also be said that, in strengthening individual self-confidence and self-assertion, the union campaign gave some women in destructive relationships or failing marriages the strength to leave.)

COMPARABLE WORTH AND THE FEMINIZATION OF POVERTY

By declaring its strike as among the first to be a national test case for the principle of comparable worth, the union created an issue with persuasive appeal for the press, as well as for workers on campus. Historically, women have gravitated toward struggles for social reform of all kinds, especially those that recognize women's special needs as wives and mothers, a condition that most trade union organizing discounts. At Yale, unionized "blue-collar" workers, mainly men, who are custodians, dining hall workers and truck drivers, earn more than female clerical and technical workers who often do work that requires more responsibility and specialized knowledge. Activists at Yale contended that the university discriminated against its female employees and that as one of the wealthiest universities in the country, it could well afford to pay clerical and technical staff wages higher than the average of $13,424.

"Say 'female poverty'," an article in *The Nation* magazine read, "and most people think of mothers on welfare. But female poverty has other, less expected faces. They belong to the thirty-four-year-old assistant editor [at Yale] whose work requires a reading knowledge of French and German but whose $13,600 salary allows her to buy only one meal a day, and the forty-three-year-old editorial assistant with a master's degree who lives with her fourteen-year-old daughter in a studio, whose rent absorbs almost half of her $13,000 salary."[14]

The "feminization of poverty" is a phrase that most often refers to the plight of the growing numbers of single female heads of household with children in the United States who are on welfare or in dire financial need. But as the *Nation* article suggested, the definition of the phrase might be expanded to include the young single secretary at Yale who will in all probability marry later than her counterpart in past decades and spend more of her adult years as a single woman and supporting herself on a Yale clerical worker's salary; she finds that she is barely able to manage. Furthermore, the phrase might apply to the single heads of households who find it impossible to survive on Yale wages and must work two jobs or collect food stamps to supplement their income; or even to women who define themselves as coming from middle-class backgrounds, who find that two incomes are increasingly necessary and are becoming the norm in order for a family to maintain a middle-class standard of living and not plunge into a cycle of downward mobility. In short, the term might encompass several groups of women at Yale and other places like it across the country who are faced with new and urgent economic contingencies.

Many Yale employees believed that the university was waging an all-out anti-union campaign. Their fears seemed confirmed when the administration at Yale hired two outside firms to combat unionization: first Segal O'Conner and Kanin and later in mid-1983, the Chicago based law firm of Seyfarth, Shaw, Fairweather and Geraldson. Although many women at Yale felt particularly vulnerable to management resistance because they were aware of how easily they could be replaced, as the union on campus grew more powerful and politically effective, employees believed that they had the strength to protect their jobs.

THE TOWN-GOWN CONTROVERSY

The union capitalized upon the town-gown controversy that had plagued the university almost from its inception. Long standing local hostilities towards Yale were an expression, in part, of a working-class antagonism towards Yale as a landowning Yankee institution for the wealthy.[15] The union skillfully exploited this tradition and manipulated the media to create a larger climate of public opinion in support of the striking workers. Bumper stickers read, "Beep, Beep—Yale is Cheap"; money poured in for a union hardship fund for striking workers most in need. The victory at Yale seemed to be not only the culmination of a town-gown controversy, a reaction of the New Haven community to the elitism and privilege of the university, but an attack upon the very meaning of the notion of a "non-profit" corporation.

By the time of the strike, New Haven had gained the dubious reputation of being the sixth poorest city in the country with a population over 100,000, according to United States Census reports. Striking workers who gathered community support for their cause no longer looked upon Yale, a non-profit institution, as charitable or benevolent. In the eyes of workers, Yale had become a big business. Its management had grown large and impersonal, and workers exhorted Yale to behave responsibly as a humane institution of higher learning, and grant employees fair wages and promotional opportunities. But at the same time that workers attacked Yale, they also embraced Yale as their home. For the most part, those who supported the union, hoped to remain at Yale and took pride in their role in maintaining the university as a great institution. Their message seemed to be, if you want us to do our jobs well, pay us well, respect us, and give us hope for the future.

HIGH PRESSURE TACTICS

For all I have said, the union's tactics were sometimes double-edged. While many employees were drawn to the union by the organizers' enthusiasm for grassroots democracy, home visits, and involving husbands in the process of organizing, others complained that their passion sometimes bordered on fanaticism. The union successfully built group solidarity but sometimes at the expense of individual freedom. Workers who complained that the union's high pressure organizing tactics intruded upon their personal and private lives became alienated from the union movement. The union's high pressure tactics, ironically, threatened to undermine the balance between the group democracy and individual self-empowerment that the union itself tried so hard to maintain.

Local 34's strategy was particularly effective at placing group peer pressure upon an employee and ostracizing that employee if she or he failed to support the union. One pro-UAW Sterling Memorial Library worker told me that her office had become an uncomfortable place to work because many of her coworkers, Local 34 supporters, had begun to ignore and avoid her on the job and during lunch hours. Moreover, her social circle on weekends that had revolved around the same set of individuals had begun to dissolve as coworkers dropped her from their social set.

UAW supporters accused Local 34 of behaving like a cult and they viewed their use of high-pressured tactics critically and with alarm. Employees, they said, who had expressed just passing or moderate interest in the union were quickly drawn into a whirlwind of organizing activity. UAW supporters claimed that before employees were knowledgeable about the union or fully understood its implications, they were placed on the steering committee of Local 34 and accorded a status and level of responsibility that was blown far out of proportion to their actual level of commitment. According to this view, employees who refused to cooperate and succumb to Local 34 pressure were contacted by the union again and again until the union succeeded in breaking down the employee's resistance to unionization. Stories circulated about workers who loudly and angrily objected to the continual onslaught of union propaganda and the lack of deference accorded their wishes to be left alone. Confronted by union supporters during lunch hours, mid-day breaks, strolls down hallways, and at home visits, some employees began to experience these unsolicited attempts to convert them as a form of harassment. Some were genuinely angered by Local 34's home visits and regarded unannounced organizers' visits as a serious violation of their privacy. Other employees were actually intimidated by the appearance of the organizers on their doorstep during the evening hours. One woman reportedly confronted Local 34 organizers who approached her home with the comment, "I didn't ask the Pentecostals to come here, and I didn't ask you," and slammed her door.

Critics of Local 34 said that the continual reiteration of Local 34's union pitch, the constant repetitive refrain bidding workers to become active and join the union, had the impact of a cultist's chant. An employee might eventually succumb to union pressure as her defenses broke down under stress, or as one worker told me, "The path of least resistance to get people to stop bothering you" is just to give in to the union pressure.

The union drive at Yale created a culture of politics, power and persuasion. A new rank and file leadership emerged that, precisely because it was so successful as an instrument of cultural change, also threatened sometimes to compromise the very values of collective participation that were at the core of that change. Women at Yale, new to union organizing, were particularly sensitive to maintaining a balance between individual empowerment and social solidarity. They viewed paid organizers' and indigenous leaders' use of high pressure tactics as a threat to this balance. During this period of social action, women engaged in a process of cultural self-definition, of negotiating gender, that encompassed the individual, social, and political aspects of their lives. They recognized their importance as workers, the power of the group, and the need for action. On the whole, these different levels of redefinition reinforced and supported each other. It would be a mistake, however, to assume that this was or could always be the case, or that the process would produce no casualties.

CONCLUSIONS

By the time of the Local 34 victory and certainly by the time of the Yale strike, fundraising campaigns to increase the university's endowment had reached an all-time high and Yale President Giamatti was beginning to pull the university out of the red. Operating deficits that had plagued the school for a decade were disappearing and new stability on campus reigned. Employees at Yale had the assurance that Yale, unlike a manufacturing concern or an insurance company, was not going to leave the community, and that the formation of a union or the occurrence of a strike was not going to induce the firm to close up shop and vacate the premises.

In December 1984, after almost 10 weeks of striking, Local 34 voted to suspend the strike for six weeks. This plan, which was at the time controversial among workers, allowed the union to avoid picketing empty buildings during school vacation. The union decided that the strike would be resumed at the start of the new semester unless it could reach a settlement with the administration. Finally on January 22, 1985 about 900 members of Local 34 in a mood of euphoria almost unanimously agreed to a tentative contract worked out by negotiators.

The contract among other gains established a new adjusted salary scale that recognized the years of service of employees and gave them substantial raises. The average salary would go up 35 percent over 3½ years, from $13,424 to about $18,000 over the life of the contract. In the fall of 1987 when contract negotiations once again seemed deadlocked, the pending clerical and technical workers' strike attracted media attention, and public figures like Jesse Jackson spoke at union rallies. Contract negotiations were extended past the strike deadline and the union and Yale management managed to forestall a strike and agree upon a contract.

When unions devote more of their energies to organizing women, more union drives undertaken by women in this country may culminate in success. Unions do not create the underlying historical conditions that give rise to organizing activity but they may play an important role in stimulating protest and shaping demand at a particular historical time.[16] Research on why men in the United States outnumber women in unions by a ratio of over two to one ought to focus more on the role unions play in shaping protest, attracting female employees and giving support to women's union efforts.

The union campaign at Yale was particularly effective because it linked issues of gender and class; it got women to see that *as women* they were confined to low paid, dead end jobs despite promises of status, but that they also shared a struggle in common with the blue-collar workers on campus. The union, moreover, during the strike, managed to rally workers around the issues of comparable worth and the feminization of poverty, without creating a sense of female exclusivity barring male workers, husbands, and supportive men on campus (students and professors) from the union struggle. It did this by working with family units and by focusing on the ways in which the two unions could mutually strengthen each other.

Local 34, through constant debate and discussion, created an awareness among clerical and technical employees that gender inequality was not just a feature of their socialization or familial situation, which the UAW emphasized, but a condition of the workplace, in which a division of labor created low paid "female jobs." During the course of organizing, women became aware of the way in which the social context of the workplace limited their options, salaries, and prospects for promotions and how these limitations made it difficult for them to provide adequately for themselves and their families. To women at Yale who collected food stamps or had to work two jobs in order to make ends meet, the university became an enemy of the home. Women who may have once borne their plight as a personal problem recognized that they shared their lot with other women workers. The union affirmed women's status as single heads of household, wives, and mothers; sensitive to their special needs, it won their support and devotion.

NOTES

1. See Nina Shapiro-Perl, "The Piece Rate: Class Struggle on the Shop Floor: Evidence from the Costume Jewelry Industry in Providence, Rhode Island," in *Case Studies in the Labor Process,* ed. Andrew Zimbalist (New York: Monthly Review Press, 1977), 277–98; Helen Safa, "Women, Production, and Reproduction in Industrial Capitalism: A Comparison of Brazilian and U.S. Factory Workers," in *Women, Men, and the International Division of Labor,* eds. June Nash and Maria Patricia Fernandez-Kelly (Albany: SUNY Press, 1983), 95–116; Karen Brodkin Sacks and Dorothy Remy, eds., *My Troubles Are Going to Have Trouble with Me: Everyday Trials and Triumphs of Women Workers* (New Brunswick, New Jersey: Rutgers University Press, 1984); Ann Bookman and Sandra Morgen, eds., *Women and the Politics of Empowerment: Perspectives from the Workplace and the Community* (Philadelphia: Temple University

Press., 1987); Louise Lamphere, *From Working Daughters to Working Mothers: Immigrant Women in a New England Industrial Community* (Ithaca, New York: Cornell University Press, 1987); Patricia Zavella, *Women's Work and Chicano Families: Cannery Workers of the Santa Clara Valley* (Ithaca, New York: Cornell University Press, 1987).

2. The statistics in text are taken from U.S. Bureau of Labor Statistics, Bulletin 2105, *Earnings and Other Characteristics of Organized Workers*, May 1980, 1981, p. 9. See also Jean Tepperman, *Not Servants, Not Machines: Office Workers Speak Out* (Boston: Beacon Press, 1976); Louise Kapp Howe, *Pink Collar Workers* (New York: G. P. Putnam's Sons, 1977); Evelyn Nakano Glenn and Roslyn L. Feldberg, "Clerical Work: The Female Occupation," in *Women: A Feminist Perspective*, ed. Jo Freeman (California: Mayfield Publishing Co., 1979), 313–39; Phyllis Marynick Palmer and Sharon Lee Grant, *The Status of Clerical Workers: A Summary Analysis of Research Findings and Trends*, Women's Studies Program, George Washington University, Business and Professional Women's Foundation, Washington, D.C. 1979.

3. Roberta Goldberg, *Organizing Women Office Workers: Dissatisfaction, Consciousness, and Action* (New York: Praeger Publishers, 1983). Ruth Milkman, "Women Workers, Feminism and the Labor Movement since the 1960's," in *Women, Work and Protest: A Century of U.S. Women's Labor History*, ed. *Ruth Milkman* (Boston: Routledge and Kegan Paul, 1985), 300–22.

4. Harry Braverman, *Labor and Monopoly Capital* (New York: Monthly Review Press, 1974), 297–98.

5. Office and Professional Employees International Union (OPEIU), 1976, "Employees Speak Out," Union flyer, Personal Collection.

6. *Yale Break*, 1970, Yale University Sterling Memorial Library, New Haven, Connecticut, Manuscripts and Archives.

7. Rosabeth Moss Kanter, *Work and Family in the United States: A Critical Review and Agenda for Research and Policy* (New York: Russell Sage Foundation, 1977), 262.

8. Toni Gilpin, Gary Isaac, Dan Letwin and Jack McKivigan, *On Strike for Respect: The Clerical and Technical Workers' Strike at Yale University (1984–85)* (Chicago: Charles H. Kerr Publishing Company, 1988), 25.

9. Karen Brodkin Sacks, "Two Faces of Leadership," Paper presented at the 81st annual meeting of the American Anthropological Association, Washington, D.C., 1982; Karen Brodkin Sacks, *Caring by the Hour*, (Urbana and Chicago: University of Illinois Press, 1988), 129–31.

10. Ruth Sidel, *Women and Children Last* (New York: Penguin Books, 1986), 63.

11. Sidel, 63.

12. Milkman.

13. June Nash, "Women in Resistance in Bolivia," in *Women Cross-Culturally: Change and Challenge*, ed. Ruby Rohrlich-Leavitt (The Hague: Mouton, 1975), 261–75.

14. *The Nation* 239, no. 18 (December 1, 1984): 572.

15. Raymond E. Wolfinger, *The Politics of Progress* (New Jersey: Prentice-Hall, Inc., 1974).

16. Frances Fox Piven and Richard A. Cloward, *Poor People's Movements: Why they Succeed, How they Fail* (New York: Vintage Books, 1977).

CHAPTER TEN

Two Faces of the State: Women, Social Control, and Empowerment

SANDRA MORGEN

Gender is one of the most hotly contested issues in contemporary politics in the United States. Public policy debates and social programs are both arenas in which changing conceptions of gender are articulated, challenged, and shaped. If we are to understand the complex dynamics of the political and cultural construction of gender in this society, our theories must comprehend the role of the state in that process.

Feminist, and particularly Marxist-feminist, theories of the state have tended to focus on the ways that the state reproduces capitalist and patriarchal social relations. The theoretical emphasis of this literature has been to implicate the state in the oppression of women primarily "through its support for a specific form of household: the family household dependent largely upon a male wage and upon female domestic servicing."[1] Mimi Abramovitz's recent historical study of social welfare policy in this country shows a persistent, albeit changing, social welfare policy, which is based primarily on preserving the "traditional family ethic."[2] This point is also central to Zillah Eisenstein's influential work on the specific efforts of the Reagan administration to restore traditional family values, structures, and functions through its neoconservative family, welfare, and abortion policies.[3] Rosalind Petchesky's excellent study of abortion policy echoes this theme, demonstrating how gender ideology and women's lives are deeply etched by state policy on the family and reproduction.[4]

However the role of the contemporary capitalist state in the political/cultural construction of gender goes beyond its function as preserver and shaper of patriarchal nuclear families. In fact, one of the most important dimensions of women's relationship to the contemporary state is as a worker in state or state-supported social welfare activities:

[S]ince 1960 the social welfare industry has generated jobs for two out of every five women compared with only one out of every five men. In 1980, women held fully 70% of the 17.3 million social service jobs on all levels of government, including education. Nearly one-third of women worked in the human services compared to only 10% of men.[5]

In this paper I examine women brought into the welfare state as workers, albeit as marginal and temporary workers, addressing this aspect of the state's role in the historically situated production of gender. The site of my research for this paper was a women's center, one of many thousands of community-based organizations that benefitted from the dramatic expansion of state social services in the late 1960s and early 1970s.

In an essay written in 1985, Frances Fox Piven noted that much feminist theory "evinces an almost categorical antipathy to the state," which Piven regards as ironic because, "while women intellectuals characterize relationships with the state as 'dependence,' women activists turn increasingly to the state as the arena for political organization and influence."[6]

In the last few years feminist theories of the state have begun to change, moving away from this kind of reductionist antipathy—with a singleminded focus on the reproductive functions of the state—toward an exploration of what Abramovitz calls the paradoxical character[7] of the state. This newer perspective views the state as a powerful force in shaping both women's lives and cultural constructions of gender. It also sees the state as a primary arena of contestation and the target of resistance by women who challenge state action (and inaction). What I hope to make clear is that although much state policy reinforces traditional gender roles and values, state support of human services, particularly community-based programs, can also have unexpected consequences. It can help promote conditions that allow women to develop alternative conceptions about women in general, feminism, and social relations of power.

THE WOMEN'S HEALTH CENTER

Of the millions of women employed in social welfare work in this country, only a tiny portion work in agencies with explicit social goals. The Women's Health Center (WHC) is one such organization.[8] The WHC is located in a mid-sized industrial city in the northeastern U.S. It was founded in 1972 by a group of women who had been meeting together as a consciousness-raising group for a year. The women in this group were feminists, and the organization they envisioned was designed to empower women. However, they did not publicly identify the WHC as a feminist organization, but as a place "to help ourselves and all women control their own lives as much as possible."[9] They described the Center as "a place where women can get together to talk, to share, to relax, or to get involved in collective action." A major theme of their early descriptions was "openness"—to new members, new ideas, and new options and choices for women.

By 1977, when I joined the group as a participant-observer, the organization had grown from a small volunteer health information and referral center housed in the basement of a church, to an organization that employed six paid staff, hosted twice-weekly family planning and routine gynecology clinics, and provided an array of counseling and referral services. None of the founders of the Center were among its volunteer or paid staff at that point. Some of the staff had joined the Center because of an ideological commitment to feminism; others had joined because they wanted to work with other women or because they had a positive experience when they had contacted the Center themselves for a service or through an outreach program.

From its earliest days, the WHC "philosophy" stressed a feminist approach to women's health (emphasizing self-help and services designed to empower women to make decisions for themselves); an egalitarian organizational model (the center was to be run collectively "by women and for women"); and the goal of serving as both a model of and base for the advocacy of alternative social relations and services. This ideology was put into practice by organizational structures and routines and a training program that reflected it. Despite a commitment to feminist goals and ways of organizing Center activities and programs, the staff most wanted to build an organization that would attract a broad base of women to services and programs. They believed that a general statement of feminist principles combined with their alternative services was appropriate to the needs of women in the city.

In its first several years of operation, the center operating budget was funded by a combination of fees (for services), income from small-scale community fundraising, and a few small subcontracts from the local Department of Social Services. This combination of sources of funding allowed the center to gradually provide peer counseling in new areas—abortion and health care, prescription and non-prescription drug abuse, and "family life" counseling (this latter was the program label of the funding agency). A small group of volunteers and first one, and then two and three paid staff, provided lay health and counseling services and ran the center as a collective with an egalitarian division of labor and a participatory decision-making structure.

In order to secure the first small subcontracts from a local human service agency, the group had to agree to hire one staff person as "Director." Although this flew in the face of their egalitarian ethic, they resolved the problem by naming her as director "on paper only;" she was to have no greater say in staff decisions than the volunteer staff and was to do the same kind of work as the volunteers. Over the next two years, additional monies permitted the hiring of the other paid staff. While the group continued to think of themselves as a collective, some differences began to emerge between the paid and volunteer staff members in the information available to them and their influence in decision making.

The group felt considerable pressure to seek larger and more stable sources of money to hire new staff. This was because the demand for services was high and because the collective realized that until they could pay salaries they would be unlikely to attract working class women or women of color to the staff, since few could afford to work without being paid. A decision was made to "go for state money" and over the course of two years (1977 to 1979) the center developed an increasingly direct and expanded relationship with the state. The center secured service contracts and grants from federal and state agencies and was granted the right to bill Medicaid for eligible clients. All of this involved becoming more greatly enmeshed in the social service and health care bureaucracy. The WHC budget grew substantially, enabling the staff to provide more diversified services. But accompanying this growth were changes in how the center operated and in staff activities and outlook.

THE DYNAMICS OF COOPTATION

In another paper, I examine in detail the dynamics of what I show to be the cooptive effects of state funding and regulation on the WHC.[10] Here, I will discuss these changes briefly as part of examining the contradictory impact of state funding and regulation on the WHC. The most obvious and powerful way in which the state shaped the direction of this grassroots organization was through the selective funding of activities, a process that served to channel activities towards direct service provision and away from advocacy, organizing, or community outreach. Not only did grants channel organizational activities towards service provision, they tended to underwrite the very kinds of social relations feminist health activists sought to change—hierarchical, one-on-one, provider-client relationships. Because most of the grants and contracts reimbursed the center on the basis of individual contact units/hours, there was an insidious movement towards more individual counseling rather than the group and self-help strategies that had been the norm. Moreover, as the Center began to apply for additional grants a rhetoric of paraprofessionalism began to overshadow the more egalitarian ethos of "women helping women."

The structure of the state funding apparatus directly affected the organizational structure of the center by creating the need for full-time administrative and clerical professionals. The Center typically received a series of small grants and contracts from different agencies, each requiring separate proposals, budgets, billings, and reports. Successful grantsmanship almost depends on a full-time fundraiser who could respond to RFP's (Requests for Proposals) in the often short time between announcement and the deadlines for grants. This time pressure also makes it difficult for groups who function collectively to involve themselves in discussion or preparation of proposals in the time available. The gradual institutionalization of a specialized division of labor within the staff, the increasing power of the director with her privileged relationships with funding agencies, and the sheer amount of administrative work associated with the Center's receipt of external funding each undermined collectivity.

Because successful grantsmanship tends to involve an "I'll scratch your back if you'll scratch mine" mentality between agencies in a community, the escalating drive towards external funding changed the relationship of the WHC with other social service and health facilities in the community. The WHC had a goal of changing the way human services were provided in its early days; it gradually became more "cooperative" (the director's word) with other agencies. This involved activities, such as serving on the Boards of Directors of other organizations and participating in other agency's staff training sessions. These "in-service sessions" did not inculcate feminist principles like the staff training at the WHC, but tended to conform to traditional and bureaucratic norms of professionalism and service. On more than one occasion, the WHC had to get letters of support from other community agencies as part of a grant application. This fostered a disinclination to criticize other agencies' handling of women's needs and services and actually became an obstacle to advocacy work within the social service and health care arena.

The state's control over the critical resources needed by an organization committed to serving women ultimately allowed it to influence the growth and direction of the WHC in ways that diverged from the WHC's political goals and principles. This process was not always overtly coercive. Often, center staff made decisions to compromise organizational and political principles with the good faith intentions of trying to meet the very real needs of women in the community for affordable and humane services. But the effect of this process was to frustrate the attempts of women to create an organization that fulfilled the promise of its feminist ideological goals.

During this time, the WHC was also subjected to more direct and coercive pressure by the state in the form of right wing political attempts to sharply regulate the activities of grassroots and specifically feminist health organizations. In 1978 the well-financed anti-abortion lobby in the state passed a bill which required organizations that received money from the state department of public health to obtain a clinic license. The process of winning licensure was both costly and designed to undermine the autonomy of health organizations. The ultimate goal of this bill was to put feminist clinics/health centers out of business, in the process decreasing the accessibility of abortion information, counseling, and service. Although the WHC fought and eventually won the battle against licensure (they did not have to get a license), this process was time consuming and it reinforced a growing faction within the staff who believed it was best for the Center not to take public political stands—for abortion, or for other issues that might "get them into trouble." Along with the more subtle, but no less undermining, effects of the developing relationship between the state and the WHC, this set of political pressures contributed to the process of containment—the use of state funds and regulation to weaken the oppositional character and potential of a grassroots organization.

The story I have told to this point is not a unique one. Countless other stories can be told of community and social movement organizations that have begun with lofty and often militant goals, and have been transformed over time into the very kinds of organizations they originally sought to change.[11] In this case, however, the cooptive pattern was ultimately reversed. In the next section of the paper I examine in some detail the *unintended* impact of state support of the WHC, which, I argue, laid the basis for progressive change in the Center and a new consciousness concerning gender among the staff.

THE CETA GRANT: SEEDS OF DIVERSITY, CONFLICT, AND RESISTANCE

The first, and one of the largest grants the WHC received from the state in the late 1970s was a CETA grant from the Department of Labor.[12] When the staff became aware that the local CETA consortium (Comprehensive Employment and Training Act) had funds available to local agencies to run training projects for low-income women, the director approached CETA with a plan to hire six or seven women to join the staff as lay health workers. The director of CETA suggested that their chances of getting the grant were better if they proposed a larger project, and if there was some kind of survey component to the project. The staff agreed to conform to those suggestions. The Center was successful, securing a $100,000 grant to hire 15 women for a year-long health education and service project that also involved canvassing the health needs and attitudes of low-income women in the community.

The CETA grant was responsible for the immediate tripling of the Center's staff, the doubling of its annual budget, and the catapulting of the Center into an ambitious project that entailed a dramatic increase in both administrative and service work. In the months following the inauguration of the CETA project, the staff of the Center found themselves on a frequent collision course between the Center's espoused goals (of participatory democracy and egalitarian social relations) and their practice. While the grant provided funds to hire 15 new staff, it also entailed spiralling increases in record-keeping, book-keeping, clerical work, and the filing of reports. At the same time, the Center was finally successful in negotiating with the state and the local hospital the conditions that enabled the Center to begin seeing Medicaid patients and billing the state for those services. This contributed to a growth in the demand for services at the same time that the administrative work had become so demanding.

Under these conditions the divisions of labor and social distribution of knowledge within the staff became more hierarchical. For the first time in the Center's history, specialized work characterized different segments of the staff: the "regular staff" (as they called themselves) continued to do health and counseling work; most of the CETA staff were put to work on the health survey and on training; and several women hired on the CETA grant did full-time clerical work. The "regular staff" also decided that it did not make sense to involve the new staff in the (now) weekly staff meeting until after they had finished the survey and their several month training program and were incorporated in the health and counseling work of the Center. So another first for the center involved the exclusion of a significant portion of the staff from participation in the collective decision-making process.

The first six months of the CETA project was a period of low morale for the staff, and a time of intensified conflict within the "regular staff"[13] and between the regular and the CETA staffs. Some of the explanation for these problems is due to the very real difficulties of incorporating so many new staff into the small organization and of sustaining collective processes under the conditions of direct pressures from the state. However, the fact that the new members of the staff were predominantly poor women and women of color and that the "regular staff" were largely white and middle-class was also a crucial factor in the conflicts that followed. Before the CETA project only one of the staff or volunteers of the Center was a woman of color, and middle-class women predominated in the ranks of both paid and unpaid staff. The hirings with CETA funds changed the staff balance so that now the staff was predominantly working-class women, one-third women of color. In effect, the CETA grant allowed the center to become a multi-racial, cross-class organization. In other words, it could become what Center staff had envisioned as a more ideal representation of the larger community. But the fulfillment of the promise of diversity brought with it dilemmas of difference. The growth and diversification of the staff, combined with the pressures of providing service and the requirements and regulations of state funding created difficulties and dilemmas that constituted a serious challenge for the staff.

While the erosion of participatory democracy had begun before the CETA grant, inequalities within the staff became institutionalized during that project. Moreover, the basis of inequality changed and was more easily named— more and more it followed the lines of race and class, with the CETA staff excluded from the structures of decision making. Race and class-based tensions punctuated a period already perceived as a "crisis" revolving around the future directions of the Center.

In early 1978, several months after the inauguration of the CETA project, the Department of Labor planned and sponsored a conference in the community to address the specific concerns of low-income women. They hired as a consultant to coordinate this conference a white middle-class woman I'll call Cynthia, who had been a long-time member of the Board of the WHC. The incidents that surround this conference illustrate how state resources, such as the CETA grant and the DOL conference, created the conditions that contextualized and fostered race and class tensions within the Center.

Cynthia met several times with the CETA staff before the conference to discuss the aims and possible outcomes of the conference. Throughout the planning meetings she often used the inclusive term "we" when discussing

goals and opportunities the conference offered low-income women, for example, "It's a great opportunity for us to tell them how we feel about their
policies." After this meeting, one of the CETA staff remarked to the others
that Cynthia had no right to use the word "we," that she had nothing in
common with low-income women. She stated clearly that she believed Cynthia should not have been hired to coordinate this conference because she
was neither poor nor a "minority" woman, and she did not seem to understand their needs.

At a meeting the week before the conference Cynthia reported proudly
on a battle she was waging with the DOL over the automatic deduction of
$5 (to pay for lunch) from the $15 stipend low-income women were to
receive for attending the conference. She suggested to the CETA staff that
they bring a "bag lunch" rather than lose the $5.00 adding,

Let's let the men pay their $5, you bring your sack lunches, and I'm sure there
will be plenty of leftovers, and for sure we can go up after awhile and have
some food and coffee. I'm sure there will be plenty of food since they know
there will be middle-class men from the agencies there.

This remark offended a number of the CETA staff. One Black woman said
"I'm going to pay for my lunch like everyone else." Another said, more
pointedly, "I've been eating leftovers all my life and I don't have to eat
them at this conference." After Cynthia left, the discussion continued, with
references to how "things like this always happen when women like that
get involved."

This incident exemplifies both the ways women of color and working-
class women experienced unequal social relations within the Center and
how they identified race and class as shaping differences among women. In
contrast to Cynthia's inclusive "we" is the perceived difference between
themselves and "women like that," and the refusal to set themselves apart
by eating leftovers. While this may not have been the first time they experienced racism or class prejudice at the WHC, it was the first time these
concerns were aired openly at a meeting. This incident ushered in a period
of more explicit discussion of racism and class prejudice within the staff,
and it underscored how much the Center's everyday practice diverged from
its egalitarian feminist ideology. Moreover, as the racism and class prejudice
of the white and middle-class staff were exposed, the power and influence
of women of color and working-class women increased.

Several months later, rumors circulated through the city that the Department of Labor was going to allocate several million dollars to a coalition
of grassroots organizations in the city as an experimental alternative to
CETA. The director met with the ad hoc coalition about including the WHC
in the package of proposals designed to target programs for minorities. The
"regular staff" decided that the women of color on staff should meet among
themselves to discuss priorities and plans for a proposal from the WHC.

This was the first time in the Center's history that there was a perceived need for a meeting exclusively for women of color. That the idea for this meeting came from the "regular staff" suggests a growing awareness that merely incorporating women of color into "their" organization was not enough. Rather, the "regular staff" acted to symbolize their willingness to relinquish a degree of control over the process of program development and to foster autonomous action by minority women.

At this meeting, the women of color not only developed their ideas about possible projects for the proposal, they also shared their feeling of distrust and discomfort of white women. They expressed the belief that the WHC was regarded primarily as a white middle-class organization by the larger community. Despite those concerns, they were also very clear that, on the whole, their involvement at the WHC had been an invaluable experience. They were anxious to develop programs within the WHC that would increasingly reach out to and involve more women of color, and would expand the community base for the WHC.

During this period the CETA staff completed the health survey and the counselor training program. They began doing health work and peer counseling, and were integrated into the staff decision-making process. But even with the larger staff the group felt unable to meet the demands for services by women, and particularly low-income women in the community. The staff felt a considerable pressure to find funds to keep the CETA staff employed at the Center, and to meet the need for services symbolized by a phone that "never stopped ringing."

During this period the meetings of the "collective" became highly charged. Tensions had been growing among "regular staff" members, a group of whom were very discontented about the disproportionate power of the director and other hidden dimensions of hierarchy within the staff. Consensus became harder to reach in conflict-ridden meetings, and increasingly, conflict revealed divisions within the staff regarding Center goals and priorities.

Among the issues that generated the most conflict were those that involved questions about grants and contracts, particularly when receiving external funding might compromise Center ideology or practice. For example, the staff was very divided about whether to apply for money from the state department of public health because new agency regulations would prohibit organizational support for abortion. In another instance several staff members, including the Director, had agreed to hold election signs for a local political candidate who had supported the Center in its recent efforts to get the city to donate a building for the Center's use. A number of staff felt that this decision was wrong because the candidate did not have a good record of supporting issues of concern to low-income women, and others believed it was "just wrong" for Center staff to get involved in an "exchange of political favors." This discussion quickly became factionalized, with the director and her supporters arguing that this compromise was made in the "long term interest of the Center" and the opposition angrily countering that this decision was made without the full endorsement of the staff.

Initially, this period of conflict underscored both the growing awareness of hierarchy and power differentials within the staff and an emerging resistance to that "hidden hierarchy." Whereas many previous decisions had been made by the director and a small group of full-time staff and essentially just rubber-stamped at meetings, decisions were now discussed and often debated at staff meetings. Once meetings became forums for political disagreement and debate, all staff were challenged to think about their own positions on issues and on questions about the Center's political identity. The frequency and intensity of conflict fostered a growing political sophistication in the staff, and led to a leveling of the disproportional power of the director and the old group of paid "regular" staff.

REVITALIZING AND REDEFINING FEMINISM

Ultimately, the grant-writing efforts of the staff paid off. Over the next year most of the ex-CETA staff were hired as full-time staff, thanks to several new grants. The Center developed two new programs: a battered women's project and a legal services project. In light of the Center's programmatic growth and the renewed commitment to collectivity among the staff, a "Restructuring Committee" proposed structural changes in the Center. This restructuring led to the creation of three units of the center: the health services; the battered women's project; and legal services. Each functioned as a collective. Each unit of the Center had representatives on an "Administrative Committee," which served as the over arching policy-making body of the staff.

In the midst of these changes in the Center, the Director announced that she was going to leave the position she had held for five years. The process of the search for a new Director reflected and reinforced the movement towards greater participation and control by the larger staff in the decision-making forums of the Center. Examining the advertisement for the new director, the Center's description of itself, which it sent to prospective applicants, and the questions used in interviewing candidates for the position, it becomes clear that the conflict within the collective had led to a revitalization of its social movement orientation and a redefinition of its feminist identity.

The WHC defines itself as a "collectively run non-profit organization." Collectivity is further defined as "worker-run projects," "collective and informed decision making by the staff and board," and "community representation in the collective." Questions asked of finalists for the job went beyond their ideological commitment to collectivity, searching for the applicants' actual experience working collectively, assessments of how their strengths and weaknesses would foster or undermine collective processes, and their views on "integrating constructively critical process within a collective." Additionally, candidates were asked specifically to discuss the problem of sustaining collectivity with a staff that was made up of women from different racial, ethnic, and class backgrounds.

The Center's presentation of itself in rhetoric and action indicated changes in how feminism was conceptualized by the WHC. These changes suggest that there was both a greater willingness to identify as a feminist organization and to root feminism in the community base of the Center. Earlier documents of the WHC had sidestepped the label feminist, instead referring to the Center as "woman oriented, woman controlled." By the late 1970s feminism had become a "firm political base undergirding the WHC." And the Center was clear about its goals:

In trying to seek active community involvement, provide high quality services and programs, and function as a worker-controlled collective the [WHC] is committed to growing as a feminist grassroots organization.

Even as the Center's feminist identity was re-invigorated, feminism was also redefined, expressing a vision of "sisterhood" that entailed an understanding of race and class differences among women.[14] For example a pamphlet developed by the WHC to celebrate International Women's Day (March 8, 1980) illustrates the changing consciousness of the staff regarding issues of racism and diversity among women:

We have also realized that women's struggle for equality is closely connected with the struggles of other oppressed groups . . . Some of these struggles [that the WHC had been involved in that year] do not concern narrowly defined "women's issues . . ." That's because women cannot achieve equality or decent lives unless all working people get a better deal, nor will women be liberated until racism is eliminated . . . The struggle for women's liberation includes all women, including women struggling for equality and a better life as workers, as Black people, as Puerto Ricans, as lesbians, or other oppressed groups.

The new and broader conception of feminism was also nurtured by the new director, a woman who had considerable experience working collectively and in multiracial organizations, and whose vision of the WHC went beyond social service provision to encompass advocacy and community organizing. She recognized the importance of consciously building the leadership of the women of color and working-class women on the staff, though she herself was a professional white woman from a middle-class family in the city.

Over the next several years, the Center was able to maintain most of the funding which supported the health and battered women's programs of the Center. A new "Social Action" project was established to support the Center's now increased involvement in community organizing and in working with other community groups on a variety of issues. More women of color were brought into the WHC as staff and as board members. As the Reagan era promoted the slashing of human service programs and the growing backlash against women's gains and women's organizations, the Center struggled and managed to retain its political direction. When the director decided to leave the WHC several years later the staff and board selected a new director from within the ranks of the staff. The new director had been first hired on the CETA grant in 1978. She became the first woman of color to serve as the Center's director.

CONCLUSION

It is difficult to convey the complex dynamics of change in the WHC over the more than ten-year organizational life span covered in this paper. Nevertheless, it is clear that substantial changes accompanied the staff's initial decision to expand, and particularly to diversify the staff by race and class. The state funds that allowed the Center to hire more working-class women and women of color helped to shape the conflict and political struggle within the staff, and brought into the Center strong proponents of an activist orientation, and a conception of feminism grounded in the experiences of women of color and poor women.

Needless to say, these effects of state funding were unintentional. Even as state resources created the conditions which brought white, Black and Hispanic, middle-class and working-class women together as staff of the Center, the social control functions of state funding and regulation continued to exert powerful cooptive influences on the Center. The women who worked at the WHC were dependent on the state for their own livelihoods, for support of their alternative model of human services, and for the basic operating expenses necessary to serve exactly those women in the community most in need of services and least likely to turn to a feminist center for ideological reasons. In the Center's first years of receiving state funds this dependency had fostered changes in organizational structure and goals, changes that undermined the Center's feminist identity and goals. During those years the staff experienced the "loss of control" (one staff member's words) over the Center, a feeling that was precisely the opposite of one of the Center's primary goals—self-determination for women. This tension between a recognized dependency and the goal of self-determination influenced many of the decisions the staff made as they struggled to balance their conflicting commitments and goals.

The impulse to found and then to maintain the WHC was profoundly oppositional. It was intended to empower women by creating a woman-controlled center. Because of race and class divisions among women in the contemporary U.S., the challenge of making this woman-controlled center also multi-racial and representative of different classes of women embroiled the staff in a complex relationship with the state and with each other. This bringing together of women with very different backgrounds and experiences profoundly challenged the presumed commonality of women's interests and the hopeful vision of women sharing and helping one another that was the core of Center ideology.

The process of redefining feminism at the WHC involved denying the assumed commonality of women's needs and interests; recognizing the persistence of inegalitarian assumptions and beliefs—racism and class biases—in women who claimed to value "sisterhood;" and finally re-examining and changing Center structures, routines, and ideologies so that they reflected the realities of different women's lives and values. For the women involved with the WHC this had to be accomplished in the context of external pressures from the state to conform to the norms of social service defined through professionalism, bureaucracy, and hierarchical social relations.

This case demonstrates how important it is to develop theories of the state that comprehend both the different sorts of relationships groups of women have with the state and the complex meaning of the increased reliance of women on the state for transfer payments, wages and salaries, and institutional and legal backing for the political gains the women's movement has wrought. There is no question that in the decade of Reaganism slashed human service budgets, weakened enforcement of civil rights legislation, and invigorated attacks on women took its toll on people of color and the poor. Nevertheless, the story of the WHC serves as a reminder that the contest over resources, meaning, and political power is more complicated than meets the eye.

That state resources underwrote the efforts of women to revitalize and redefine feminism in this community demonstrates that the impact of state policies on gender practice and ideology cannot be assumed but must be investigated. In this case women, supported and constrained by their relationship to the state used state resources in ways that challenged and transformed dominant gender, race, and class ideologies and practices.

NOTES

1. Mary McIntosh, "The State and the Oppression of Women," in *Feminism and Materialism,* ed. Anette Kuhn and Ann Marie Wolpe (London: Routledge and Kegan Paul, 1978), 258.

2. Mimi Abramovitz, *Regulating the Lives of Women: Social Welfare Policy From Colonial Times to the Present* (Boston: South End Press, 1988).

3. Zillah Eisenstein, *Feminism and Sexual Equality: Crisis in Liberal America* (New York: Monthly Review Press, 1984).

4. Rosalind Petchesky, *Abortion and Woman's Choice: The State, Sexuality and Reproductive Freedom* (Boston: Northeastern University Press, 1984).

5. Abramovitz, 377.

6. Frances Fox Piven, "Women and the State: Ideology, Power and the Welfare State," in *Gender and the Life Course,* ed. Alice Rossi (New York: Aldine Publishers, 1985), 265.

7. Abramovitz, 35.

8. The Women's Health Center (WHC) is a pseudonym for a feminist health clinic in which I did fieldwork from April 1977 through early 1979. For additional ethnographic description of the feminist organization and the larger community in which it is located see Sandra Morgen, *Ideology and Change in a Feminist Health Center: The Experience and Dynamics of Routinization* (Chapel Hill, North Carolina: Department of Anthropology, doctoral dissertation, 1982).

9. Because I have used a pseudonym for the city and center which are the subject of this work, I will not footnote documents specifically in the remainder of this paper. Rather, I will note that the quotation is from a WHC document only.

10. Sandra Morgen, "The Dynamics of Cooptation in a Feminist Health Clinic," *Social Science and Medicine* 23, no. 2 (1986): 201–210.

11. For example, see Phillip Selznick, *TVA and the Grassroots: A Study in the Sociology of Formal Organizations,* (New York: Harper Torchbooks, 1966); Meyer Zald and Roberta Ash, "Social Movement Organizations: Growth, Decay, and Change," *Social Forces* 44 (1966): 327–340; Diane Bush, "The Routinization of Social Movement Organizations: China as a Deviant Case," *Sociological Quarterly* 19 (Spring 1978): 203–217; Miriam Galper and Carolyn Washburn, "A Woman's Self-Help Program in Action," *Social Policy* 6, no. 5 (1976): 46–52; and Katherine Newman, "Incipient Bureaucracy: The Development of Hierarchies in Egalitarian Organizations," in *Hierarchy and Society: Anthropological Perspectives on Bureaucracy,* ed. Gerald Britan and Ronald Cohen (Philadelphia: Institute for the Study of Human Issues, 1980).

12. The Comprehensive Employment and Training Act (CETA) was enacted in 1973 with the goal of providing education and training programs to reduce "structural unemployment." Funds were allocated for vocational training, general high school equivalency degrees (GED), and other forms of adult education, and for the Public Service Employment (PSE) project which created jobs in public sector and non-profit organizations such as the WHC. PSE programs were eliminated by the Reagan administration in 1981 and in 1982 CETA was replaced by the smaller and much less ambitious Job Training and Partnership Act (JTPA).

13. Sandra Morgen "Contradictions in Feminist Praxis: Individualism and Collectivism," *Comparative Social Research: A Research Annual,* Supplement 1, 1990 eds. T.M.S. Evens and James Peacock: 9–59.

14. Black feminist theorists have been incisive critics of feminist ideological insistence on the commonality of women's experiences. See especially, Bonnie Thornton Dill, "On the Hem of Life: Race, Class and the Prospects for an All-Inclusive Sisterhood," in *Class, Race, and Sex: The Dynamics of Control,* ed. Amy Swerdlow and Hannah Lessinger (Boston: G. K. Hall, 1981); Angela Davis, *Women, Race, and Class* (New York: Random House, 1981); and bell hooks, *Feminist Theory: From Margin to Center* (Boston: South End Press, 1984).

CHAPTER ELEVEN

Delicate Transactions: Gender, Home, and Employment among Hispanic Women

M. PATRICIA FERNÁNDEZ KELLY

The days have vanished when scholars could comfortably speak about the roles of men and women as if they were immutable biological or temperamental traits. More than a decade of feminist thought and research in the social sciences has brought about a complex understanding of gender as a process reflecting political, economic, and ideological transactions, a fluid phenomenon changing in uneasy harmony with productive arrangements. The theoretical focus of this essay is on the way class, ethnicity, and gender interact.

I compare two groups of Hispanic women involved in apparel manufacturing: One includes native- and foreign-born Mexicans in Southern California; another, Cuban exiles in Southern Florida.[1] All the women have worked in factories at different stages in their lives, and they have also been involved in industrial work in the home. In a broad sense, women's incorporation into the work force is part and parcel of economic strategies that have allowed manufacturing firms to compete in domestic and international markets. From a more restricted perspective, it is also the result of personal negotiations between men and women in households and workplaces. Combining these perspectives, it is possible to compare the two groups of women to see the influence of economic resources and immigration histories on conceptions and institutions of gender. Despite sharing important characteristics, the two groups represent distinct economic classes and social situations. I use the cases to examine how economic and social factors can reinforce or undermine patriarchal values and affect women's attitudes toward and relationships with men.

A complex conceptualization of gender has emerged over the past two decades from the dialogue between Marxist and feminist scholars. In this dialogue, theorists have focused on the relationship between productive and reproductive spheres to uncover the varied content of gender relations under differing conditions of production and in different periods.[2] Here "gender" refers to meshed economic, political, and ideological relations. Under capitalism gender designates fundamental economic processes that determine the allocation of labor into remunerated and non-remunerated spheres of production. Gender also circumscribes the alternatives of individuals of different sexes in the area of paid employment. Women's specific socioeconomic experience is grounded in the contradiction that results from the wage labor/unpaid domestic labor split.

In addition, gender is political as it contributes to differential distributions of power and access to vital resources on the basis of sexual difference. The political asymmetry between men and women is played out both within and outside of the domestic realm. In both cases it involves conflict, negotiation, and ambivalent resolutions which are, in turn, affected by economic and ideological factors.

Finally, gender implicates the shaping of consciousness and the elaboration of collective discourses which alternatively explain, legitimate, or question the position of men and women as members of families and as workers. While all societies assign roles to individuals on the basis of perceived sexual characteristics, these roles vary significantly and change over time. Gender is part of a broader ideological process in constant flux. Moreover, adherence to patriarchal mores may have varying outcomes depending on their economic and political context.

This interplay of economic, political, and ideological aspects of gender is particularly evident in studying the relationship between women's paid employment and household responsibilities. Women's work—whether factory work, industrial homework, or unpaid domestic work—always involves negotiations of gendered boundaries, such as the line between wage labor and domestic responsibilities, and the arrangements that tie household organization and family ideals. Industrial homework, for example, both contradicts and complies with the ideological split between "work" and "family" as this sets standards for male-female differentiation; women who do homework work for wages but do not leave their homes and families.

Employers rely on homework to lower the wage bill, evade government regulations, and maintain competitiveness in the market;[3] none of these goals seem consistent with women's attempts to raise their economic status. Yet homework has been used by women to reconcile the responsibilities of domestic care with the need to earn a wage. Furthermore, women use and interpret homework as a strategy for bridging employment and family goals in a variety of ways. Women move between factory work, homework, and unpaid domestic labor on different trajectories, depending on both household organization and class-based resources.

Some conceptual clarification is needed for this analysis. It is necessary to distinguish "family" and "household." "Family" is an ideological notion that includes marriage and fidelity, men's roles as providers and women's roles as caretakers of children, and the expectation that nuclear families will reside in the same home. Rayna Rapp notes the prevalence of a family ideal shared by working- and middle-class people in the United States.[4] While "family" designates the way things should be, "household" refers to the manner in which men, women, and children actually join each other as part of domestic units. Households represent mechanisms for the pooling of time, labor, and other resources in a shared space. As households adjust to the pressures of the surrounding environment, they frequently stand in sharp, even painful, contrast to ideals regarding the family.

Class accounts largely for the extent to which notions about the family can be upheld or not. The conditions necessary for the maintenance of long-term stable unions where men act as providers and women as caretakers of children have been available among the middle and upper classes but absent among the poor. Nuclear households are destabilized by high levels of unemployment and underemployment or by public policy making it more advantageous for women with children to accept welfare payments than to remain dependent upon an irregularly employed man. The poor often live in highly flexible households where adherence to the norms of the patriarchial family are unattainable.

Class differences in the relation between household patterns and family ideals are apparent in women's changing strategies of factory work, homework, and unpaid labor. Homework, for example, can maintain family objectives or help compensate for their unattainability. In describing two contrasting ways women link household organization, paid employment, and gender and family ideals, my study creates a model for class and ethnic specific analyses of gender negotiations.

THE HISPANIC COMMUNITIES IN MIAMI AND LOS ANGELES

Although there are many studies comparing minorities and whites in the U.S., there have been few attempts to look at variations of experience *within* ethnic groups. This is true for Hispanics in general and for Hispanic women in particular; yet contrasts abound. For example, Mexicans comprise more than half of all Hispanics between eighteen and sixty-four years of age living in the U.S. Of these, approximately 70% were born in this country. Average levels of educational attainment are quite low with less than 50% having graduated from high school. In contrast, Cubans represent about 7% of the Hispanic population. They are mostly foreign-born; 58% of Cubans have 12 or more years of formal schooling.[5]

Both in Southern California and in Southern Florida most direct production workers in the garment industry are Hispanic. In Los Angeles most apparel firm operatives are Mexican women, in Miami, Cuban women.[6] The labor force participation rates of Mexican and Cuban women dispel the widespread notion that work outside the home is a rare experience for Hispanic women.[7] Yet the Los Angeles and Miami communities differ in a number of important respects. One can begin with contrasts in the garment industry in each area.

The two sites differ in the timing of the industry, its evolution, maturity, and restructuring. In Los Angeles, garment production emerged in the latter part of the nineteenth-century and expanded in the 1920s, stimulated in part by the arrival of runaway shops evading unionization drives in New York. The Great Depression sent the Los Angeles garment industry into a period of turmoil, but soon fresh opportunities for the production of inexpensive women's sportswear developed, as the rise of cinema established new guidelines for fashion. During the 1970s and 1980s the industry reorganized in response to foreign imports; small manufacturing shops have proliferated, as has home production. In contrast, the apparel industry in Miami has had a shorter and more uniform history. Most of the industry grew up since the 1960s, when retired manufacturers from New York saw the advantage of opening new businesses and hiring exiles from the Cuban Revolution.

The expansion of the Los Angeles clothing industry resulted from capitalists' ability to rely on continuing waves of Mexican immigrants, many of whom were undocumented. Mexican migration over the last century ensured a steady supply of workers for the apparel industry; from the very beginning, Mexican women were employed in nearly all positions in the industry.[8] By contrast, the expansion of garment production in Miami was due to an unprecedented influx of exiles ejected by a unique political event. Cubans working in the Florida apparel industry arrived in the United States as refugees under a protected and relatively privileged status. Exile was filled with uncertainty and the possibility of dislocation but not, as in the case of undocumented Mexican aliens, with the probability of harassment, detention, and deportation.

Mexican and Cuban workers differ strikingly in social class. For more than a century, the majority of Mexican immigrants have had a markedly proletarian background. Until the 1970s, the majority had rural roots, although in more recent times there has been a growing number of urban immigrants.[9] In sharp contrast, Cuban waves of migration have included a larger proportion of professionals, mid-level service providers, and various types of entrepreneurs ranging from those with previous experience in large companies to those qualified to start small family enterprises. Entrepreneurial experience among Cubans and reliance on their own ethnic networks accounts, to a large extent, for Cuban success in business formation and appropriation in Miami.[10] Thus, while Mexican migration has been characterized by relative homogeneity regarding class background, Cuban exile resulted in the transposition of an almost intact class structure containing investors and professionals as well as unskilled, semiskilled, and skilled workers.

In addition to disparate class compositions, the two groups differ in the degree of their homogeneity by place of birth. Besides the sizable undocumented contingent mentioned earlier, the Los Angeles garment industry also employs U.S.-born citizens of Mexican heritage. First-hand reports and anecdotal evidence indicate that the fragmentation between "Chicana" and "Mexicana" workers causes an unresolved tension and animosity within the labor force. Cubans, on the other hand, were a highly cohesive population until the early 1980s, when the arrival of the so-called "Marielitos" resulted in a potentially disruptive polarization of the community.

Perhaps the most important difference between Mexicans in Los Angeles and Cubans in Florida is related to their distinctive labor market insertion patterns. Historically, Mexicans have arrived in the U.S. labor market in a highly individuated and dispersed manner. As a result, they have been extremely dependent on labor market supply and demand forces entirely beyond their control. Their working-class background and stigma attached to their frequent undocumented status has accentuated even further their vulnerability vis-à-vis employers. By contrast, Cubans have been able to consolidate an economic enclave formed by immigrant businesses, which hire workers of a common cultural and national background. The economic enclave partly operates as a buffer zone separating and often shielding members of the same ethnic group from the market forces at work in the larger society. The existence of an economic enclave does not preclude exploitation on the basis of class; indeed, it is predicated upon the existence of a highly diversified immigrant class structure. However, commonalities of culture, national background, and language between immigrant employers and workers can become a mechanism for collective improvement of income levels and standards of living. As a result, differences in labor market insertion patterns among Mexicans and Cubans have led to varying social profiles and a dissimilar potential for socioeconomic attainment.

THE WOMEN GARMENT WORKERS

These differences between the two Hispanic communities have led to important differences between the two groups of women who work in the garment industry. For Mexican women in Southern California, employment in garment production is the consequence of long-term economic need. Wives and daughters choose to work outside the home in order to meet the survival requirements of their families in the absence of satisfactory earnings by men. Some female heads of household join the labor force after losing male support through illness, death, and, more often, desertion. In many of these instances, women opt for industrial homework in order to reconcile child care and the need for wage employment. They are particularly vulnerable members of an economically marginal ethnic group.

By contrast, Cuban women who arrived in Southern Florida during the 1960s saw jobs in garment assembly as an opportunity to recover or attain middle-class status. The consolidation of an economic enclave in Miami, which accounts for much of the prosperity of Cubans, was largely dependent upon the incorporation of women into the labor force. While they toiled in factories, men entered business or were self-employed. Their vulnerability was tempered by shared goals of upward mobility in a foreign country.

Despite their different nationalities, migratory histories, and class backgrounds, Mexicans and Cubans share many perceptions and expectations. In both cases, patriarchal norms of reciprocity are favored; marriage, motherhood, and devotion to family are high priorities among women, while men are expected to hold authority, to be good providers, and to be loyal to their wives and children. However, the divergent economic and political conditions surrounding Mexicans in Southern California and Cubans in Southern Florida have had a differing impact upon each group's ability to uphold these values. Mexican women are often thrust into financial "autonomy" as a result of men's inability to fulfill their socially assigned role. Among Cubans, by contrast, men have been economically more successful. Indeed, ideological notions of patriarchal responsibility have served to maintain group cohesion; that offers women an advantage in getting and keeping jobs within the ethnic enclave.

Cuban and Mexican women both face barriers stemming from their subordination in the family and their status as low-skilled workers in highly competitive industries. Nevertheless, their varying class backgrounds and modes of incorporation into local labor markets entail distinctive political and socioeconomic effects. How women view their identities as women is especially affected. Among Mexican garment workers disillusion about the economic viability of men becomes a desire for individual emancipation, mobility, and financial independence as women. However, these ideals and ambitions for advancement are most often frustrated by poverty and the stigmas attached to ethnic and gender status.

Cuban women, on the other hand, tend to see no contradiction between personal fulfillment and a strong commitment to patriarchal standards. Their incorporation and subsequent withdrawal from the labor force are both influenced by their acceptance of hierarchical patterns of authority and the sexual division of labor. As in the case of Mexicans in Southern California, Cuban women's involvement in industrial homework is an option bridging domestic and income-generating needs. However, it differs in that homework among them was brought about by relative prosperity and expanding rather than diminishing options. Women's garment work at home does not contradict patriarchal ideals of women's place at the same time as it allows women to contribute to the economic success that confirms gender stratification.

The stories of particular women show the contrasts in how women in each of these two groups negotiate the links among household, gender, and employment arrangements. Some of the conditions surrounding Mexican home workers in Southern California are illustrated by the experience of Amelia Ruíz.[11] She was born into a family of six children in El Cerrito, Los Angeles County. Her mother, a descendant of Native American Indians, married at a young age the son of Mexican immigrants. Among Amelia's memories are the fragmentary stories of her paternal grandparents working in the fields and, occasionally, in canneries. Her father, however was not a stoop laborer but a trained upholsterer. Her mother was always a home-maker. Amelia grew up with a distinct sense of the contradictions that plague the relationships between men and women:

All the while I was a child, I had this feeling that my parents weren't happy. My mother was smart but she could never make much of herself. Her parents taught her that the fate of woman is to be a wife and mother; they advised her to find a good man and marry him. And that she did. My father was reliable and I think he was faithful but he was also distant; he lived in his own world. He would come home and expect to be served hand and foot. My mother would wait on him but she was always angry about it. I never took marriage for granted.

After getting her high school diploma, Amelia found odd jobs in all the predictable places: as a counter clerk in a dress shop, as a cashier in a fast-food establishment, and as a waitress in two restaurants. When she was 20, she met Miguel—Mike as he was known outside the barrio. He was a consummate survivor, having worked in the construction field, as a truck driver, and even as an English as a Second Language instructor. Despite her misgivings about marriage, Amelia was struck by Mike's penchant for adventure:

He was different from the men in my family. He loved fun and was said to have had many women. He was a challenge. We were married when I was 21 and he 25. For a while I kept my job but when I became pregnant, Miguel didn't want me to work any more. Two more children followed and then, little by little, Miguel became abusive. He wanted to have total authority over me and the children. He said a man should know how to take care of a family and get respect, but it was hard to take him seriously when he kept changing jobs and when the money he brought home was barely enough to keep ends together.

After the birth of her second child, Amelia started work at Shirley's, a women's wear factory in the area. Miguel was opposed to the idea. For Amelia, work outside the home was an evident need prompted by financial stress. At first, it was also a means to escape growing disenchantment:

I saw myself turning into my mother and I started thinking that to be free of men was best for women. Maybe if Miguel had had a better job, maybe if he had kept the one he had, things would have been different, but he didn't . . . We started drifting apart.

Tension at home mounted over the following months. Amelia had worked at Shirley's for almost a year when, one late afternoon after collecting the three children from her parents' house, she returned to an empty home. She knew, as soon as she stepped inside, that something was amiss. In muted shock, she confirmed the obvious: Miguel had left, taking with him all personal possessions; even the wedding picture in the living room had been removed. No explanations had been left behind. Amelia was then 28 years of age, alone, and the mother of three small children.

As a result of these changes, employment became even more desirable, but the difficulty of reconciling home responsibilities with wage work persisted. Amelia was well regarded at Shirley's, and her condition struck a sympathetic cord among the other factory women. In a casual conversation, her supervisor described how other women were leasing industrial sewing machines from the local Singer distributor and were doing piecework at home. By combining factory work and home assembly, she could earn more money without further neglecting the children. Mr. Driscoll, Shirley's owner and general manager, made regular use of home workers, most of whom were former employees. That had allowed him to retain a stable core of about 20 factory seamstresses and to depend on approximately 10 home workers during peak seasons.

Between 1979, the year of her desertion, and 1985, when I met her, Amelia had struggled hard, working most of the time and making some progress. Her combined earnings before taxes fluctuated between $950 and $1,150 a month. Almost half of her income went to rent for the two-bedroom apartment which she shared with the children. She was in debt and used to working at least 12 hours a day. On the other hand, she had bought a double-needle sewing machine and was thinking of leasing another one to share additional sewing with a neighbor. She had high hopes:

Maybe some day I'll have my own business; I'll be a liberated woman . . . I won't have to take orders from a man. Maybe Miguel did me a favor when he left after all . . .

With understandable variations, Amelia's life history is shared by many garment workers in Southern California. Three aspects are salient in this experience. First, marriage and a stable family life are perceived as desirable goals which are, nonetheless, fraught with ambivalent feelings and burdensome responsibilities.

Second, tensions between men and women result from contradictions between the intent to fulfill gender definitions and the absence of the economic base necessary for their implementation. The very definition of manhood includes the right to hold authority and power over wives and children, as well as the responsibility of providing adequately for them. The difficulties in implementing those goals in the Mexican communities I studied are felt equally by men and women but expressed differently by each. Bent on restoring their power, men attempt to control women in abusive ways. Women often resist their husbands' arbitrary or unrealistic impositions. Both reactions are eminently political phenomena.

Third, personal conflict regarding the proper behavior of men and women may be tempered by negotiation. It can also result in the breach of established agreements, as in the case of separation or divorce. Both paths are related to the construction of alternative discourses and the redefinition of gender roles. Women may seek personal emancipation, driven partly by economic need and partly by dissatisfaction with men's performance as providers. In general, individuals talk about economic and political conflict as a personal matter occurring in their own homes. Broader contextual factors are less commonly discussed.

The absence of economic underpinnings for the implementation of patriarchal standards may bring about more equitable exchanges between men and women, and may stimulate women's search for individual well-being and personal autonomy as women. However, in the case at hand, such ideals remain elusive. Mexican garment workers, especially those who are heads of households, face great disadvantages in the labor market. They are targeted for jobs that offer the lowest wages paid to industrial workers in the United States; they also have among the lowest unionization rates in the country. Ironically, the breakdown of patriarchal norms in the household draws from labor market segmentation that reproduces patriarchal (and ethnic) stratification.

Experiences like the ones related are also found among Cuban and Central American women in Miami. However, a larger proportion have had a different trajectory. Elvira Gómez's life in the U.S. is a case in point. She was 34 when she arrived in Miami with her four children, ages three to twelve. The year was 1961.

Leaving Havana was the most painful thing that ever happened to us. We loved our country. We would have never left willingly. Cuba was not like Mexico: we didn't have immigrants in large numbers. But Castro betrayed us and we had to join the exodus. We became exiles. My husband left Cuba three months before I did and there were moments when I doubted I would ever see him again. Then, after we got together, we realized we would have to forge ahead without looking back.

We lost everything. Even my mother's china had to be left behind. We arrived in this country as they say, "covering our nakedness with our bare hands" (*una mano delante y otra detrás*). My husband had had a good position in a bank. To think that he would have to take any old job in Miami was more than I could take; a man of his stature having to beg for a job in a hotel or in a factory? It wasn't right!

Elvira had worked briefly before her marriage as a secretary. As a middle-class wife and mother, she was used to hiring at least one maid. Coming to the United States changed all that:

Something had to be done to keep the family together. So I looked around and finally found a job in a shirt factory in Hialeah. Manolo (her husband) joined a childhood friend and got a loan to start an export-import business. All the time they were building the firm, I was sewing. There were times when we wouldn't have been able to pay the bills without the money I brought in.

Elvira's experience was shared by thousands of women in Miami. Among the first waves of Cuban refugees there were many who worked tirelessly to raise the standards of living of their families to the same levels or higher than those they had been familiar with in their country of origin. The consolidation of an ethnic enclave allowed many Cuban men to become entrepreneurs. While their wives found unskilled and semi-skilled jobs, they became businessmen. Eventually, they purchased homes, put their children through school, and achieved comfort. At that point, many Cuban men pressed their wives to stop working outside of the home; they had only allowed them to have a job, in the first place, out of economic necessity. In the words of a prominent manufacturer in the area:

You have to understand that Cuban workers were willing to do anything to survive. When they became prosperous, the women saw the advantage of staying at home and still earn additional income. Because they had the skill, owners couldn't take them for granted. Eventually, owners couldn't get operators anymore. The most skilled would tell a manager "my husband doesn't let me work out of the home." This was a worker's initiative based on the values of the culture. I would put ads in the paper and forty people would call and everyone would say "I only do homework." That's how we got this problem of the labor shortages. The industry was dying; we wouldn't have survived without the arrival of the Haitians and the Central Americans.

This discussion partly shows that decisions made at the level of the household can remove workers, actively sought and preferred by employers, from the marketplace. This, in turn, can threaten certain types of production. In those cases, loyalty to familial values can mitigate against the interests of capitalist firms. Interviews with Cuban women involved in homework confirm the general accuracy of this interpretation. After leaving factory employment, many put their experience to good use by becoming subcontractors and employing neighbors or friends. They also transformed so-called "Florida rooms" (the covered porches in their houses) into sewing shops. It was in one of them that Elvira Gómez was first interviewed. In her case, working outside the home was justified only as a way to maintain the integrity of her family and as a means to support her husband's early incursions into the business world:

For many long years I worked in the factory but when things got better financially, Manolo asked me to quit the job. He felt bad that I couldn't be at home all the time with the children. But it had to be done. There's no reason for women not to earn a living when it's necessary; they should have as many opportunities and responsibilities as men. But I also tell my daughters that the strength of a family rests on the intelligence and work of women. It is foolish to give up your place as a mother and a wife only to go take orders from men who aren't even part of your family. What's so liberated about that? It is better to see your husband succeed and to know you have supported one another.

Perhaps the most important point here is the unambiguous acceptance of patriarchal mores as a legitimate guideline for the behavior of men and women. Exile did not eliminate these values; rather, it extended them in telling ways. The high labor force participation rates of Cuban women in the United States have been mentioned before. Yet, it should be remembered that, prior to their migration, only a small number of Cuban women had worked outside the home for any length of time. It was the need to maintain the integrity of their families and to achieve class-related ambitions that precipitated their entrance into the labor force of a foreign country.

In descriptions of their experience in exile, Cuban women often make clear that part of the motivation in their search for jobs was the preservation of known definitions of manhood and womanhood. Whereas Mexican women worked as a response to what they saw as a failure of patriarchal arrangements, Cuban women worked in the name of dedication to their husbands and children, and in order to preserve the status and authority of the former. Husbands gave them "permission" to work outside the home, and only as a result of necessity and temporary economic strife. In the same vein, it was a ritual yielding to masculine privilege that led women to abandon factory employment. Conversely, men "felt bad" that their wives had to work for a wage and welcomed the opportunity to remove them from the marketplace when economic conditions improved.

As with Mexicans in Southern California, Cuban women in Miami earned low wages in low- and semi-skilled jobs. They too worked in environments devoid of the benefits derived from unionization. Nevertheless, the outcome of their experience as well as the perceptions are markedly different. Many Cuban women interpret their subordination at home as part of a viable option ensuring economic and emotional benefits. They are bewildered by feminist goals of equality and fulfillment in the job market. Yet, the same women have had among the highest rates of participation in the U.S. labor force.

CONCLUSIONS

For Mexican women in Southern California, proletarianization is related to a high number of female-headed households, as well as households where the earnings provided by women are indispensable for maintaining standards of modest subsistence. In contrast, Cuban women's employment in Southern Florida was a strategy for raising standards of living in a new environment. These contrasts in the relationship between households and the labor market occurred despite shared values regarding the family among Mexicans and Cubans. Both groups partake of similar mores regarding the roles of men and women; nevertheless, their actual experience has differed significantly. Contrasting features of class, educational background, and immigration history have created divergent gender and family dilemmas for each group.

This analysis underscores the impact of class on gender. Definitions of manhood and womanhood are implicated in the very process of class formation. At the same time, the norms of reciprocity sanctioned by patriarchal ideologies can operate as a form of social adhesive consolidating class membership. For poor men and women, the issue is not only the presence of the sexual division of labor and the persistence of patriarchal ideologies but the difficulties of upholding either.

Thus, too, the meaning of women's participation in the labor force remains plagued by paradox. For Mexican women in Southern California, paid employment responds to and increases women's desires for greater personal autonomy and financial independence. Ideally, this should have a favorable impact upon women's capacity to negotiate an equitable position within their homes and in the labor market. Yet these women's search for paid employment is most often the consequence of severe economic need; it expresses vulnerability not strength within homes and in the marketplace. Indeed, in some cases, women's entry into the labor force signals the collapse of reciprocal exchanges between men and women. Women deserted by their husbands are generally too economically marginal to translate their goals of gender equality and autonomy into socially powerful arrangements. Conversely, Cuban women in Southern Florida have more economic power, but this only strengthens their allegiance to patriarchal standards. The conjugal "partnership for survival" Elvira Gómez describes is not predicated on the existence of a just social world, but rather an ideological universe entailing differentiated and stratified benefits and obligations for men and women.

NOTES

A different version of this essay appears in Women, Work, and Politics, *Louise Tilly and Patricia Guerin, eds. (New York: Russell Sage Foundation, 1990).*

1. This essay is based on findings from the "Collaborative Study of Hispanic Women in Garment and Electronics Industries" supported by the Ford Foundation under grant number 870 1149. Initial funding for the same project was also provided by the Tinker Foundation. The author gratefully acknowledges the continued encouragement of Dr. William Díaz from the Ford Foundation.

2. Joan W. Scott, "Gender: A Useful Category of Historical Analysis," *The American Historical Review,* 91, 5 (1986): 1053–75; Felicity Edholm, "Conceptualizing Women," *Critique of Anthropology,* 3, 9/10: 101–30. For a relevant analysis of class, see Michael Buroway, *The Politics of Production* (London: New Left Books, 1985).

3. M. Patricia Fernández Kelly and Anna M. García, "Informalization at the Core: Hispanic Women, Homework and the Advanced Capitalist State," in *The Informal Economy: Comparative Studies in Advanced and Third World Societies,* eds. Alejandro Portes, Manuel Castels, and Lauren Benton (Baltimore: Johns Hopkins University Press, 1989).

4. Rayna Rapp, "Family and Class in Contemporary America: Notes Toward an Understanding of Ideology," in *Rethinking the Family,* eds. Barrie Thorne

and Marilyn Yalom (New York: Longman, 1982). See also Eli Zaretsky, *Capitalism, The Family and Personal Life* (New York: Harper and Row, 1976).

5. Frank D. Bean and Marta Tienda, *The Hispanic Population of the United States* (New York: Russell Sage Foundation, 1987). There are almost twenty million Hispanics in the United States, that is, 14.6% of the total population.

6. Approximately 75% and 67% of operatives in Los Angeles and Miami apparel firms are Mexican and Cuban women respectively.

7. Note 54.2% of native-born and 47.5% of foreign-born Mexican women were employed outside the home in 1980. The equivalent figure for the mostly foreign-born Cuban women was almost 65%. Non-Hispanic white women's labor force participation in 1980 was assessed at 57.9% (U.S. Census of Population, 1980).

8. Peter S. Taylor, "Mexican Women in Los Angeles Industry in 1928," *Aztlán: International Journal of Chicano Studies Research*, 11, 1 (Spring, 1980): 99–129.

9. Alejandro Portes and Robert L. Bach, *Latin Journey: Cuban and Mexican Immigrants in the United States* (Berkeley: University of California Press, 1985), 67.

10. Alejandro Portes, "The Social Origins of the Cuban Enclave Economy of Miami," *Pacific Sociological Review*, Special Issue on the Ethnic Economy. 30, 4 (October, 1987): 340–372. See also Lisandro Perez, "Immigrant Economic Adjustment and Family Organization: The Cuban Success Story Reexamined," *International Migration Review*, 20 (1986): 4–20.

11. The following descriptions are chosen from a sample of 25 Mexican and 10 Cuban women garment workers interviewed in Los Angeles and Miami Counties. The names of people interviewed, and some identifying characteristics, have been changed.

PART FOUR

Stereotypes of Difference and Strategies of Identity

CHAPTER TWELVE

Claims to Motherhood:
Custody Disputes and Maternal Strategies

ELLEN LEWIN

This custody thing traumatized me, maybe more than the children. It was like the most frightening experience of my life. And I'm afraid to have another child. I'm afraid someone's going to try and take them away from me.
—*Thirty-four-year-old mother of two*

Custody battles between mothers and fathers are increasingly routine features of divorce negotiations. Despite the proliferation of "no-fault" divorce laws, the incidence of divorce-related litigation has grown in recent years, with a substantial proportion of these disputes centering on child custody. Until children reach majority, or the disputing parties exhaust their financial resources, nearly any change in the situation of either parent may be viewed as a "material change of circumstances" worthy of renewed legal inquiry.[1]

Although only a small percentage of men actually seek custody in court, as many as one-third of divorced women report custody litigation threats being raised in the course of divorce negotiations.[2] The outcome of negotiations once custody threats have been instituted (or even hinted at) shows that, fathers' stated motivations notwithstanding, the threat of a custody action serves to enforce compliance with other paternal demands—for low child and spousal support awards,[3] for a larger share of the marital property, or for visitation arrangements that are convenient for the father.[4]

Even when they feel that they are "good mothers," women tend to capitulate to husbands' demands when custody becomes an issue. There are a number of reasons for this. First, mothers know—or are advised to this effect by their attorneys—that the traditional judicial preference for maternal custody has been breaking down in recent years. Although the absolute number of fathers who actually become custodial parents remains small, this is because so few fathers attempt to win custody. Once a father brings a custody matter to trial, his chances of winning are about equal to those of his former wife.[5] Women are at a disadvantage in custody litigation because their post-divorce employment may be seen as being in conflict with their maternal obligations, because they have less to offer their children economically, or because their behavior may be more carefully scrutinized for evidence of immorality. Second, custody litigation is expensive, and women are more likely to agree to a compromise, or even to give up custody, because they cannot afford a long court battle. Finally, disputed custody can take a terrible toll on children, and mothers are apt to compromise to spare their children a potentially traumatic ordeal.

Lesbian mothers are particularly vulnerable to such litigation. Judges tend to view them as unsuitable custodial parents solely because of their sexual orientation, even in the absence of any direct evidence of improper parental behavior.[6] Because they are aware of their poor chances in a court of law, lesbian mothers are even more concerned about custody challenges than are other formerly married mothers. Lesbian mothers thus tend to develop careful and consciously crafted strategies aimed at protecting themselves from custody litigation. More frequently than heterosexual mothers, lesbians may perceive a threat to exist even when no direct challenge has been made.[7]

MOTHERHOOD AND GENDER

Being a mother has generally been viewed as a sort of default option—as the natural, essential outcome of being a woman, as a status ascribed, not achieved, and as the "cause," in one way or another, of women's predicament in the world.[8] Threats to custody, however, compel women to define and codify the qualities that make them suitable parents, to be self-conscious and reflective in ways otherwise rarely required. Ties assumed to be based on sentiment become basic elements of strategies that will help avoid custody litigation, or when litigation does occur, facilitate a successful outcome.

Courtroom battles over custody and the other legal machinations, which may accompany, precede, or substitute for them can arise only in a context in which motherhood has come to be viewed as an achieved characteristic. The courts no longer assume that there is something essential about being the female biological parent that destines a woman for custody of her children.[9] Rather, parenthood is seen, though not always explicitly, as a set of skills and resources, and, in the case of women, moral entitlements, which insure adequate care of minor children. Custody disputes, then, depend on contradicting the notion that motherhood, and therefore gender itself, is natural; claimants to custody must display their skills, prove to others what would otherwise be assumed to emanate from biology.[10]

As already mentioned, when lesbianism is raised in a custody situation, other factors tend to slip into the background. It is difficult enough to prove one's maternal capabilities, but to do so under conditions that view two aspects of one's identity as inherently opposed is even more difficult. Judges and others who make decisions about family policy tend to assume that homosexuality cannot be compatible with parenthood under any conditions.[11] The assumption that homosexuality and parenthood cannot be harmoniously or morally combined emerges, of course, not only in custody determinations but in decisions about adoption and foster family policy, visitation rights for gay fathers, and even concerns about homosexuals working in such fields as teaching and child care.[12]

The increase of custody challenges by fathers would seem to indicate greater paternal interest in childrearing and increasing social recognition of the importance of fathers as caretaking parents, a goal which has been at the heart of some feminist recommendations.[13] I will argue, however, that the strategies mothers employ to protect themselves from custody threats, and the social organization that evolves in the context of these threats, act instead to strengthen a matrifocal emphasis in families facing custody challenges. When the possibility of custody litigation throws its shadow over the divorced mother and her children, mothers tend to define parenthood as a solitary maternal venture, with little room for paternal contributions.

Ironically, this outcome differs little from the picture that continues to emerge of two-parent families even in "post-feminist" times. Despite much celebration of the growing importance of fathers as primary parents and caretakers, studies reveal that maternal employment notwithstanding, fathers spend only marginally more time caring for children and doing housework than they did in earlier times.[14] Thus, custody challenges have converged with other factors which produce family patterns in which mothers serve as primary, if not sole, caretakers of children.

MATERNAL STRATEGIES

In this paper, I will describe some of the strategies[15] divorced mothers, both lesbian and heterosexual, devise for managing the threat of custody litigation.[16] Central to most mothers' efforts to protect themselves from custody challenges are what we might call strategies of appeasement. Strategies of appeasement describe efforts made by mothers to influence fathers not to bring custody actions. Mothers who fear such litigation typically keep a "low profile" (particularly if they are lesbians or have a co-resident lover), abandon claims to marital property, child and spousal support, and make compromises on issues like visitation.

Strategies of appeasement are fundamental to most mothers' efforts to avoid custody litigation. No matter how respectable a woman may be, and no matter how much she really needs the economic or interactional involvement of her former husband to manage her childrearing obligations, she tends to become extremely fearful when custody is raised as a point of contention, regardless of how oblique the possibility of legal action may be. Mothers who confront custody challenges often feel that they have to defend their very being, that their essential value as persons is somehow under scrutiny.

Lesbians' fears of being totally vulnerable to custody litigation are even more intense, as most lesbian mothers are familiar with cases of mothers who have lost their children solely because of their sexual orientation. Ironically, accusations about lesbianism are quite common in custody litigation, even, as we shall see below, when there is no foundation for them. Thus, it is not unusual for a heterosexual mother to have to confront charges of lesbianism when her husband seeks custody, charges which can be quite difficult to disprove once they have been introduced.

As appeasement requires abandoning or reducing claims not only to paternal involvement but to financial support, it can be difficult to achieve without tapping other network resources. Mothers' ability to maintain strategies of appeasement when they face custody challenges can be enhanced by the availability of strategies of support, that is, by access to female friends or kin who can offer affective and instrumental support.

However, in the absence of a strong, effective network, particularly one which can cushion economic uncertainty, mothers may come to believe that they can depend only on themselves. Self-reliance, competence and individual ingenuity become key elements of their approach to adversity—a strategy of autonomy. Like many other aspects of the marriage-divorce system as it is emerging in American culture, maternal self-reliance has paradoxical benefits. At the same time that divorce represents the breakdown of the family and a personal failure for women, it provides an important opportunity to establish one's self-reliance, to avoid the expected, but morally ambiguous, dependence marital life implies for women. At the same time that marriage and motherhood represent entry into adult status,[17] the independence gained at divorce may be seen as further progress toward the cultural ideal of achieving individual autonomy.[18]

In the examples that follow I will indicate the ways in which mothers who face actual or potential custody challenges use strategies of appeasement, support, and autonomy in the course of protecting the integrity of their families. These data illustrate the ways in which these three strategic emphases intersect, producing, in many instances, unintended consequences for mother, father, and child. In particular, the claim to being a "good mother," a key element of female gender identity in American culture, is transformed from a natural attribute into the product of self-conscious achievement. This occurs at the same time that assumptions and behaviors displayed by these mothers are, in fact, drawn from elements and oppositions already in place in two-parent families.

STRATEGIES OF APPEASEMENT

Interviews with mothers who had experienced actual custody litigation or who regarded themselves as having been threatened with it at some point before or after their divorces consistently indicate that the mere mention of a custody challenge can dominate the proceedings. Most are aware that avoiding a battle during the divorce does not provide a permanent resolution, as a husband can return to court at any time in the future to seek a new custody ruling. This means that strategies for avoiding litigation must remain in operation at least until children turn eighteen.

Although Linda, a law student at the time of her divorce, is not a lesbian and has no specific reason to fear being declared "unfit," she was intimidated by the threat of a custody battle. Her psychologist husband raised the possibility of a custody suit during their settlement negotiations.

When I said you're not giving me enough money . . . he said, "Well, if we have to have a fight over money, we might as well have a fight over custody." So I got real panicked and real scared, and I didn't want to fight a custody battle with him. So I agreed just down the line with his financial arrangements. I was real scared. Although he didn't file a custody suit at that time, I knew it was going to come sooner or later. I hoped I could postpone it until I was out of law school and could fight back.

Linda believed that conciliatory behavior would make her husband less willing to pursue a custody challenge. But for lesbians, conciliation may not be enough. Appeasing a former husband and avoiding a custody suit frequently hinges on secrecy, maintaining strict separation of private and public lives, and, in some cases, deceiving the children. Mothers must weigh the potential damage of their children "letting something slip" to their father or the strain of the children having to keep a secret against the psychological effects on the family of clouding their identities in secrecy.

Shortly before Elaine, a suburban school teacher, filed for divorce, she had become lovers with another married woman. Her husband hired a private detective to observe her activities, and she soon found herself at the center of a custody trial.

That only got resolved because I lied on the stand, and said it had been a passing phase but it was over. Interestingly enough, the shrink . . . got on the stand and also said he thought it was a passing phase and he thought I was cured. So I got the kids.

Because Elaine lied at the trial, and also because her teaching position could be threatened by disclosure of her sexual orientation, she has had to be extremely cautious in the years since the divorce and has felt unable to challenge any of the financial arrangements which were worked out with her former husband.

Here I am leading this double life. Publicly I'm a flaming heterosexual, when in truth I'm a lesbian and my kids don't even really know about it. To go back to court over child support would give my ex-husband the opportunity to bring in the lesbian issue again, so I just figured I'd make it. And I did make it financially. I took in boarders, rented out the garage.

Theresa, the mother of a nine-year-old son, went through a lengthy custody trial, which left her virtually bankrupt. She was not a lesbian at the time of the trial and John, her former husband, was unable to substantiate his accusations that she was. Since the custody dispute, however, she has come out[19] and now feels that she must carefully separate her life as a mother and as a lesbian in order to protect herself from more litigation. She does not perceive her husband's history of psychiatric illness and her own record of social stability and professional accomplishment as improving her chances in any way.

Now that I'm gay, I'd lose. There's just no way in the world I would win, after having my fitness questioned when I was Lady Madonna, let alone now. So I would just simply tell him, no, I won't go to court, if you want custody, take it . . . I've done everything to keep my ex-husband or my son from finding out.

The precautions Theresa has taken include living in a middle-class suburban area and arranging her house in a way she considers unimpeachably "bourgeois." The Bay Bridge, which separates her home from San Francisco, where she works and meets lesbian friends, has become a symbol to her of her divided life. She undergoes a transformation as she travels the bridge homeward or toward the city, experiencing the commute as an opportunity to prepare herself for the requirements of her destination. The most vital aspect of her strategy is preventing her son from discovering her lesbianism, not wanting him to bear the burden of keeping her secret.

Ironically, avoidance of her former husband, which would enable Theresa to relax her vigilance a bit, is the very thing that she has not been able to arrange. She considers John, who has a disability which keeps him from regular employment, a model father, and has accepted his offer of childcare in her home while she works. On one level, this arrangement saves her a great deal of money and also insures that her son has regular contact with his father, something she sees as desirable. On another level, the childcare arrangement has eliminated any possibility of privacy for Theresa. She must not only restrict the kinds of friends who visit her home, but must make sure that no compromising material of any sort can be found in the house.

In many instances, the husband only indirectly threatens to bring the mother into court and to use lesbianism as a weapon. Jean, a lesbian mother of two daughters, describes the negotiations surrounding her divorce, which terminated with her sacrificing nearly all of the money she had contributed to the purchase of a house.

He never brought it into the negotiations directly. But he would like call me and harass me, and by innuendo suggest that there were many issues that he *could* bring up if he wanted to . . . So basically, I traded my equity in the house for that issue not being raised at that time.

Besides the loss of her share of the house, Jean was unable to get Richard to agree to contribute to the children's education or their medical expenses. Although she has considered returning to court to change the agreement, the possibility that her ex-husband would raise the issue of her lesbianism has discouraged her from doing this. Richard nearly always sends his child support payments late and, in a recent dispute, has refused to contribute to the costs of orthodontia for the children. In an effort to improve relations with him, Jean offered to send him a monthly written narrative about the children's activities. He said that he would like her to do this, but refused to consider doing the same thing for the time the children spend with him in the summer.

In another case, Rita, a clerical worker who lives with her woman lover and her eight-year-old son, reports that she has no way to enforce the child support and visitation agreement made at the time of her divorce because of her fear that a custody challenge might arise. Although her ex-husband, Jim, was supposed to pay her $100 a month and see their son every other weekend, he has never made a single payment and has almost never visited the child, failing even to remember his birthday. Despite this history, Rita still thinks that Jim might become interested in custody, perhaps if he were to remarry.

Rita believes, though, that as long as Jim does not pay child support, her position in a possible custody case is strengthened; as a further gesture toward self-protection, Rita has not directly discussed her lesbianism with her son. She lives openly with her lover, sharing a bedroom with her, and explained during the interview that nearly all of their friends are gay. Nevertheless, she feels sure that her son is unaware of the situation and thus protected from having to keep a secret.[20] Rita does not believe that Jim's record of violent behavior toward her (which once resulted in an arrest for battery) would help her in a custody battle.

In some other instances, custody threats are even less explicit, but still serve to affect the way mothers manage their relations with their former husbands. Judy, the mother of a nine-year-old son, left her marriage after she got involved in the women's movement and began a relationship with a woman. Judy works part-time in an office and is active in local feminist organizations.

I figured I should tell the lawyer I was gay, since he was really pushing to get a lot of money out of my husband . . . [but] I was saying no, don't push it, to the lawyer, because I'm gay and I don't want a custody hassle. And the lawyer really got off on that, and started asking me all these questions about did I lust for women, and all that crap. It was really awful.

Judy's son, Michael, spends each summer with Bill, and each summer Bill raises the possibility of having the boy live with him year round. Judy has given some thought to this request, seeing it as evidence of Bill's commitment to their son. However, a lawyer she recently consulted has advised her that allowing such an arrangement, even on a temporary basis, would open the door to a permanent custody change. Judy also perceives any challenge to the existing financial arrangement as too provocative to consider. Since the divorce, Judy's husband has remarried and is doing very well financially. He has never increased his small financial contribution, and has refused to help pay for any unusual expenses, such as music lessons, claiming that this is in line with Judy's feminist principles.

He's said that since I made this feminist decision to live on my own and not be dependent on a man, why should he give me more money? Which I sort of agree with in a lot of ways. I don't really want to be dependent on him financially.

Bill knows that his son will not be deprived of anything he really needs, because Judy's parents, who are well-to-do, are willing to help her with expenses beyond her means.

The effect of Bill's custody threat, subtle though it has been, is to limit the amount of contact he has with his son and to make quite unlikely any sort of authentically "joint" custody arrangement.[21] Were Judy not fearful, for example, that Bill might launch a custody battle once he had "possession" of Michael during the school year, she might be willing to allow an arrangement that would give her son longer, and more meaningful, exposure to his father. She also might be more aggressive in seeking child support payments that would reflect the actual cost of raising her son and correspond more accurately to her ex-husband's income. In addition, however, to her fear of a custody challenge, Judy's knowledge that she can depend on her parents for assistance mitigates her need to make further financial claims on her former husband. In the same vein, Rita makes no effort to obtain a more significant financial and personal commitment from her former husband while Jean accepts the asymmetrical arrangement she has worked out with her children's father.

IMPACT ON FATHERS

The impact of these strategies is to reinforce the mother's role as the sole support of the household, to limit the contact between father and child, and to accentuate differences between the cultural and economic climates of the maternal and paternal homes. For most mothers, the need to keep distance from their former husbands means that the father is the last person with whom issues affecting the child are discussed; to share real problems with him would be to admit to weakness or error, and the mothers whose custody claims are in doubt cannot risk such exposure. Thus, while the father's interest in custody implies an interest in participating in childrearing, the actual effect of his custody bid is to exclude him from most aspects of parenting.

Carol, a lesbian mother of a son and a daughter, lost custody of her children for several months but finally regained it after a lengthy trial. Although her children visit regularly with their father, she never discusses any of their problems with him.

I do not want to talk with him about any of that kind of stuff because I think he would use it against me. I don't trust him still and I do feel that he would like custody of our son for sure.

Similarly, Linda, the law student described earlier, is conscious of not being able to rely on her ex-husband for any level of material or emotional support. She characterizes her husband as a "spectator" in his approach to fatherhood. He sees himself as doing a good job if he takes the children on excursions, but is unable to manage any of the problems that arise when they make their weekly visits.

If he has a headache, the kids come home. If one of the children has the sniffles, the kids come home. He puts up with the fun, but he doesn't quite know how to handle the inconveniences. In fact, at times he's just dropped them off on the doorstep and pulled away.

Because of the continuing history of custody threats since the end of the marriage, Linda does not feel that she can discuss any parental matters with him.

When I do present problems to him, he points out what I'm doing wrong. And it makes me feel that he's gathering evidence for another custody suit. He will reveal nothing of what he perceives as problems to me. So we don't communicate at all. Luckily, I have friends that I can talk to about my concerns about the kids. The man that I'm involved with, I talk to about them. My happiness I want to share as much as the problems, and it makes me sad that I can't share that with him. But there's too much of a wall of bitterness to talk about us sharing the good things about our kids. And there's not trust enough to share the problems, so there's just no communication around that.

While paternal interest in gaining custody would seem to indicate that fathers are eager to play a fuller role in their children's formative years, not only actual threats of custody litigation but even expressions of interest in spending more time with children can cause mothers to become fearful. On the one hand, mothers often suspect that custody threats are made cynically in order to reduce the amount of child support paid, to negotiate a more favorable property settlement, or to otherwise influence mothers to accept less than adequate economic arrangements. Because custody decisions are never final, the threat of renewed litigation can persist, even after a mother has won custody in court. On the other hand, even fathers who have a sincere interest in their children may find themselves distanced from them, as mothers seek to avoid any kind of contact that might generate evidence usable in a custody challenge.

SOURCES OF SUPPORT

When mothers who face custody challenges can use their networks for ongoing material or emotional support, the exclusion of the father from their support system is less likely to leave them either isolated or impaired in their ability to manage unexpected situations.

In Rita's case, for example, the financial difficulties caused by Jim's failure to pay child support are eased by the regular support she receives from her family. Despite the fact that Rita's mother is uneasy with her lesbianism (including being actively hostile toward Rita's lover, Jill), they have developed a daily childcare arrangement, which makes it possible for Rita to manage quite well on a low income.

Rita's relationship with her mother is not one-sided. Her mother depends on her for support when there is a family crisis, and Rita has a strong sense of responsibility toward the entire family. She also has a close relationship with her father, sometimes spending hours talking with him when something bothers her. He helps her with her car and advises her on household repairs. Rita's sister is another source of emotional support. They often talk on the phone, and sometimes care for each other's children for extended periods.

For many mothers, friends, rather than relatives, form the core of the support network. Linda, as mentioned earlier, is able to discuss problems and concerns both with her boyfriend (whom she is planning to marry) and with two close women friends. The emotional support she receives from these friends is supplemented, in the case of her boyfriend, with financial assistance. She describes her women friends as being "like sisters"; both have children close in age to her children and this means that they are ideal people with whom to discuss various parenting dilemmas, the very issues she is afraid to raise with her former husband.

Rosemary, a forty-year-old mother of five, now going through a divorce after twenty years of marriage, often finds herself in need of emotional support. Ironically, though Rosemary is not a lesbian, her husband is gathering evidence about her friendships with other women to allege that she is. No less than women who are lesbians, Rosemary is fearful about defending her "fitness" in court.

Intellectually, I realize that they're not going to be taken from me. But emotionally, I feel like I'm in a panic, because how the hell do I go around and prove I'm a good parent? You can find a hell of a lot of proof to find you're bad. But you can't find proof that says you're good.

Besides the custody challenge, Rosemary is facing financial disaster in the wake of her husband's departure. The marriage had been quite traditional, so until it was over, Rosemary was not familiar with family finances and the way in which her husband managed his income. Now that she is alone, she has discovered that her husband, Carl, left her in serious debt, forcing her to move from their large house to a small apartment and leaving her unable to obtain credit on her own. The situation is not helped by Carl's hostility when she attempts to communicate with him, nor by his refusal to pay child support until ordered to do so by the court. He has a large income and continues to maintain a comfortable, even luxurious, lifestyle, a contrast Rosemary finds especially painful when her children return from visits and compare her household unfavorably with his.

A number of friendships have helped sustain Rosemary through the difficult period following the collapse of her marriage, but one woman friend has had a particularly central role during this time. Every night at a prearranged time, she and her friend Charlotte (a divorced mother who lost custody of her children) have agreed to talk on the phone. They both discuss their problems, but in recent times Rosemary often cries while Charlotte listens. Rosemary helped Charlotte go through the trauma of her divorce and the loss of her children; now Charlotte is reciprocating. But the support Rosemary receives from this friendship goes beyond these telephone conversations. On occasions when Rosemary feels that she cannot cope with her children alone, she can call Charlotte and ask her to join them for dinner. In addition, without much explicit discussion of Rosemary's serious financial difficulties, Charlotte often arrives at Rosemary's door with a turkey or other food which she "doesn't need."

Strategies of appeasement and strategies of support can dovetail neatly, with support systems enhancing mothers' efforts to appease ex-husbands. But in some instances, these two strategic emphases may conflict, as when the way to appease a litigious father appears to be including him in the day-to-day family routine. Arrangements of this type create particularly stressful situations for mothers, as successful maintenance of a "low profile" is difficult when one's former husband is constantly on the scene.

For example, Theresa's situation, which gives her little choice but to involve her husband as her son's regular caretaker, undermines her efforts to incorporate friends into her support system. The result is a fragmented, highly specialized network. She gets her main emotional support from her friends at work, who accept her as a lesbian and respect her as a skilled professional. But these friends do not cross the bridge into her personal life.

Theresa's lover also provides some needed emotional support, but this is compromised by the secrecy that shrouds their relationship; the relationship itself is as much a source of stress as a support, since it is the most likely point at which secrecy might be breached. Nor can Theresa look to her family for substantial support. She has a warm and affectionate relationship with them, but counts on them for little concrete as they live in an Eastern city and are quite poor. Rather, she is protective toward them, and hesitates to share any information with them that might be alarming.

Similarly, the price of the extensive emotional and economic support Rita receives from her family has been the peripheralization of her tie with her lover, Jill. Her parents refuse to visit her home or to include Jill in family events; at the same time, however, their assistance makes it easier for Rita to maintain a relationship which could discredit her in a custody action.

MAXIMIZING AUTONOMY

For some mothers, insulating themselves from threats to custody depends on self-reliance; these women find it difficult to form supportive networks, particularly when caution restricts their contacts with relatives and with their ex-husbands. As one lesbian mother said:

I feel like I'm some kind of a spy-agent, or something like that, with a secret assignment that I have to be protecting. Like the state secrets or something. It's a pressure on me.

Similarly, Theresa's inability to maintain sufficient distance from her ex-husband to bring supportive others into her life has essentially pushed her toward a strategy of autonomy. In other instances, women describe disappointments in efforts to sustain supportive networks among friends, perceiving non-mothers as selfish and insensitive to the problems faced by mothers.

Not uncommonly, mothers who describe themselves as sole parents see this as a condition which began during their marriages. For example, Rosemary, now embarking on a custody battle with her husband of twenty years, sees little difference between her circumstances as a married and as a single mother.

I consider that I was a single parent for twenty years of the marriage. He wasn't there for birthdays, he didn't show up for christenings, it was not uncommon for me to stand in the doorway Christmas day and say, goddamit, mister, it's Christmas, please don't go out sailing today . . . Going to PTA meetings, getting involved in their Brownies, their Cub Scouts—it was all my job. I did all of that. Discipline, I did all that. I did the cooking, the cleaning, the shopping. I took care of everything. I took the kids to the doctors, I made the appointments. If they had any emergencies, I took care of it. I still do. That's no different.

While for some women, then, self-reliance implies the absence of an effective, reliable support system, for others it reveals competence and skill which they were never able to display before, or which they couldn't acknowledge. Carol, the lesbian mother of two, who won her children back from their father in a lengthy custody suit, described becoming a single mother in terms of personal growth and development.

I felt before that I was in a jar. There were a lot of things cooking around inside, but the lid was on. And now I feel I've had the opportunity to really think for myself, find out what I can do for myself, make the decision myself . . . I am the head of the household. I can feel it. That feels good to me. I was the head of the household essentially when he was here, but there was a deference to him . . . I feel more grown up [now] than I ever did.

Carol's feelings were echoed by Susan, a heterosexual mother who is cautious in her dealings with her former husband because of oblique threats he has made about custody. Although she has close relationships with her sisters and has several women friends, she does not feel that she can easily depend on any of them for ongoing assistance. She also has established an intimate relationship with a man who gets along well with her son, but she believes that there is a limit to what she can expect from him because he is not, and never can be, the "real father."

Despite an initial period of intense loneliness, a feeling that she was "part of nobody," at the time that she left her marriage, Susan has come to view the end of her marriage and the need for self-reliance it has engendered as the "greatest thing that ever happened to me."

Independence . . . As an adult to have control over my own life. To make my own decisions, to not to have to ask anybody to do anything. To do whatever I want without having to consult. In terms of raising my child, to do it the way I see fit, and not to have to fight somebody else over that. My image of that is a flower that's tightened within itself. After the divorce, it opened up like— have you ever seen a slow-motion of a flower opening? That's what I felt like. My personality and my strength just really blossomed.

CONCLUSION

Custody threats tend to eclipse differences among mothers. In the cases discussed here, lesbian and heterosexual mothers coping with potential or actual custody litigation devise strikingly similar strategies for managing threats to family integrity. Whether they bear the additional legal handicap of lesbianism or not, mothers feel able to survive the custody challenge only by bargaining with scarce resources. This generally means both abandoning rights to material benefits that might be obtained from the former husband and peripheralizing him as a parent.

Rather than just "being" mothers, women involved in custody disputes come self-consciously to define their maternal achievements, to break down their roles into specific components and skills which fathers cannot—or will not—perform. Instead of looking to nature to legitimate claims to motherhood, women must depend both on demonstrating competence, as well as on invalidating paternal claims, whether they do this in the formal legal system or through informal negotiation.

The mothers that I interviewed have lost the financial support once available to them from their children's fathers but few suggest that divorce had deprived them of a collaborator in the business of parenting. For those women who face or fear a custody battle, the need to defend their centrality as parents adds a bitter irony to their situations: they know that the custody challenge is, in many instances, a strategy for providing less, rather than more, care for their children. Even when paternal interest in the children is sincere, mothers understand that they will not survive the custody challenge if they offer what their former husbands ostensibly desire—more involvement in the daily business of parenting—as this will only make them more vulnerable to litigation.

Instead, appeasement, accession to paternal demands to an extent that discourages a custody challenge, along with successful use of supporting strategies, marks maternal competence. Being a "good mother" is thus transformed from a state of being, a natural attribute, into evidence of skill, rewarded by preventing fathers from gaining custody or, better yet, by keeping custody disputes from arising.

At the same time, then, that custody threats exacerbate the pressures on these families, they provide a context within which women can demonstrate their competence and achieve not only the status of "good mother" but that of autonomous adult woman. In establishing their claims to motherhood, women facing custody disputes also explicitly negotiate gender, deriving pride from their struggles and defining motherhood as achievement and strength.

NOTES

Research for this paper was supported by NIMH Grant MH-30890 and by a grant from the Rockefeller Foundation Gender Roles Program. The author wishes to thank Terrie A. Lyons for her contribution to the research and analysis, and Faye Ginsburg, Carol Shepherd McClain and Anna Tsing for their comments on earlier drafts of this paper.

1. Phyllis Chesler, *Mothers on Trial* (New York: McGraw-Hill, 1986); Nancy D. Polikoff, "Gender and Child-Custody Determinations: Exploding the Myths," in *Families, Politics, and Public Policy: A Feminist Dialogue on Women and the State*, ed. Irene Diamond (New York: Longman, 1983), 183–202; Lenore Weitzman, *The Divorce Revolution* (New York: Free Press, 1985).

2. Weitzman, 310.

3. Single mother families already derive little income from child and spousal awards, as numerous studies have shown. About 40% of divorced fathers are not required to make payments, and of the 60% who receive support orders, about half do not comply. See B. R. Bergmann and M. D. Roberts, "Income for the Single Parent: Child Support, Work and Welfare," in *Gender in the Workplace,* ed. Clair Brown and Joseph A. Pechman (Washington, DC: Brookings Institute, 1987), 247–270.

4. Terry Arendell, *Mothers and Divorce* (Berkeley: University of California Press, 1986).

5. Polikoff, 184.

6. Nan D. Hunter and Nancy D. Polikoff, "Custody Rights of Lesbian Mothers: Legal Theory and Litigation Strategy," *Buffalo Law Review* 25 (1976): 691–733; Ellen Lewin, "Lesbianism and Motherhood: Implications for Child Custody," *Human Organization* 40, no. 1 (1981): 6–14; Rhonda R. Rivera, "Legal Issues in Gay and Lesbian Parenting," in *Gay and Lesbian Parents*, ed. Frederick W. Bozett (New York: Praeger, 1987), 199–227.

7. Terrie A. Lyons, "Lesbian Mothers' Custody Fears," in *Women Changing Therapy,* ed. Joan H. Robbins and Rachel J. Siegel (New York: Haworth Press, 1983), 231–240.

8. Carole H. Browner and Ellen Lewin, "Female Altruism Reconsidered: The Virgin Mary as Economic Woman," *American Ethnologist 9,* no. 1 (1982): 61–75. See also Judith K. Brown, "A Note on the Division of Labor by Sex," *American Anthropologist 72* (1970): 1073–78; Nancy Chodorow, *The Reproduction of Mothering* (Berkeley: University of California Press, 1978); Sherry B. Ortner, "Is Female to Male as Nature is to Culture?" in *Woman, Culture and Society,* ed. Michelle Z. Rosaldo and Louise Lamphere (Stanford: Stanford University Press, 1974), 67–87; Michelle Z. Rosaldo, "Woman, Culture and Society: A Theoretical Overview," in *Woman, Culture and Society,* ed. Michelle Z. Rosaldo and Louise Lamphere (Stanford: Stanford University Press, 1974), 17–42, for classic interpretations of the impact of motherhood on women's social and cultural status.

9. Custody law has shifted since the nineteenth-century from a primary concern with parental rights (associated with the notion that children are the property of the father), to a maternal preference (by which mothers could only lose custody, particularly of children of "tender years," if they were deemed "unfit"), to the current standard of "best interests of the child," purported to be gender-neutral. See Committee on the Family, Group for the Advancement of Psychiatry, *Divorce, Child Custody and the Family* (San Francisco: Jossey-Bass, 1980); Weitzman, 36.

10. Along similar lines, it might be noted that the culture increasingly views reproduction itself in this light. The interests of pregnant women and fetuses, for example, are commonly supposed to be separate and antithetical, reflected both in the normalization of a variety of technological interventions during pregnancy and birth and in recent approaches to such matters as "surrogacy." See Barbara Katz Rothman, *The Tentative Pregnancy* (New York: Viking, 1986) and George Annas, "Baby M: Babies (and Justice) for Sale," *Hastings Center Report 17,* no. 3 (1987): 13–15, for discussions of recent developments in these areas. In "Reproductive Technologies and the Deconstruction of Motherhood," her chapter in her edited volume, *Reproductive Technologies: Gender, Motherhood and Medicine* (Minneapolis: University of Minnesota Press, 1987), 10–35, Michelle Stanworth has pointed to the ongoing development of guidelines to insure that women who avail themselves of new conceptive technology are heterosexual and married. Not coincidentally in the same period, the law has come increasingly to resolve custody disputes by making mothers demonstrate their qualifications. Gender, as well as motherhood, must be achieved in all of these contexts.

11. Lewin, 7.

12. See Wendell Ricketts and Roberta Achtenberg, "The Adoptive and Foster Gay and Lesbian Parent," in *Gay and Lesbian Parents,* ed. Frederick W. Bozett (New York: Praeger, 1987), 89–111; and Rhonda R. Rivera, "Our Straight-Laced Judges: The Legal Position of Homosexual Persons in the United States," *Hastings Law Journal 30,* no. 4 (1979): 799–956.

13. See, for example, Chodorow, 211–219; and Dorothy Dinnerstein, *The Mermaid and the Minotaur* (New York: Harper and Row, 1977). Authors representing the perspective of "fathers' rights" generally question what they

consider an unwarranted maternal preference in most custody awards, as well as complain about the size of divorce settlements, alimony and child support payments. Many guides for fathers who wish to seek custody have been published, and the theme of paternal nurturance has been popularized by such films as *Kramer vs. Kramer*. See, for example, Mel Roman and William Haddad, *The Disposable Parent* (New York: Holt, Rinehart, Winston, 1978); and Gerald A. Silver and Myrna Silver, *Weekend Fathers* (Los Angeles: Stratford Press, 1981) for examples of this perspective; see also Polikoff, 183–197 for a critique.

14. See Heidi I. Hartmann, "The Family as the Locus of Gender, Class, and Political Struggle: The Example of Housework," *Signs* 6, no. 3 (1981): 366–394.

15. I have spoken elsewhere of the ways in which becoming a mother may be used strategically to enable women to achieve goals with broader cultural significance. Forging links with particular categories of people, notably with children, may be central to maternal agendas in some contexts, as shown by Browner and Lewin, 61–73. In other situations, as for lesbians who use donor insemination, the formation of a particularly valued personal identity appears to define varied approaches to becoming a mother. See Ellen Lewin, "By Design: Reproductive Strategies and the Meaning of Motherhood," in *The Sexual Politics of Reproduction,* ed. Hilary Homans (London: Gower, 1985), 123–38. Maternal strategies are characteristic not only of the process of becoming a mother (with or without a conscious decision) but of subsequent behavior and choices.

16. Data presented here are excerpted from 135 interviews with lesbian and heterosexual single mothers conducted in the San Francisco Bay Area between 1977 and 1981. Informants' names and some descriptive details have been changed to preserve their anonymity.

17. See Lois W. Hoffman, "Effects of the First Child on the Woman's Role," in *The First Child and Family Formation,* ed. Warren B. Miller and Lucile F. Newman (Chapel Hill: Carolina Population Center, 1978), 340–67.

18. See, for example, Robert Bellah, et al., *Habits of the Heart* (Berkeley: University of California Press, 1985).

19. "Coming out" can refer to one's first homosexual experience, but also describes the point at which one defines oneself as a lesbian or gay and/or acknowledges this identity to others. See, for example, Jeannine Gramick, "Developing a Lesbian Identity," in *Women-Identified Women,* ed. Trudy Darty and Sandee Potter (Palo Alto, CA: Mayfield, 1984), 31–44.

20. Interestingly, Rita's son was present during most of the interview. She did not appear to censor her remarks or to feel that his presence altered his "unawareness" of her sexual orientation.

21. See Roman and Haddad, 123–148, 173–174; C. Ware, *Sharing Parenthood After Divorce* (New York: Viking, 1982); Lenore Weitzman and Ruth Dixon, "Child Custody Awards: Legal Standards and Empirical Patterns for Child Custody, Support and Visitation After Divorce," *UC Davis Law Review* 12 (1979): 473–521.

CHAPTER THIRTEEN

Passing Notes and Telling Jokes: Gendered Strategies among American Middle School Teenagers

JOYCE E. CANAAN

Why do teenagers develop strategies in gendered groups? What do these strategies reveal about their constructions of femininity and masculinity? How do findings about these strategies contribute to the gender literature, in which there is a near silence about teenagers? This paper explores these questions by showing how American middle-class teenage boys and girls respectively use the gender-marked strategies of joke-telling and note-passing to elaborate gender-specific peer group systems. It suggests that teenage prestige hierarchies draw on class, status and gender division within the community in which they live, and from the community's status regionally and nationally. In this sense, these hierarchies reproduce social hierarchies that structure American social relations more generally.

During my fieldwork[1] among teenagers in the American upper middle-class suburban community of Sheepshead,[2] I found that the classroom in particular and the school in general provided key sites where teenage girls and boys implicitly elaborate gendered understandings of themselves. This is especially true during middle school—the first of two secondary schools for teenagers between 11 and 14 in grades six through eight. Middle school teenagers, unlike their high school elders who go out with friends on weekday evenings and on weekends, have few public spaces other than school for meeting friends.[3]

I found that middle school students develop an explicit and exclusive three-tiered peer group system. They call these three components the "top" or "popular," "middle" and "low groups." Middle school boys, especially those in the top group, interrupt their teachers by making fun of other boys, especially those in the "low groups." I also found that girls—in all three of their peer groups—more quietly interfere with the teacher by writing and passing notes to others in the same group. These intra-peer group interactions, I will suggest, provide a basis with which both boys and girls explore and elaborate their gender-specific social hierarchies.[4] This paper argues that although teenagers formulate gendered identities as part of peer group strategies that seem to establish them as separate from and even "rebelling against" adults, in fact in many ways they mirror their parents' social world.

THE COMMUNITY OF SHEEPSHEAD

Sheepshead is a mostly white (97%), predominantly upper middle-class community of about 13,000 near a major American city on the eastern seaboard. Community leaders tend to be Roman Catholic; other religious groups include Protestants, Jews, and members of the Russian Orthodox church. About 75% of community members are of American parentage while the rest are of Italian (16%), German (14%), or Polish (9%) descent. Many families are *nouveau riche*, recently moved from lower middle-class communities on the other side of the city to this more spacious and wealthy community. Sheepshead is not a community that esteems so-called "high" cultural values associated with the established middle-class.[5] For example, parental contributions to and teenagers' participation in athletic programs far exceeds that for more "cultural" programs like music and art. The town has a chapter of the John Birch society, an indication of the strength of conservative political values in Sheepshead. The homogeneity of the community by race and class leads to a general consensus in values. The high race and class status of Sheepshead both regionally and nationally encourages teenagers to reproduce, rather than repudiate, their parents' values.[6]

Sheepshead has the third highest per capita income in the state.[7] With 70% of the male work force holding white collar jobs that pay at least 50% more than the blue collar jobs held by nearly 30% of male workers, the gap between the two groups is significant, giving the community a decidedly upper middle-class aura. While 30% of all women in the community work outside the home,[8] this percentage and the salaries these women receive are well below the national average, yet another sign of Sheepshead's general conservatism.[9]

Sheepshead's schools have the third highest per pupil income in the state, which is not surprising, given the town's high per capita income. Its five public schools include three elementary schools, a middle school (of about 600 students) and a high school. As Bourdieu,[10] among others, has shown, in Western capitalist cultures academic qualifications indirectly contribute to and affirm a dominant group's position. This privileged background enables these children to enter school with more of the skills required for success, and to attend schools with the best equipment and staff. Thus it is not surprising that Sheepshead high school teenagers whose parents hold white collar jobs tend to go to four and two year colleges (about 70%). Nor is it surprising that the 30% whose parents hold blue collar jobs tend to go to business/secretarial, art or technical school (7%), blue and pink collar work (14%), or that about 8% of them are undecided about their future.[11]

Middle school students' positions in their gendered, three-tiered peer group systems, like their later career plans, are strongly influenced by their parents' career paths. Mainly children of professional managerial fathers are in the "middle" and "top" or "popular" groups and mainly children of fathers holding blue collar jobs are in the "low" group. The former groups have the monetary power and cultural knowledge necessary to consume the key objects and activities with which popularity is constructed.[12] In other words, the existence of a number of ranked "middle-class sectors" within Sheepshead—business, professional, clerical, and sales—shapes the prestige hierarchies of teenagers.[13] Within these hierarchies, gender differentiation is created and reproduced through the kinds of activities that are the focus of this paper.

THE GENDER AND YOUTH SUBCULTURES LITERATURES

Gender in contemporary U.S. society has been described as involving a differentiation between men's "public" and women's "domestic" orientations. In mid-nineteenth-century America, the dominant view of middle-class white women gave primacy to their roles as mothers and homemakers, who socialized children and developed their moral character—and affirmed that of husbands—so that their husbands could survive and maintain their own moral integrity and economic position in the heartless and unstable world of industrializing America.[14] During the twentieth century, primacy has been given to women's role as supervisors of expressive functions in the home, as those primarily responsible for the "intimacy" of the marital relationship and for children's psychological development.[15]

Although women increasingly work outside the home, and domestic work and services are increasingly available in the market, the structural separation and assymetry of gender relations, and the association of women with the home and men with work, still remains in Western cultures today. While most women now work after marriage, their jobs tend to be less powerful and prestigious, pay less, and have fewer fringe benefits than those of men. Not surprisingly, married middle-class women and men view women's jobs as supplementary to their domestic responsibilities and to the primary job of the male breadwinner. Thus, despite women's work outside the home, the dominant notion of femininity is "specifically linked with the private realm of the home and the bedroom."[16]

Concomitantly, masculinity remains linked with the public sphere. It is, as Connell suggests, a hegemonic form "constructed in relation to various subordinated masculinities as well as in relation to women"[17] and it sets the agenda with which gender and gender relations are constructed, negotiated, and transformed.[18]

I am suggesting, then, that for white American middle-class people today, women's orientation to the private sphere refers to their focus on the home as both physical and emotional space. Men's orientation to the public sphere refers to their focus on work and performance in most contexts. Although there is greater acceptance of women working outside the home, in communities like Sheepshead they are still thought to be supplementing the family income rather than pursuing a career; their orientation to the home is seen as motivating them to work. They are still seen as less committed to work and their lower pay is often justified on these grounds. Finally, women are thought to take care of the supposedly "innermost" aspects of home life, their family's psychological make-up and their husband's sexuality. As I will show in this paper, teenage girls and boys are reproducing these orientations in their own activities.

I would argue that the identities and expectations for male vs. female behavior that these teenagers enact helps to reproduce a gendered division of labor and, therefore, American capitalism as we know it.[19] In moving beyond an analysis that views gender difference as biological or otherwise a natural outcome of motherhood, it is important to understand how gender identities are formed, reproduced, and possibly renegotiated between generations.

The youth subcultures' literature makes some promising directions from which to address these issues. It posits that young peoples' rebelliousness depends not just on historical circumstances or on a generation's consciousness of itself, as sociologists claim, but on young people's social class position. It explores how the capitalist mode of production shapes Western youth, especially those from working-class backgrounds. These youth, who experience most inequality, are also most resistant to dominant adult dictates.[20] However, as later research in this tradition illustrates, the early work focuses almost singularly on young white boys,[21] ignoring people of color, girls, or the relationship between girls and boys in peer group formation. This is thought to be due either to male bias[22] or to girls being "mute" in male-dominated public spheres because they develop a "bedroom culture" at home.[23] More recent research explores whether bedroom culture is as "potentially subversive" as prior researchers posited.[24] In my work on gender among middle-class teenagers, one can see how the formation of peer group identities and hierarchies create male orientations toward public drama and female orientations toward private intimacy. To better understand how this process takes place, I will first evaluate the Sheepshead middle-school structure and the way students respond to it in forming their peer group system. This structure, like community social relations, provides a basis for students' gender-based social hierarchies.

THE MIDDLE SCHOOL STRUCTURE AND STUDENTS' RESPONSE TO IT

For Sheepshead teenagers, peer group formation is established within the possibilities of the everyday practices of middle school life. Elementary school students in Sheepshead spend most of the day in a structured class-room with one teacher. Middle school students, in contrast, spend their days in up to eight classrooms with up to eight teachers, each of whom devotes time to bureaucratic matters like taking attendance, which gives students more unstructured time together during classes than before.[25] Since adults no longer supervise their movement from class to class as directly or strictly as before, students also spend more time together between classes which develops their awareness of themselves as a group. In addition, middle school classes are ranked at one of three 'levels' of purported academic ability. It is in the context of ranking and growing peer group awareness that students begin developing a comprehensive, three-tiered peer group system of their own.[26]

Middle school students heighten and formalize these and other differences by developing exclusive and ranked "top," "middle" and "low" gender-specific groups into which all can be placed. Top group members enact this system by making themselves positively outstanding and those they consider most subordinate negatively outstanding.[27] For example, in hallways be-tween classes, one of two top group males "accidentally" pushes the other into a low group male, making the latter's books fall on the floor. Or, a top group female, watched by her friends, tells a low group female that she is ugly and should bathe more often.[28] Actions like these explicitly designate those in the top and low groups and implicitly designate those in the middle group. In the following section on boys' joke-telling and girls' note-passing, I will show how in Sheepshead teenagers use such activities to elaborate gender-based social hierarchies.

BOYS' CLASSROOM JOKING

One of the primary ways in which top group males develop peer groups and their understanding of masculinity in classes is by telling jokes in class, usually about low group males. If successful, these jokes disrupt but do not anger the teacher and demonstrate the teller's strength and control relative to the subordinates they mock, and to girls. Their descriptions of joking reveal how they make this activity masculine. John Monroe, a seventh grader near the top group, compares his joke telling to that of low group Mikey Baritelli:

JM: A crack is as good as nothing if it's [delivered] too late. I mean, kids will say, like, Mikey Baritelli's got some good jokes. I'll give him that credit. But his timing sucks.
JC: Why?
JM: Like, like um, after all the jokes are made [in class], he'll say, "Hey, so-and-so, ha, ha." Or else he'll say a totally unfunny joke. To make no joke at all, and to make an unfunny joke is the worst thing of all, 'cause you'll get so mocked out. "Ah, Mikey, shut up, you scrub puppy!" They'll tear you apart . . . I'm not the best joke teller, but I've got good timing. I know when

and when not to pitch a good joke. Like if there's a roll going, where everybody's [going] bang, bang, bang, I'll throw in a couple. Usually the class cracks up.

JC: That helps you to be popular, doesn't it?

JM: Yeah. I think I'm climbing up from the middle group.

According to John, his own joke-telling differs from Mikey's in two respects; he knows good jokes and delivers them with "good timing." He realizes this partly because the class laughs or "cracks up" when he tells jokes. Mikey faces a rather different response. He is "mocked out" because his jokes are "unfunny" and his "timing sucks." John suggests that timing is the more critical factor; while he may not have the best joke repertoire, he, unlike Mikey, knows "when and when not to pitch" jokes. John's comments indicate that another factor also contributes to good joke-telling: audience awareness of the speaker's status. John's acknowledgement of his rising status indicates that he knows that his audience is likely to be receptive to his jokes, no matter what their quality. Low group Mikey, in contrast, is more likely to face a hostile audience no matter how good or bad his jokes are.

Using the language of sport indexes joke-telling as a masculine activity. John notes that jokes are "pitch[ed]" and "throw[n]," like balls in baseball, one of the most popular (and predominantly male) sports in America, which he plays. Like baseball, joke-telling is a 'game' that is publicly visible, seen by other boys, girls, and the teacher. Sport provides a key site where boys elaborate masculinity:

Sport is the central experience of the school years for many boys . . . What is learned by constant informal practice, and taught by formal coaching, is for each sport a specific combination of force and skill . . . What it means to be masculine is, quite literally, to embody force, to embody competence.[29]

Constituting joke-telling as masculine contributes to John's ability to rank himself and other boys. The three-tiered male group system thus partly gets its shape by boys' relative ability to tell jokes about others and respond to those told about them. While joke-telling delineates degrees of masculinity, the way John describes this activity obscures this process both for himself and others. He compares only boys' joke-telling abilities, yet talks about "kids" and "everybody." Making distinctions among boys and ignoring girls places the latter beneath the former while still enabling both genders to maintain that they are equal. Indeed, this strategy of only making distinctions in the dominant category and ignoring all others is an effective means by which Sheepshead teenagers, and dominant Americans more generally, rank people yet proclaim universal equality.[30]

This strategic game of masculinity occurs at the same time as the teacher is organizing another "game," to carry John's analogy further. Joke-telling interrupts classroom instruction. Top group boys wrest control of the oral verbal form with which the teacher teaches them 'serious' 'factual knowledge' and subvert it by making 'funny' jokes about the 'knowledge' they are developing about themselves as peer group members. If they success-fully control this verbal form—that is, do not anger the teacher and get peers to laugh with them at a subordinate—they show their force and skill relative to peers *and* adults. They demonstrate that their masculinity is powerful enough to dominate in this context usually controlled by the teacher.[31]

Joke-telling is only one step in demonstrating top group dominance, low group subordination, and the criteria of masculinity. In the following con-versation, John Monroe relates how the rather rotund Andy Maneri, fre-quently mocked for his obesity, tells a joke and is quickly put in his subordinate place by two top group males. This verbal assault is followed by a physical assault which confirms his low position. "Everybody"—which, as I observed, includes middle and top group boys[32]—gangs up on the victim by hurling spitballs and erasers at him when the teacher's back is turned:

JM: Like today in social studies . . . Andy Maneri started cracking off to the class, so, um, Pete Kruska and Ronald Whitney . . . turned right around and zapped him. A couple of good shots.

JC: What did he [Andy] say?

JM: When you were young, your mother took you to the market and the fruit man said, "Here, have some apples for your family. And here's a banana for the monkey." [laughs] . . . And, um, Ronald came back with a maternal joke. He said, "I saw your mother. She was in the orangutan cage." [laughs] . . .

JC: They said this in class?

JM: Mr. Mann, Mr. Mann was standing there smiling. And he's like, "Okay, that kind of mocking isn't bad as long as it doesn't hurt anybody's feelings." And Andy's [sitting] over there. And whenever Mr. Mann turns around, every-body gets their wasps ready and shoots Andy. Today he, he got black and blue spots.

JC: What do they do?

JM: They take rubber bands, okay, and they fold pieces of paper up to this shape, a V-shape, and they shoot them, just like a sling shot. And they sting. And, and they threw erasers at him . . .

JC: Doesn't the teacher know this is going on?

JM: He's got his back turned. He doesn't hear a thing. Paper doesn't make a lot of noise.

Here top group boys dramatically enact their fairly substantial power relative not only to Andy but also to the teacher. This occurs more frequently with teachers like Mr. Mann who have little idea how hurtful mocking is and who, as many kids told me, have little control over their classes. Such demonstrations also take place in front of male and female peers. Female peers usually serve as audience for, rather than object of, such public spec-tacles. Especially during their first two years of middle school, boys are most concerned about their relations with other boys and consider girls marginally interesting.[33] In addition, as top group seventh grade Jeff Danner indicates, girls are thought to be unlikely to tell jokes because joke-telling is considered masculine, "[I]ts not possible, I think . . . [for girls to make] wise-ass remarks to the teachers because I don't think the girls are . . . [as] apt to say that in class, to go out on a limb".

Girls probably are unlikely to "go out on a limb" in this manner because, as Seidler[34] notes, taking ever greater risks which put one further "out on a limb" exemplifies masculinity. Girls, less concerned about publicly demonstrating strength and control in front of and relative to the teacher (as the next section shows), are not very likely to make such remarks in class.

Male risk-taking is not, however, fail safe. The result can be public humiliation—if the teacher is in a bad mood and has a low threshold for disruption, if one's timing is off, or if one's joke is not funny. A boy must be able to hide his feelings of failure if his joke is unsuccessful. Thus the version of masculinity that these top group boys are developing is not just about taking risks. It is also about concealing vulnerability from others. Jeff Danner notes that a "tough" or masculine boy:

wouldn't let things affect him. Like he would . . . withstand pain pretty well. Like a cut or something, he would kind of look at it and, you know, not think much of it. And even if he would feel pain inside he would, you know, withhold it and he wouldn't let it out . . . [And h]e would exhibit his strength, often.

As I suggest elsewhere,[35] Jeff's discussion of this male capacity to "kind of look at" that which pains him physically or emotionally gives him the distance he needs to stifle and thereby control this pain. Hegemonic masculinity requires that a boy deny his feelings so that he appears invulnerable. Insofar as intimate feelings are thought to belong to the female, private realm, boys effectively sever themselves from the private sphere in which girls primarily act. They thereby place this sphere, and girls more generally, subordinate to themselves.

This capacity to create a drama in the classroom context, in which these boys are on center stage and all other students are their audience, is one of the most striking features of this top group male strategy for enacting inequality. It occurs in other contexts, such as the gym locker room where top group boys physically assault a subordinate while boys in other groups watch. The classroom strategy is perhaps the most dramatic because it plays with teacher and student power simultaneously and directly. It also expands the notion of masculinity to include verbal, as well as physical domination.

Why do top group males publicly humiliate a subordinate in situations in which the latter has little, if any, chance of winning? I suggest that they do so because they are just beginning to elaborate masculinity in the middle school context. As Jeff Danner notes, "nobody realizes you have that much control unless you exercise it." It is not enough, as social critic John Berger maintains, that "[a] man's presence is dependent upon the promise of power which he embodies".[36] Perhaps especially as boys are learning how to be men, this promise must be fulfilled. Top group male students who strive to elaborate what being a man is about enact hegemonic understandings of masculinity by showing their strength and control over themselves and others in public contexts. Doing so allows them to place other boys' and girls' gendered constructions of themselves beneath their own.

These dominant males thus are reconstituting classroom space in their own terms. Males in other groups cannot help but realize, by observing or being the brunt of top group male actions in these spaces, that the most powerful and determining form of masculinity is constructed here.

Teenage boys take control of public space and thereby leave to girls the space already designated as theirs, the social relations and subjectivity of the purportedly female private sphere. My data about social composition also indicate that girls' orientation toward the private sphere is probably stronger among Sheepshead upper middle-class girls because their mothers are less likely than other American upper middle-class women to work outside the home. Teenage boys take control of public space and thereby leave to girls the space already designated as theirs.

In the United States and other capitalist cultures, domestic and public spheres of labor are not just separate, but the domestic sphere is considered "invisible" and:

has no value because it cannot be put on the market and it cannot be put on the market because of the [marriage] contract by which her [the wife's] labour power is appropriated by her husband.[37]

The public sphere is then construed as the only visible and real sphere because here production—that is, men's work as wage-earners—occurs.

For this particular gendered division of labor to work, it must appear "natural" to its participants. I am suggesting that an ideological framework in which this particular gendered division of labor appears natural is being incorporated in teenagers' social relations. Teenage boys emphasize their performance in the public sphere and deny the private dimensions in themselves and their social relations. This construction of masculinity has implications for what teenage girls can articulate and where they can do so. As I shall show below, teenage girls' stress on the private and intimate in their note-passing adds to broader gender ideologies by creating a web of hardly visible relationships that focus on the supposed "innermost" aspects of personality.

TEENAGE GIRLS' CLASSROOM NOTE-WRITING AND -PASSING

The Sheepshead teenage girls in *all* groups primarily express themselves as gendered subjects and peer group members by frequently writing and passing notes to the girls in the *same* group during school. These notes vary in intent. Some notes may affirm bonds or express differences between girls; others aim to subvert teacher authority. High school junior Melissa Boudin states that in middle school note-passing was:

MB: *the* fad. To sit down in study hall and write like thirteen notes to all your girlfriends. And every note said the same damn thing in it ... Like, "Hi, how are you? What's new? What did you do? What are you doing after school? You know, I'm in study hall, its real boring. There's nothing to do ... " One right after the other. I mean, nothing gets accomplished. I mean you don't, you know, resolve fights between the two [girls].

Despite Melissa's claim that "nothing gets accomplished," her comments indicate that notes indicate how a girl feels, what happens in class and what might happen after school. While Melissa maintains that "you don't ... resolve fights" by passing notes, during my fieldwork I observed that two girls verbally fought one another when one reportedly "stole" the other's boyfriend. The one whose boyfriend was stolen wrote a vitriolic note to the other in which she scathingly analyzed the psychological make-up of the other. Clearly, note-passing is more powerful than Melissa claims. Melissa's comments and my observations of middle school girls more generally suggest that note-passing is a key means by which girls in all groups expand their elementary school strategy of developing close intra-group relationships. For example, those knowing why a powerful, top group girl acts cold and distant or warm and friendly, are thought to have "inside" information on this girl. This indicates their ability to manipulate the components of the social hierarchy to get closer to this girl and thereby enhance their peer group position. These activities differ from male joke-telling in which primarily top group boys target those most subordinate to themselves. Top group girls, like boys, impose their perspective on others but generally not in ways that confront teachers.[38] In the gym locker room, for example, the only school space where teachers do not directly supervise students and where the genders are separated, top group girls publicly mock low group girls and those in their own group whom they dislike. They also try making up and performing songs and dances about sexuality—but only in contexts where boys are absent. Note-passing, then, is one of several activities with which young women enact their concern with intimate matters.[39] To understand these differences, I will examine the contents and contexts of notes.

With regard to note contents, middle group eighth grader Rebecca Bennett states that she and her new friend Jane pass notes in which they mock Rebecca's former friend Pam Stelle's dress:

RB: I mock out Pam ...
JC: To her face?
RB: No, I couldn't to her face. I guess I'm scared of her ...
JC: What do you say behind her back, when you mock her out?
RB: Especially about things she wears, you know, her taste in clothes (laughs).
JC: Like what?
RB: How things don't match. Well, one [day] (laughs), okay, she wore, she had a pink oxford [shirt] and a navy blue skirt and tan knee socks and, a scarf? Okay. And it [the scarf] was little purple flowers on an orange background? (laughs) With a pink shirt?

JC: Yeah.

RB: And it looked so bad. And she had it, like, draped . . . with the two ends in back. It looked really weird. So we were mocking her out. She didn't know it . . .

JC: How did you dissect her?

RB: (laughs) Uh, well, it was in [musical] band so we couldn't talk that much. And Jane was writing on her music. And she was saying (sarcastically) "Isn't that scarf beautiful? (laughs) Doesn't it match perfectly with her clothes?"

JC: Mmhmm.

RB: Sarcastically, you know?

Rebecca fears insulting her prior best friend Pam directly so she does so indirectly by passing notes with her new best friend Jane. By belittling Pam together, they affirm their friendship and place Pam beneath them. They do so when Pam is present, when *they* know that *Pam* probably knows that they are passing notes to each other about Pam. This suggests that girls, like boys, use a strategy which pits two dominants against one subordinate. This strategy provides critical—in both senses of the word—means for dominants to demonstrate their power. Yet in some ways the female object of derision is more powerless than the male. She cannot intervene to present herself favorably in this activity. On the other hand, because the rest of the students and the teacher do not have their attention drawn to note-passing, its object is not publicly humiliated, as is the male object of derision. The absence of a public audience also means that note-passers risk less than joke-tellers and do not have to cover their vulnerabilities. I now shall show how these similarly structured strategies differ in meaning.

Rebecca's comments indicate that note-passing partly fabricates a language of style with which girls construct their own and others' identities. She and Jane delineate their criteria of good dress, acknowledge its superiority to that of Pam and posit that Pam's mismatched clothing speaks of her "inner self." Pam herself elsewhere makes the point that outer appearance speaks of "inner" identity, "If I find something I know I like, if I know I like certain kinds of clothes, then I know I'm that kind of person."

Other research suggests that women use clothes as signs of inner identity in contemporary Western capitalist cultures. Work on appearance is also thought to provide a basis for establishing an intimate relationship with a man so that women project their "[d]esires, hopes and longings . . . onto the surface of the commodity"[40]. Because my upper middle-class white female subjects negotiate their work on appearance with note-passing (and other activities), it provides one means of further inculcating ideas about intimacy and emotions that are associated with appearance.

Since the peer group system provides the structure through which teenage girls start linking their identities to commodities, and since the top group sets the terms for consumption, teenage girls give primacy to top group girls' dress sense. At the time when the dominant version of feminity is just being constructed, most girls do not yet express significant intentional var-

iation from this version. Moreover, top group girls can be brutal in establishing their dress code as dominant. Cool group girls mock subordinates'
clothes "to hurt" them rather than tease them "for fun." As Pam states:

I know who I am, but, like, I have to present an image to everybody else, you
know . . . You don't want to wear things that like, everybody else isn't wearing . . . The cool kids might get teased [if they wear something that no one else
wears] but that would be for fun, you know, not to hurt.

Pam's comments suggest that girls carefully package their public presentations to fit with external dictates. As I show elsewhere,[41] this packaging
is also constrained by what girls of different social classes can afford. These
upper middle-class girls in Sheepshead are developing a form of femininity
appropriate to their class. They have benefitted from school thus far and
see themselves continuing to do so in the future. They recognize school
knowledge as legitimate and want to learn it. They differ from working-
class girls to whom schooling seems hardly relevant or beneficial, and who
also develop a "culture of femininity" which emphasizes work on
appearance[42], but which more actively defies teacher authority. My upper
middle-class female subjects, in contrast, defy teacher authority less actively
and pay more attention to academic excellence, which indexes their class
position.

Most of the Sheepshead top group boys also know that they are more
likely to have professional careers, which pay higher salaries than their
working-class counterparts who will probably have manual labor jobs paying more limited wages. They also know that academic excellence is necessary for entry into the professional world. As Jeff Danner says:

[Y]ou've got to start paying attention . . . if you're going to get anywhere beside
menial labor. Academically, you have to be up there . . . You've got to take it
seriously just now.

They realize as well that school has been and increasingly will be targeted
to meet their middle-class needs and marginalize working-class teenagers[43].
Such knowledge probably prevents them from pushing teachers to the
point of getting angry, as occurs more frequently among working-class
teenagers[44]. Like teenage girls, their social class position prevents them from
taking too many risks in the classroom.

The contexts of note-passing demonstrate how these upper middle-class
girls are less likely to challenge authority than boys, while enacting the
importance of "private" social relations. Seventh grade middle group Tracy
Curtis points out that most note-passing occurs in study hall:

JC: How many notes do you get a day?
TC: I don't know. It depends. Including study? In study notes?
JC: Yeah.
TC: Oh, about twenty.
JC: Really?

TC: Because, because we write short notes then we pass them around in study. It's so funny. Mr. Vitale, oh it's such a riot because he never catches you.
JC: He doesn't see you?
TC: No, it's such a riot.
JC: What's he doing while you're passing notes, marking stuff?
TC: Reading the paper.

In study hall, where students supposedly do homework and teachers do not evaluate them or even command their attention, "short" notes are passed frequently. This contrasts with longer ones passed less frequently in and between other classes. Tracy's delight in passing notes without getting "caught" by the teacher suggests that she views this activity as defiant. Yet it occurs in the one class where boys do not try to wrest control from teachers because here teachers lack such control. Because note-passing uses the less powerful written form, it does not directly challenge boys' or teachers' classroom power.

Tracy's comments point to other differences between girls' and boys' gendered strategies in the classroom. Boys directly usurp the oral verbal form that the superordinate teacher uses to instruct and control the class, introducing the world of their peers that they fashion more fully in other school contexts[45]. Significantly, boys *never* use the written form of note-passing. By contrast, girls only occasionally use the male oral form of joke-telling in class. This further affirms the dominance of joke-telling over note-passing as subversive genres, and confirms girls' relatively lower position.

These teenage girls' note-passing indicates their contradictory position in contemporary American culture. They develop an alternative view of the world to that which males elaborate in public contexts, stressing more private dimensions of personal relations. Although these girls view education as beneficial to their present and future positions, they give primacy to intimate social relationships. Although, increasingly, girls are growing up to act in both the domestic and public spheres, those whom I studied are less likely to have such as orientation because of the more conservative view of gender in Sheepshead. I found that most of my female subjects only plan to pursue careers before marriage and after their children grow up or if they are divorced. They primarily focus on their future roles as mothers and wives at home, as the emotional caretakers of their husbands and children. Clearly they are their mother's daughters. My female subjects' use of the subordinate verbal genre in the classroom context, both reflects and reproduces, at least for the time being, their gendered understanding of a particular fraction of middle-class American culture in Sheepshead.

CONCLUSION

This paper suggests that American upper middle-class teenagers develop strategies in the classroom that express and affirm their notions of masculinity and femininity. The version of masculinity that top group boys constitute through joke-telling centers on remaking and dominating social relations in public space. Their primary usage of the powerful oral form for joke-telling helps distinguish them as active creators of masculinity, as "more masculine" than other boys and as defiant of adult authority. It also differentiates masculinity from femininity and subordinates the latter to the former. Girls' primary usage of the less confrontational written form for note-passing places them beneath boys and hardly contests teacher power. They use it to construct a version of femininity that centers on appearance, which itself is used to explore and expand their understanding of emotions and to prepare them for intimate social relations. Both genders' strategies, which only somewhat contest teacher authority, indicate their shared dominant class position as present and future beneficiaries of schooling.

The understandings of gender that these teenagers build prepare them for their future roles as upper middle-class women and men (from a particular fraction of this class). These girls develop through note-passing and other activities a notion of femininity that stresses close attention to personal relationships, and to style as an index of class, thereby preparing them for a primary orientation to nurturance of others and the home. Young men, in contrast, who see themselves as the primary organizers of and actors in public space as adults, construct a gender role through joke-telling, which enacts and extols public performance, and hardly recognizes the other, female sphere.

These findings suggest that at least for some upper middle-class white young people and in at least some public contexts in American culture, the division between public and private remains gendered. Even though both genders act increasingly in both spheres, and as women in particular spend more of their lives working for wages, each gender remains oriented to one sphere, nonetheless. The structural asymmetry between the genders and the spheres with which they are primarily linked continues, even as some women, at least, are straddling the two domains.

Finally, these findings indicate that even as teenagers seem to be resisting adult authority, they often end up reproducing the conventional class, status, and gender hierarchies of the "parent culture." Teenage "goofing off" in school helps create gender identities that orient young men to public drama; young women to the creation of intimate social networks that monitor nuances in appearance and consumption. These differentiations, which they unselfconsciously produce, have been essential to reproducing the gender and class hierarchies of capitalism as we know it in contemporary American culture.

NOTES

I would like to thank Faye Ginsburg and Anna Tsing for their helpful comments. I would also like to thank Dave Rogers for making me say things more clearly.

1. Fieldwork was conducted from September 1979 to November 1980 and for one month (March) in 1981.

2. Sheepshead is a pseudonym for the community. All names of persons used in this paper also are pseudonyms.

3. They may meet friends in their homes, and occasionally at the local bowling alley or pizza parlour, but generally remain at home in the evening.

4. While Everhart also noticed that American working class middle school boys tell jokes and girls pass notes, he did not explore how these strategies were gendered. See Robert Everhart, *Reading, Writing and Resistance* (Boston: Routledge and Kegan Paul, 1983).

5. Pierre Bourdieu, *Distinctions* (Cambridge: Harvard University Press, 1984).

6. Bureau of Government Research, *1980 Legislative District Data Book; Municipal Data Book,* 1981 (names deleted to preserve community anonymity); Dorothy Unrath, "A School-Community Study of Sheepshead," 1977.

7. The largest and most visible group are the families whose male heads (40%) hold professional managerial jobs and own spacious, new homes at some distance from the town center. Nearly 30% of employed men hold sales and clerical jobs, and own less spacious but still very comfortable and well-furnished homes. Nearly 30% of the employed men who hold manual labor jobs—as craftsmen, operatives, laborers and service workers—tend to live in homes either in or near the town center or at its peripheries.

8. About 45% of these are clerical workers, 22% hold professional or technical jobs like nursing or teaching, 12% work in sales, 12% are service workers, 5% are laborers, and 4% hold managerial and administrative jobs. Many of these women work part-time and earn salaries which average two-thirds less than those that men receive.

9. Bureau of Government Research, Municipal Data Book.

10. Pierre Bourdieu and Jean Passeron, *Reproduction in Education, Society and Culture* (London: Sage Publications, 1977).

11. Bureau of Government Research, Municipal Data Book, Unrath.

12. There are exceptions, of course. In addition, my research suggests that sibling position contributes to peer group position. Younger siblings enter the peer group world with greater knowledge of how to act than do peers without older siblings. See Joyce Canaan, *Individualizing Americans: The Making of American Suburban Middle Class Teenagers* (Ph.D. dissertation, University of Chicago, Department of Anthropology, 1990).

13. Canaan (1990).

14. Mary Ryan, *Womanhood in America* (New York: Franklin Watts, 1975); Barbara Welter, "The Cult of True Womanhood: 1820–1860," *American Quarterly* 18 (Summer 1966).

15. See Ryan, 173.

16. See Robert Connell, *Gender and Power* (Oxford: Polity Press, 1987) 187.

17. Connell, 183.

18. Women, for example, either accommodate themselves to this notion of masculinity and thereby elaborate its female complement, which Connell calls "emphasized femininity," or resist it and develop an alternative form.

19. Connell, *Gender and Power;* Christine Delphy, *Close to Home* (Amherst: University of Massachusetts Press, 1984); Ryan.

20. Stuart Hall and Tony Jefferson, eds., *Resistance Through Rituals* (Lon-

don: Hutchinson, 1976); Dick Hebdige, *Subcultures* (London: Methuen), 1979; Paul Willis, *Learning to Labor* (New York: Morningside Press, 1977).

21. This focus on white people is present in both literatures. Cultural studies began to explore the issue of race in the Centre for Contemporary Cultural Studies [CCCS] Women's Studies Group book, *Women Take Issue* (London: Hutchinson, 1978); in Valerie Amos and Pratibha Parmar, "Resistances and Responses: The Experiences of Black Girls in Britain," in *Feminism for Girls,* Angela McRobbie and Trisha McCabe, eds. (London: Routledge and Kegan Paul, 1981); and, more directly, in *The Empire Strikes Back* (London: Hutchinson, 1982). In the early 1980s black and Third World women challenged the white, middle-class First World bias of feminist theory. See Angela Davis, *Women, Race and Class* (London: The Women's Press, 1981); and Cherrie Moraga and Gloria Anzaldua *This Bridge Called My Back* (New York: Kitchen Table Women of Color Press, 1981).

22. Angela McRobbie, "Settling Accounts with Subcultures," *Screen Education* 34 (1980).

23. McRobbie and Jenny Garber, in Hall and Jefferson 209–222; Rachel Powell and John Clarke, "A Note on Marginality," in Hall and Jefferson, 223–230.

24. Erica Carter, "Alice in Consumer Wonderland," in *Gender and Generation,* Angela Carter and Mica Nava, eds. (London: Macmillan, 1984), 187; Christine Griffin, *Typical Girls?* (London: Routledge and Kegan Paul, 1985).

25. Philip A. Cusick, *Inside High School* (New York: Holt, Rinehart and Winston, Inc., 1973).

26. For a discussion of how these patterns are initiated in elementary school, see J. Brooks-Gunn and W. S. Matthews, *He and She* (Englewood Cliffs: Prentice-Hall, 1979), and J. Lever, "Sex Differences in the Games Children Play," *Social Problems* 23 (1976).

27. Canaan (1990).

28. Ibid.

29. Robert Connell, *Which Way Is Up?* (North Sydney: George Unwin and Allen, 1983), 18.

30. Canaan (1990).

31. This is especially true if the teacher is male. If the teacher is female, different interactive forms may develop (Canaan [1990]).

32. While my data indicate that young women participate in such activities when the victim is female, I am uncertain if they do so when the victim is male.

33. Canaan (1990).

34. Vic Seidler, "Fear And Intimacy," in *The Sexuality of Men,* Andy Metcalfe and Martin Humphrey, eds. (London: Pluto Press, 1985).

35. Canaan (1990).

36. John Berger, *Ways of Seeing* (Harmondsworth: Penguin, 1972), 45.

37. Delphy, 95.

38. For instance, one low group sixth grade young woman sometimes interspersed her oral classroom contributions with a "tsk" sound. Other top group young women frequently added their own "tsk" sounds as this young woman spoke—but hardly loud enough for the teacher to hear. Unlike young men, they studiously avoided being caught by the teacher.

39. Canaan (1990).

40. Frigga Haug, ed., *Female Sexualization* (London: Verso, 1986), 135. Winship and McRobbie suggest that in women's magazines, appearance is considered a key means by which women express their "individual" identities and "independence" and simultaneously are constituted as objects of and for male desire. See Janice Winship, "Woman Becomes an 'Individual': Femininity and Consumption in Women's Magazines 1954–69," *CCCS Stencilled Papers* (1981), 23; McRobbie, "Working Class Girls and the Culture of Femininity," in CCCS Women's Studies Group, 1978.

Making oneself attractive is tricky business; it requires that one "tread the precarious line between discrete and glamorous femininity" (Winship), that one sexualize one's appearance, but not too much. As my work and that on British girls suggests, the category of "slut" or "slag"—that is, a sexually "easy" girl— develops during the early teenage years as girls begin sexualizing their appearance. See Joyce Canaan, "Why a 'Slut' is a 'Slut': Cautionary Tales of American Suburban Middle Class Teenage Girls' Morality," in *Symbolizing America*, Hervé Varenne, ed. (Lincoln: University of Nebraska Press, 1986); Canaan (1990); Celia Cowie and Sue Lees, "Slag or Drag," *Feminist Review* 9 (1981); Sue Lees *Losing Out* (London: Century Hutchinson, 1986). A girl so labelled is thought to have an exterior appearance that speaks of an overly sexualized interior—that is, of her being "too receptive" to male sexual advances. More generally, appearance provides the basis for a girl's reputation (Canaan [1990]); it is thought to indicate how she *responds to* advance that a boy initiates. As I suggest earlier, my female subjects' wish to sexualize their appearance indicates that they are reproducing wider cultural values.

41. Canaan (1990).

42. McRobbie, "Just Like a 'Jackie' Story," in McRobbie and McCabe.

43. Canaan (1990).

44. Everhart, Willis.

45. Canaan (1990).

CHAPTER FOURTEEN

Catching Sense: Learning from Our Mothers To Be Black and Female

SUZANNE C. CAROTHERS

My mama was a midwife. She and the other midwives taught each other. Sure, there was a community doctor but, my mama and the other women delivered those babies by themselves. If they had any complications, they'd call the doctor. 'Course, I've never known my mother to lose a case.
—A sixty-four-year-old woman

Black parents are required to prepare their children to understand and live in two cultures—Black American culture and standard American culture.[1] To confront the bicultural nature of their world, these parents must respond in distinctive ways. In the following essay, I show how this can be seen in the practices and beliefs of several generations of Black women through their descriptions of seemingly ordinary and commonplace activities.

The first setting in which people usually experience role negotiations is the home. Boys and girls will draw from important lessons learned at home

On the plantations of the St. Helena Island off the coast of South Carolina, one would rarely hear, "Where were you born?" More likely, one would be asked, "Where did you *catch sense?*" The people on this island do not assume that the place where a person was born is the same as the place where that person was raised and socialized. Nor is birthplace viewed as equivalent to the setting, context, or situation in which people begin to make meaning about and understand the world in which they live. "Catching sense" was discussed in a paper entitled "Black Families on St. Helena Island," by Patricia Guthrie, delivered at The National Council of Negro Women conference *Black Women: An Historical Perspective*, Washington, D.C., November 12–13, 1979.

during childhood to negotiate their future roles as viable members of society. Distant though the lessons may seem from the perspective of an adult, they were taught directly and indirectly in the context of day-to-day family life. Of the many dyads occurring within families, the interactions between mothers and daughters are a critical source of information on how women perceive what it means to be female. I have been particularly interested in these perceptions among Black mothers and daughters because of the unique socio-economic, political circumstances in which these women find themselves in American culture. During the Fall, Winter, and Spring of 1980–81, I returned to my home town of Hemington, fictitiously named, to collect data for my study. It is the contradiction that emerged between my experience of having grown up in the Black community of Hemington and my graduate school reading of the social science literature on Black family life and mother-daughter relationships that led me to engage in this research.

BACKGROUND

Prior to the 1960s, studies on Black families in American society characterized them as pathological, dysfunctional, deviant, and matriarchal.[2] These studies emphasized Blacks' difficulties in achieving position, power, or prestige and viewed the family as a major source of weakness.

During the 1960s, new scholarship began to refute these older arguments. This new scholarship identified the strengths, stability and cohesiveness of Black families. Researchers began to re-define Black family life in its own cultural context without expectations of white middle-class nuclear family organization as the model for understanding Black family domestic units. In this research, the positive aspects of Black women's strong position in their families has become more clear.

Yet, the implications of Black women's strength has not been explored fully in the literature on American mother-daughter relationships. Black women have traditionally combined mothering and working roles, while white middle-class women in the United States until recently have not. In Western cultures, mothering is regarded as a role that directly conflicts with women's other societal roles. In response to this condition, many theorists of female status consider the mothering role to be the root cause of female dependence on and subordination to men.[3] Yet, this has not been the experience of Black mothers. As others have argued, "Women have been making culture, political decisions, and babies simultaneously and without structural conflicts in all parts of the world.[4]"

During the 1970s, a recurring theme in the United States literature on mother-daughter relationships was the ambivalence and conflict existing between mothers and daughters. The literature describes competition and rivalry and suggests a negative cycle of influences passed from mothers to their daughters. For example, Judith Arcana suggests,

The oppression of women created a breach among us, especially between mothers and daughters. Women cannot respect their mothers in a society which degrades them; women cannot respect themselves. Mothers socialize their daughters into the narrow role of wife-mother; in frustration and guilt, daughters reject their mothers for their duplicity and incapacity—so the alienation grows in the turning of the generations.[5]

The above quote is generally inapplicable to the relationship between Black mothers and their daughters. The Black cultural tradition assumes women to be working mothers, models of community strength, and skilled women whose competence moves beyond emotional sensitivity. It is through this tradition of a dual role that Black women acquire their identity, develop support systems (networks), and are surrounded by examples of female initiative, support, and mutual respect.

Black mothers do not raise their children in isolation. In contrast, Nancy Chodorow argues,

The household with children has become an exclusively parent and child realm; infant and child care has become the exclusive domain of biological mothers who are increasingly isolated from other kin, with fewer social contacts and little routine assistance during their parenting time. . . .[6]

The families to whom Chodorow refers above are child-centered. In the arrangement she describes, the needs of the domestic unit are shaped and determined primarily by those of the children. Scholars of Black family life offer evidence of other arrangements.[7] According to them, Black women raise their children in the context of extended families in which social and domestic relations, as well as kinship and residence structures offer a great deal of social interaction among adults that includes children. In addition, these researchers have shown that child rearing is only one of many obligations to be performed within Black family households. They agree that child rearing cannot be evaluated in the singular context of an individual but rather in the plural context of the household. The process through which daughters learn from their mothers in Black families, therefore, contradicts the wave of literature on mother-daughter relationships.

In order to appreciate the contrast in orientation of Black mothers, it is necessary to consider the wider social context of Black parenting. Black parents in American society have a unique responsibility. They must prepare their children to understand and live in two cultures—Black American culture and standard American culture.[8] Or as Wade W. Nobles[9] has suggested, Black families must prepare their children to live near and be among white people without becoming white. This phenomenon has been referred to as *biculturality* by Ulf Hannerz and by Charles Valentine, an idea derived from W.E.B. Dubois who wrote in the early 1900s about the idea of double consciousness: "that Blacks have to guard their sense of blackness while accepting the rules of the games and cultural consciousness of the dominant white culture."[10] Because Black parents recognize that their children must learn to deal with institutional racism and personal discrimination, Black children are encouraged to test absolute rules and absolute authority.[11] It is therefore critical to the socialization of Black children that their parents provide them with ample experiences dealing with procedures of interpersonal interaction rather than rules of conduct. The children are socialized to be part of a Black community rather than just Black families or "a fixed set of consanguinal and affixed members."[12] Beginning early in childhood, the wider social context in which Black children are raised usually involves not only their mothers, but also many adults—all performing a variety of roles in relation to the child, the domestic unit, and the larger community. Furthermore, the transmission of knowledge and skills in Black family life is not limited to domestic life but occurs in public life arenas in which Black women are expected to participate. Working outside their homes to. contribute to the economic resources of the family has been only one of the many roles of the majority of Black women. As members of the labor market, Black mothers simultaneously manage their personal lives, raise their children, organize their households, participate in community and civic organizations, and create networks to help each other cope with seemingly insurmountable adversities.

Participation in work and community activities broadens the concept and practice of mothering for Black women. How do the women learn these roles? What must they pass on to their female children if they are to one day perform these roles? An exploration of the social interactions between Black working mothers and their daughters, as well as the cultural context and content can extend our knowledge of the cultural variation in mothering roles and mother-daughter relationships and the processes by which mothers shape female identity.

THE STUDY

Several reasons prompted my decision to return to Hemington for this research. Typically, studies of Black family life have been conducted in urban ghetto communities in the north and mid-west, some in the deep rural South and most with lower class or poor people.[13] In developing my research, I wanted to avoid choosing a location where there were vast differences between the Black and white standard of living that so often characterize the research settings in which Blacks are studied. In these settings, the usual distinguishing features for the Black population are poverty, unemployment, under employment, low wages, and inadequate housing. The white communities are more varied economically, ranging from relatively wealthy managerial elites to welfare recipients living in housing projects. Yet, there are many middle-sized and large southern cities with large, varied and stable Black communities that researchers have not adequately explored. Hemington is such an example.[14]

Prior to 1960 and urban redevelopment, the Black community of Hemington was primarily concentrated in the area closest to the main business district of the city. At the time of the study, most Blacks still lived in predominantly all Black neighborhoods located on the west side of town, where a broad range of housing suggests an economically varied Black community. Blacks in Hemington live in public housing projects, low income housing (both private homes and apartments), modern apartment complexes, and privately owned homes, ranging from modest to lavish.

Although I had not lived in Hemington for more than ten years, my kinship ties to the community meant that I had access to people, situations, and information that an outsider might not have or would need a considerably longer time to acquire. My experiences of growing up there and then studying and working in educational institutions in northern white society made me sensitive to differences in cultural patterns and more eager to analyze them.

Forty-two women and nine girls between the ages of 11 and 86 from twenty families agreed to participate in the study. I asked them to help me understand the meaning of mothering and working in their lives and how this meaning was passed on from mother to daughter—generation to generation. The stories that the women and girls shared with me about the very ordinary day-to-day activities of their lives became a rich source for understanding how women found and created meaning in the less-than-perfect world in which they lived.[15]

The study was of women whom Alice Walker would call the anonymous Black mothers whose art goes unsigned and whose names are known only by their families.[16] Many of the women in the study have known me all my life. They are great-grandmothers, who have lived to see their grandchildren's children born and grandmothers who have raised their children. I grew up with some of the mothers who are raising their children. Still others, the young girls, I remember from the time they were born.[17]

Seventy-five years separate the births of the oldest from the youngest participants. According to their ages and the age at which each became a mother, informants fall into five grouping possibilities. I have identified these groups as follows:

Participant Groupings

Group	Name	Ages	# In Each Group
I	The Rural Born Ladies	68–86	9
II	The First to Pursue Schooling and Technical Training	58–67	6
III	Those Who Received Post-Secondary Education, Most Urban Born	40–57	15
IV	The Young Home Owners, All Urban Born	24–39	12
V	The Children/Unmarried Young Adults	11–23	9

Identifying these groups helps to locate the women's experiences relative to the challenges each generation confronted in an ever-changing society.

These women perceive themselves as middle-class. All are or have been employed. They are people who share a common system of values, attitudes, sentiments, and beliefs which indicate that an important measure of "class" for these Black Americans is the range of resources available to the extended family unit. This system, then—based on extensive inter-household sharing—is not synonymous with traditional criteria for social class structure which includes wealth, prestige, and power.[18]

WHAT BLACK MOTHERS TEACH: CONCRETE LEARNINGS AND CRITICAL UNDERSTANDINGS

In order to understand the teaching and learning process taking place between Black mothers and daughters, I observed the women and asked them questions about their seemingly ordinary and commonplace daily activities. When the participants in the study were asked from whom they learned, their answers included their mothers, fathers, stepfathers, stepmothers, grandfathers, grandmothers, great-grandmothers, aunts, the lady next door, an older sister, a brother, a teacher—in short, their community. When asked *what* they had learned from these people, their responses touched a range of possibilities, which can be grouped into two broad categories. Cooking, sewing, cleaning, and ironing are examples of activities that are associated with the daily routines of households that I call "concrete learnings". The regular performance of these leads to what I refer to as "critical understandings," which include such things as achieving independence, taking on responsibility, feeling confident, getting along with others, or being trustworthy. The acquisition of these is not easy to pinpoint and define. They are not taught as directly as the concrete learnings, but they are consistently expected. Their outcomes are not as immediately measurable because they usually take a longer time to develop.

What do mothers do to pass on to their daughters the understandings that are considered critical to a daughter's well being, and the skills, the learned power of doing a thing competently? Mothers teach their daughters what to take into account in order to figure out how to perform various tasks, recognizing that the individual tasks that they and their daughters are required to perform change over time. Therefore, the preparation that mothers provide includes familiarity with the task itself, as well as a total comprehension of the working of the home or other situations within which the task is being done. The women's interviews reveal that mothers teach by the way that they live their own lives ("example"), by pointing out critical understandings they feel their daughters need ("showing"), and by instructing their daughters how to do a task competently. Their teaching is both verbal and nonverbal, direct and indirect. Daughters learn not only from their mothers, but also from other members of family and the community.

The data indicate that concrete learnings teach—in ways that verbal expression alone does not—a route toward mastery and pride that integrates the child into the family and community. Daughters learn competency through a sense of aesthetics, an appreciation for work done beautifully. The women described this notion as follows: "You don't see pretty clothes hanging on the line like you used to;" "Mama could do a beautiful piece of ironing;" "You always iron the back of the collar first. The wrinkles get on the back and it makes the front of the collar smooth;" or "Now if I got in the kitchen and say I saw these pretty biscuits, I might say Mama how did you get your biscuits to look this pretty . . ." This aesthetic quality becomes one of the measures of competently done work as judged by the women themselves and by other members of their community.

As each generation encountered technological changes in household work, mothers became less rigid about teaching their daughters concrete learnings. However, like previous generations, mothers still teach their daughters responsibility through chores, which gives them opportunities to practice and get better at doing them, both alone and with others. These activities are not contrived but rather they constitute real work and contribute to the daily needs of their households. Participation in these activities encourages mastery of them.

Women across the generations boasted about having mastered chores. Take the comments of the forty-seven-year-old grandmother, Mrs. Edwina Phillips who said:

By the time I was 11, I could do a lot of stuff, I could do everything in a house. I could iron for people. I started babysitting for people the summer I was seven going on eight. . . . I was seven and I know I did a good job.

Another example can be seen in the statement of Mrs. Queen Ester Washington, a member of the Rural Born Ladies Group, who has one great-granddaughter.

Yea, we had to carry in the night wood. We had to do our night work. We had to milk the cows. We had to feed the horses. We had to do everything. You see, I was raised in the country and you know what country people do? [They] pick cotton, hoe cotton, and you learn to do it all. I know how to do almost anything in the working line.

After I become an expert in farm work in the country, I moved to Hemington and then I become an expert in domestic work.

Sixty-four-year-old Mrs. Odessa Johnson, a grandmother of two, offered these remarks,

I started working when I was in the first grade. This lady who was white lived across the fence from us. My mother used to put me across the fence. I'd wash the dishes. This would give the lady time to spend with her little girl who was sick. Then she'd put me back across the fence and I'd go home. You know people were real proud of me. I know they were because Mama's patients would say, "Jenny you going to let Odessa come and stay with me a while?"

A thirty-two-year-old mother of two said,

Grandmama is a very good cook and I watched her. Mama is a good cook and I watched her. I'd pick up on things. Gradually they'd let me do little things here and there. If I cooked something, I don't care what it was, they would eat it. I made some dumplings one day that were just like rubber balls! They ate them. They never complained about them. I enjoyed cooking. You know when people act like they enjoy your cooking, even when you know it's bad, you do it, and the more you do, you get better at it. I enjoyed cooking so much that I took over a lot of the cooking from Mama, especially during the week.

Each woman described a certain kind of pride in herself for having learned and accomplished a task well. Such mastery reinforced and established the woman's confidence in her ability to perform well. Having chores to do was the important link bridging concrete learnings to critical understandings germane to a daughter's well-being.

DEMANDS OF DOUBLE CONSCIOUSNESS OR
LESSONS OF RACISM

While mothers teach critical understandings through example, maxims, and practical lessons, they use what I am calling "dramatic enactments" as a powerful tool to teach their daughters ways to deal with white people in a racist society. Thus, daughters learn critical understandings that are specific to the Black experience.

When mothers teach by example, they enact before their daughters the particular skills necessary to achieve the task at hand. By contrast, dramatic enactments expose children to conflict or crisis and are often reserved for complex learning situations. "Learning to deal with white people," for example, was viewed by some women in the study as important to their survival, and dramatic enactment was identified as being a powerful technique for acquiring this skill. One thirty-one-year-old woman in group IV explained how she learned this critical understanding through dramatic enactments from her grandmother, who did domestic work.

My sister and I were somewhat awed of white people because when we were growing up, we did not have to deal with them in our little environment. I mean you just didn't have to because we went to an all-Black school, an all-Black church, and lived in an all-Black neighborhood. We just didn't deal with them. If you did, it was a clerk in a store.

Grandmother was dealing with them. And little by little she showed us how. First, [she taught us that] you do not fear them. I'll always remember that. Just because their color may be different and they may think differently, they are just people.

The way she did it was by taking us back and forth downtown with her.

Here she is, a lady who cleans up peoples' kitchens. She comes into a store to spend her money. She could cause complete havoc if she felt she wasn't being treated properly. She'd say things like, "If you don't have it in the store, order it." It was like she had $500,000 to spend. We'd just be standing there and watching. But what she was trying to say [to us] was, they will ignore you if you let them. If you walk in there to spend your 15 cents, and you're not getting proper service, raise hell, carry on, call the manager but don't let them ignore you.

Preparing their daughters to deal with encounters in the world beyond home was a persistent theme in the stories offered by the women in this study. By introducing their daughters and granddaughters to such potentially explosive situations and showing the growing girls how older women could handle the problems spurred by racism, mothers and grandmothers taught the lessons needed for survival, culturally defined as coping with the wider world.

THE COMMUNITY CONTEXT

As I suggested earlier, my own and other research shows distinctive patterns according to which mothers and other members of Black families relate and respond to young children. The teaching and learning processes in these families occur in an environment in which a great deal of social interaction among the adults includes children. The present study confirms Young's research[19] and takes her argument farther by suggesting how patterns of interaction between Black mothers and daughters within the context of community relationships facilitates teaching and learning.

The concept of Black family units working in concert to achieve the common goals they value, arises out of the inherent expectations of helping and assuming responsibility for each other as part of a conscious model of social exchange.[20] Thus, giving and receiving are the understood premises for participating in community life. Different from guilt, this system has been fueled by the racial and economic oppressions that have plagued Black families since their introduction into American society. Women in these family units traditionally assume a critical role in meeting these responsibilities. This does not end when children reach maturity, nor is it hierarchical, from mother to child; it is part of the larger community value that the women believe in and sustain, described by a woman in group II:

I was raised in a Christian neighborhood. That whole neighborhood was just Christian people. They looked after each other. You know, like if someone was sick in the neighborhood, they didn't have to send out nowhere for people to come in and take care of them. The people in the neighborhood would take care of them. They would iron, cook, do everything. Didn't even go in and say, "Do you need me to do anything." Folk would just come in and take hold.

This community context is especially supportive of the kind of teaching and learning that takes place between Black mothers and daughters.

Given the difficult conditions that racism and economic discrimination have imposed on the Black community (including, of course, the middle-class Black community), it is important for children to know that their parents can survive the difficult situations they encounter. Children need to trust that the world is sufficiently stable to give meaning to what they are learning. *Dependability*—based on elements of character such as hard work, faith, and the belief that their children can live a better life—provides the context for that trust and the daughters' sense of their mothers' competence to deal with the world.

Despite the conflicts that sometimes arose, daughters generally acknowledged the ongoing lessons their mothers had to teach them and that the process of *life-long learning* was central to their relationship, as Mrs. Washington's quote illustrates,

Kitty and James, either one haven't got to the place today where I couldn't tell them if they were doing something wrong. And people gets on me for that. And I say, well you never get too old to learn. I say, if I know it's right why can't I correct them? They say, "When a child gets up on his own, you ought to let 'em alone." Then I say, well I'm going to bother mine as long as I live if I see 'em doing something wrong. I'm going to speak to them and if they don't do what I say, at least they don't tell me that they aren't. They just go someplace else and do it.

This sense of teaching and learning as an ongoing part of the mother-child relationship adds an impetus to the daughters frequently expressed belief that they fulfilled their mothers' dreams and in a sense justified their mothers' lives through gaining an education.

This is what Mama was working toward [my going to college]. This was her ambition. It was just like she was going to college herself. The first summer I finished high school and every summer after that, Mama took sleep-in jobs up in the mountains to earn extra money for my college education . . . She very much wanted us to take advantage of all the things she never had. This is what she worked for.

Part of what makes increased formal education a continuation, rather than a rupture of the mother-daughter relationship is the daughters' insistence (backed up, of course, by community values) that older women had a kind of wisdom that transcended school-learning. A fifty-year-old woman said:

Even without a [formal] education, my mother has more common sense than I do. I rely on her because I can say, "Well mother, so and so is going to happen, what do you think about it?" Surprisingly, she has an answer that I would have never thought of. I respect her for that.

Another woman fifty-three years of age agreed,

Even though my mother did not get much formal education, she knew what was going on the world about her. She could read and write anything that she wanted. That was never a handicap for her. Maybe her language was not up to par, as for correctness of it [grammar], she could communicate her ideas. She knew how to say what she needed to say.

Black domestic units are centered around the needs and work of the household. Because of the necessity of so much work, though the pressures have been reduced over the generations, working together has become one of the major vehicles for learning. Learning is made attractive in this context because it represents access to adulthood and to continued membership in the family and community.

Through *shared work* activities, women give their children substance and sustenance by being available to them and providing an image and structure for them to follow. Their availability cannot be measured in terms of the amount of time mothers spend with their children. These women became skilled in using regular household work as an opportunity to spend time with their children. For example, it was not uncommon for these mothers in groups I and II especially, not to be home when their children arrived home from school. The women's lives were organized around very demanding paid-work schedules and therefore not geared to making exclusive time for children. As one woman in group IV described it, "Some of the time we spent together was like working . . . working in the yard or I would sew and my mother would clean." Shared activities included going grocery shopping, accompanying a mother to work, cleaning house, hanging clothes on the line, sitting on the porch talking, walking to the bus stop, or, getting up, getting breakfast, and getting out to school. Mothers made the best use of the limited time they had.

These shared activities did not take place in a special world that women designed for their daughters; rather, they took place in the context of the real world of their mothers. And it was these worlds that daughters were expected to understand and eventually manage on their own. As explained by one woman, the activities started early in childhood:

We bought food, clothes, or whatever we needed. We took great joy in doing it but Mama didn't tax that on us. She just raised us to be thoughtful about the household. If I was working and came home and we were out of bread, I went and bought some. My nine-year-old brother would do the same thing. He'd come from that coal house and if we didn't have any bread, he'd turn right around and go back to get some.

Thus, shared work does not necessarily mean doing the same thing at the same time. Rather, it is an awareness of what is being done by each member of the family or community that contributes to the survival and good of everyone.

Getting work done together requires in turn, a *free flow of information,* which in turn supports the teaching and learning process. It is important for mothers to teach daughters how to cope with the world; therefore, they do not hide the world from their children. Rather, information about what it takes to deal with their reality is readily available to Black daughters, which makes them quite knowledgeable about their mothers' own struggles and sacrifices. A forty-seven-year-old woman illustrated this point when she said:

Anyone of my children could have paid my bills, could have told you how much money I made, how much I was going to pay in church, how much grocery I was going to buy and what week I was suppose to buy what grocery when they were twelve years old. You see, what I did was let them in on the real facts of how we were doing it. I didn't play no games with them. We didn't pretend we had what we did not have. They knew exactly what we had.

The free flow of information creates an atmosphere of problem solving, that problems can and must be solved within the actual limits of the situation.

Black daughters learn their mothers' histories by seeing their mothers in the roles of mamas who nurture as friends, who become confidantes and companions; as teachers, who facilitate and encourage their learning about the world; and as advisors who counsel. For these women, the role of mother is not seen as "a person without further identity, one who can find her chief gratification in being all day with small children, living at a pace tuned to theirs.[21] From early on, the women in the present study see their mothers as complex beings. Knowing her mother's history intensifies the bond between mother and daughter, and helps daughters understand more about the limits under which their mothers have operated.

Getting along however, is not necessarily dependent on the women always reaching agreement, or daughters following the advice of their mothers. It would not be unusual for a mother and daughter to fall out about an issue one day and speak to each other the next. Such interactions provide continuing opportunities for daughters to practice developing and defending their own points of view, a skill useful in the outside world. These interactions insure the back and forth between Black mothers and daughters, which promotes the teaching and learning process and increases Black daughters' respect for what mothers have done and who they are.

Although respect remains a key value in mother daughter relationships and helps to foster the teaching and learning process, generational differences between mothers and daughters lead to tensions that threaten the teaching and learning context. Daughters need to *balance* their loyalty to their mothers with their own needs to grow up in accord with the terms of their own generation: realities. Mothers, on the other hand, need to balance their need for their daughters' allegiance with the knowledge that the daughters require a high degree of independence to survive and achieve in the world.

Loyalty is the unspoken but clear message in the words spoken by the mothers and daughters in this study. They describe it in terms of faithfulness and continuing emotional attachment. As loyalty defines what Black mothers and daughters expect from each other, it also is part of the conflict between them—when Black women are unable to separate the tangled threads that bind them so closely. Their obligation to each other and the deep understanding of the plight they share sometimes nurtures a desire to protect, rather than commit what would be seen as an act of desertion.

This conflict was more pronounced between women in groups I and II who are the mothers of women in groups III and IV, respectively. The conflicts experienced by mothers and daughters was tempered by the daughters' desire to protect their mothers, a belief that their mothers wanted what was best for them, and the respect they had for their mothers. A forty-five-year-old woman in group III, describing her mother in group I, explained:

I would adhere to my mama's wishes because I loved her so. You see, what she believed in got us this far. As these kids say, "if you can't think of something better, don't knock it." That's just the way I feel about it. I might sit down with my husband and get it off my chest but when my Mama says it, I'm going to listen. I'm going to respect her. I'm forty-five and I have never sassed my Mama. I am not trying to change my Mama. She is who she is.

As the quote makes clear, alienation does not characterize the kind of conflicts existing between these Black mothers and daughters. The daughters recognized the web of contradictions in which their mothers' lives were suspended. Women also have respect for their mothers' ability to overcome seemingly insurmountable situations. The women know only too well the odds stacked against them and their mothers. As one woman said,

At my age, I still would not sass my Mama. I don't dispute her because she is so dag gone strong that I don't think that I have a right to dispute her. I think that she is entitled to be wrong sometimes. I think she's earned it.

CONCLUSION

Women in this study routinely have confronted very early on the contradictions between the world in which they were born and raised and the one away from their homes. The result is that the women are not thrown by that which is different or contradictory to their home practices; rather, they can accept, understand, negotiate and deal with the differences in reasonable ways.

A high degree of mutual respect and camaraderie characterize the teaching and learning processes taking place between Black mothers and daughters. The community value of mutual responsibility makes this possible. Because of the multiple roles that these mothers play, the interactions between Black mothers and daughters require that mothers balance these roles and determine which one is appropriate in different situations. It also requires that daughters actively consider the context and purpose of the interaction and the mood of her mother to determine the appropriate response. Thus, the issue of authority that is often a major concern and obstacle in school learning for both teacher and students, shifts to mutuality in the teaching and learning process occurring between Black working mothers and their daughters.

The daughters have learned from their mothers by being exposed to the complications, complexities, and contradictions that as working women, their mothers faced in a society which has traditionally viewed working and mothering as incompatible roles. The recognition of this difference requires that Black women, as a condition of their daily existence, constantly negotiate an alternative understanding of female identity that challenges the dominant gender paradigm in American culture.

NOTES

1. Throughout this article, I use the term Black as a proper noun in recognition of a specific cultural group like, Latinos or Asians. To that end, I have chosen to capitalize the "B." For a discussion of the use of an upper case "B" denoting Blacks and the interchangeable use of Blacks with Afro-American consistent with my view, see Kimberle Williams Crenshaw's article "Race, Reform, and Retrenchment: Transformation and Legitimation in Antidiscrimination Law," *Harvard Law Review* 101, no. 7 (May 1988): 1332.

2. The 1930s ushered in a decade of studies on family life in which the *Negro family* became a focal interest. In the 1960s, when social scientists became interested in the question of poverty, the *Negro family* once again became a focus for research. Studies concerning Black family life were conducted in key industrial urban areas. For a discussion of the literature on Black family life in the United States see my unpublished Ph.D. dissertation, "Generation to Generation: The Transmission of Knowledge Skills and Role Models from Black Working Mothers to Their Daughters in a Southern Community," New York University, 1987, pp. 11–19.

3. Nancy Chodorow, *The Reproduction of Mothering: Psychoanalysis and the Sociology of Gender* (Berkeley: University of California Press, 1978).

4. Karen Sacks, *Sisters and Wives: The Past and Future of Sexual Equity* (Westport, CT: Greenwood Press, 1979).

5. Judith Arcana, *Our Mothers' Daughters* (Berkeley: Shameless Hussy Press, 1979).

6. Chodorow, p. 5.

7. Joyce Aschenbrenner, *Lifelines: Black Families in Chicago* (New York: Holt, Rinehart & Winston, 1975). Cynthia Epstein, "Positive Effects of the Multiple Negatives: Explaining the Success of Black Professional Women," in *Changing Women in a Changing Society*, ed. J. Huber (Chicago: University of Chicago Press, 1973). T. R. Kennedy, *You Gotta Deal With It: Black Family Relations in a Southern Community* (New York: Oxford University Press, 1980). E. P. Martin & J. M. Martin, *The Black Extended Family* (Chicago: University Press, 1978). Karen Sacks, *Sisters and Wives* (Westport, CT: Greenwood Press, 1979). V. H. Young, "Family and Childhood in a Southern Negro Community," in *American Anthropologist* 72 (1970), 269–88.

8. T. Morgan, "The World Ahead: Black Parents Prepare Their Children for Pride and Prejudice," in *The New York Times Magazine* (1985, October 27),

32. V. H. Young, "A Black American Socialization Pattern," in *American Ethnologist* 1 (1974), 405–513.

9. See Nobles in J. E. Hale, *Black Children: Their Roots, Culture and Learning Styles* (Provo, UT: Brigham Young University Press, 1982).

10. Dubois, W. E. B. *The Gift of Black Folk: The Negroes in the Making of America* (New York: Washington Square Press, 1970), xii. For "biculturality" see Ulf Hannerz, *Soulside: Inquiries Into Ghetto Culture a Community* (New York: Columbia University Press, 1969), and Charles Valentine, "Deficit, Difference, and Bicultural Models of Afro American Behavior," in *Harvard Educational Review* 41, no. 2 (1971).

11. Young (1974), 405–513.

12. Kennedy, 223.

13. Kennedy, 226. I recognize that one of the reasons that social scientists choose urban settings to study Blacks had to do with the large migration of Black people from the country to the city that began in the early decades of the 1900s. Once in the city, these new arrivals helped to create a new urban metropolis which represented a population vanguard that intrigued social scientists. With the decay of many urban areas, the trend has reversed: Urban dwellers are now returning to southern communities for some of the very reasons people fled the south 70 years ago.

World War II accelerated the growth in industrial areas of job opportunities, which promoted the beginning of the one-way migration from the South to the North. The South lost 1.5 million Blacks between 1940 and 1970. The migration pattern changed in the 1970s. While the majority of Blacks continued to live in the South in the 1920s, by 1970, 53% of the nation's Blacks lived in the South and 81% lived in urban areas. During the 1970–80 decade, the South and West regions which together accounted for 90% of the nation's population also accounted for an estimated 92% growth from April 1980 to July 1982. (United States Department of Commerce, 1979 & 1983).

14. According to the 1980 census approximately one-third of Hemington's population was Black. The population of Hemington County was 404,270. Blacks were 27% of this population. In the City of Hemington Blacks were 32% of the population.

15. The research consisted of 51 taped interviews of two, three and four generations of mothers and their daughters. In addition, a questionnaire was given to each of the participants on a day other than the interview.

16. Alice Walker, *In Search of our Mothers' Gardens* (New York; Harcourt Brace and Jovanovich, 1983), 231–243.

17. They represent five different sets of consanguineous generations including: 1) seven grandmothers and mothers; 2) four great grandmothers, grandmothers, and mothers; 3) two great-grandmothers, grandmothers, mothers, and unmarried daughters; 4) three grandmothers, mothers, and unmarried daughters; and 5) four mothers and teenage daughters. The method of selecting the participants was primarily through a snowball sample technique using personal contacts of women in my mother's network of friends, neighbors, and co-workers. The initial source of participants was an older subdivision call Fenbrook Park. Names of participants, when used, have been changed.

18. This study employs the definition of social class as discussed by John F. Cuber and William F. Kenkel in *Social Stratification in the United States* (New

York: Appleton-Century-Crofts, 1954). They suggest that "*Social class* has been defined in so many different ways that a systematic treatment would be both time consuming and of doubtful utility. One central core of meaning, however, runs throughout the varied usages, namely, the notion that the hierarchies of differential statuses and of privilege and disprivilege fall into certain clearly distinguishable categories set off from one another. Historically, this conception seems to have much better factual justification than it does in contemporary America . . . Radical differences, to be sure, do exist in wealth, privilege, and possessions; but the differences *seem to range along a continuum with imperceptible gradation from one person to another,* so that no one can objectively draw 'the line' between the 'haves' and 'the have nots,' the 'privileged' and 'underprivileged,' or for that matter, say who is in the 'working class,' who is 'the common man,' or who is a 'capitalist.' The differences are not categorical, but continuous" (p. 12). For an in-depth discussion of class see Rayna Rapp's article, "Family and Class in Contemporary America: Notes Toward an Understanding of Ideology," *Science and Society* 42(3): 278–300.

19. In 1970, Young studied child rearing practices among Black families. She observed southern Black family organization and child rearing systems of household supports. She documented distinctive patterns in which mothers and other members of Black families relate and respond to young children identifying the value that these families place on children's autonomy, initiative, and their ability to fend for themselves. In her 1974 study, Young identified distinctive processes involved in Black parenting. She points out that Black parents must teach their children "techniques of adaptation to persons and situation, while at the same time [they must teach their children how to] maintain . . . a strong sense of [an] independent self" (p. 405). Young's work was concerned with the socialization of young children. The present study has dealt with the socialization of children as they grow older and the interactions between mothers and their daughters.

20. See I. G. Joseph and J. Lewis, *Common Differences: Conflicts in Black and White Feminist Perspectives* (Garden City, NY: Anchor Books/Doubleday, 1981), 76–126.

21. A. Rich, *Of Woman Born* (New York: N. W. Norton, 1976), 3.

CHAPTER FIFTEEN

Rage and Representation:
Jewish Gender Stereotypes in American Culture

RIV-ELLEN PRELL

Jewish mothers, for more than fifty years, and Jewish princesses for the last decade, are well-known and pervasive stereotypes of Jewish women held by Jews, as well as by many other Americans. In combination, the two stereotypes provide opposing, if related, images of women who overwhelm men, respectively, by excessive nurturance or acquisitiveness.

According to these stereotypes, Jewish mothers give too much, whether it is food or demands for success. They suffer and induce guilt in their ever disloyal children, particularly sons. They behave like martyrs and constantly deny their own needs and wishes. The Jewish mother's character is captured well by the ethnic variant on the light bulb jokes of the 1970s.

How many Jewish mothers does it take to change a light bulb?
None, "I'll sit in the dark."[1]

Martyred, willing to sacrifice, yet miffed at those who neglect her and forget her sacrifices, the stereotypical Jewish mother exaggerates all forms of maternal nurturing only to invert them by her demand to be compensated through the constant love and attention she will never directly request.

By contrast, Jewish American Princesses (JAPs) require everything and give nothing. In jokes about them, they are completely focused on themselves and their overwhelming needs. They do not nurture, but require others to meet their constant demands. They do not take responsibility, or cook, or clean for their families. They are particularly obsessed with their physical attractiveness, although not in the interest of sexual pleasure. A widely circulating joke about JAPs conjures up the stereotype.

"How do you get a JAP to stop having sex? Marry her."

In this paper I examine pervasive Jewish gender stereotypes held by Jewish men about Jewish women. They appear in popular, widely circulated jokes, as well as in canonized literature written by American Jewish men. These gender stereotypes are changing. Jewish mothers are yielding to Jewish American Princesses, and a male stereotyped persona, the Jewish American Prince, is appearing on the scene for the first time. Stereotypes, then, change because they are sensitive to changing issues of relations between ethnic and majority groups. I will argue that the changing humor and stereotypes reveal the conflicts experienced by Jewish men as they negotiate their difference from and continuity with American culture.

These stereotypes certainly reveal a particular form taken by Jewish men's ideas and anxieties about women. What is less apparent is that the women of these jokes may also symbolize many facets of American Jewish life for men. The culture that gave rise to and nurtured these widely known gender images communicated powerful constructions of what constituted success, Americanization, loyalty, and Jewishness. Gender and ethnicity are linked in this humor because how Jewish men think about Jewish women may well reveal how they think about themselves as Americans and Jews.

Scholars of ethnicity, normally committed to the study of boundaries and differences, in this case between Jews and Christians, systematically overlook the *intra*-group differentiation between men and women who share an ethnic group. Gender and ethnicity are rarely, and only recently considered together. Men and women, for example, may be joined by ethnic ties, but they often experience the consequences and meaning of their ethnicity differently. Feminist anthropologists, historians, and sociologists have demonstrated the significance of these differences in a variety of cultures and historical periods.

Gender is significant not only because it forms the basis of social relationships within ethnic groups, but also because it frequently symbolizes the ethnic group for its members, as well as outsiders. Long suffering, nurturing mothers and distant fathers are each gender-coded symbols, which may represent an entire ethnic group in the mass media and to its members. Interpreting these stereotypes provides clues for understanding what links gender to ethnicity and how that link operates to establish both differentiation from outsiders and within groups.

Gender can be made to represent ethnic experience because it is so closely associated with relationships—self and other, child and parent—that quite explicitly portray one's place in a group. Gender, then, can be linked to intimacy or outsiderhood, or versions of both, and is a powerful symbolic vehicle for constructing, and reconstructing, the significance of ethnicity for minority men and women within a dominant culture.

Stereotyping is inevitable when groups, differentiated by a variety of factors, meet within a single social system. Stereotypes simplify and concretize difference. Sometimes humans admire others from afar, creating positive stereotypes, but more often stereotypes denigrate and differentiate groups to the advantage of those who hold these ideas. In neither positive nor negative cases are stereotypes accurate depictions of reality. Rather, they are representations of others, sometimes created out of limited shared experiences, and sometimes out of fears projected on others one may know well. Gender stereotypes are more likely the latter. In combination with ethnicity, gender stereotypes may be decoded to understand how difference is expressed not only between groups, but within them, as well.

Jewish stereotypes, like all other cultural stereotypes, rely on broad social categories. For example, both European and American Jewish humor have employed culturally significant categorical differences, such as social class, region of origin, and level of religious and secular education. Contemporary American Jewish humor, however, particularly since the 1960s, seems singularly focused on gender. The Jewish mother is the most prominent figure of contemporary Jewish humor[2] and jokes about her began before the Second World War. Jokes about Jewish American Princesses developed in the 1960s and flowered in the 1980s. As a result, the joke repertoire about Jewish women includes wives and potential marriage partners, as well as mothers. As Susan Schnur wrote about students, Jewish and non-Jewish, whom she taught at Colgate University in 1987, "I had been raised on moron jokes; *they* had been raised on JAP jokes."[3] Jokes about Jewish women have become a common coin of American life, as well as the central province of American Jewish humor. The subjects and numbers of jokes about women are expanding, but the images are redundant. The Jewish mother and princess reflect one another. The jokes often rest on simple inversions of characterizations thought to be ridiculous.[4]

Gendered jokes have dominated American Jewish humor, but women rather than men are consistently the subjects of these jokes. There are no Jewish father jokes, and the Jewish American Prince is just developing as a stereotype, not yet the subject of a series of jokes. Both the prominence of women in the humor and the absence of men from it require explanation as much as the roles (mother and princess) that are featured, to the exclusion of any other type of woman. Gender stereotypes, and the humor that makes use of them, seem neither random nor idiosyncratic. They depend on a narrowed, yet consistent set of messages and ideas. Jewish women are, for example, associated with a number of roles and activities, as well as social movements that range beyond mother and potential wife. The presence of Jewish women in unions, Socialist movements, and contemporary politics from feminism to anti-war activism conceivably could have yielded a stereotype of a political activist. Many Jewish women have, like their middle- and upper-class counterparts in the larger society, been active participants in voluntary and charitable associations, but no stereotype of a "society lady" has emerged. Linking Jewish women to men through these two stereotypes is an issue to be understood rather than assumed.

Marilyn Strathern, an anthropologist who writes about New Guinea, has put the problem of gender stereotypes well by differentiating between "the ideal" and the "actual,"[5] urging us never to read from stereotype to behavior, or idealized images to actual social relations, because representations are not actualities. Gender stereotypes are symbolic representations of the sexes, underpinning formal relations of authority or power. While typifications may tell us about many features of a society, how women and men actually function in a particular social system cannot be predicted by the stereotype alone. In Strathern's research among New Guinea Hageners, men and women may well be associated with either gender stereotype. Stereotypes must be "read" for cultural notions and then interpreted in light of how men and women behave. The inevitable inconsistencies can aid our understanding of cultural prescriptions, as well as the realities of social existence.

In a pluralistic and literate society the matter of stereotypes is more complex. Stereotypes are often written into literature, which is then read by members of the subculture, as well as by those outside of it. Inscribed in print, these stereotypes take on reality for people inside and outside a subculture. At the same time, male and female stereotypes may stand as cultural symbols for a series of relationships between opposites. They may also symbolize intra-psychic conflicts about belonging and rejection, associating women, for example, with negative ethnic group qualities, such as aggression, and distancing males from these associations. All of these possibilities only underscore Strathern's caution, that gender stereotypes cannot be read literally but must be understood in a series of contexts.

Strathern's insight is crucial for understanding American Jewish gender stereotypes. The popular and scholarly studies of these stereotypes consistently discuss whether or not they are "true" or "provable." While Jews have long been engaged in combatting anti-Semitic stereotypes, their encounter with gender stereotypes is of a different order. Jewish gender stereotypes are largely held among and generated by Jews themselves. They tend, then, to articulate internally held constructions. Yet, they bristle with the hostility and degradation that are associated with anti-Semitism. To read the stereotypes as actualities moves us away from the task of understanding what they mean.

Some argue that the stereotypes are untrue, others that they are true, and others still that they are both true and untrue.[6] Those that argue they are untrue claim, by way of sociological and quantifiable studies that, for example, Jewish mothers are not measurably more protective than others, or that Jewish college aged women are not different from their peers.[7] They claim, particularly in the cases where these stereotypes are also held in the wider society, that these caricatures are codes for anti-Semitic accusations masked by gender.[8] And indeed, some suggest that gender slurs seem to function to overshadow the transparent anti-Semitism.[9]

Nevertheless, there are those who argue that the stereotypes are based on accurate descriptions of behavior, and link their "truth" to cultural and historical developments. They explain that a history of uncertainty and oppression creates a preoccupation with safety, hence the Jewish mother with her suffocating behavior.[10] Others argue that a long religious tradition of sexual repression leads to certain attitudes toward the body and pleasure, hence the Jewish woman characterized as the frigid Jewish princess.[11] Or, as folklorist Alan Dundes suggests, more recent Jewish American Princess stereotypes suggest a rejection of middle-class norms that idealize complicit women devoted to denying their own needs in order to satisfy those of their families.[12]

Finally, there are those who write that the stereotypes are *both* true and untrue. For example, several writers who have looked at the stereotypes of Jewish women's sexuality suggest that Jewish men may denigrate women's sexuality out of their fear of inadequately competing with gentile men.[13] Others argue that these stereotypes constitute a Jewish internalization of anti-Semitism expressed by the larger culture. This more profoundly psychological analysis recognizes the complex process by which minorities represent themselves to themselves as outsiders in a majority culture. These typifications involve internalized negative stereotypes held by others about one's own group. The very popularity of the JAP jokes with some non-Jews may well support this point. The implicit anti-Semitism of JAP jokes means one thing within the Jewish community and another outside of it, but both associate Jews with an unfair and undeserved affluence.[14] Indeed, the JAP humor of the late 1980s is more hostile and, by implication, violent than previous decades.

> What is the difference between a JAP and a vulture?
> Painted Nails.
> What do you call 48 JAPs floating face down in a river?
> A start.[15]

Jokes, such as these, wish the death of people who are both women and Jews. The graffiti about JAPs reported on college campuses suggests that these stereotypes share much in common with racist ones. The line between "self-hate" and anti-Semitism is becoming harder to draw.

My point is not to support or deny these analyses of stereotypes. Rather, it is to suggest that virtually all approaches to the study of Jewish gender stereotypes invoke an unexpectedly positivist base that assumes they are capable of being accurate reflections of reality, or at least partially true, or generated from seekers of truth. What is missing in this conversation is some sense of these gender stereotypes as symbolic representations of American Jewish experience, and any inquiry into why relations between men and women are a medium for constructing Jews' relationships to other Jews and to American culture.

The humor, as I read it, suggests a fundamental incompatibility at the core of American Jewish culture. To be an American and a Jew necessitates relinquishing one or another of those identities. Social class, career aspirations, styles of interaction and sexuality—separately and together—are codes for and symbols of how one is American. I suggest that the stereotypical suffocating mother or whiny and withholding wife express ideas about how Jewish men understand their own place in American society. These stereotypical women represent the anxiety, anger, and pain of Jewish men as they negotiate an American Jewish identity. Jewish women, in these stereotypes, symbolize elements of "Jewishness" and "Americanness" to be rejected. Jewish women represent these features precisely because of their link to Jewish men, whom they do and do not resemble. Like a distorted mirror, Jewish men see Jewish women as inaccurately reflecting themselves. These stereotypes suggest that women may be represented as "too Jewish" or "too American," through their pattern of sexuality, nurturance, and consumption. Because gender and ethnicity are about sameness and difference, these stereotypes associate certain features of American and Jewish life with women that Jewish men fear and wish to abandon.

AMERICAN CULTURE AND THE JEWISH AMERICAN PRINCESS

No one is certain where this stereotype began, but a princess-like character appears in Herman Wouk's novel *Marjorie Morningstar*,[16] and the character of Brenda Patimkin in Philip Roth's short story "Goodbye Columbus" some years later.[17] Both works of fiction were made into popular films. This stereotyped young woman is a figure of post-war American Jewish affluence, whose key features concern consumption and sexuality, activities that figure as structural opposites in the humor and stereotype. The JAP is as rapacious and eager a consumer as she is unwilling to engage with her husband in an animated and mutually satisfying sexual relationship. When she is sexually active it is as a lure to entrapment.

The JAP can be both a wife and a daughter in the humor, and both relations make possible her insatiable desire to consume through acquiring expensive things and going to expensive places. Perhaps the most often told "consumption joke" asks, "What is a JAPs' favorite wine?" The punch line ranges from, "Take me to Florida" to "Buy me a mink." The answer not only may interchange various luxury consumer items for one another, but can vary depending on the person to whom it is directed. Some versions specifically include "Daddy, take me to . . ." in the joke. Such jokes use consumption to link a woman to her husband and her father as vehicles for achieving her desire. JAP jokes about sexuality only link husband and wife and assume her to be withholding and uninterested, or portray the JAP as sexually active because she is an unmarried woman. One JAP joke makes the complex links disturbingly clear. "How do you give a JAP an orgasm? Scream 'Charge it to Daddy'."[18] There is no mutuality in any of these relations. The JAP takes but does not give. She takes because she is dependent and may give only to create dependence.

What is particularly striking about the humor as Jewish humor is how it portrays the butt of the jokes. Jewish humor in Europe and America typically has been iconoclastic. It is anti-authoritarian, mocking all authorities, including God. Jews have often used their sharp humor to puncture the authorities within and without their community, who could not otherwise be criticized. Little people tended to emerge triumphant by the punch line of the joke.[19] This humor often ridicules the grandiose as offending a fundamentally democratic spirit. By contrast, the JAP, almost always the butt of the joke, is a whiner and a consumer, but she is neither powerful nor authoritative. Paradoxically, she, not the males who support her, is open to ridicule. As American Jewish humor focuses on gender, its sharp edge is directed at a relatively powerless figure. If the JAP is grandiose, the others in her world of affluence are free of ridicule and not the butt of the joke.

JAP jokes are atypical Jewish humor for a second reason. They are unmarked by any specific Jewish characteristics. There is no Yiddish in the jokes, or even dialects, both of which have been essential features of many generations of American Jewish jokes. The JAP has few qualities in common with other Jewish characters in Jewish humor. She is neither the fool, nor a clever deceiver. There is only a small measure of parody in the humor and some irony. If there is one humorous device it is, of course, exaggeration, but little else.

JAP jokes are constructed around completely American figures in American settings, behaving like Americans, in other words: consumers. Indeed, even the name of the stereotype, the JAP, is interesting because of the position of "American" in it. "Jewish mothers," or "German Jews," or "rabbis," or "schnorrers" (hangers on), never carried a cultural designation specific to the United States. The JAP stereotype is overwhelmingly marked by the American experience; the post-war American experience, in particular. Although there is evidence in earlier immigrant novels of vulgar bourgeois women, in Yezierska's *Bread Givers*[20] and Gold's *Jews Without Money*,[21] they were neither young, nor on the verge of marriage. Even married JAPs do not have children. Brenda Patimkin's mother in Roth's "Goodbye Columbus" was a woman of the suburbs, but she was not a princess, for all her wealth and attractiveness. The JAP, then, has no accent, and no history marred by suffering, hunger, or want, all typical of immigrant experiences. She is not only fully American, but epitomizes American success; she is affluent.

THE CONSTRUCTION OF THE JAP STEREOTYPE

The JAP is in every way American, and yet she is the butt of contemporary Jewish humor. What, then, is funny about the Americanness of the JAP? The answer lies in part in understanding from whose perspective the JAP is constructed. The JAP is a different type of Jew and American than the teller of the joke. Folklorist Alan Dundes' analysis of the JAP implies that Jewish women have created the image as a protest. He writes, "For women, the JAP joke cycle pinpoints what's wrong with the traditional roles women were expected to accept cheerfully in the American upwardly mobile, middle-class."[22] However, these jokes are not told from the point of view of women. They are always told *about* women. Women are the butt of the jokes.[23] Although women may tell these jokes, they tend to tell them about others. Although some women may call themselves "JAPs," or wear gold necklaces that say "JAP," they are typifying themselves from another's point of view.

Dundes draws a peculiar conclusion about the JAP joke from the point of view of women when he insists that the disinclination of women to engage in oral sex is because it "presumably give(s) primary pleasure to males."[24] Nowhere do the jokes suggest that any form of sex is pleasant for women. And Dundes also argues that the humor portrays autonomous women because the JAP is free to shop and beautify herself. This conclusion is hardly convincing if we are to believe that this joke cycle appeals to middle-class women as an expression of protest against their lack of autonomy and self-expression.

In JAP jokes women are passive, except for engaging in those activities done for the purpose of making themselves attractive—shopping, staying thin, and beautifying themselves—which depend on leisure and affluence. A greeting card that consists of JAP jokes portrays a JAP: She is standing, dressed in tennis whites. She wears high heeled shoes, drapes a mink coat over her shoulder, wears a long strand of pearls at her neck, and a Diet Pepsi with a straw stands before her. The diet beverage and tennis attire suggest a preoccupation with staying thin, but the portrayal of her as a physically active or competent woman, even for leisure, is undermined by the presence of jewelry, mink coat and, above all, high heeled shoes. Affluence and consumption undermine her physical vigor.

These stereotyped women are emulating culturally prescribed standards of beauty associated with the highest social strata. Whether this form of beauty—obsessively thin and highly styled—is directed toward men may be debatable. Nevertheless, this appearance depends on affluence and leisure, the combination of which is most likely acquired through marriage.

The jokes and images present women as non-sexual and narcissistic. More to the point, they make men victims of prey of women because men finance consumption but get nothing in return. In the jokes JAPs withhold sex and victimize men. These jokes, their images, their anger, and exaggeration are constructed by males about women. The perspective of the joke teller and the butt are quite straightforwardly differentiated by gender. What appears to be funny about the jokes, what constitutes a "protest" in the humor, is that men saddled with demands for producing economically to finance consumption reveal their true oppressors. The message of the humor is that Jewish wives or potential wives are slave drivers and ridiculous in their unceasing consumption. For all of their apparent beauty JAPs are frauds, sexless and childish. Men tell these jokes as an apparent protest against their fate with these women.

Paul Cowan's memoir about his journey to become a Jew articulates a related perspective.[25] He wrote about events that occurred decades before he became committed to feminism and Judaism. Consequently, we must read this passage about his relationship to Jewish women as a young man in light of his "new" consciousness. In the memoir he describes why he avoided young Jewish women after reading *Marjorie Morningstar*. In this novel he discovered "Shirleys," stereotyped Jewish women feared by the novel's initially appealing male character, Noel Airman, who wants a career in theater. For Wouk and Cowan the "Shirley"—a predecessor of the JAP—had the potential to ruin a man's life. Cowan writes:

I feared that Jewish women would imprison me. It left me feeling scared that my idealized version of my adult self as a latter day James Agee or John Dos Passos would be stifled by some Shirley who outwardly encouraged me to adventure, but who privately planned to trap me in a stifling suburban home. By contrast, the blondes to whom I was attracted were golden girls who would help me act out my journalist's version of the frontiersman's dream. They would provide me with protective coloration . . .[26]

Cowan makes explicit that the JAP stereotype is a gender stereotype held by Jewish men about Jewish women. It is constructed by a Jewish man in opposition to his immediate world. He does not want to exist within his family's expectations. He does not want to be forced to work or live like his father, who achieved affluence for the family. He does not want to be constrained by the expectations or narrowed vistas of American Jews hurtling themselves toward suburban success.

Precisely as the Jewish male rejects the Jewish American Princess as the embodiment of middle-class Jewish life, he does so with another woman and another life in mind. I would argue that JAPs are always constructed in contrast to a concealed stereotyped Christian woman who Lenny Bruce called "the shiksa goddess," or Philip Roth portrayed as "the monkey" in *Portnoy's Complaint*.[27] If Jewish women consume, then there is an unnamed stereotyped woman who does not. If the JAP avoids oral sex, as in the single minded preoccupation of JAP jokes, there is a stereotyped woman who apparently delights in it. Cowan implies this general opposition between Jewish and Gentile women when he writes of the "protective coloration" of the "golden girl," who is decisively not Jewish. If the JAP is accessible and the expected partner of the Jewish man, the Shiksa may be interesting in part because she, like many aspects of American culture, may not be attainable.

In the published text of a performance piece, "The Last Jew in America," Susan Mogul reflects Cowan's and Wouk's construction of Jewish men's attitudes toward Jewish women by dramatizing a Jewish woman's view of this relationship in the following monologue:

My mother said, "You know, Susan, you could be the last Jew in America, with the way all your brothers and sisters are intermarrying." I thought I owed it to my research, at least to try to go after a Jewish guy and see what it's like. Who knows?

Anyway, I went out to the Beverly Hills singles bars one night, and I had absolutely no luck. Christian guys would come up and we talked, but no Jewish action whatsoever. So I called up my friend Carol Mike on the phone and I said, "You know, Jewish men just don't want to date Jewish women, I'm convinced of it. We'll conduct a scientific experiment. I'll prove I'm right."

I went down to Woolworth's and I picked up this cross for $5.95, and of course, I scratched the words "not really" on the back to protect myself from the wrath of my father and of God as well. (She hangs the cross around her neck.)

Well! You would not believe the action. You think I'm exaggerating, but really. I'd never gotten so much attention from Jewish men *in my life*, or from men at all.[28]

Cowan and Mogul both reveal a construction of Jewish gender relations in which Jewish men reject Jewish women. A woman is not essentially attractive or unattractive. What makes a woman attractive to a Jewish man is that she is identifiably non-Jewish. As a non-Jew she will not be focused on consumption, her husband's productivity, and success, either because she already has it or because she is so poor and undemanding she cannot imagine it.

The asymmetry of the identifiers "American" (desirable) and "Jewish" (undesirable) reflects a second asymmetry between male and female. What is constructed in these male generated Jewish gender stereotypes is not a simple, more familiar mirror image. We do not find oppositions, such as male is to female as strong is to weak or aggressive is to passive. Rather, we find a triangulated relationship. Jewish men are to Jewish women are to Christian women as successful is to demanding is to acquiescent, or as sexual potency is to frigidity is to sexual desire. The third term is ever present but always invisible. It is the JAP's Jewishness and its relationship to her Americanness that the stereotype and humor feature. Jewishness is what she shares with the constructor of the stereotype. As he seeks his counterpart, he must construct two females, one like him and one unlike him, rejecting the Jewish woman and their shared qualities in favor of the American woman. Frederic Cople Jaher argues that in American Jewish fiction, Jewish protagonists are inevitably punished for their liaisons with gentile women. He writes that "Jewish boys who forsake Jehovah and virtuous women of their own faith for Dionysius and gentile temptresses inevitably get punished."[29] Jewish gendered humor, as well as the stereotype itself, demonstrates that Jewish men also perceive themselves as punished for liaisons with "virtuous women of their own faith." The punishment results from associating Jewish women with the American economic success that deprives men of the sexual rights associated with Gentile women.

CONSUMERS AND CONSUMED:
THE REFIGURING OF AMERICAN AFFLUENCE

The JAP stereotype describes married, but apparently childless women, or women in search of a marriage partner at the age of marriageability.

Like the princess of fairy tales, the JAP always stands on the threshold of womanhood. The JAP's link to marriage is the most salient feature in her portrait as entrapper. Middle-class American Jewish men, not unlike most American men in the middle-class, see adult status, ambition, career, and marriage as linked. Mainstream American Jewish culture has successfully encouraged its young adults to make choices that lead to careers that guarantee, at minimum, a middle-class life. The American Jewish family has made this career pattern for men its highest priority since immigration, certainly emphasizing education and success over religious observance and Jewish education. Not only are American Jews economically successful ethnics, they have achieved their success through education leading to a limited number of professional and career choices. They do so with remarkable loyalty to their ethnic group, demonstrated by their choice to live among Jews and maintain Jewish friendships. This pattern is particularly true of second and subsequent generations of men who have been in the work force for a longer time than Jewish women and whose careers are determinative of family social class status.[30] Although, as a group Jewish women are well-educated, until recently they stayed at home with their children and entered the labor force much later, if at all.[31] These Jewish patterns are, of course, shared with the white middle-class. Major demographic studies of New York, Boston, and Rhode Island demonstrate that Jewish success and Jewish identification, although not religious adherence, have been achieved.[32]

In American culture, success is associated with and symbolized by consumption, particularly since the Second World War. Jokes centering on JAPs' preoccupation with consumption, T-shirts that proclaim "I live to shop," and all the caricatures of spending to excess are the products of this pervasive American pattern. Warren Susman[33] and William H. Whyte,[34] among others, have written about the transformation of American society to a consumption rather than production oriented culture. Nothing characterizes the suburban family more completely than shared consumption. And Elaine May's recent book on the post-war family maintains that consumption was a critical element in maintaining families against divorce in the 1950s.[35] Indeed, her discussion of the Nixon-Kruschev debates in the 1950s demonstrates that even global policy was argued on the grounds of who had better consumer items and would be likely to maintain them over time.

The JAP stereotype, then, articulates the epitome of middle-class life and family oriented consumption, whether owning the proper designer labels, spending a great deal of time in restaurants, or redecorating a home. The humor moves back and forth in its portrayal of the JAP as American (focused on consumption) and Jewish (narcissistic, sexually withholding, and manipulative). The jokes in no overt sense differentiate Jewish and American, but the humor depends on identifying against the JAP. The ironic juxtaposition of consumption and frigidity make clear that the JAP is the consummate consumer who cannot herself be consumed. A series of jokes, in fact, juxtapose shopping and sex.

How does a JAP fake an orgasm? She thinks of going shopping.
What's a JAP's favorite position? Bending over credit cards.
What's a JAP's favorite position? Facing Neiman-Marcus (or Blooming-dale's).[36]

All that has been achieved by American success has been showered on the JAP, who inexplicably resists the sexual relationship that assures her continued affluence. This stereotype-driven humor, of course, does not *describe* Jews' social class, women's shopping habits, or sexual relations. Rather, it *represents* Jewish men's distress about becoming American men. Jewish women are portrayed as a barrier to adult male life because they withhold sex and demand production. Men are victimized by both demands and refusals. What appears to be the normal steps to adult life—education, career, marriage—in jokes and stereotypes are perilous steps on the way to disaster because of who waits in the wings as the appropriate marriage partner. Marriage will not ensure sexuality, and will lead to a career that will drive one toward giving and receiving nothing in return. JAP jokes are only peripherally about women. Rather, women's demands and refusals symbolize what will become of men as they enter adulthood, only to be deprived of their dreams.

LINKS AND SPACES BETWEEN JEWISH MOTHERS AND JEWISH AMERICAN PRINCESSES

To understand these key elements of the stereotype—consumption and the refusal to be consumed—requires reconsidering the older, more conventional female gender stereotype of the Jewish mother. Dundes' discussion of this stereotype attempts to generate the new acronym JAM, Jewish American Mother, but it is his invention and has not yet caught on in the culture. The Jewish mother has no geographic specificity. Novak and Waldoks, in their *Big Book of Jewish Humor,* suggest that the humorous figure of the Jewish mother appears only after migration to America.[37] This view is only partially correct. There has always been a Jewish mother or "Yiddishe mama," but she was not a butt of humor until the second generation of immigrant society. Henry Roth's *Call It Sleep*[38] and Michael Gold's *Jews Without Money* both enshrine a perfect mother. She is present everywhere in the immigrant experience, from music to theater and film to novels. But she is the representation of the lost world, the fantasy perfect mother, who is characterized above all by total and complete self-sacrifice for others, particularly her sons. Indeed, Novak and Waldoks argue that it is the Jewish mother's changing economic role that is responsible for her becoming a figure of ridicule. In Europe, she was a productive member of the family. In America, she no longer actively contributed to its economic survival. Rather, her inactivity became a sign of the financial success of her husband.[39]

These changes may well contribute to the stereotype. Nevertheless, it is not her financial dependency but her preoccupation with her children and concern for them, the very aspects of the once romanticized Jewish mother, which are the subjects for ridicule. Her characteristics change less than the perceptions of them held by her sons. By the second generation, she became the butt of humor because Jewish men were now the products of families focused on acculturation and these sons rendered self-sacrifice as suffocation. Jewish men did not want to sacrifice and could not bear the sacrifices apparently implied by their mother's behavior. The all-giving mother was revealed as the all-demanding mother.

Ironically, for all of their differences, mother and princess present the same dangers to Jewish males. The Jewish mother cannot give her children enough food. The classic JAP joke about her ability to nurture states that what she makes best for dinner is "reservations." Over a period of a mere two decades the stereotype of the Jewish woman became two stereotypes; a nurturer and a person unable to cook, feed, or care for her family, particularly her husband. Jewish mothers were separated from Jewish wives. The Jewish mother, however, bears a partial resemblance to the "shiksa" who gives all and asks nothing. The difference between "shiksa" and "mother" is that there are hidden demands in the mother's gift, and that the mother is not Gentile, American, or mainstream. Shiksas are not associated with food and they are less nurturant than undemanding. Ultimately, then, what unites the Jewish mother and the Jewish princess is that each is a threat to the Jewish male; son and potential husband. These women are entrappers and seducers. Neither will give without asking for something in return. They are also bound to one another by their relationships to men.

Are Jewish mothers represented as having special alliances with Jewish princesses? Are these gender representations linked? I would suggest not. In literature, humor and folklore Jewish mothers are primarily tied to their sons. Jewish princesses seem to be made by their fathers in the humor I have reviewed. In all types of literature, humor, and folklore there is an ever present sexual antagonism between men and women of the same generation, and an over attachment across generations. What cannot or will not be expressed between men and women of the same generation is played out between parents and opposite sex children as intimacy without a sexual component. Mothers indulge their sons and fathers indulge their daughters. Mothers hold out high aspirations for their sons, apparently expecting them to be different from the men they married. Fathers withdraw from their wives, and delight in creating a royal daughter, despite the fact that they are never portrayed as kings.[40] The father-daughter link portrayed in JAP humor and stereotypes reflects the sudden affluence of many Jews following a major economic depression and World War Two.[41]

ACCULTURATION AND ITS COSTS

In these gender stereotypes we see at work both the representations of profound contradictions in American Jewish life, and the process of trans-mitting those very contradictions. In these stereotypes one finds consumption and success bought at the price of lost sexuality. We see women who demand and never reciprocate, leaving men successful yet betrayed. We see men feeling themselves under constant threat of annihilation, either in the person of the suffocating mother or the parasitic wife. The success that makes consumption possible satisfies the mother but does not provide the avenue for adult sexuality or mutuality. The promises of American culture pay off only in liaisons with the other, the shiksa or Gentile, who then makes it impossible to continue Jewish life.[42]

The cultural costs and implications of an economic system in which men produce and women consume is well-documented. From Thorsten Veblen to feminist Barbara Ehrenreich, social critics have noted the inevitability of men's resentment and women's portrayal as parasites built into this division of labor.[43] Elisa New's analysis of a recent book about the trial of a husband who murdered his wife because she was a "Jewish princess" effectively argues that Jews have collapsed American Jewish culture with American success, to such an extent that they have become indistinguishable.[44] Female representations among Jews—mother and princess—then clearly share much in common with other middle-class representations of women as narcissistic and sexually withholding.

These analyses do not, however, address other implications for male-female opposition within the family. In the case of American Jews the Jewish family is associated with the continuation of the Jewish people. To marry a Jewish partner is increasingly seen as the most certain insurance for trans-mitting a culture and history. Sociologists have documented thoroughly the fact that when they form families American Jewish adults become synagogue members and ritual participants. The center of Jewish life has moved from community to family to the individual. The individual is the center of gravity for Judaism. The choices leading to economic success and endogamous marriage are the most powerful promise for a continuing Jewish people.

The individualism of the American Jew, however, is rather different from the individualism of American culture, which idealizes the freedom to move anywhere, unfettered by any past. Unlike the quintessential American com-munities of the 1970s described by Frances FitzGerald, American Jews do not make up their lives free of a history.[45] The American Jew is, of course, no longer closely tied to a community bound by shared religious obligations and a single status hierarchy, as was the case for many centuries for Jews throughout the world. American Jews do not deny one another a place in their communities if they desecrate the Sabbath or violate various laws of purity. Nevertheless, neither are they free of a past nor do strongly identified Jews hope that their children will set out in search of an uncharted future. American Jews' persistent identification with Judaism despite their non-observance of Jewish religious practice makes clear to their children that they should continue to be Jews. Individuals are autonomous and free to make their own choices. But these choices include the proper marriage partners, having children who understand that they are Jews, and being successful. These choices are expected, even overdetermined. They seem to be the minimum requirement for remaining within the normative Jewish community. Approval, love, and acceptance, qualities often associated with Jewish families, are typically withdrawn when individuals exercise their "autonomy" to make the wrong choices. Undeniably, American Jewish families emphasize these issues as they raise their children, and it is these cultural demands that are represented in the humor.

To be free of JAPs is to assert one's freedom from obligation, responsibility, and productivity, but it is also to negate the Jewish people, the family, and hence the self. To be linked to a JAP is to undermine the self linked to community. The Jewish mother who nurtures, protects, and rewards makes one Jewish and successful. The JAP takes and withholds and is constructed as the poisoned reward for success. This terrible dilemma is normally associated with the "wrong" choices made by Jewish men who are attracted to the forbidden outsider, the shiksa, who symbolizes an unambiguous Americanization. Intermarriage, however, implies abandoning one's own family and people. The stereotypes that are increasingly apparent in the 1980s suggest that Jewish men construct Jewish women as representations of a vision of American success associated with their parents' dreams for them. In this sense, the JAP is another version of the Jewish mother, bent on blocking access to unfettered autonomy precisely because she represents American expectations for consumption and success. This culturally acceptable union continues the Jewish people both by promoting the achievement of success and producing another generation. Obviously, men share these cultural norms or the choice would not entail such conflict and agony. Marriage, women, and gender relations all symbolize this generationally transmitted conflict between the Jewish man's wish to enter adulthood and reproduce the Jewish people, and a fear of that course as destroying his development as an autonomous male.

Jewish gender images, then, represent the tension between reproducing Judaism, maturing and assuming responsibility, and pursuing one's destiny. That men were trained for careers and women for marriage was one common pattern for success that appears to evoke this inevitable tension. However, stereotypes are not sociological road maps for describing how American Jews became who they are. Rather, they symbolize, through one gender's perspective, the association of sexuality, acculturation, family, and consumption, the key themes of American Judaism in the post-war period. These could not be European or immigrant stereotypes because they assume affluence; they reflect and construct choices and possibilities unavailable until the period of increasing assimilation. Indeed, Jewish intermarriage skyrocketed in the 1960s when these stereotypes were just taking shape.[46] They speak most centrally to the association of Judaism and suburban success, and the projection of that desire for success onto women. Americanization as a middle-class aspiration appears to be feared by men, who associate Americanization with Jewish women. The other, the Gentile woman, remains a counterbalance fantasy partner for freedom from this connection, but at the cost of a future.

ARE THERE PRINCES IN THE ROYAL FAMILY?

I have emphasized female stereotypes in this chapter. I emphasize the perspective of the stereotype because it provides the key to understanding why these gender representations appear when they do and in the form that they do. There are stereotypes about Jewish men, but few are named. There is no Jewish father, for example, although there is the pervasive stereotype of the Jewish male as passive. Only recently has a defined stereotype of the Jewish prince emerged. The writer Nora Ephron describes him in her book *Heartburn*. He wants attention and service lavished upon him. She writes,

You know what a Jewish prince is, don't you? If you don't, there's an easy way to recognize one. A simple sentence, "Where's the butter?" Okay. We all know where the butter is, don't we? The butter is in the refrigerator . . . But the Jewish prince doesn't mean "Where's the butter?" He means "Get me the butter." He's too clever to say "Get me" so he says "Where's." And if you say to him (shouting) "in the refrigerator" and he goes to look, an interesting thing happens, a medical phenomenon that has not been sufficiently remarked upon. The effect of the refrigerator light on the male cornea. Blindness. "I don't see it anywhere." . . . I've always believed that the concept of the Jewish princess was invented by a Jewish prince who couldn't get his wife to fetch him the butter.[47]

The Jewish prince is simply the son of the Jewish mother. He has become the butt of the joke and stereotype. The presence of this stereotype simply inverts the mirroring images of one male and two women, one Christian and one Jewish, for one woman and two males.

These direct inversions—prince and princess—emerge as stereotypical parallel figures as Jewish mother and father did not. The culture generated a marked Jewish mother and left Jewish males entirely unmarked. Perhaps the newest gender stereotypes speak to a change in family relations, in part created by the fact that both men and women are likely to be employed. Changing family relations are unlikely, however, to be the sole explanation for these stereotypes. Gender representations continue to express the tensions and conflicts surrounding assimilation, acculturation, and success which continue to be associated with one's family of origin and choice of marriage partner.

I have argued that Jewish gender stereotypes are a strategic site for the analysis of American Jewish culture. I suggest that the focus of American Jewish humor on gender relations requires that we understand why these relations effectively symbolize how Jews attempt to remain Jews and live in the American mainstream. Understanding that the point of view of the stereotype is male, I have argued that Jewish women are associated with the desire for prestige, consumption, the continuity of the Jewish people, and the absence of erotic desire. Gender stereotypes are a rich vein to be mined for understanding American culture and the ways in which social class, ethnicity, gender and culture guide the construction of American lives.

These stereotypes suggest that Jewish men and women do not experience their Judaism in precisely the same way. Both are clearly affected by the association of Judaism with social class, but women, until recently, were dependent on husbands' and fathers' successes to achieve Americanization and mobility. Men reacted to that dependence in the portraits they made of wives and mothers as demanding and suffocating. The link of class and ethnicity is a close one for American Jews, who seek success without assimilation. Since cultural uniqueness is guaranteed by marriage choice, it should not be surprising that the dangers and enticements of assimilation are expressed in representations of Jewish women, both young and mature, as dependent, insatiable consumers with devastating power.

NOTES

I appreciate the helpful, often witty, always insightful comments of Howard Eilberg-Schwartz, Sara Evans, Steven Foldes, Amy Kaminsky, Elaine Tyler May, Cheri Register, Anna Tsing, and Barbara Tomlinson on a previous draft of this chapter.

1. William Novak and Moshe Waldoks, *The Big Book of Jewish Humor* (New York: Harper and Row, 1981).

2. William Novak and Moshe Waldoks, *The Big Book of Jewish Humor* (New York: Harper and Row, 1981).

3. Susan Schnur, "When a J.A.P. is not a Yuppie? Blazes of Truth," *Lilith: The Jewish Women's Magazine* 17 (1987): 10–11.

4. Alan Dundes "The J.A.P. and the J.A.M. in American Jokelore," *Journal of American Folklore* 98 (1985): 456–475. Dundes has also noted the link between these two stereotypes; as I note, our approaches differ on several points.

5. Marilyn Strathern, "Self Interest and the Social Good: Some Implications of Hagen Gender Imagery," in *Sexual Meanings; the Cultural Construction of Gender and Sexuality,* Sherry Ortner and Harriet Whitehead, eds. (Cambridge: Cambridge University Press, 1981), 166–91.

6. Dundes, 466–68, addresses these issues of Jewish women's stereotypes and some of the literature on the stereotypes.

7. See Zena Smith Blau, "In Defense of the Jewish Mother," *Midstream* 13 (2): 42–49 and Sherry Chyat, "JAP-Baiting on the College Scene," *Lilith: The Jewish Women's Magazine* 17 (1987): 42–49.

8. Chyat, 7.

9. Francine Klagsburn, "JAP: The New Anti-Semitic Code Words," *Lilith: The Jewish Women's Magazine* 17 (1987): 11.

10. Charlotte Baum, Paula Hyman and Sonya Michel, *The Jewish Woman in America* (New York: Plume, 1975), 242.

11. Susan Weidman Schneider, "In a Coma! I Thought She Was Jewish!: Some Truths and Some Speculations About Jewish Women and Sex," *Lilith: The Jewish Women's Magazine* (1979): 5–8.

12. Dundes, 470.

13. Schneider.

14. Jewish gender stereotypes have captured some interest of late. Graffiti was found in 1986 at Syracuse University throughout the library slurring Jewish American Princesses. These incidents have been discussed by Chayat 1987, Schnur 1987, and Judith Allen Rubenstein, "The Graffiti Wars," *Lilith: The Jewish Women's Magazine* 17 (1987): 8–9.

15. Cited in *Lilith* 17 (1987).

16. Herman Wouk, *Marjorie Morningstar* (Garden City, N.Y.: Doubleday, 1965).

17. Philip Roth, *Goodbye Columbus* (New York: Houghton Mifflin, 1959).

18. From Noble Works Greeting Card.

19. Novak and Waldoks, xx–xxi.

20. Anzia Yezierska, *Bread Givers: A Struggle between a Father of the Old World and a Daughter of the New* (New York: Pera Press, 1975). Originally published in 1925.

21. Michael Gold, *Jews Without Money* (New York: Avon Books, 1965). Originally published in 1930.

22. Dundes, 470.

23. The significance of gender for the perspective of the joke is also noted by Gladys Rothbell, "The Jewish Mother: Social Construction of a Popular Image," in *The Jewish Family: Myths and Reality,* Steven Cohen and Paula Hyman, eds. (New York: Holmes and Meir, 1986), and E. Fuchs, "Humor and Sexism," in *Jewish Humor,* Avner Ziv, ed. (Tel Aviv: Papyrus Publishing House, 1986).

24. Dundes, 470.

25. Paul Cowan, *An Orphan in History: Retrieving a Jewish Legacy* (Garden City, New York: Doubleday, 1982).

26. Cowan, 112.

27. Philip Roth, *Portnoy's Complaint* (New York: Random House, 1969).

28. Susan Mogul and Sandy Nelson, "The Last Jew in America: A Performance by Susan Mogul," *Images and Issues* 4 (1984): 22–24.

29. Frederic Cople Jaher, "The Quest for the Ultimate Shiksa," *American Quarterly* 35 (1983): 529.

30. See Steven M. Cohen, *American Assimilation or Jewish Revival?* (Bloomington: Indiana University Press, 1988) and Calvin Goldscheider and Alan S. Zuckerman, *The Transformation of the Jews* (Chicago: University of Chicago Press, 1984).

31. Sidney Goldstein and Calvin Goldscheider, *Jewish Americans: Three Generations in a Jewish Community* (Englewood Cliffs, N.J.: Prentice-Hall, 1966).

32. See Steven M. Cohen, *American Modernity and Jewish Identity* (New York: Tavistock, 1983), Cohen, and Goldstein and Goldscheider.

33. Warren I. Susman, *Culture as History: The Transformation of American Society in the Twentieth Century* (New York: Pantheon Books, 1984).

34. William H. Whyte, *The Organization Man* (Garden City, NY: Doubleday, 1956).

35. Elaine Tyler May, *Homeward Bound: American Families in the Cold War Era* (New York: Basic, 1988).

36. Dundes, 464. In the third joke, an obvious reference is made to Jews facing east when they pray in remembrance of their allegiance to ancient Israel

and Jerusalem, which was the center of worship. In the joke shopping is associated with prayer and sex is stimulated by facing a substitute sacred center.

37. Novak and Waldoks, 268.

38. Henry Roth, *Call It Sleep* (New York: Avon, 1976). Originally published in 1934.

39. Novak and Waldoks, 268.

40. Patricia Erens' study of the portrayal of Jews in American films demonstrates that in the 1920s the patriarchal father was the source of power and villainy in films. He grows weaker and virtually disappears from films as the mother grows more powerful and suffocating. See *The Jew in American Cinema* (Indiana University Press: Bloomington, 1984), 256–257.

41. Writers about eastern European Jewish life have emphasized the very powerful link between sons and mothers. Some have suggested a link between daughters and fathers as well, but in general the father is characterized as remote. Both the mother-son attachment and son-mother-in-law hostility are articulated in folklore, but far less exists around the daughter-father tie. See Marc Zborowski and Elizabeth Herzog, *Life is With People: The Culture of the Shtetl*, 8th ed. (New York: Schocken Books, 1971).

42. In a related argument regarding Roth's *Portnoy's Complaint*, Alan Segal notes that Portnoy can only escape his condition by "shedding" a Jewish identity which dominates and controls him. His means of escape is "sex with the goyim" or "shikses" on "a compulsive scale which both emancipates and imprisons him because its pleasure derives from it being forbidden." Segal does not focus on Roth's female contemporaries, but only the Jewish mother. Alan Segal, "Portnoy's Complaint and the Sociology of Literature," *British Journal of Sociology*, xxii (1971): 267.

43. *The Hearts of Men: American Dreams and the Flight From Commitment* (New York: Doubleday, 1983).

44. "Killing the Princess: The Offense of A Bad Defense," *Tikkun* 2 (1989): 17.

45. Frances FitzGerald, *Cities on a Hill: A Journey Through American Cultures* (New York: Simon and Schuster, 1986).

46. Cohen, *American Assimilation*.

47. Nora Ephron, *Heartburn* (New York: Knopf, 1983).

PART FIVE

*Unbecoming Women: Tricksters, Monsters, and
Unendurable Contradictions*

CHAPTER SIXTEEN

"Drastic Entertainments": Teenage Mothers' Signifying Narratives

SHARON THOMPSON

Under the world where Earthmaker lives, there is another world just like it, and of this world, he, Trickster, is in charge.
—Paul Radin, The Trickster[1]

1

Promiscuous, comic, taboo-splitting trickster camps through myth and folklore in women's clothes. He takes his penis off and throws it in the lake. He gets pregnant. But he is never interpreted as that most common and credible inversion from a practical point of view, the female whose phallus is constructed or appended. Even analyses that emphasize trickster's femininity quickly revert to the pronoun "he." Perhaps we cannot truly imagine women in this extreme state of desocialization.

Like the culture hero, trickster is independent, motherless, "free." He represents separation at its most fantastic extreme. In this sense, to tell trickster tales is to joke on the theme of masculinity. A female analogue is the witch, but trickster is streetwise; and while trickster belongs to adolescence, she is supposedly finished, a hag. Disorderly woman is perhaps the closest female relative of trickster. She is a lusty and unruly dominatrix who sometimes crossdresses.[2] But while disorderly woman makes the most of her humanity, she doesn't strategize.

In African-American folklore, trickster is known as the Signifying Monkey. He is a figure so marginal that he has no vested interests of his own—nothing to win, nothing to lose. Trickster often appears with a wife in African tales, literary critic Carra Hood has pointed out. In these tales, trickster works to dupe the community out of its food supplies, while his wife urges distributing the food fairly: More generally, trickster tales are about leveraging human nature against itself, provoking others to get themselves into trouble or expose their own self-interest, stupidity, or hypocrisy. These tricks are often conversational—hints, innuendoes, and rumors.

To play a trick is to "signify." To fall for one is to be "signified on." As Henry Gates has synthesized, the art of signifying survived the Middle Passage, slavery, abolition, the hope of civil rights movement, and the breaches of the 1980s to become a vital part of contemporary African-American oral and written literature. In contemporary usage, signifying is a varied and complex rhetorical practice of indirection and coding that multiplies meanings by blurring the distinctions between implication and assertion, fact and fiction, wish and joke. With splendid ethnographic studies, both Claudia Mitchell-Kernan and Geneva Smitherman have shown that in African-American culture women as well as men are "signifiers."[3] Their informants did not represent themselves as tricksters in any other respect, however.

This paper draws on their work, and trickster literature generally, to illuminate the narratives of an extraordinary group of African-American teenagers who both signify and represent themselves as tricksters. I met these narrators near the end of a study of teenage girls' narrative practice. In the course of the six-year study (1980–86), I gathered 400 narratives about sex, romance, and pregnancy, using a snowball technique to generate the sample, which includes African-American, Puerto Rican, Chicana, and white girls, middle-class and poor, lesbian, bisexual, and heterosexual from the Northeast, Midwest, and Southwest. The interviews were long and open ended. Frequently interview sessions lasted three to four hours, and I spoke with some narrators several times. The sample described in this paper is small—ten informants. I have had qualms about presenting their material for this reason, but I promised these narrators that I would make known what they told me, and they represent a uniquely subversive and rebellious perspective. These interviews were gathered, and this piece was originally written, before the direction of the AIDS epidemic became clear to the subjects. At the time of the interviews, they had received no public health information about AIDS. Given the problems that confront many teenage mothers, and the problem they are thought to constitute, narrative analysis may seem beside the point.[4]

2

Esu, do not undo me,
Do not falsify the words of my mouth.
—Yoruba invocation cited by Ayodele Ogundipe[5]

As Barbara Babcock-Abrahams has observed, tricksters "emerge from or imply" anti-structural states. They are liminal: They live with or come from or remind us of change, marginality, and inferiority.[6] Similarly, the narrators I work with here are adolescent, poor, stigmatized, left out. Teenage mothers, they represent one of the most baffling categories of adolescents in the 1970s and 1980s. As members of adolescence, they are children. As members of their gender, they are adults. They can set up a separate household but not vote, procreate but not work. They live on the periphery of survival and possibility. They are poor. They don't have high school degrees. The training programs that give them hope are ephemeral. Their living arrangements with friends and family are temporary and shaky. They aren't married, and they know that marriage to a man who can't get work would not stabilize or improve their situation.

Many girls' lives are circumscribed by the disjunctive conditions above. Most rationalize their experiences, in order to prove goodness or coherence. Only a few choose the trickster's path out of the options that tradition offers. These few multiply contradictions, play all sides of paradox, stretch probabilities and pleasures to the limit, and make a joke out of dualism. Although their existence is shot through with marginality, they downplay it as they do all vulnerability. With slow glimmering smiles and sharp laughs, they brag that they are difficult to pin down; moody; nasty; slick. They are good mothers, but that is it for them with goodness, girls' special and suspect province. Like folkloric tricksters who shift from one anti-structural state to another during a tale, they declare themselves chameleons, and they describe negotiating some of the hardest passages of gender and marginality and responding to realistic problems—battery and two-timing, for example—with the resources of cunning, hyperbole, and rebellious hilarity. In their stories, they brush off the unstable conditions of their lives that constitute weaknesses but celebrate other liminal states as options and disguises—particularly, adolescence and pregnancy. From such quicksand, they build their lives and stories, transforming weakness into strength, blame into affirmation, oppression into confusion. They are not shaped by their experiences, they insist. They shape themselves. They exclaim over their nerve, boldness, and autonomy.

They savor the story of themselves in action: shellgaming, trumping, one-uping, calling every question, turning every table. When they want autonomy, they argue that they are "adults." But they defend their claim to freedom and pleasure on the grounds that they are still "kids." They declare themselves fully conscious and self-interested in playing off adolescent ambiguities, going "up and down," acting young and mature, strong and weak: fooling about these qualities, being slick.

A great aspect of adolescence, they report, is that men and boys who come on to them have a fifty-fifty chance of getting their quarry's age wrong.

> He was talking to me. He was asking me different questions.
> "Do you know how old I am?"
> He goes, "You're probably about seventeen, eighteen."
> I said, "Do I look that old?"

He says, "Yeah," he says, "bodywise you do."
I says, "I'm only fourteen."
He's like, "Oh my god. What do I do now?"
I said, "I'm only fourteen."
"So what?"
But I knew he was like kind of funny about saying anything else to me.

Being half-child, half-adult is to control two languages:

Then sometime I would go beyond my level, and I'd talk to him like I was up there with him. I'm saying to him . . . when I'm sitting down talking serious, I can talk to you like if I was a grown woman myself. Then again, I can talk to you like I was a child.

Men assume young women are naive. These narrators know this, and they delight in using the presumption of innocence like a poker face. If innocence is a great ruse, so is knowingness, as Bell's narration demonstrates repeatedly. Bell is a large-boned, forceful young women with deep brown skin, who fixes her eyes hypnotically when she speaks. She engaged in combative repartee with other students who tried to come into the school kitchen where we were talking, but she didn't appear to have close friends in the program. Her performance sequences—passages in which she quoted dialogue and imitated the participants—suggest that her social relations are mainly familial and romantic. Brash and comic, Bell tells a classic seduction story with a switch: After getting herself drunk to shortcircuit anxiety about having first sex, she pretended sobriety so her lover would assume she knew what she was doing.

As much as she loves the secrecy that ambiguity affords, she embraces its flip side: sudden disclosure that she is an object of misunderstanding. Bell was so flat in the early stages of her pregnancy, she claims, that her lover didn't discern the bulging life within the body he caressed. This account at once recounts a signifying coup—fooling a lover—and indicates how paradoxical a maternal and romantic figure she was (young, flat, but pregnant; sarcastic and pregnant but attractive.)

What happened was, I went down into the laundromat and he was sitting in the laundromat and he was watching me. Because when I was pregnant, I was flat as this table. You couldn't tell nothing. So he was busy trying to talk to me, and I wasn't paying him no mind. This was going on for about two weeks. I say, he was really cute and everything.
Q: And he was always at the laundromat?
A: Yeah! Every time I would go down there, it was like either he was coming in or he was going out. And it was like this is—too much of a coincidence. Every time I'm bumping into this guy. So one day he took me out and . . . he took me to the movies. We had fun that night.
So he goes, "You got a man?"
I goes, "No."
He says, "You don't?" I says, "No. I got rid of him."

He goes, "Why?"
I said, "He wasn't pleasing me. He wasn't satisfying me."
He says, "Do you want a man?"
I said, "I'm looking for one."
He says, "Do you think I qualify?"
I said, "First of all I've got to tell you something."
He goes, "What?" I go, "I'm five months pregnant."
He goes, "YOU'RE WHAT?"
I said, "I'm five months pregnant."
He ain't believe me until I was seven months. I started blowing up all of a sudden. He goes, "You really was pregnant."
I said, "I told you. I was five months pregnant when you met me."
He goes, "Well, I really like you. You got a nice attitude about yourself."
I said, "I'm putting on a front for you. I'm being nice."

NASTINESS: COLDNESS AND INSATIABILITY

For these narrators, being "nasty" rather than nice is a matter of pride. A rhetorical and sexual attitude, being nasty involves talking back to boys and men; exchanging courtship insults; engaging in willful, stubborn or irrational acts; performing and receiving oral sex; having sex with both genders; taking part in orgies. Nastiness goes along with being cold to sex or love; being able to take or leave lovers. Cold, nasty girls are beyond romance and the reach of fatal attractions.

I said now, "If love is that blind, then I don't never want to fall in love." I don't never want to fall in love. Not that bad. Not that bad at all.

Like Zen masters, they have given up on expectations. They have no hope. They have let go. As a matter of principle and practicality, they act and talk as if they could care less. Bell has never tried to attract lovers, and she won't lift a finger to keep them enthralled:

My mother said, "What do you do to them?"
I said, "Nothing. That's the whole problem."

Courtship is his job, not hers. She takes the convention—men want women—at face value; plays it as a trump card. She doesn't practice the passive of arts of attraction or positioning (being in the right place at the right time). She doesn't try to hold him with affirmations of love. She embraces coldness as a strength.

He says, "You're no fun. You're not romantic."
I says, "I'm not. I'm cold!"
He goes, "Why do you consider yourself cold?"
I go, "Didn't you just tell me I was cold?"
"Yeah. All right then."
"The reason why I'm cold is because I don't do the things you want me to do."

To be cold to love is proof against emotional and erotic blackmail. When these narrators say they can "take or leave sex" or "your romance doesn't phase me," they position themselves beyond male persuasions. In a state of romantic alienation, they won't take shit, and they cannot be talked into buying or selling love.[7]

Giving up on expectations and being prepared to cut one's losses do not require passing up a good thing. On the contrary, they involve taking what comes for what it's worth—pleasure at face value, for example. Explicit sexual intentionality distinguishes this group of narrators. They acknowledge sexual curiosity, adventurousness, desire, and bisexuality. They "explore" the body and sexuality. They enjoy oral sex. Again, they are in it for the game: "Sex is fun to me."

TEACH ME TO HAVE SEX

Trim and quick, Suzette characteristically represents herself as naive. She looks upon appearances as clues, or screens. What is behind things, she wants to know. As a toddler, she used to look through the keyhole of her mother's bedroom door to find out what was going on, and she experimented with intercourse well before puberty. She talked about her involvement with an older man as "a sexual education." Here she focuses on what she learned in her older lover's bed, not on Oedipal obsession or victimization:

So I asked him. So he took me to his house. So we had sex and everything. So that first time wasn't really nothing. But afterwards! I started learning all these crazy positions, all these movements—I'm like a regular walking magazine.

These narrators describe sexual appetites as insatiable as their need for affirmation and opportunity. They propose that this insatiability drives them to break taboos—having oral, anal, and group sex—and being slick.[8]

Cause I can have sex and not be satisfied. Never get enough.

Bisexuality is a trademark of the folkloric trickster. By definition, bisexuality makes monogamy unlikely. In exchange, it offers pleasure and an additional gear with which to play with expectations and appearance; disorient, throw off guard, confuse, trick. Long after the ambiguous years of puberty, bisexual girls retain a flexible identity with which to continue to maneuver expectations and appearances. These narrators see it simply as a trick to double their pleasure, as Suzette's vignette illustrates.

When Suzette learned that her cousin had had sex with women and multiple partners, she pricked up her ears. "I knew I was going to do this. . . . from the time my cousin told me she was bisexual." To wangle an invitation, she gave her cousin the impression that she was much more experienced than she actually was. With the expectation of being pleasured by Suzette, her cousin invited her to come along to an orgy. First there was music and plenty to drink. Then:

Everybody started working their way over to the bed. Here, I'm just like, you know, what am I doing? So they performed on me, because, you know, all of them knew something new to me, right? So they was performing on me, kissing me, sucking on my chest. Everything. The works!

Her cousin, whom I also spoke with, was furious because Suzette received all the pleasure and attention. Suzette looked upon the whole event as hilarious and rich, a high point in her sexual career.

TWO-TIMING WOMEN

Usually, I'll try somebody while I'm going with somebody and see if they better and then if they are, then I'll leave them.

No sooner are these girls out of sight than their lovers are out of mind, and they are on to the next one. They are "slick," they say—that is, fast, smooth, hard to hold on to, quick to wriggle out of trouble. Part of the pleasure, and the trick, is secrecy. Suzette has an established practice of "trying" a new partner before breaking up in order to make sure that the new partner will be "better," more knowledgeable and endowed. Knowledgeable lovers know about oral sex and the clitoris, which Suzette and her cousins discovered in childhood and named "the little man in the boat."

Romantic betrayal doesn't *signify* at all, the trickster narrators insist. Yet they tell stories about deceiving others as they have been deceived—going out on lovers, for example—with particular enthusiasm.

Q: Mmmhmm. Now does Donald know about your older man lover and does the older man know about Donald?
A: Okay. This is how I work this in, right? Okay, Donald, I told him. . . . I never dwelled on that guy again. But with this one, okay, he knows he's the father, right. He knew we had a couple of fights while we was talking and everything. He knows all about him, but he don't know I'm still dealing with him. In the beginning I confessed one time that I slept with him while me and him was dealing. But he overlooked that. . . . He don't know Donald calls me every night at 11 o'clock, talks nasty talk, talks all kind of crazy things to me.

With relish, daughters of separated or divorced parents relate slipping out of their houses in the middle of the night to meet secret lovers, killing two narrative birds with one story.[9]

And sometimes—I mean, most of the time now we sneak out in the middle of the night to have sex. Three o'clock, two o'clock in the morning, four o'clock. Knowing I have to go to school the next morning. All hours of the night, we're having sex. I come to school so sleepy, so tired. Nobody knows—.

MORE THAN HE CAN HANDLE

While these narrators claim that they don't care what happens to their suitors and lovers, they make it very hard for lovers to leave or two-time them. Bell, for example, who represents herself as totally cold to the claims of love, describes an extraordinary struggle to keep her man that includes being in two places at once. (In folklore, doubling the self is a trickster maneuver.) Bell provides a realistic explanation for how she made her lover think she had the capacity to be in two places at once.[10]

Let me tell you, every time—between me and that other girl, between the two of us, he couldn't take it. And I don't know why he took on more than he could handle. That's the way I see it. . . . Everywhere I go, that's where he was. And he didn't know where I was going to pop up. One day he took her out in Queens. He didn't know I was out in Queens. Because he had just called me. And what happened was, I had my calls transferred to my aunt's house. So he's thinking that he's calling in Brooklyn and he's calling in Queens. And I'm busy talking to him. "Yes, isn't that nice. You home? Mmmhmm. I'm home." Walked down the boulevard and who do I see turning the corner, but John Henry. I'm standing there. He's like, "I just finished talking to you." He says "You know, I never can tell where you're going to be." He says, "I don't know why I even thought about getting involved with another woman."

Bell follows her first example with a less realistic account. As if by magic, everywhere she goes, he is, and vice versa. They are each other's guardian angels. She is not the only one who has observed this phenomenon. She cites witnesses.[11]

He said, "Even when you was pregnant, you was there." He said, ". . . we talking, gambling, carrying on—who pulls into the garage?" . . . I said, "I already know that he pulled into the garage because I know the sound of his car." They like, "Well, how do you know that?" I'm saying, "Easy. Because everywhere I go, he's there."

Suzette's strategy reverses Bell's. She doesn't track her lover down; she lets him "explore." Her secret power is her knowledge of his desire. "Cause see he goes with these different girls but he's still waiting to bed me." She just keeps her door open. He always comes back.

KILLING THEM SOFTLY

Conceptualizing themselves as dangerous sexual actors, these narrators describe their sexual appetites and practices as potentially deadly weapons. Talking about her secret affair with an older man, Suzette worries that he might die trying to satiate her. She has heard about this happening, and she wondered repeatedly what precisely might kill.

So I was like, How did that happen? To this day I don't know how she gave him that heart attack. What all it was consist of when they was making love for him to have a heart attack like that.

She wants to know, she says, because she doesn't want her older lover to die on her: "I swear I don't." By "being so nasty," she "might be giving this man a heart attack," she fears, her tone suspiciously exuberant. I asked if there had ever been a man she wouldn't mind having killed. Sometimes she'd like to kill her younger boyfriend, she said.

Bell has an even more original conceptualization of herself as a dangerous sexual actor. Reversing the proposition that the young need to be protected from the old, she hypothesizes:

Being that I'm young and I deal with older men, I can pull them because my body pulls more. If an older woman goes with a younger man, she can pull from his body. [sic] And then it can work vice versa. . . . But mainly a younger woman pulls from an older man. You know what I'm saying?. . .
Q: Pulls energy?
A: Yeah. Makes them look old. They can be young and then they can look very old. Because I remember before, when I met him? Perfect. I mean he looked like he could pass for sixteen or seventeen years old. Look at him now, you'd be like—.

She advances a "pulling theory" of sexual resistance as well:

What they don't understand is, being that I was in different classes, how to work with your body, different nerves and the muscles in your body . . . if I feel there's something wrong, like "what are you doing to me," . . . I'll pull them. . . . And I can hurt them that way and they know it.

FORGETTING GENDER FOR SEX

The Winnebago trickster whom Paul Radin represented in *The Trickster* forgot to take part in one of the most primary acts of masculinity—war—because he was so busy having sex. In this sense, he forgot to be a man. The narrators represented here fight with their lovers as vigorously as they go to bed, and they vehemently recall scenes of battle. But in the aftermath of sex and struggle, they "forget" to do what women do—to cry. They never describe themselves—as girls most commonly do—as passive victims of inconstancy, callousness, or aggression. Rather, they portray themselves as strong women who take their pleasure and defend their bodies and their rights. When they talk about pain, they focus on their courage and imperviousness. Superwomen, they cannot be injured.[12]

And you know, I don't care who I get, they can't hurt me.

And:

So he's like, Mmm. Nothing I do to this girl hurts her. I got to find me a higher step for her. You know, because, I mean, things he be thinking be hurting me, they don't hurt me.

Bell's body is as invulnerable as her feelings, she claims; she is a resistant surface. She describes emerging unscathed from a brutal fight with her lover in a parking lot that the police had to break up. "He didn't leave no scratches or no marks, and they said he was hitting me hard. I said, " 'Well, I ain't got no black eye.' " He, on the other hand, sustained multiple injuries. "He had scratches! He had a black eye!"

3

These teenage girls seem to do well for themselves in mining entertainment and support out of the meager resources that come their way. As cold women, they successfully protect against being pimped, sucked dry, or disappointed in love. As conniving women, they get and keep the pleasures of sex and romance. As nasty women, they leverage male insecurity with their willingness to go elsewhere. To a degree, of course, they are claiming rhetorical triumphs they may not pull off in life while downplaying losses and humiliations. The narratives in this group are unquestionably "drastic entertainments"—words, lives, thrust in the face of despair. In the course of proving how tough and invulnerable they are, these self-conscious and disenfranchised narrators refer many times to violence, abuse, and betrayal. Their babies' fathers pled with them to carry their pregnancies to term and then left them without resources. Several were homeless for lengthy periods of time, and they often went hungry at lunchtime. Under such harsh circumstances, nourishing and proclaiming a lusting, irrepressible, greedy, and plural self preserves a sense of power and freedom.[13]

Is there a public—political—aspect to their disorder as well? Might early sexuality and fertility itself constitute in some sense a trickster strategy—a social decision to mine the body, as almost sole resource, for everything that it can divulge—sexual play or public resources? In a period in which social resources to mitigate the imbalances of racism have been continuously withdrawn, training programs and social services for teenage mothers have constituted virtually the only sector of social welfare in which experimentation and development have taken place. To that extent, teenage sexuality and reproduction itself do constitute a successful rebellion of the trickster variety—a recourse that has astoundingly forced the public hand.[14]

But like all symbolic inversions, the triumph is marginal and unstable. When we talked, the narrators were in the full flush of adolescence. Experience had not yet totally worn out their hope. They were in vocational training programs, and they believed that hard work would enable them to make a much better life for their children. Several told me that after they obtained their G.E.D.'s, and became electricians and word processors, they would go back to school to become architects, doctors, and astronauts. Then they would have more children. Some *will* have the lives they dream of; many will not. As diligently as they study, the job of remediation is difficult, and it seems unlikely the failing economy or the health care system will furnish the leeway they deserve. Good jobs are fewer and farther between; the housing problem is worse; they are already burdened with sexual and reproductive problems.

Tricksters are tolerated as a "margin of mess," Babcock-Abrahams has argued, because their negations generate new alternatives and ideas.[15] At present, this country is increasingly suppressing marginal examples. *These* tricksters are tolerated, I fear, because their rebellions are private and invisible, and they are not expected to live for long. The poor grew much poorer and sicker in the last decade under a social policy fairly described as malign neglect. Trickster's hemisphere shrank. To alleviate the injustices these narrators so brilliantly and bravely gloss over, to afford them something beyond the body to mine, the world must turn upside down.[16]

NOTES

An earlier version of this article was presented at the 1985 American Anthropological Association panel, "The Mirror of Social Reproduction: Representations of American Teenagers," organized by Joyce Canaan and Nancy Lesko. Carra Hood, Edna Haber, Robert Myers, Ruby Rich, Ann Snitow, Christine Stansell, and Carole S. Vance commented sagely on a longer version of this paper in record time. I wish I could also name the teenagers who contributed their drastic entertainments, but I have, rather, changed their names as I promised them I would.

1. Paul Radin uses the phrase "drastic entertainment" in *The Trickster: A Study in American Indian Mythology* (New York: Schocken Books, 1972), 180. The epigraph is Radin's rendering of the Sam Blowsnake's 1912 trickster account, 53.

2. The opening paragraphs of this piece combine a number of trickster traditions—Winnebago, Yoruban, and African-American. A comparative analysis of the original texts and their ethnographic history would undoubtedly uncover important distinctions. Since this work takes up a contemporary line of inquiry, I intend no more than a loose illuminating metaphor. The paragraphs draw upon Barbara Babcock-Abrahams, " 'A Tolerated Margin of Mess': The Trickster and His Tales Reconsidered," *Journal of the Folklore Institute,* edited at Indiana University, 11 (3): 147–186 and "Liberty's a Whore: Inversions, Marginalia, and Picaresque Narrative," in *Reversible World: Symbolic Inversion in Art and Society,* ed. Barbara A. Babcock (Ithaca: Cornell University Press, 1978), 95–115; *Mother Wit from the Laughing Barrel: Readings in the Interpretation of Afro-American Folklore,* ed. Alan Dundes (Englewood Cliffs: Prentice-Hall, Inc., 1973); Natalie Zemon Davis, "Women on Top: Symbolic Sexual Inversion and Political Disorder in Early Modern Europe," in *Reversible,* 147–190; Robert D. Pelton, *Trickster in West Africa: Mythic Irony and Sacred Delight* (Berkeley: University of California Press, 1980); Enid Welsford, *The Fool and the Trickster* (Cambridge, England: D. S. Brewer; Totowa, NJ: Rowman & Littlefield, 1979). The evolutionary relation of trickster and culture hero was plucked from Robert H. Lowie, "The Hero-Trickster Discussion," *Journal of American Folklore* 22 (1909), by Babcock, 162–63.

3. On signifying, see Henry Louis Gates, Jr., *The Signifying Monkey: A Theory of Afro-American Literary Criticism* (New York: Oxford University Press, 1988) and Gates' essay "The blackness of blackness: a critique of the sign and the Signifying Monkey" in his anthology *Black Literature and Literary Theory* (New

York and London: Methuen, 1984), 285–321. Carra Hood, Yale University, made the observation about trickster's marital disputes in a personal conversation, June 1989. Her Master's thesis, "The Challenge of African Literature: A Preliminary Study," (Yale University, 1988) treats African trickster stories in detail. Tellingly, American ethnography has largely ignored both the theme of greed vs. liberality and trickster's wife. On women and signifying, see Claudia Mitchell-Kernan, *Language Behavior in a Black Urban Community* (Monographs of the Language-Behavior Laboratory, University of California, Berkeley, No. 2); Geneva Smitherman, *Talkin and Testifyin: The Language of Black America* (Boston: Houghton Mifflin, 1977).

4. Shirley Brice Heath shows this in her *Ways With Words: Language, Life, and Work in Communities and Classrooms* (Cambridge: Cambridge University Press, 1983) and "What No Bedtime Story Means: Narrative Skills at Home and School," *Language in Society* 11 (1): 49–76. For a more representative depiction of growing up black and female, see, for example, the work of Joyce Aschenbrenner, Molly C. Dougherty, Joyce Ladner, and Carol B. Stack.

5. Gates, *Signifying,* cites the signifying couplet from Ayodele Ogundipe's Ph.D. dissertation, "Esu Elegbara, the Yoruba God of Chance and Uncertainty: A Study in Yoruba Mythology," 2 vols. (Indiana University, 1978), (II), 135.

6. Babcock-Abrahams, " 'A Tolerated Margin,' " 151. For most maternity equals reform and settling down—i.e.: (a) Living with a baby's father or with a male lover who has taken on paternal financial responsibilities. (These girls drop out of school more often than any other group of teenage mothers.) (b) Being absorbed into family. (She may occasionally see her baby's father. Often she goes back to school or to work.) (c) Living with a female lover who accepts the economic and parenting responsibility of co-mother or of a father. (d) Going it alone. (She has her own apartment or she and her baby are homeless together. Her primary relationship, for now—she may say "forever"—is with her baby.) The literature on teenage pregnancy and motherhood is vast. See, especially, Ayala Gabriel and Elizabeth R. McAnarney, M.D., "Parenthood in Two Subcultures: White, Middle-Class Couples and Black, Low-Income Adolescents in Rochester, New York," in *Adolescence* 18 (Fall 1983): 595–607; Cheryl D. Hayes, *Risking the Future: Adolescent Sexuality, Pregnancy and Childbearing* (Washington, DC: National Academy Press, 1987); *Teenage Pregnancy in a Family Context: Implications for Policy,* ed. Theodora Ooms (Philadelphia: Temple University Press, 1981); Rosalind Petchesky, *Abortion and Woman's Choice* (New York: Longman, 1984); "Teenage Pregnancy: A Critical Family Issue," Mott Foundation Special Report, 1981; the work of Catherine Chilman, Constance Lindemann, Greer Fox Litton, and Kristin Luker; and the many reports in *Family Planning Perspectives.* For a more general discussion of teenage mothers' narratives, see Thompson, "Pregnant on Purpose: Choosing Teen Motherhood," *The Village Voice,* December 23, 1986, 1, 31–34, 36–37. A summary of lesbian teenage mothers' accounts appears in "Now You See Her, Now You Don't: The Lesbian Teenage Mother," in "Current Issues," 1987 International Scientific Conference on Gay and Lesbian Studies papers, December 15–18, 1987, Free University, Amsterdam.

7. Patricia Cleckner describes what males conventionally say to convince a lover to go on the street in "Jive Dope Fiend Whores: In the Street and in Rehabilitation," in *Women in Ritual and Symbolic Roles,* ed. Judith Hoch-

Smith and Anita Spring, (New York and London: Plenum Press, 1978), 269–85.

8. For a comparative perspective on girls' pleasure in teenage sex, see Thompson, "Search for Tomorrow: On Feminism and the Reconstruction of Teen Romance," in *Pleasure and Danger: Exploring Female Sexuality,* ed. Carole S. Vance (Boston: Routledge & Kegan Paul, 1984), 362–69.

9. In African folktales, three steps make a figure into a trickster, Alan Dundes argued in "The Making and Breaking of Friendship as a Structural Frame in African Folk Tales," in *Structural Analysis of Oral Tradition,* ed. Pierre Maranda and Elli Konas Maranda (Philadelphia: University of Pennsylvania Press, 1971), 171–188: (1) False friendship; (2) Contract; (3) Contract violation.

10. On the trickster's doubling, see Babcock-Abrahams, 159.

11. On the use of performance speech as supporting evidence, see especially Nessa Wolfson, "A Feature of performed narrative," *Language,* and generally *Folklore, Performance, and Communication,* eds. Dan Ben-Amos and K. Goldstein (The Hague: Mouton, 1975).

12. Radin, *Trickster,* 55. For a description of the tendency to cry over the spilt milk of love that most teenage girls' tendency exhibit but Trickster narrators avoid, see my essay, "Search," 369–71.

13. In "Negotiating Respect: Patterns of Presentation Among Black Women," in *Talking Black* (Bowley, Mass: Newbury House Publishers, Inc., 1976), 58–80, Roger D. Abrahams discusses the concept of "testimony," among black women. Heath, *Ways,* 170, discusses the tendency of the inhabitants of a rural black community to cast personal stories as victories. In "Sexuality, Schooling, and Adolescent Females: The Missing Discourse of Desire," *Harvard Educational Review* 58 (February 1988): 29–62, Michelle Fine argues for the importance of developing the "female sexual subject" for teenage girls.

14. For example, programs generated by the 1978 Adolescent Health Services and Pregnancy Prevention and Care Act and the 1981 Adolescent Family Life Act.

15. Babcock-Abrahams, "Tolerated," title.

16. On the increasing economic difference between rich and poor in the U.S., see, for example, "Richest Got Richer and Poorest Poorer in 1979–87," *The New York Times,* March 23, 1989, 1 and 24. A growing literature attests to the sexual and reproductive health risks facing girls and women of color. On AIDS transmission, see the Centers for Disease Control, *HIV/AIDS Surveillance* (Washington, D.C.: U.S. Department of Health and Human Services, 1989).

CHAPTER SEVENTEEN

Monster Stories:
Women Charged with Perinatal Endangerment

ANNA LOWENHAUPT TSING

The last decade has been a heady time in the United States for public discussion of women's roles in parenting. Motherhood has returned as one of the more publicly visible goals for women. At the same time, debates about women's reproductive rights, appropriate birthing technologies, and social policies to deal with child abuse have problematized motherhood. Pregnancy, childbirth, and child rearing are no longer seen as easy and "natural" routes to womanhood, but as fraught with sacrifices, perils, and challenges that women must surmount.

Women's strategies to face these challenges are shaped in part by stories of other women. Personal stories of mothers and aunts are supplemented by more public stories that tell of successful or frustrated superwomen with careers and children, sacrificing but satisfied "postfeminist" mothers, or monster mothers who stuff their children in garbage bags and take them out with the trash. Monster stories, in particular, advise women of a new public agenda in which children, like fetuses, must be saved from their own mothers. As the "interests" and "rights" of both fetuses and children increasingly have been posed in opposition to those of adult women, tales of women who endanger their babies have spread warning of women's potential as aborters and child abusers. Like other cautionary tales, these stories advise and inform about acceptable ways to live. In inverting all that is proper, endangering "anti-mothers" join female monsters of the 1960s and 1970s—monsters such as the fat woman (the anti-beauty) and the female boss—in the ongoing production and negotiation of gender.

Since 1986 I have been conducting research on U.S. American women charged with endangering their newborns during, or due to, unassisted birth.[1] My interest in these cases developed with my surprise at public reactions to them. Unassisted childbirth, it seems, earns women a characterization as calculating criminals. Journalists, psychologists, and neighbors who had never met these women were ready to describe them as callous murderers. In most of the cases I have studied, I found the events surrounding the childbirth open to varied interpretations. Often the cause of death of the infant was unclear, with no evidence of trauma; these women were not accused of striking or strangling their babies. Many of the women charged claimed they did not know they were in labor; some were unaware they were pregnant. Yet rather than leading to a discussion of these ambiguities, the fact that a woman gave birth alone was seen as evidence or cause of her criminal neglect of the newborn. As a feminist, I was disturbed by the way these ambiguous events were being transformed into monster stories. As an anthropologist, I was curious about the emerging cultural assumptions that underlay these moral narratives.

A variety of sources compete and combine to construct representations of women charged with endangering newborns. I collected stories from interviews with legal and medical personnel, reporters, community members, and defendants, as well as from newspaper articles, police reports, court files, and psychiatric, medical, and probation records. The stories were far from homogeneous, even within a given case, but, again and again, I found the women's specific history eclipsed by a broader question: What kind of a woman could endanger her own offspring at the moment of birth, the moment which should most excite her maternal sentiments? This question generated its own answer: Only a person completely lacking in parental—and human—sensibilities could commit such an act. To those who considered their cases, these women were, as one prosecutor put it, "unnatural," "bizarre," and "without basic human emotions."

As women who endanger babies, the defendants become enemies of nurturance and affection. Furthermore, their stories exemplify a broader cultural scenario in which the forces of compassion and morality must intervene to save a child from selfish neglect.

The image of the vulnerable infant, endangered by its maternal environment unless rescued by altruistic outsiders, has emerged at the conjunction of a number of contemporary U.S. debates. The anti-abortion movement has used such images most systematically, but the cultural theme of endangered children also must be viewed in relation to the state's developing interest in preventing and punishing child abuse. Discourses on fetal and child protection overlap with medical preferences for a supervised birth process; together these build the assumption that healthy babies can be delivered only under a doctor's supervision. The criminalization of unassisted birth draws from each of these semi-autonomous sources.[2] The endangered newborn is an exceptionally persuasive image in an overlapping evocation of these discourses; symbolically, birth is the intimate moment in which the infant's new visibility gives rise to parental love.

The cultural centrality of these issues is attested to by the powerful emotions provoked by the cases I have studied. Everyone with whom I have discussed the cases has responded with strong feelings, whether of shock or sympathy. For those not directly involved, both shock and sympathy stimulate curiosity to know more about the woman's experience: How could she have not known she was in labor? Why didn't she call for help? My study offers an alternative focus: on the overlapping, competing discourses that construct the publicly available story, rather than on the woman's subjective experience. This alternative alerts us to the ways that our demands for the "truth" of experience involve naturalizing conventions that can obstruct our appreciation of the cultural construction of the crime. Most everyday talk of crime, for example, follows "detective story" conventions in which justice is served when the criminal has been properly identified. In mining a woman's experience to uncover "what really happened," we forget to question the definition of the crime. Because these are maternity cases, we also turn to another American standard of "truth": the "truths" of a woman's direct intuitive knowledge gained from her bodily experiences. Within this convention, a woman unaware of her pregnancy or labor must be a physical or psychological anomaly. Yet, in searching for individual pathologies, we confirm cultural standards. A cultural analysis of endangering mothers must not only avoid but denaturalize these conventions connecting subjectivity, truth, and justice.

Stories about the death of newborns raise difficult moral dilemmas. They disturb, and they arouse sympathy. My analysis of stories told about these women does not even come near the formidable problems of how to create a better situation for women and infants in unwanted and unplanned births. Yet, a first step in this direction must surely involve a critical rethinking of the 1980s romanticization of motherhood. Both feminist and nonfeminist ideologies that glorify nurturant mothering in opposition to male-dominated technologies and political styles encourage as their hidden complement the conceptual space of the "anti-mother." Its monsters are created, and women are condemned, in the very real space of courtrooms and prisons.

CONSTRUCTING THE "ANTI-MOTHER"

Ideas about appropriate and inappropriate birthing practices and definitions of "infanticide" vary widely cross-culturally and cross-historically.[3] The !Kung San of southern Africa, for example, are reported to regard unassisted childbirth as brave and responsible, rather than criminal.[4] U.S. American legal and medical standards in the first half of this century implied that "natural death" overtook a fraction of newborns, despite the best attentions; only more recently has it become impossible for a newborn without obvious prenatal defects to die "naturally" outside of the attendance of a physician.[5] Stories of "criminal" childbirths thus illuminate changing cultural standards for parenting and women's roles.

The culturally specific features of contemporary charges of perinatal endangerment become especially clear when compared to those of an even earlier era. In Puritan New England in the 1690s—the time of the Salem witch trials—a spectacular rise occurred in cases of "lewd women" indicted and convicted of infanticide.[6] Rates of conviction surpassed those for all other forms of homicide. By the late 1690s, both Massachusetts and Connecticut had adopted Jacobean English infanticide law, which criminalized any woman who gave birth without a witness to a bastard child who died. Under the law, it was irrelevant whether the infant was stillborn, whether the mother was conscious and able-bodied, and whether she harmed it either by action or inaction. Concealment was the crime; hanging was the punishment.

Thousands flocked to see women hung for infanticide in early 18th century New England as religious leaders turned their cases into moral lessons.[7] Judges and preachers alike stressed transgressions against sexual morality as the key element of the crime. Historians Hoffer and Hull write that the most important evidence in these women's trials involved not the death of the infant, but "first the concealment of sin, second, prior sexual wantonness, and third, the disobedience of women to community standards."[8] Ministers framed the crimes in a progression of sins, one leading to the next: "from *solitary* Filthiness . . . unto *social;* and from secret *Fornications* to secret *Murders;* and at length to an untimely and shameful Death . . ."[9]

This discourse is not totally unfamiliar, yet the stakes have changed.[10] The Puritan criminals offended standards of female chastity; the contemporary cases are crimes against motherhood. Concealment is a crime in the contemporary cases for a reason quite different from secret vice: it shows a selfish, anti-maternal autonomy, and it defies the prerogatives of the medical system in establishing life and death. In supporting medical prerogatives, the cases I have studied are tied less to sexual sins than to other crimes against (appropriate) pregnancy: "prenatal child abuse" by using unauthorized drugs or disregarding doctors' orders; late miscarriage, seen as homicide when tied to "prenatal child abuse"; and vaginal birth, interpreted as itself a form of child abuse in cases of court-ordered caesarians.[11]

The vehemence of contemporary stories generated about women charged with endangering newborns is in part an artifact of the process in which the criminal justice system creates crime stories. Both defense and prosecution must fashion an explanation of the "crime" that can convince a jury; these are stories tailored for persuasion within dominant or emergent community standards. Even if a case is settled without a trial, it is settled in relation to lawyers' beliefs about how a jury would respond to their stories.

The stories persuade because they give an identity and a history to the woman charged with a crime. As a particular type of individual, she can fit into our expectations for guilt or innocence. Her life stories proliferate: the defense and prosecution create competing versions; judges, psychologists, probation officers, medical examiners, and reporters offer their insights and interpretations. Public discussion takes off from news reports, rumors, memories of old cases, and other scraps. The one voice that is unlikely to be heard publicly is that of the defendant. Her identity and her story are constructed by the "experts" around her; she rarely has an opportunity to articulate her own version. Rather than revealing the authenticity of experience, these stories show a subjectivity constructed from the discourses of others.

In contrast to images of endangered babies lifted outside of social or historical context, stories of "anti-mothers" depend on the interpretation of particular events. Details of circumstance and identity heighten the believability of "unnatural" acts; they create plots that dramatize the predictable tale of selfish rationality and manipulation leading to an unhappy end. The stories create a negative example for *all* women to avoid. Yet they are not homogeneous; how a monster is formed depends on what kind of woman the defendant is perceived to be. Indeed, most of the stories I have collected so far fall into two somewhat discrete clusters. In one, young white "innocent-looking" schoolgirls are revealed as perverse products of a distorted maturation process. In the other, somewhat older, poor white women, as well as women of color of all ages, are described as obstinate and cunning refusers of medical knowledge and routine health care. These appear to be two separate kinds of characterization, rather than two points on a continuum of what the legal system finds criminal. Their divergence is a reminder that the cultural construction of the "female" is never a unitary process. Even an essential "anti-woman" is created from symbolic scraps of race, class, age, and ethnic difference.

To show how the interpretation of particular cases creates a cultural agenda that extends far beyond the case itself, I turn to stories of two women, drawn respectively from each of the clusters I have just identified. I have changed names and disguised places and features of personal identity to protect both the chronicled women and the storytellers. My narration of events in each case presents the publicly available evidence through which stories were built; of course, I can make no claims to being a neutral voice. In both the cases I present here, I spoke at length to the woman charged, about both the birth and the ensuing legal entanglements, but in neither case is this a presentation of her voice or her experience. The women's own accounts raise issues of consciousness and authority that deserve separate discussion. Here, however, I am most concerned with the "official" versions.

"COLLEGE STUDENT ADMITS GUILT . . ."

In 1985, Donna Sloan was a nineteen-year-old sophomore at a state college. She was a shy, "straight A" student, majoring in psychology and planning to attend law school after college. She had a steady boyfriend, whom she intended to marry after graduating, and she lived with a roommate in a large dormitory. One night, Sloan left her roommate and her boyfriend, who was asleep in her dorm room bed, to use the dormitory bathroom. Some time later, she came back and climbed into bed.

The next day, a janitor at the dormitory found a placenta in the bathroom trash and reported it to the campus police. Soon after noon, the police found the body of a full-term female newborn in the dormitory dumpster. By that evening, Sloan and her boyfriend had been questioned by the police, and she had been confined to the campus infirmary.

On autopsy, the infant showed no signs of trauma, except for a minor bruise on the forehead; the lungs floated, suggesting that the infant had breathed at least once. The medical examiner ruled that the cause of death was asphyxiation. No evidence, however, suggested the infant had been suffocated or otherwise injured.

Criminal charges of murder, felony child abuse, and concealing a death were formally brought against Sloan almost two months later, but public reaction was much speedier. Both college and city officials were aware of public talk that compared Sloan's case to a well-known earlier case in which a mother had refused to cooperate with the authorities in locating her three-year-old child, who had been beaten to death by her boyfriend. Many felt she had been "let off too easy," and they pressured the police and prose-cutors to be tougher on child abusers. Sloan was the next "baby murderer" in line. Indeed, many felt Sloan's crime was worse; as even her defense attorney put it, that earlier baby "lived for three years, this baby lived for three minutes. . . . the baby just had no chance." "The public was becoming unglued about this case," he recalled.

The lawyer remembered, too, his own initial reaction as he was assigned to the case. "When I first read about a baby in a trash can I had probably the general public's reaction of 'Oh my God, that's horrible.' You know, dead baby in a trash can, what kind of a cruel person, what kind of a sick person, or something, could do something like that." Even after he met Sloan, he was "pretty appalled," particularly because, he felt, "Donna was convinced at that point that she hadn't done anything wrong." "Donna was being very, very cold about what happened. . . . She wasn't communicating that much. She was expressing no emotion, no grief. She didn't seem to be grieving at all."

Sloan's lack of public grief was the keystone of her negative public image. It was reported that the day after the incident she had attended a movie and a picnic with her boyfriend; for many, this proved her callousness. The calm and reserve attributed to her signaled an anti-maternal identity: a woman who could dispose of a newborn without a care. Indeed, this made it impossible for many to take her version of the incident seriously. Few paid attention to her contention that she didn't know she was pregnant and that she thought the infant was stillborn because it never moved or cried. Her lawyer could see that her "emotionless" image was losing her case before they could even consider a trial. "And I started leaning on her pretty hard at that point," he recalled, "saying, 'Donna, you have got to start showing some remorse to the public about this case.' "

Sloan's image as cold legitimated a narrative about her actions that turned public sentiment against her and made it impossible, according to her law-yers, to bring her case to trial. In this respect, her case was not isolated. Most all the women I studied who were charged with endangering newborns were described at some point in the proceedings as cold. They did not care; they did not cry. "There was never a time the remorse was there . . . She just was not doing the things that a mother that had just lost her child [would do]," said the sheriff who charged one young woman. "She showed no real emotion about the thing," remarked a district attorney, describing another. Moreover, if they were not "emotional," they must be its opposite: calculating. "She knew exactly what she was doing," recalled a probation officer, "She said, 'This is an inconvenience to me, and I don't want it'. . . . She had no conception that she had done anything wrong." These are women described as too autonomous and self-oriented to ask for or accept help. But, of course, this is a description of the *crime,* not the woman charged: she should have "asked for help," but she gave birth alone. The women's descriptions as without emotions seem to have less to do with their distinctive personal characteristics than with the criminal narrative involved in bringing charges against them.

Sloan's lawyers urged her to avoid a trial by accepting a plea bargain: in exchange for dropping the murder charges, she pled guilty to child abuse (a felony) and concealing a death (a misdemeanor). Defense efforts moved to arguing against a severe prison sentence. These efforts were successful, the lawyers believe, largely because of a videotape shown at the sentencing hearing in which Sloan cried as she spoke of the birth in the bathroom stall. Sloan's tears make it possible for the judge and onlookers to listen to a more sympathetic story of that night's events. An obstetrician testified that the infant, emerging from an exceptionally fast delivery, had probably landed in a position that allowed it to take a first breath, but not to expel the breath or take another; it may have died before Sloan would have been able to pick it up. A psychologist testified that Sloan showed severe symp-toms of "denial," which, articulated as a medical syndrome, legitimized her ignorance of her pregnancy.

Sloan herself, on videotape under hypnosis, related the following version of the events: she did not know she was pregnant, nor had anyone around her suggested it; she had gone to the bathroom thinking she had gas pains; she was shocked and frightened when suddenly she delivered a baby; the baby was cold, grey, and motionless, and she assumed it was dead. Weak, scared, and confused, she had wrapped the baby's body in toilet tissue and placed it in the trash can. (The body was presumably transferred to the dumpster when the janitor emptied that trash can.) "And by the end," her lawyer recalled, "the [District Attorney] was saying, 'I don't even want her to go to jail. I just want her to get the treatment.' " The story had been recast: Sloan was a victim as much as an aggressor. She was sentenced to four years probation and 400 hours of community service.

In fact, long before the sentencing hearing, both Sloan's supporters and detractors were aware that she was young, confused, and, during the incident, in shock and pain. No one debated these characterizations; the difficulty was what to make of them. Did her naivete and pain make her any less criminal?

Rather than uniformly inspiring support and empathy for the defendant, youthful innocence has increasingly become a feature of a new criminal profile. Thus, for example, when a journalist discovered that six women in one area had been criminally charged in relation to neonatal deaths in the first six months of 1987, he described the phenomenon as a new "syndrome." "Experts say the syndrome begins with a sexually confused young mother. . . . 'It often happens to the overweight, shy, self-conscious girl who has one or two sexual experiences'. . . . The girl is usually horrified at the prospect of having children. . . . She 'disposes' of the cause of her troubles—the baby." Although the portrait is sympathetic, the "girls," he implies, have earned their punishment. In the logic of this new criminal identity, the fact that Sloan was young and confused made her more deserving of criminal charges rather than less.

Criminalization gains its importance within a cultural setting in which the unsupervised death of a newborn is a public tragedy that cannot be resolved without a renewal of the state's civilizing authority. Unless blame is fixed and punishment meted, society might be held to blame for not protecting human life. Thus, in a 1987 case in which the fetus of a nineteen-year-old high school senior probably died *in utero* before an unassisted premature birth, the liberal county attorney still insisted on the importance of criminal charges: "It just, just didn't get through to her, the significance of the act of human life. . . . I did want to show the community, to show her that indeed this isn't right." (The student gave birth alone and deposited the dead infant/fetus in the trash.) "You can't be doing it. . . . [I]f we don't do anything, we don't address formally and officially and then suddenly we're going to have infanticide out there. We really are. Suddenly we're going to be killing babies."

In Sloan's case, the image of criminally warped innocence gained its relevance from an intersection of public discussion of child abuse, on the one hand, and abortion, on the other. Following a national trend, child abuse had become a major issue in Sloan's area since the late 1970s.[12] New legislation created new criminal outlines around child abuse and toughened penalties; new policies alerted social service and medical workers to the "hidden" crimes of abusive parents; the media kept the issue in the public eye. In the discourse that emerged from these trends, troubled young mothers were potential abusers who must be kept—whether by discipline or education—from harming their children. Their own vulnerability did not mean that they deserved more services, more rights, or a better society. Instead, it situated them more clearly as objects of social control.

Sloan's case was defined not only as "child abuse" but also as "late abortion." Anti-abortion activists had recently scored a major legislative victory in Sloan's state. The college was in a liberal community, but pro-choice activists and medical workers were on the defensive.

From the first, Sloan's case was interpreted from within abortion battle lines. One letter to the editor pointed out: "A few hours earlier the child would have been labeled a fetus rather than a baby." The writer continued,

This child, though dead, was at least fortunate enough to have died in a manner that still causes outrage among society. Her mother must at least face charges. Millions of this child's murdered peers have not even this consolation. Their deaths go unnoticed—no headlines, no funeral, just the trash bin or to the laboratory to be used for research.

For community members who sympathized with Sloan, the logic of "abortion taken to its obvious conclusion" smothered the possibility of raising issues of women's reproductive rights in relation to the case. Since pro-choice activists were already being labelled murderers, it seemed too dangerous a time for them to debate fundamental issues of the definition of this "crime." Instead, sympathizers turned to imagery of vulnerable pregnant teenagers—imagery that had been brought to prominence by the abortion debate earlier in the decade. When feminists first used this imagery to counter anti-abortion forces, it was intended to inspire commitment to equal rights and opportunities for young women. Portrayals of young women as victims of a sexist and repressive society were directed toward increasing their access to social services and to knowledge about their own bodies. But, at least by 1985, the concern over endangered babies had overshadowed public empathy for these young women. What remained was a sympathy—which, indeed, helped reduce Sloan's sentence. But it never occurred to her defense lawyers that a jury might turn their social concern to find Sloan not guilty.

Value statements from the abortion debate have emerged in practically every case I have found in which a white high school or college student has been charged with perinatal endangerment. For those who oppose abortion, the connection is simple. As the sheriff who arrested one college student put it, "This was just a nine month abortion to her. She's been told that it's legal and she stretched it all the way." But even for those with pro-choice positions, the abortion debate has opened a space for new ethical issues and images of endangerment. Two aspects of the discussion of these cases impressed me as influenced by abortion discourse. First, those involved with the cases continually stress their recognition of "the value of human life." The young woman's crime, for many, revolves around her lack of respect for this abstract value; one kind of lack of respect, it is argued, leads readily to another. Second, the women are depicted by both the horrified and the sympathetic in imagery that evokes "any young American woman." Like the feminist images of the pregnant "everywoman" that began the abortion debate, these young women are depicted as looking and acting like "the girl next door." Indeed, from the perspective of those eager to punish them, this is why these girls are threatening, and why an example must be made of their cases to instruct the others.

Liberals and conservatives coming to issues of child protection from different directions thus make some common space in creating an ambivalent criminal identity for these young white women. The terms of legal, psychological, and journalistic discussion vary, yet each creates imagery of a perverse naivete—perhaps a distortion of maturation. This is an imagery that explains both the young women's familiarity and their difference: Although they start out like ordinary girls, they fail to develop an appropriate womanhood. They are reproductively mature, yet selfish—like babies—and unwilling to nurture others. They accept no help. Without feminine abilities to accept paternal love or give maternal love, they are the monstrous creations of a female autonomy that threatens every young girl in school.

For the lawyers, judges, journalists, doctors, and psychologists who shape their stories, this is not an irredeemable criminality. Most have reasoned that the shock of felony charges and convictions is necessary, not only to show the defendants the dangerous path they have taken, but also to startle the others who still manage to pass as normal teenage girls. At the same time, most have argued, imprisoning them for many years is probably unnecessary. Once the shock of their criminal convictions has brought them to a more appropriate developmental course, therapy, education, and understanding can finish their rehabilitations as women and as mothers.

"HARRIS GETS 10 YEARS IN INFANT DEATH . . ."

Donna Sloan's case was not isolated; within a year of her sentencing, three other women in her area had been charged in related cases. One of these was twenty-five-year-old Marlene Harris, who worked for a temporary maid service in a rural resort town. Harris, like Sloan, was charged with murder and felony child abuse. Like Sloan, she pled guilty to child abuse, and the murder charges were dropped. But unlike Sloan, she was sentenced to 10 years in the penitentiary.

Like Sloan's case, Harris' was covered extensively and rather unsympathetically by the media. As for Sloan, many of those who knew of the case were horrified; but some were sympathetic. What accounted for the striking difference in sentencing?[13] A host of local factors including the personalities and strategies of lawyers, prosecutors, and judges were certainly relevant. But interviews with the police, prosecutor, and probation officer in the case also revealed that Harris had given those who constructed her case a rather different impression than Sloan and the other white high school and college students whose cases I have studied. (Harris is also white.) She was cast as a rather different kind of monster.

Unlike Sloan, Harris had known she was pregnant. She even got her sister to drive her to the closest abortion clinic, which was three hours away, only to find that she was six months pregnant; the closest clinic that could give her an abortion was several states away. She decided to bear the child and give it up for adoption. She talked with a friend who had given up a baby, and she thought she could do the same.

Her greatest anxiety about the process was her friend's story that when she delivered the baby, the medical personnel took it away without letting her see or hold the child she had produced. She said it was this anxiety that impelled her, when her water broke in the middle of the night, to drive past the hospital where she had planned to deliver and check into a motel. She wanted to hold the baby for a moment. "When my water broke, it was just really weird," she recalled in an interview. "[I] didn't want no one to take him away from me."

She delivered the baby on the motel bed. Weak and cold from loss of blood, she drew a warm bath and crawled in with the baby. She lost consciousness, and when she came to, the baby had drowned in the tub.

Not everyone believed this version of how the baby died—the version Harris told the police, her lawyers, her court-appointed therapist, and her probation officer. Some argued that Harris must have gone to the motel specifically to drown the baby. For most of those involved in the case, however, it didn't matter how the baby had died.

What established Harris' guilt was not the manner of death, but a larger "pattern" of Harris' actions and nonactions. The district attorney recalled in an interview, "[T]here had never been any prenatal concerns. It showed to us . . . a deliberate pattern of secrecy surrounding the birth and a deliberate decision not to get any medical attention. There was a pattern of, what we believed, were false truths, falsehoods given to medical personnel after the event." (Harris had gone to the hospital the next day because she was still hemorraging and the placenta had not descended; she had been evasive to doctors about the location of the baby she had delivered.) The district attorney continued, "My time frame [for understanding her culpability] begins on the day that she finds out she can't have an abortion. . . . If she had gotten prenatal care that obviously would have gone against our theory that she had made her mind up for the child not to survive. . . . At the moment of birth, if she'd called for a doctor or even called out to the front desk, that would have changed some things. . . . We see a total lack of action and that ends up in an unattended birth. . . ."

Like Donna Sloan, Harris was described as "cold," "uncaring," and lacking in remorse (although when I met her she cried copiously over the death of her infant, whom she had named Jeffrey.) Unlike Sloan, and despite her girlish manner, she was also described as devious and a liar. Moreover, while she was derided for having "average" or lower intelligence ("Marlene's probably not the brightest person in the world," explained one police officer), her ignorance was endowed with a kind of animal cunning that looked out for self-survival at any moral expense. The district attorney explained, "My overwhelming impression of Marlene Harris is that if you took ten people and put them on a deserted island, and there were limited resources for survival and you came back in a year that Marlene would be healthy and fine and you probably wouldn't find the other nine people."

Like Sloan, Harris was condemned because she had not sought help. She had also chosen to give birth alone. "What type of a person would really go through childbirth alone?" asked the probation officer. A police officer explained his sense of the legal basis of this condemnation: "A reasonable person, which is something the law has a lot to do with and which is something that cops kind of use as a basis for deciding things, a reasonable person would have not gone to the motel, they would have at least stayed home. In that case, a reasonable person would have . . . [called] somebody. You get an ambulance over there. 'My goodness sakes, I'm having a baby, help.' You don't do this kind of thing alone, it's too dangerous for you, it's definitely too dangerous for the kid. . . . [A] normal, a reasonable person would have gone to the clinic. . . ." To the police officer, the clinic is a safe, warm environment staffed with doctor protectors. The sense that all "reasonable" people would go to the hospital for protection was so strong that no one was able to hear Harris' anxiety that the hospital would be an alienating place where she would lose contact with her own labor and birth. As another police officer put it: "[S]he drove past the clinic to get where she was going to this motel. . . . It's just not a normal thing. . ." "Even animals have a nesting instinct," said the probation officer.

Again and again in the interviews, Harris was condemned for a bad attitude toward the medical system. As one rereads the quotes above, it becomes clear that her refusal of medical assistance is, for those who constructed her case, the key element of her crime. This is why the manner of the infant's death was irrelevant. Not only had she avoided prenatal checkups, she had also given birth without a doctor's assistance, and diagnosed her infant's death by drowning without a medical expert. Furthermore, she "lied" to doctors about the baby the next day.

This interpretation of the crime was successfully conveyed to Harris during the legal proceedings. When interviewed later, she spelled it out:

Q: Where did they say the negligence or recklessness came?
MH: Well, for not going to the hospital.
Q: When, when your water broke?
MH: Yea, and no prenatal care. And not calling an ambulance afterwards.
Q: When you saw the baby on the bottom of the tub, your thought wasn't "call an ambulance."
MH: No, just to grab him.

An analysis of how Harris was cast as a medical non-complier leads to the perceptions those who worked on the case held of her class status and background. Harris is a highschool dropout, with a highschool equivalency degree; she was working as a maid and living in a trailer with a male roommate. Accounts of her family offer glimpses of sporadic unemployment and alcoholism, and hints of domestic abuse. She herself had moved and mated too often for "middle-American" standards. Unlike Sloan and the other college girls, she was not a young woman with whom a "nice family" would want their daughters to identify—even as a negative example.

In fact, Donna Sloan was also not from a well-off family. Her divorced mother had supported the children on a secretary's salary. Like Harris, Sloan was represented, of necessity, by public defenders. But Sloan had plans for education and dreams of upward mobility; she was respectable, morally presentable, and at least "aspiring" middle-class. In U.S. American understandings of class, respectability and aspirations are as important as income in one's ability to be classified as "middle-class" and therefore "normal." In contrast to Sloan, Harris was easy to classify as one of the "hard living" poor. The differences between how Sloan and Harris were treated had more to do with *perceptions* of class than with economic resources.

Class was never brought up explicitly in discussions of either Sloan's or Harris' guilt, but just as Sloan's position as a college student made it possible for both detractors and supporters to portray her as an "average girl gone wrong," Harris' exclusion from middle-class respectability framed her crime as resistance to medical aid. Contemporary U.S. standards of middle-class respectability require respectful attention to "modern," "scientific" conventions of health and personal care. Despite grumblings against the medical system, middle-class people expect themselves and others to follow the advice of the medical experts. The use of preventive health care, including dentistry, check-ups, and perinatal obstetric care, has become an especially important class marker. Those who do not use these services are, according to the voice of respectability, stupid, lazy, and irresponsible—precisely the qualities seen as causing poverty itself. While it may be merely reprehensible to let these qualities control one's self-care, it is seen as *criminal* to operate with these traits around children.

Class issues entered into the construction of Harris' case without anyone ever mentioning the costs of health care. (A hospital delivery, like a late-term abortion, would have put Harris into serious debt. As a maid, she had neither health insurance, nor state assistance.) Instead, perceptions of the poor as ignorant and irresponsible influenced descriptions of Harris' character. ("Pure laziness stopped her from going and getting more birth control pills," said one police officer.) As "reasonable" and "respectable" actions were equated, Harris was cast outside conceivable moral standards. She had selfishly gone to a doctor when she herself was hemmoraging, but she had refused preventive medical care for her child. Thus, it was reasoned, she was not only ignorant but also dangerous and devious. Cunning, rather than naivete, was seen as the cause of her crime.

All the women of color and the post-school age white women seen as poor, whose perinatal endangerment cases I have studied, have been characterized in one way or another as medical non-compliers. These women are seen as unfamiliar, alien beings. They are identified not as educable products of a defective maturation, but as outside of middle-class, "normal" values. They can be controlled but not changed. Following the recommendations of police, prosecutors, and probation officers, and the decisions of judges, they tend to be sentenced to long terms in prison.

Several women who attempted to obtain medical assistance were greeted with arrests and charges that seem explicable only in the logic of non-complier imagery. Twenty-eight-year-old Sarah Berkley, a white woman on welfare, fetched her boyfriend from the other room and had him call "911" emergency services when, unaware that she was pregnant, she delivered a baby in the toilet. No one—including the boyfriend (father of the child) and the medical personnel who quickly arrived—attempted to revive the infant, who never breathed. But Berkley was immediately arrested for "failure to provide health care"; she was eventually sentenced to 20 years in prison for "child endangerment" and "neglect of a dependent person." Twenty-one-year-old Candice Smith, a black woman on welfare, also delivered in the toilet at home; her mother called "911." A court-ordered psychiatric report focused mainly on her history of consulting with doctors but misunderstanding or refusing their advice. As a result, the psychiatrist accused her of "conscious lying" and diagnosed "borderline mental retardation." Smith was sentenced to twenty-five years in prison.

Helen James, a twenty-eight-year-old black woman, actually went to the hospital to have her baby. She delivered in a toilet; the infant was resuscitated by nurses, but James was charged with attempted murder. Not only had she had no prenatal care, police explained, but she had made up the name of a physician when nurses initially quizzed her about her prenatal care. And although doctors and nurses who took her off the toilet on to a wheelchair said she had come quietly, the story soon developed that she had resisted with considerable force. The screaming woman forced from an inappropriate birth place is a powerful image of non-compliance.

Because these women are considered ignorant and obstinate, the legal authorities worry about their conduct in the future. Helen James, for example, was ordered to undergo mandatory pregnancy testing every six months for ten years. As the prosecutor explained, "You can't order them to be sterilized. There are lots of defendants we wish we could, but we can't, and we thought that this would be, not saying to her, 'You can't have any more children' but just in case she does get pregnant again, it would ensure, hopefully ensure, adequate prenatal care and that the baby afterwards was going to be taken care of appropriately."

Middle-class white girls, and those who can pass as such, are not appropriate objects for monitoring. Instead, both supporters and detractors agree that the case is an isolated incident in the young woman's life. She must move beyond it and learn from it. Compare, for example, the case of an eighteen-year-old white student, whose newborn died: "I don't think she'll ever want to live through that again," said the prosecutor, as the judge suggested that five years probation was "very lengthy under the circumstances."

CHILDBIRTH AS A CULTURAL AGENDA

That the legal system discriminates against poor people and people of color is hardly news. What I am suggesting here is that women charged with endangering newborns are differentiated through distinctive characterizations of what *kind* of "criminal" is involved. Stories of inappropriate mothering are built from diverse symbolic resources. What brings them together is their cultural opposition as "unnatural" alternatives to more appropriate forms of womanhood and maternity. By setting a "bad example," these women, in all their diversity, direct those who hear their stories toward the singular path of propriety.

What are the assumptions about proper gender and parenting behavior that these cases help to build? I heard two very basic assumptions reiterated throughout discussion of these cases. First, pregnant women alone—and not, for example, boyfriends, parents, or community services—are held responsible for the health and safety of the fetuses they carry and the newborns they deliver. Second, this responsibility does not put the woman "in charge"; instead, it is the basis of her dependency. To be a good mother, a woman must recognize and internalize the connection between responsibility and dependency.

In the cases I studied, no serious suggestions were ever made to file charges against anyone besides the woman who delivered. In contrast to cultures in which husbands may be blamed for difficult deliveries, fetal deaths, or maternal deaths in childbirth, the cultural assumption in these cases seems to be that men (and female family members) are interested observers but not participants in the process of creating healthy infants.[14] The singularity of women's responsibility for infants, certainly not new in U.S. American culture, has perhaps been further encouraged by the medical focus on the mother's body as the source of danger for the developing fetus, as well as the increasing willingness of the state to deal with women as social adults independent of families.

Responsibility becomes appropriate female nurturance only when it is tied to an acceptance of female vulnerability. In no case that I studied was a woman blamed for not asking for help and protection from the father of the child, but women *were* condemned for not seeking help and protection from the state and the medical profession. They were also condemned for not demonstrating a yielding femininity in this relationship. If police, judges, and doctors are outraged when a woman does not cry for them, mourn her loss in front of them, or otherwise show her vulnerability, perhaps it is because their "paternal" responsibility for her child encourages them to claim a husband-like authority and protectiveness over her sexuality and reproduction.

These assumptions about women's maternal responsibility and dependence are not new creations of the last decade. The American feminist analysis of the 1970s that opened up questions about the cultural construction of motherhood repeatedly invoked the twin dilemmas of female responsibility and vulnerability.[15] However, the vigor with which these cultural elements have been reasserted as ethical universals since the mid-1980s depends on an historically specific cultural agenda. The importance of this form of mothering is asserted in reaction to the female "selfishness" encouraged by public approval for women's participation in wage labor, career development, and political activity. The crimes I have been discussing are considered particularly "unnatural" because the women's irresponsibility is associated with rationality, self-centeredness, and lack of emotional display. These crimes seem worse than those of mothers who murder in passion (who could be "psychotic"), for the "selfish" murderer's traits flourish in the dangerous climate created by career women and feminists. Ironically, the defendants, for the most part, are neither.

Along with the even newer drug-related prenatal child abuse charges, these cases contribute to new standards of perinatal vigilance. Through the ways they define criminals, they also reformulate understandings of gender to build cultural commitments to particular forms of maternal nurturance. This is an agenda that seems to speak sympathetically to feminist goals of instilling appreciation for devalued "women's work," including raising children, and for the distinctive female perspectives that grow out of women's everyday activities. In the last decade, feminists have become especially alert to the importance of revaluing mothering. Analysis has moved from overgeneralized criticisms of the burdens of parenting toward a new appreciation of its empowering challenges.[16] Yet, in the current political climate, this reevaluation easily slips into step with a variety of programs and proposals that attempt to renaturalize ideas of maternal nurturance as the essential trait of decent womanhood. The new perinatal vigilance calls attention to one such agenda. It is an agenda that isolates female reproductive experiences from every other aspect of women's lives, requiring that pregnancy be a transcendant moment that can carry every woman outside the complexity of her particular history. Feminists cannot afford this romanticization of motherhood. They must attend instead to the social and historical circumstances that both create these expectations for what it means to be a "woman," and constrain women's choices about whether and how to bear or raise children.

NOTES

This essay is based on data gathered by Suzanne Bernhart, Rena Fischer, Roberta Nieslanik, Mary Orgel, and Barbara Zollars, as well as myself. The essay has benefited from discussions with project members as well as with Betsey Chadwick, Paulla Ebron, Elizabeth Evans, Sylvia Forman, Faye Ginsburg, Diane Gifford-Gonzales, Sandra Morgen, Mary Patvaldnieks, Troels Petersen, Lisa Rofel, David Schneider, Joanne Wyckoff, and Sylvia Yanagisako.

1. This essay is based on material on 25 cases, in which women were charged with endangering newborns in unassisted births between 1984 and 1988, as well as three cases from this period in which newborns died in unassisted births but no charges were filed. To protect the privacy of both the defendants and those who spoke about them, I have chosen not to discuss locations. This means that I am unable to consider locally and regionally specific social dynamics that were relevant in each case; however, I believe the "stories" make sense as part of a nationwide phenomenon.

2. For careful readings of these three discursive fields, see Faye Ginsburg, *Contested Lives: The Abortion Debate in an American Community* (Berkeley: University of California Press, 1989); Linda Gordon, *Heroes of their Own Lives: The Politics and History of Family Violence: Boston, 1880–1960* (New York: Viking Press, 1988); Emily Martin, *The Woman in the Body: A Cultural Analysis of Reproduction* (Boston: Beacon Press, 1987).

3. Lynn Morgan ("Cross-Cultural Perspectives on Life and Personhood," unpublished manuscript) compares ideas about infanticide and the beginning of life cross-culturally. For a sample of different cultural approaches to birthing and infanticide, see also, Hiroshi Wagatsuma, "Child Abandonment and Infanticide: A Japanese Case," in *Child Abuse and Neglect: Cross-Cultural Perspectives*, ed. Jill Korbin (Berkeley: University of California, 1981); Philip Bates, "Legal Criteria for Distinguishing Between Live and Dead Human Foetuses and Newborn Children," *University of New South Wales Law Journal* 6 (1983): 143–151; Judith Leavitt, *Brought to Bed: Childbearing in America, 1750–1950*, (New York: Oxford University Press, 1986).

4. Marjorie Shostak, *Nisa: The Life and Words of a !Kung Woman*, (Cambridge: Harvard University Press, 1981), 179.

5. This conclusion is drawn in part from interviews with medical examiners on changing standards for autopsies. A reading of appeal decisions for infanticide convictions since the 1890s also suggests shifts in the basis for both legal and medical definitions of "natural" neonatal death—gradually since the late 1940s, and more definitively since the late 1970s.

6. Peter Hoffer and N.E.H. Hull, *Murdering Mothers: Infanticide in England and New England 1558–1803* (New York: New York University Press, 1984), 56–57.

7. Ann Jones, *Women Who Kill* (New York: Fawcett Columbine, 1981), 46–48.

8. Hoffer and Hull, 49.

9. Foxcroft in 1733, quoted in Jones, 46.

10. A few direct connections can be seen in contemporary cases. Massachusetts, for example, still has a law against concealing the death of an *illegitimate* child. The law, classified under "Crimes Against Chastity," retains the Puritan emphasis on concealment of sin (*Annotated Laws of Massachusetts* 272 #22).

11. Recently, nationally publicized cases involving drug and alcohol use have moved perinatal endangerment cases in new directions as influenced by the "war on drugs." One effect has been to push criminalization to earlier gestational

periods. Several of the cases I have been studying may be criminalized miscarriages; in some the gestational period is unknown. In 1988, one woman was charged with two counts of first degree murder—through cocaine use—when she miscarried five month twin fetuses. Bonavoglia ("The Ordeal of Pamela Rae Stewart," *Ms.*, July/August 1987) and Irwin and Jordan ("Court-Ordered Cesarian Sections: An Anthropological Perspective," paper presented at the annual meetings of the American Anthropological Association, 1985) discuss cases of prenatal child abuse charges and court-ordered cesarean sections, respectively. See also, "Maternal Rights and Fetal Wrongs: The Case Against the Criminalization of 'Fetal Abuse'," *Harvard Law Review* 101 (1987–88): 994–1012; Lawrence Nelson, Brian Buggy, and Carol Weil, "Forced Medical Treatment of Pregnant Women: 'Compelling Each to Live as Seems Good to the Rest' " *Hastings Law Journal* 37 (1985–86): 703–763.

12. In 1974, a federal statute on child abuse (United States Code Title 42 Chapter 67 Section 5103) required states to institute new reporting procedures for child abuse in order to qualify for federal funding. By the late 1970s and early 1980s, many states had increased child abuse penalties and made reporting mandatory for medical, mental health, and educational system workers.

13. Harris' sentence was reduced in a sentence reconsideration. A new team of lawyers created an image for Harris in which her age and class background were deemphasized in favor of childlike traits that made her appear much more like Sloan.

14. In contrast, male involvement in pregnancy and birth has been described in an extensive cross-cultural literature on "the couvade," or male birth observances.

15. Adrienne Rich's contrast between the "experience" and the "institution" of motherhood (*Of Woman Born* [New York: Bantam, 1976]) and Nancy Chodorow's contrast between pre-Oedipal and Oedipal mother-child relations (*The Reproduction of Mothering* [Berkeley: University of California Press, 1978]) are two examples in which the power of female responsibility, on the one hand, and its helpless encompassment by patriarchal constraints, on the other, are described as the two central features of mothering.

16. Examples of recent feminist revaluation, and sometimes glorification, of mothering and nurturance include: Miriam Johnson, *Strong Mothers, Weak Wives* (Berkeley: Univ. of California, 1988); Mary O'Brien, *The Politics of Reproduction* (Boston: Routledge and Kegal Paul, 1981); Carol Gilligan, *In a Different Voice: Psychological Theory and Women's Development* (Cambridge: Harvard University Press, 1982); Phyllis Chesler, *Sacred Bond: The Legacy of Baby M* (New York: Times Books, 1988). For more careful reevaluations see, Sara Ruddick, "Maternal Thinking," in *Mothering: Essays in Feminist Theory*, Joyce Trebilcot, ed. (Totowa, NJ: Rowman and Allenheld); Deborah Rosenfelt and Judith Stacey, "Second Thoughts on the Second Wave," *Feminist Studies* 13, no. 2 (Summer 1987): 341–361.

CHAPTER EIGHTEEN

The Ideology of Reproduction: The Reproduction of Ideology

EMILY MARTIN

In American society, as in most societies, there are forms of thought and practice that are so natural to some members that they seem simply to be common sense; to other members they are constraining and shackling. Thought and practices that are especially constraining to women can be found within the institutions of contemporary American science. It is urgent for feminists to discern the way science scrutinizes and constructs women's bodies and senses of self to the public and to women themselves. The first task is to identify structures in medical science that contribute to the domination of women. The second task is equally important: to identify our own class perspectives, so that while we isolate and identify patriarchal ideology we avoid unintentionally reproducing our own class perspectives.

In this essay I will discuss the medical construction of birth as an aspect of control over women. I will focus on whether the dominant medical model is accepted or resisted by women giving birth and whether there is difference in the nature of resistance among women in the United States from different classes. For example, the campaign for twilight sleep in the early 1900s and the current women's health movement both originated in the middle-class.[1] With these movements, as with the birth experiences I will analyze below, it is crucial to recognize specific class bases to certain forms of resistance.

Medical control of birth essentially involves control over the contents of the woman's uterus, and control over how those contents emerge from her body. Three related domains in which there have also been ongoing struggles for control over women in western history are: the mouth, the vagina, and the home. Who or what gets in, and who or what comes out, as well as how such events are described and constructed, have been fiercely contested.[2]

The link between control of the female mouth, vagina-womb and the threshold of the house was forged in the Renaissance.[3] During the 16th century, there was a dominant conceptual opposition between the "classical" body and the "grotesque" body. The classical body was an image of "finished, completed" man. The "opaque surface" of the body was seen as the "border of a closed individuality that does not merge with other bodies and with the world" but is under the jurisdiction of the absolutist state. The head of this body was emphasized as the locus of reason, and its language was the language of the official literature of the ruling classes, governed by hierarchy and etiquette of formal institutions.[4] The grotesque body, in contrast,

is not separated from the rest of the world. It is not a closed, completed unit; it is unfinished, outgrows itself, transgresses its own limits.[5]

Those parts of the grotesque body that were open to the outside world were emphasized: the open mouth, genitals, breasts, nose. This body favored the marketplace, where it had the liberty to speak the language of obscenity and abuse.[6]

The problem women posed within this dichotomy was that they came to be seen as "*naturally* grotesque."[7] As such, they required constant surveillance in three areas: the mouth, the vagina, and the threshold of the house. Laxity in one of these areas was often taken as a sign of laxity in another: "the signs of the harlot 'were her linguistic fullness' and her frequenting of public space"; the signs of the normative woman were the enclosed body, the closed mouth, the locked house.[8]

These themes have taken different forms in subsequent historical periods.[9] In the late 19th century, one of the chief symptoms of the disorder "hysteria," which mostly affected middle- and upper middle-class women, was complete silence, the inability or refusal to speak at all.[10] A woman's mouth was to be controlled, but no speech at all would seem too much like withdrawal from the reach of control. Fittingly, part of the treatment for hysteria was confinement at home, even restriction to one room or, in the extreme case, to a bed.[11] Later, the "talking cure" developed by Freud and Breuer in collaboration with Bertha Pappenheim, would attempt to return hysteric women to normal speech, by investigating and scrutinizing the inner unconscious language of their dreams and associations.[12] Although these treatments used confinement at home and penetration of inner language to treat the symptoms of hysteria, the cause behind these symptoms was often thought to be an errant uterus.[13] The link between control of the mouth, vagina-womb and home is clear.

How does this link continue in the present? As we saw, Renaissance imagery focused on women's sexuality, which ideally was to be controlled by husbands. A large body of recent research and theoretical examination shows us how control over women's sexuality continues to be a central issue in our society.[14] The aspect of that control that involves birth depends heavily on scientific knowledge, which in turn depends on medical scrutiny of the interior spaces of the vagina and uterus, as well as the fetus. This scrutiny has been increasing in intensity since the late 18th century.[15]

Scrutiny of the internal female organs has led to greater medical control of women's bodies, and scrutiny of birthing and labor has led to the same result. Contemporary medical control of labor depends on a series of central metaphors taken from the realm of production. Medically, the uterus is seen as an involuntary muscle, which accomplishes most of the labor of birth by itself. The labor the uterus does is expressed as mechanical work, as defined in physics, a narrow conception of force working against resistance. As a standard medical school textbook puts it,

Labor is work; mechanically, work is the generation of motion against resistance. The forces involved in labor are those of the uterus and the abdomen that act to expel the fetus and that must overcome the resistance offered by the cervix to dilation and the friction created by the birth canal during passage of the presenting part.[16]

Treating the uterus this way amounts to breaking down what is actually a complex and interrelated process into simple mechanical components. In much the same way, scientific time and motion studies in industry break down work, such as screwing in a screw, into simpler actions. In the case of time and motion studies, the object is clearly to control the exact movements of the worker, so as to increase production.[17]

The language applied to labor contractions sounds very much as if doctors' uppermost concern was control. Uterii produce "efficient or inefficient contractions"[18] good or poor labor is judged by the amount of "progress made in certain periods of time".[19] In Friedman's famous representations of average dilatation curves, the amount of time it takes a woman's cervix to open from four to eight centimeters is described as a "good measure of the overall efficiency of the machine".[20] Presumably the "machine" referred to is the uterus.

By what means is the uterus held to a reasonable "progress", a certain "pace"[21] and not allowed to stop and start.[22] A woman's labor, like factory labor, is subdivided into many stages. Each stage and substage is assigned a rate of progress; deviation from these rates can produce a variety of "disorders". Obstetrics handbooks list the proper management of these disorders; administration of medication (to sedate or stimulate); x-ray or sonogram to determine whether an obstruction is present; forceps, or c-section.[23]

In the effort to control birth, the doctor is predominately seen as the "manager" of the labor process; given all this it would be expected that the baby would be seen as a "product." It is surely significant that cesarean section, which requires the most "management" by the doctor and the least "labor" by the uterus and woman is seen as providing the best products.[24]

This particular construction of birth, which presents women with verbal descriptions and evaluations, as well as sees to it that they behave in certain ways, has contributed to statistics representing high rates of induction, particularly in England[25] and cesarean section, particularly in the United States. Historically, this control depended on moving birth from the home to the hospital. As Judith Leavitt has shown, the transfer of birth from home to hospital (virtually complete in the U.S. by now) meant a loss of women's domestic power base, from which they had been able to shape even medically attended births, and include the attendants they wished.[26]

When hospital routines usurped a woman's ability to determine who could accompany her through labor and delivery, or to decide what procedures she would endure, they took away an essential ingredient of a woman's identification as a woman and as a mother-to-be. They erased a woman's powers over the processes of childbirth, which to her marked the beginning of her maternal responsibilities, and thus threatened her competence for her new job of motherhood. They obliterated millennia of women's own birthing traditions.[27]

If control over birth is related to moving the place of birth out of the domain of the house, how is it related to the third member of our triad, control over the mouth, in particular, women's utterances during and about birth? In general in American society, it is well known that control of women's speech is a continuing issue in the politics of gender. Stereotypes that women are wont to speak more than they ideally should are with us still; holding up this stereotype critically against women is only one of the many ways the attempt can be made to silence women. Sociolinguistic research has shown women speak less in mixed sex groups than men, succeed in establishing the topic of conversations less often than men, and are far more likely to be interrupted by men than to interrupt.[28] One way women have confounded efforts to control them has been to stop talking altogether. For example, the impenetrable silence of hysterics was probably one threatening aspect of their condition. So with conversations: women must still speak *some* in order to be interruptable. It cannot be accidental that interruptions are defined linguistically as "penetrations," "intrusions," "deep incursions" into the "internal structure of a speaker's utterance".[29]

Despite the frequent constraints applied to women's speech, when it comes to birth as a subject of discourse, organized efforts by women to talk back to the medical establishment about its treatment of birth began almost as soon as the medical management of birth was established.[30] The contemporary organizations that attempt to redefine medical treatment of birth have developed new key metaphors that counter the central medical images of birth as production.[31] These include such images as a river: "the continuous flow of labor narrows into an intense stream of life-filled birth"; a ripening fruit: "like fruit ripening on a tree, birth takes time. If we start too soon or try to rush, it will be like picking unripe fruit: harder work, longer hours, and possible damage to the crop".[32] Other metaphors stress birth as something a woman does rather than passively has happen to her: like running a marathon, climbing a mountain, swimming an Olympic race;[33]

"like moving a grand piano across the room: that hard, but that satisfying, to feel it moving along".[34]

These efforts to redefine birth come from women active in the middle-class women's health movement. What forms of resistance to the medical model of birth are there among those who are not activists, and how do these forms vary by class? I came to these questions after doing a study of how 165 women of different ages and both working-class and middle-class backgrounds perceive menstruation, birth and menopause in contrast to medical models of these events.[35] "Middle-class" was taken to include: self-employed business people, white-collar or blue-collar salaried professionals and managers, salaried administrative sales and clerical employees, super-visory employees, fire fighters, and police. For the most part these occupations give workers greater autonomy, responsibility, security, mobility, and prestige than working-class occupations. "Working-class" was taken to include skilled craft workers, clerical office workers, retail sales clerks, factory laborers, and service workers, all occupations that have increasingly suffered loss of autonomy and control. In that study, class background turned out to differentiate women's descriptions of certain events, such as menstruation. For example, all the middle-class women we interviewed spoke of menstruation in terms of the medical model: internal body parts that shed debris or waste when they fail to produce a baby. But all the working-class women spoke of it in terms of what it was like to experience menstruation (how it looks, feels, smells, how bothersome it is) or how significant it is as a marker in becoming a fully adult woman. When I did this study, I wondered whether the interviews would reveal any class differences in how women respond to the medical definition of birth, but I could not find a pattern of such differences. When I looked at the interviews again, with broader issues of control in mind, patterns I had not seen before began to emerge.

At first glance, of the seventy middle-class and working-class women who described recent birth experiences in my own study,[36] twice as many middle-class women as working-class women used metaphors that gave the woman herself an active role in birthing.[37] Here are some examples from middle-class women:

Hard work:
I said, "This one's mine. I've earned it. I worked too hard for it. I've earned it and it's mine" (Sarah Lasch).[38]

Riding the contractions:
While I was in a lot of pain I wasn't anxious about [the baby's] safety. And the doctor and my husband was with me and I had a friend who was really helpful in keeping me breathing. I felt like I fell into riding the contractions, but they were really uncomfortable and pretty intensive (Carol Gleason).

Powering her out:
I felt so grateful to have had a vaginal delivery, to be able to put forth the

effort. Feeling the pain . . . to be the one who powered her out, even though it was cut short because of the episiotomy (Laura Hurst).

Skiing:

It was snowing out. [I said] I'm going to ski this baby out. I'm gonna ski down that hill and I'm going to open and push him out, so I did. I skied. I went up in the chair lift as the contraction went up and went off and skied, shushed right down the hill. It was great fun . . . I really flew: one push and I went straight down the hill, a straight hill, I picked a mogul hill" (Wendy Berger).

Fewer working class women used expressions of this general kind:

"I was triumphant. I can do it, I already did it" (Janice Sanderson).

"I have never felt more powerful in my whole life than when I was giving birth, because this magnificent thing was happening, which was like the whole center of life to me. It was like, this is it, man! And I'm doing it: I'm really involved in it! This is it!" (Ann Morrison).

Although it may appear at this point that middle-class women define birth in more active terms than working-class women, the overall picture is far more complicated. As I will argue below, for middle-class women, what may appear to be in one way a form of defiance against medical models, is in another way a form of exertion of control over one's own body in the public domain of the hospital. For working-class women, what may appear to be a relative lack of defiance against medical models of birth is in another way a rejection of both medical *and* middle-class ideals of decorous and controlled behavior during birth. To see this we must shift from the reproductive organs back to the mouth, in particular to actual vocalization during childbirth. In my study, many women expressed a connection between being in control of the uterus and being in control of the mouth. Nearly a third (twenty-two) of the seventy women who described recent birth experiences explicitly made this connection, even though we did not ask them about it directly. Indeed, such a connection had not at the time occurred to any of us who were doing the interviews. All but one of the thirteen middle-class women in this group viewed energetic vocalizations, such as yelling and screaming, as an abhorrent loss of control and as associated with not being in control of birth.

I'm worried about giving in, being completely out of control. You see the movies where the women are screaming and ripping the sheets off . . . where people are very out of control and you see their mouths wide open as they can possibly be, really, in physical pain (Sally Xenos).

They have only curtains to partition off the rooms for labor. You can hear the different ways people react. Some who have had natural childbirth are relaxed and in control and other people are just yelling and screaming because they are so frightened and that's very disconcerting (Lucy Dorset).

(Looking ahead to her first birth:)

Then I think that I will be screaming and yell at him [her husband] not to touch me. My sister-in-law when she was in transition didn't want anyone around her. She couldn't relax. I try to psyche myself and say that I am not going to scream. My sister said a few times that she wanted to, but hearing a woman down the hall screaming, it really psyched her into not doing it. She really concentrated more (Theresa Anthony).

We went to the hospital where they put me in the labor room. I was not one of these screaming, hollering, I'll kill my husband for doing this to me women. I was very calm. I was relaxed (Rebecca Warren).

Of the nine working-class women who made a connection between mouth and uterus, five viewed screaming or making loud noise during labor as neutral or positive. Some examples:

The things my mother had to go through in childbirth. It was outrageous. I mean, like a nurse coming in and telling her to shut up because she was screaming. I mean, it's just not right. I told nurses to get out of my room when I was pregnant, because *they* made too much noise (Ann Morrison).

The only thing that I could think about when the pains got that bad was that I would never have another child. Because I don't think that I deal too well with pain sometimes. And I forgot everything that they taught in class. About breathing in, and if you have to scream turn the scream inside. Go with the contractions. *I* was screaming *outside* (April Hobbs).

Labor was so ungodly, I screamed through the whole thing. My husband said I did real good, instead of going [pants silently], I went [makes loud sound while panting] (Pamela Hunter).

These women did not condemn themselves for making noise, even though their vocalizations often ran up against the different sensibilities of the medical staff, who often tried to squelch them,

They come in to see how many centimeters you are dilated. [The nurse] was putting in this big speculum, you know how you get your pap smear, [but] the one that she was putting in me was not like a regular one. It was big and she was putting it in when I was having a contraction. And I screamed, right? And I said, "Where is my mother?" and she said, "You are getting ready to be a mother yourself, don't call yours." And I said, "Look, Miss, do you have any children?" And she said, "No." She didn't have any children and didn't know what I was going through (Crystal Scott).

At the change of shift the nurse coming on was a little less sympathetic. She was, like, "Oh, God, you are doing all of this screaming. Shut the hell up." She didn't say that but it is like the impression that I got (April Hobbs).

The other four working-class women were more negative about screaming during labor, but not for the same reasons as the middle-class women. One described being a "good girl" for not screaming during a very difficult transition in which she was being injected with spinal anesthetic during contractions. But she then went on to describe later events which finally justified her screaming:

I was telling them to leave me alone and to not stick me during my contractions. They wouldn't listen. So I called really loud. And [the doctor] walked into the room and I said that I want some peace during my contractions. He said, "Don't stick her during the contractions, let her breathe." I had not cried. I had gone through transition, but I had not cried or cussed. I was so proud of myself. I was so good and so composed. Well, after that second stick I just lost it. I was hysterical. I was in tears. They hurt me that bad. That was real pain. They were trying to numb me but they hit a nerve or something. I started crying and the one who was sticking me said, "Oh, come on you are getting upset. I think you are starting to imagine pain." I had had it and they stuck me one more time. I let out a scream that they heard down the hall in the waiting room (Becky Sololov).

Another attributed her screaming to her extreme youth at the time and judged it negatively because the pain "wasn't that bad."

When I think about it I don't think my labor pains was that bad. But I was so scared inside that my reaction to it was worse than the actual pain. It didn't last that long. I was only in labor for about six hours, so that was good. I did cry a lot. As a matter of fact, I screamed. I hollered. Now that I think about it I think it was totally ridiculous, because like I said, it wasn't that bad . . . But I was scared, sixteen-years-old, I was totally terrified. I really was . . . during the whole time I was alone (Stephanie Naylor).

For both these women, screaming is less a sign of loss of control than a justifiable expression of extreme pain.

What was central for the two other working-class women was that they were frightened early in their own labors by the screaming of a nearby woman who they presumed to be farther along in labor. One determined not to do likewise (Ginny Barrows), and the other was warned by others not to: "They told me, 'Don't you scream anything.' I didn't want to scream anyway. [My boyfriend said,] 'You scream, I'm gonna make you remember it. I'm gonna stick a tape recorder and let you hear yourself scream.' I said, 'Oh, boy I ain't gonna scream, because he might really get a tape recorder.' So I didn't scream, I just pushed" (Adrian Davis).

Let us see whether these differences in emphasis on control over utterances in labor are paralleled in what women say about control over birth in general. Of our seventy women, nine mentioned explicitly that they were afraid of losing control in birthing, had felt out of control, or had been firmly in control. For example,

I thought that I was going to be in control all the time. I wasn't completely out of control, but I didn't know everything that I was doing. It was really hard to relax (Judy Kirschner).

I did kind of lose control during transition. The whole thing was that I didn't realize that I was there. They said in class that that was the worst time and if you were going to lose it you would lose it there (Vivian Mitchel).

I think I've gotten the impression that the calmer you remain, the better off you are and the more in control you are of your physical condition (Sally Xenos).

Of these nine women, all of whom brought this issue up spontaneously in the course of telling the stories of their pregnancies or deliveries,[39] eight were middle-class and one was working-class. This, together with the material on vocalization, suggests a difference concerning the importance of controlling and being controlled among middle-class women than among working-class women. Part of that difference may relate to the different experiences working-class and middle-class women have at work. There is pervasive emphasis on control in contemporary American workplaces.[40] Some people are concerned about exerting control; others are subjected to this control. As I have defined them in my study, working-class women (such as clerks, factory workers, service workers) are subjected to control of their time and behavior by others, while the middle-class women (such as salaried managers, administrators or supervisors) are often responsible for exerting control.[41] Sometimes managerial employees must exert this control over others and sometimes they must exert it over themselves. They may become what Foucault called "self-affirming subjects"[42], as they take on control and management of their time and their responsibilities on the job. I wonder if loss of control might seem far more of an anathema for middle-class people that are responsible for maintaining control, than for those in the working-class that are more often held under control by other people.[43]

The largely middle-class women's health movement emphasizes control over birth. Partly, this takes the form of the familiar breathing techniques of Lamaze, used to "control" contractions. It also takes the form of emphasis on consumer choice. This model is one of the individual in the marketplace of birth options; a woman becoming as informed as possible, and exercising relatively free choice among these options.[44] In one sense this is radical because it treats practices medical science would have us think of as impartial, scientific progress just like any other commodities offered for sale and profit in the market place. If so, the buyer (the birthing woman) seems in control because she can take it or leave it.[45] However, one problem with adopting this stance is that it forecloses on the option to relax and let events unfold. The birthing woman and her supporting partner must maintain almost constant vigilance and control over the pregnancy as it develops, and over the labor and its various stages.

As one middle-class woman expressed it,

I wanted to be prepared. I didn't want to go into the hospital completely blind like I had the first time. I wanted to be ready. We took childbirth classes. We spent most of the time preparing for the hospital rather than preparing for the labor. Knowing our hospital rights and what we had a right to demand and to refuse. And just getting prepared for what we would have to deal with (Sue Jackson).

Another middle-class woman expressed this as a regret:

There were a lot of options. I knew exactly what I wanted. Natural birth. I didn't want any medication, unless it was real necessary. I didn't want to have a cesarean. I didn't want to have my labor induced. I didn't want to get anything. I just wanted to do it natural. I wanted things to fall into place. I felt that there was a lot of options, too many. It just seemed like such a natural thing. I wouldn't need anything. I felt there was a lot available to me, but I already knew what I wanted (Pamela Nugent).

In a sense the effort to wrest control away from the medical organization of birth has resulted in middle-class women becoming controlled themselves, being the agents of exerting control over themselves, as silent, except for certain controlled forms of breathing, they perform birth in the public arena of the hospital. Letting "things fall into place" or events unfold in a spontaneous way as they might in a conversation or a courtship is precluded. The metaphors from the women's health movement I discussed above contain imagery that invites spontaneous development (a river, ripening fruit). Although some of these images appear in the interviews, and at times doubtless help empower women in the face of medical intervention, what appears *more* often is concern with controlling the event and being controlled.

Of course, being in control has a far deeper meaning than just breathing quietly. In birthing, losing control can mean having one's body physically penetrated. This concern is not an abstraction, as the cesarean section rate, which involves cutting open the mother's abdomen to remove the baby, is now over 20% in many states.[46] Here is the rub: to feel empowered and in control in this setting through breathing may be an illusion.

My material indicates at least in a preliminary way that middle-class women more readily exaggerate the extent to which any woman can be in control of birthing. In so doing they may be ignoring other aspects of their experiences, which are less easily articulated because they are (as our culture sees them) more physical and less controllable. Working-class women more readily articulate precisely these kinds of experiences: I am in pain; this hurts; it is enough to make me scream; I am not really in control of this situation, *and no one could be.*

Middle-class women in my study commonly said that they were seeking an aesthetically beautiful or spiritual experience of birth. In contrast, working-class women emphasize more often what they see as the substantial reality of birth: its extreme pain:

It was just constant contractions for 14 hours and I hated it I remember, while it was happening. It was very painful. I was aiming for natural. I had done Lamaze. But somehow I didn't think Lamaze would make it through this whole thing. I think Lamaze is good, but it was too long. Just too long (Pamela Nugent).

[What was labor like for you?] "Hell, hell" (Crystal Scott).

I was in so much pain that I could hardly watch. But I enjoyed watching the first baby coming out and I wanted to watch her come out. It was so painful that I could barely see her come out. The nurse was taking my hand and pulling away, I was squeezing so hard. It was a lot. I don't know. . . . They were talking about breathing and panting and—what are you talking about, it hurts!!" (Anita Duke).

These kinds of statements could contribute to rejecting with vehemence, or with humor, the pretensions of the middle-class. Think of the difficulty a middle-class teacher of a Lamaze prepared childbirth class would have in responding to statements that "birth is hell," "Lamaze wouldn't take you all the way" and "what are you talking about [breathing], it hurts!" Similarly, when working-class women "lose control" by screaming or calling for their mothers while in labor, they may be resisting both the control of hospital staff over the event of birth and the control of the middle-class health movement over their voice and breath. Further research could show whether they are explicitly resisting aspects of the women's health movement, or whether they are primarily using "out-of-control" behavior (screaming loudly rather than breathing quietly) as the only dependable way to get the attention of hospital staff.

Why should there be such a difference between working- and middle-class women? We are all familiar with processes that occur in the division of labor in industrial society that lead to separation of intellectual from manual functions. As Frederick Winslow Taylor puts it: "we propose to take all the important decisions and planning which vitally affect the output of the shop out of the hands of the workmen, and centralise them in a few men, each of whom is especially trained in the art of making decisions and in seeing that they are carried out."[47] Given that this is one of the ways life experience tends to differ between those women I define as working class and those I define as middle class, what we see in birth may be an extension of this: perhaps in birth as in their work places, middle-class women more than working-class women advocate and practice 'mind over matter' and seek mental concentration that does not allow the body to dictate events.[48]

Judith Leavitt comments that the hospital in the twentieth century acts as the great leveller, making women's experiences more alike than in the nineteenth century.[49] Perhaps so, but we must not make the mistake of assuming uniformity in what women are resisting or how they do it. Many women may agree about the desirability of overcoming the medical control of birth, but within that agreement may be enormous diversity. While resisting the medical ideology of reproduction, some middle-class women may be reproducing the ideology and practice of control, in this case by exerting control over themselves. By enacting "out-of-control" behavior, some working-class women may be resisting both the treatment they expect from medical managers and middle-class ideology about the desirability of always being in control. That middle-class women find the idea of going out of control in labor repellent and even grotesque is evidence of an opposition among women that does not serve our common interests. As medical control of women's bodies evolves with the help of new technologies, it remains to be seen whether the most effective resistance will be to labor quietly and in control or loudly and out of control, or indeed whether women will labor themselves at all. Surely we would all gain if we saw these different strategies not simply as success or failure to remain in control, but as the result of complex negotiations via the body that are produced by different class and work experiences.

NOTES

I owe thanks to Hy van Luong who suggested to me there might be more to class differences in birth experiences than I had seen in The Woman in the Body, *to members of the Upstate New York Feminist Seminar, and to the members of the Anthropology department of the University of Michigan for many helpful suggestions. Faye Ginsburg and Anna Tsing have my warmest appreciation for their editorial help.*

1. Lawrence G. Miller, "Pain, Parturition, and the Profession: Twilight Sleep in America," in *Health Care in America,* eds. Susan Reverby and David Rosner (Philadelphia: Temple University Press, 1979), 19–44; Margot Edwards and Mary Waldorf, *Reclaiming Birth: History and Heroines of American Childbirth Reform* (Trumansburg, New York: The Crossing Press, 1984).

2. Paul Friedrich, *The Meaning of Aphrodite* (Chicago: University of Chicago Press, 1978), 392, suggests the "complex concept of orifice-(curved) edge" is probably operative to some extent in all grammars. Jean Comaroff, "Bodily Reform as Historical Practice: The Semantics of Resistance in Modern South Africa," *International Journal of Psychology* 20 (1985): 541–567, has argued for the "widespread existence of categories associated with the perception of 'orifice'—a seemingly universal marker of the threshold between 'inside' and 'outside', 'self' and 'other' and controlled (and hence cultural process) as against unbounded, asocial flux".

3. Peter Stallybras, "Patriarchal Territories: The Body Enclosed," in *Rewriting the Renaissance: The Discourses of Sexual Difference in Early Modern Europe,* eds. Margaret W. Ferguson, Maureen Quilligan, and Nancy J. Vickers (Chicago: The University of Chicago Press, 1986), 123–142.

4. Ibid, 123–24.

5. Mikhail Bakhtin, *Rabelais and His World* (Cambridge: MIT Press, 1968), 26.

6. Ibid, 154.

7. Stallybrass, 126.

8. Ibid, 127.

9. See L. J. Jordanova, ed., "Naturalizing the Family: Literature and the Bio-Medical Sciences in the Late Eighteenth Century," in *Languages of Nature: Critical Essays on Science and Literature* (London: Free Association Books, 1986), 86–116, esp. 99, for a late 18th century version.

10. Elaine Showalter, *The Female Malady: Women, Madness, and English Culture 1830–1980* (New York: Pantheon, 1985), 159–61; Carroll Smith-

Rosenberg, *Disorderly Conduct: Visions of Gender in Victorian America.* (New York: Oxford University Press, 1985), 201.

11. Smith-Rosenberg, 208; Barbara Ehrenreich and Deidre English, *For Her Own Good: 150 Years of the Experts' Advice to Women.* (New York: Anchor Books, 1979), 131–133.

12. Showalter, 155.

13. Smith-Rosenberg, 204, 206. Ehrenreich and English, 138.

14. Adrienne Rich, "Compulsory Heterosexuality and Lesbian Existence," *Signs* 5, no. 4 (1980): 631–660, argues that a central aspect of this control is the cultural assumption that normal sexuality is heterosexuality.

15. L. J. Jordanova, "Naturalizing the Family: Literature and the Bio-Medical Sciences in the Late Eighteenth Century," in *Languages of Nature: Critical Essays on Science and Literature,* ed. L. J. Jordanova (London: Free Association Books, 1986), 86–116. *Also:* Ann Oakley's history of the medical treatment of childbirth sees the development of this aspect of science as ever greater and more sophisticated incursions into the previously hidden inner space of the womb. From the nineteenth century efforts to know what was inside from a distance—feeling early contractions, hearing the fetal heartbeat from outside the body. Ann Oakley, The Captured Womb: A History of the Medical Care of Pregnant Women. (Oxford: Blackwell, 1984), 25–26—medical science rapidly moved in the twentieth century to 'seeing' and knowing the fetus and uterus with x-rays, Oakley, 28, then with ultrasound, fetoscopy, amniocentesis, external and internal fetal monitoring. Oakley summarizes:

At times it has seemed that the nature and limits of technological innovation have been inspired simply by a global impulse to expose as much of the fetus's intrauterine life to the physician's gaze as is both technically and humanly possible (Oakley, 182).

16. Jack A. Pritchard and Paul C. MacDonald, *Williams Obstetrics,* 16th ed. (New York: Appleton-Century Crofts, 1980), 382.

17. Harry Braverman, *Labor and Monopoly Capital* (New York: Monthly Review Press, 1974).

18. Kieran O'Driscoll and Michael Foley, "Correlation of Decrease in Perinatal Mortality and Increase in Cesarean Section Rates," *Journal of the American College of Obstetricians and Gynecologists* 61 (1983): 1–5.

19. Kenneth R. Niswander, *Obstetrics: Essentials of Clinical Practice,* 2nd ed. (Boston: Little, Brown and Co., 1981), 207.

20. Pritchard and Macdonald, 385.

21. O'Driscoll and Foley, 5.

22. Barbara Katz Rothman, *In Labor: Women and Power in the Birthplace,* (New York: Norton, 1982), 269.

23. Charles R. B. Beckmann and Jeffrey W. Ellis, *A Clinical Manual of Obstetrics* (Norwalk, Connecticut: Appleton-Century-Crofts, 1983), 501–6.

24. Helen Marieskind, "Cesarean Section," *Women and Health* 7, no. 3–4 (1982): 179–98. *Also:* For a more detailed discussion of these points, see Emily Martin, *The Woman in the Body: A Cultural Analysis of Reproduction* (Boston: Beacon Press, 1987).

25. Ann Oakley, *The Captured Womb: A History of the Medical Care of Pregnant Women* (Oxford: Blackwell, 1984).

26. Judith Walzer Leavitt, *Brought to Bed: Childbearing in America 1750–1950* (New York: Oxford University Press, 1986), 107.

27. Ibid, 194.

28. Elizabeth Aries, "Interaction Patterns and Themes of Male, Female, and Mixed Groups," *Small Group Behavior* 7 (1, 1976): 7–18; Alette Olin Hill, *Mother Tongue, Father Time: A Decade of Linguistic Revolt* (Bloomington: Indiana University Press, 1986); Paula A. Treichler and Cheris Kramarae, "Women's Talk in the Ivory Tower," *Communication Quarterly* 31, no. 2 (1983): 118–132; Candace West and Don H. Zimmerman, "Women's Place in Everyday Talk: Reflections on Parent-Child Interaction," *Social Problems* 24 (1977): 521–529; Candace West and Don H. Zimmerman, "Small Insults: A Study of Interruptions in Cross-Sex Conversations between Unacquainted Persons," in *Language, Gender and Society,* eds. Barrie Thorne, Cheris Kramarae, and Nancy Henley (Rowley, Massachusetts: Newbury House, 1983), 103–117; Don H. Zimmerman and Candace West, "Sex Roles, Interruptions and Silences in Conversation," in *Language and Sex: Difference and Dominance,* eds. Barrie Thorne and Nancy Henley (Rowley, Massachusetts: Newbury House, 1975).

29. West and Zimmerman, "Small Insults", 104.

30. The campaign for twilight sleep in the U.S. in the early 1900s was an effort by middle-class women to insist on painless childbirth, by demanding that doctors administer a combination of analgesics and amnesiacs used in Europe (Lawrence G. Miller, "Pain, Parturition, and the Profession: Twilight Sleep in America," in *Health Care in America,* eds. Susan Reverby and David Rosner [Philadelphia: Temple University Press, 1979], 32).

31. Emily Martin, *The Woman in the Body: A Cultural Analysis of Reproduction* (Boston: Beacon Press, 1987), 156ff.

32. Nancy Wainer Cohen and Lois J. Estner, *Silent Knife: Cesarean Prevention and Vaginal Birth After Cesarean (VBAC)* (South Hadley, Massachusetts: Bergin and Garvey, 1983), 120–121.

33. Ibid, 233.

34. Rothman, 20.

35. Martin, *Woman in the Body.*

36. See Martin 1987 for information about the study and the class composition of the women interviewed. By "recent" I mean births that took place since 1960. Until then women in U.S. hospitals were put to sleep during delivery (Judith Walzer Leavitt, *Brought to Bed: Childbearing in America 1750–1950* [New York: Oxford University Press, 1986], 140).

37. These patterns have to be termed exploratory because the numbers involved are not large. There were four middle-class women and two working-class women. In spite of the small size of these numbers, the pattern runs in the same direction as patterns I discuss later in this paper.

38. See Martin 1987 Appendix 2 for a brief sketch of the women interviewed. All names are pseudonyms.

39. The interview questions are in Appendix 1 of Martin 1987.

40. Ernest Mandel, *Late Capitalism,* trans. Joris De Bres (London: NLB, 1972), stresses the need for greater control over the work force in late capitalism, because the greater reliance on technological innovation means rapid turnover in the production process becomes essential.

41. Phil Blackburn, et. al., *Technology, Economic Growth and the Labour Process* (New York: St. Martin's Press, 1985), 25; Craig Littler, *The Devel-*

opment of the Labour Process in Capitalist Societies (London: Heinemann, 1982), 188.

Also see Craig Littler, *The Development of the Labour Process in Capitalist Societies* (London: Heinemann, 1982), 190ff, and Craig Littler, "Deskilling and Changing Structures of Control," in *The Degradation of Work? Skill, Deskilling and the Labour Process,* ed. Stephen Wood (London: Hutchinson, 1983) for comparisons between control of the labor process in the U.S., Britain and Japan.

42. Michel Foucault, *The History of Sexuality,* trans. Robert Hurley, vol. 1. (New York: Vintage, 1980).

Other areas of contemporary (especially middle class) American life that seem intensely concerned about control issues are: psychotherapy ("control" disorders form a major part of the diagnostic manual DSM III); time management (think of handbooks such as Alan Lakein, *How to Get Control of Your Time and Your Life* (New York: The New American Library, 1973); eating (dieting is seen as all about control of appetite or calorie intake. See Joan Jacobs Brumberg, *Fasting Girls: The Emergence of Anorexia Nervosa as a Modern Disease* (Cambridge: Harvard University Press, 1988) on anorexia nervosa as a control disorder.

43. This is complicated by recent developments in the organization of work in some industries which place workers in positions of greater control. In cybernetically organized continuous process industries, workers control the controls rather than being controlled by them (Larry Hirschhorn, *Beyond Mechanization* [Cambridge: The MIT Press, 1984], 2, 52). Workers become "persistently vigilant and often nervous, feeling that though they execute few tasks they have become more responsible for the entire process. 'You have to think more about the job you're doing. You can't look around. In the old mills, the job got so you didn't have to think, no mental effort. This job is very touchy, you have to watch all the time, think every minute . . . Even when the mill is turned on automatic, you still have to think all the time' " (Hirschhorn, 71). Still, these automatic industries currently form a small proportion of all industries (Phil Blackburn et. al., *Technology, Economic Growth and the Labour Process* [New York: St. Martin's Press, 1985], 145).

44. Diony Young, *Changing Childbirth: Family Birth in the Hospital* (Rochester, New York: Childbirth Graphics, 1982); Edwards and Waldorf.

45. Edwards and Waldorf, 65, 107.

46. Craig Tanio, et al., *Unnecessary Cesarean Sections: A Rapidly Growing National Epidemic* (Washington, D.C.: Public Citizen Health Research Group, 1987).

47. Alfred Sohn-Rethel, *Intellectual and Manual Labor* (Atlantic Highlands, New Jersey: Humanities Press, 1983), 151.

48. This was certainly true in an earlier time in our history. The early twentieth century advocates of birth control, Margaret Sanger and Marie Stopes, explicitly sought for the middle classes, a kind of ethereal sexuality, and reserved the need for birth control for the "grossly unchaste" lower classes (Carol Bachhi, "Feminism and The 'Eroticization' of the Middle-Class Woman: The Interaction of Class and Gender Attitudes," (paper given at the University of Delaware Seminar in Women's Studies, 1988).

49. Leavitt, 82.

CHAPTER NINETEEN

Incongruities: Dissonance and Contradiction in the Life of a Black Middle-Class Woman

IRMA MCCLAURIN-ALLEN

My life abounds in incongruities. Fresh from a vacation in Paris, I may, a week later, be on the milk-run Trailways bus in Deep South backcountry attending the funeral of an ancient uncle whose world stretched only 50 miles and who never learned to read. Sometimes when I wait at the bus stop with my attaché case, I meet my aunt getting off the bus with other cleaning ladies on their way to do my neighbors' floors.
—Leanita McClain

When a young black woman dies, it is usually of passing interest, except to those who knew her. When the same black woman has traversed the usual social boundaries and established a place for herself in professional and political spheres traditionally occupied by white males, then her death calls our attention to questions about her life. This is true of Leanita McClain, a gifted, black journalist who worked for the *Chicago Tribune*. By studying her life I hope to bring out the contradictory elements that emerge as a result of the complex interactions of race, class, and gender and the positioning of the individual in the construction of social reality. Throughout her life and with her choice of death at the age of thirty-two, at the height of success in society's terms, Leanita demonstrated an understanding of the injustices and dilemmas of our society. She was articulate, in a way most of us never manage to be, about both her life and anticipated death. It is this explicitness that gives me the means to discuss the relationship between identity and social structures. The act of suicide can be interpreted in many different ways: as resolution or capitulation; as cowardice or courage; as anger internalized or rage externalized. Some view her death as the ultimate form of self-criticism codifying the vulnerability and self-doubt she expressed in private writings. Others read it as an attempt to exert some measure of control and authority over her life. In my view, it was the product of contradictions experienced by this sensitive woman (both journalist and poet), in effect becoming her most powerful statement on the complex social arena in which her identity was constructed.

It is in understanding and explicating such a life that feminist scholarship comes to terms with its greatest challenges. Leanita McClain was not a "typical" woman. The "typical" women of feminist scholarship have too often been white and middle-class. But Leanita was also not a "typical" black woman, and certainly not a "typical" professional woman. Her life, in her own words, was full of "incongruities"—of gender, class, and racial status, and of personal and professional personas. Such incongruities allow us to move beyond stereotypes in understanding differences among women.

Feminist debates through the 1970s acknowledged the influence of race and class in the production of gender, but often treated them as "epiphenomenal," ignoring the fact that the particular way in which women define themselves and experience gender oppression arises out of a cultural history shaped and determined by race, class, and particular events. In the lived reality of individual women, these three aspects of social identity are inextricable from one another. Black feminists, it seems, have understood the necessity of developing such a theoretical viewpoint.

A careful review of the emerging black feminist literature reveals that many Black intellectuals, especially those in touch with their marginality in academic settings, tap this standpoint in producing distinctive analyses of race, class, and gender.[1]

Following in this tradition, I argue for an approach to the study of gender as a dynamic creation, always historically and culturally specific—and dialectically constituted together with other aspects of social stratification, including race and class. Such a framework allows us to see the coherency of Sandra Harding's thesis that "in cultures stratified by both gender and race, gender is always also a racial category and race a gender category."[2] By viewing race and gender as inextricable, Harding points the way to an analytic framework that assumes the simultaneous production of race, class, and gender. To understand this dialectical process of gender formation, it is useful to look at the relationship between sociality and subjectivity, and between individuals and institutions. How are different kinds of *women* formed within the dialectical interrelations of race, class, and gender?

THEORIZING BLACK WOMEN'S LIVES

The theoretical models currently available to feminist social scientists have focused on structures and systems but paid less attention to the complex process within which gender and other forms of social inequality are created, manipulated, and incorporated into individual identities. By focusing on the individual, we can gain a new perspective on the contradictions within systems of social inequality.

To understand and explicate multiple forms of oppression, one needs a dynamic model of the experience of social inequalities within which race, class, and gender are accepted as interactive realities that assert themselves to varying degrees in complex and contradictory ways. The model must also attend to how individual identities are formed within the historically and culturally specific contexts of these structures of social inequality.

Instead of assuming the homogeneity of women's experiences, these analytical tools allow us to acknowledge the distinctiveness of cultures and the universal presence of social inequality without always having to specify the practices and products in the terms employed by western feminists. Thus, it becomes possible to accept as a point of departure "the concept of a multiple, shifting, and often self-contradictory identity . . . an identity made up of heterogeneous and heteronomous representations of gender, race, and class, and often indeed across languages and cultures."[3] In this analytical context, the lives of black and other women, whose social realities produce "fractured identities," form the critical juncture for feminist inquiry. As Bonnie Thornton Dill asserted in her essay, "The Dialectics of Black Womanhood," "it is the potential synthesis of [the] contradictions [in black women's lives] which embraces the future problems and possibilities of a new definition of femininity for *all* American women."[4]

I would like to elaborate on Dill's idea of the importance of certain kinds of contradictions that emerge in the production of social inequality. Leanita McClain pointed to this condition of her life and social world by speaking of having a "foot in each world." She was born and socialized into a milieu in which people have little power except in the day-to-day regulation of their lives. She later gained access to a different world, by virtue of talent and historical circumstances, whereby she found herself in a position to exercise authority over others and participate in the kind of power that affects society. Emotionally tied to her past in which her values and expectations were formed (and where family and friends still resided), yet drawn into a different arena as a result of class status, professional training, and personal choice, Leanita found herself confronted by contradictions at many levels. Such dissonance alone does not necessarily precipitate particular forms of consciousness. However, in Leanita's case the intensity and frequency of the contradictions coalesced to impel her toward a certain social awareness. The disparities between the world she came from and the world she lived in manifested themselves most noticeably in her decision to live in a white neighborhood and in her selection of whites as closest friends, with a few exceptions. Despite her claim to live in both the black and white world, in fact she was viewed ambivalently by both communities and experienced ambivalence toward them. Operating in a power sphere usually only accessible to white males, she witnessed social inequality as it was constituted and practiced. Leanita was reminded daily and in various interactions that her social standing and the security she derived from it were at best precarious. Her writings on the contradictions in her life offer a glimpse of a black professional woman caught between the domains of power of her adult life and the disenfranchised world of her early personal history.

Within feminist research, autobiographies, diaries, letters, novels and poems have provided the important materials for describing and explicating women's experiences. By using Leanita's own works about herself, she ceases to be merely a *subject or object* but becomes *co-commentator*—albeit post mortem—in the analysis of her life. Engaging in this process, what Clifford and Marcus call the "dialogical mode," ensures that my (the author's) voice, rather than assuming an authoritative and objective position, is balanced by other voices, namely, that of the life history's subject. As Clifford points out, using this mode "obliges writers to find diverse ways of rendering negotiated realities as multisubjective, power-laden, and incongruent."[5]

This interpretative approach enables Leanita's words to *speak for her* while I, as a black female anthropologist, am able to examine, challenge, and empathize with my subject/object, allowing the reader access to our different views. Contributing to my understanding of her text is the fact that we were both shaped by a particular cultural history. We share age, race, and gender cohorts, were reared under similar conditions, and even attended the same public high school. Yet our responses to these conditions diverged. I am alive to write the story, and she is the one who requested that:

When my death comes,
Let me be unlike anyone else.
Let my death be felt.[6]

INTERPRETING PERSONAL AND POLITICAL REALITIES: A LIFE HISTORY APPROACH

Leanita McClain was born October 3, 1951 in the city of Chicago. Like most urban centers, it is a city full of deep contradictions. In 1784, John Baptiste Point du Sable, a black man, was the first settler; yet, in recent times Chicago has been called the "most residentially segregated city in the United States where a Negro dare not step outside the environs of his race."[7] Yet some have stepped outside the prescribed racial boundaries. Gwendolyn Brooks, a black female poet and Pulitzer Prize winner, has made Chicago her home. She now resides there as poet laureate of Illinois, her presence an indication of the individual's ability to transcend narrow categories that constrict and dampen the aspirations of the majority of blacks. Ironically, in 1969, the year Brooks was honored by the state of Illinois, two young black men, Mark Clark and Fred Hampton were murdered by Chicago police. The police raid against these two leaders of the Black Panther Party is viewed, in retrospect, by historians as "a wanton and gross abuse of the civil rights of blacks."[8] But then, it was an act symbolic of the contempt held by the city's political machine and its white constituency for the black populace.

Chicago is a divided city where paradoxes abound. Skyscrapers spiral up and tower across the city's skyline, some like Marina Towers symbolizing privilege, and others oppression, like the Robert Taylor homes, one of numerous housing projects concentrated in ghettos throughout the city. It is also a place ruled by politics where race has always been a dominant factor. Although the germination may have begun sooner, racial violence in Chicago dates back to the race riots of 1919 with an evolving system of racial stratification in housing, education, and politics that controlled many city jobs and civil service jobs under a patronage system. In the recent past, hostilities between blacks and whites have been so vociferous that during a visit in the mid-sixties, the late Martin Luther King was compelled to suggest that white Mississippians should visit Chicago if they wanted to learn how to hate. Despite such polarizations, and the attendant violence and hostility, Chicago elected its first black mayor in 1983. This is a city where black versus white; rich versus poor, privilege versus oppression— and incongruities abound.

Amid such disparities, Leanita McClain, poor, black and intellectually gifted was reared. She grew up in the urban ghetto of the Ida B. Wells housing projects. The McClains were among thousands of black families who migrated to the city from Alabama and Mississippi with fertile dreams of upward mobility. They viewed the North as a mecca and thought their lives in the ghetto to be temporary. Like many children of these "immigrants" Leanita was raised to have high aspirations and to see her life in the housing projects as a stopover.[9] Education was seen as the primary key to personal success. And so, Leanita attempted to transcend the restricted experiences of her parents, and thousands of other blacks. Leanita believed in the American vision of personal struggle and equivalent rewards and pursued this symbolic promise through study and hard work. Within a short period of time, Leanita escaped the fated world of those who remained in the ghetto. She attended public elementary and high schools and began working as an ad taker at the *Chicago Tribune* in 1971 while enrolled at Chicago State College. In 1973, at the age of twenty-two, she completed her Masters of Science in journalism at the Medill School of Journalism at Northwestern University. Eight years later, at the age of thirty, she became the first black and second woman to sit on the editorial board of the *Chicago Tribune*, the oldest and, historically, the most conservative paper in the city of Chicago and one of the largest daily papers in the Midwest.

The Board was responsible for "determining and setting forth public positions on local, national, and world issues."[10] Most of the board was comprised of bright, middle-aged to elderly white men. Leanita McClain and one other member of the Board differed radically from their colleagues— they were women. And Leanita differed even further: despite her sandy brown hair, hazel eyes, and freckles, she was black. In fact, she was the first black ever to share such power in the 137-year history of the *Tribune*. The "accident" of Leanita's presence could probably be traced back directly to the riots, which had shaken the city of Chicago in 1968, devastating the west side of Chicago and leaving it a wasteland of parking lots and deteriorating storefronts. These events, coupled with an analysis of their impact in the form of the *Report of the National Advisory Commission on Civil Disorders* (the Kerner report), demanded action from all sectors of the community, including the newspaper industry. The report charged that the white press "repeatedly, if unconsciously reflects the biases, the paternalism, the indifference of white America." As one reporter hired during the late sixties recalls, the newspaper industry's response was on two levels. "We had the riots and the newspapers needed someone to go out into the black community with a pencil and pad" and they also "realized they had been ignoring the underlying problems in the black community."[11] Leanita was a member of a new cadre of black and women reporters hired after 1968 to work in every aspect of the newspaper industry.

She was not the first or even the second black reporter to be hired by the *Tribune* in 1973. That honor was granted five years earlier to two black men. Leanita was, however, the only black on the *Tribune* staff who traced her lineage back to the riots, the projects, and the people who lived in Chicago. She had been reared in the Ida B. Wells housing projects and attended Lucy Flower Vocational High School on the westside of Chicago where the riots had their genesis. Leanita directed the force of her editorial powers to this disenfranchised readership. As a member of the *Tribune's* task force, which convened in 1980 to expand their coverage of local issues, she had worked to establish a market for the paper within the black community, even though most of her black constituency considered the *Tribune* a conservative bastion of white power. Her writings displayed a sensitivity to inequality and called for a commitment to moral rightness. Whether out of conscience or other motives, she appointed herself the community's public voice.

With a wide stylistic range that could be acrimonious in one editorial and urbane and witty in another, Leanita revealed both the personal and public effects of social inequality. She wrote of the tension between values shaped by her past experiences and new ones necessary for her professional survival but which offered her no emotional sanctuary.

I have made it, but where? Racism still dogs my people. There are still communities in which crosses are burned on the lawns of black families who have the money and grit to move in.

Her recognition that her life opportunities were always configured within the matrix of race and gender is powerfully demonstrated in the following statement:

What a hollow victory we have won when my sister, dressed in her designer everything, is driven to the rear door of the luxury high rise in which she lives because the cab driver, noting only her skin color, assumes she is the maid, or the nanny, or the cook, but certainly not the lady of any house at this address.[12]

Leanita strongly believed that all women were not oppressed equally. White women accrued more privilege by virtue of race. By contrast, black women, regardless of their success, were never perceived as exercising authority over others. In an interview one month before her death, she commented:

I think progress for females [has] happened a lot faster than progress for blacks as a group. And I've said that an awful lot . . . I think Naomi Sims put it best in her book on black women and success when she said that white men that run the world and everything in it can still deal with a female of their color, then with a female or anybody of a [different] color and I think that's why white women have advanced so rapidly.[13]

What Leanita did not address in her statement above was the cause for her own advancement as a black woman over other black men with greater seniority at the *Tribune,* including her ex-husband. I believe she gained privilege as a black woman over black men because she was perceived as less threatening in the position of power and authority as editor and member of the editorial board. Yet Leanita was not so naive as to believe that she was immune from the effects of gender oppression. In the statement below she acknowledged that women's socialization to serve others is so strong and begins so early in the life cycle as to appear almost natural. This produced, she believed, fear in women once they stepped outside their prescribed roles.

We were raised to be mommies or secretaries and you find yourself on a construction crew, barking at seven men everyday, it can make you insecure.

Also, unequal conditions in the work place helped to create feelings of frustration and powerlessness, as illustrated in these recollections of a white woman who worked at the Tribune during the same time.

I really considered filing a class action suit against the paper because I felt I was still paying my dues when a lot of these guys I had trained or [who] had started out with me were department heads.[14]

But Leanita moved outside of set social expectations and found herself in the position to exercise authority over white men. Despite her status as their supervisor or editor, she was questioned because she was both black and a woman. The experience gave her a sense of having achieved against tremendous odds, but also it was an inescapable source of stress in her life.

It was traumatic and . . . I accomplished a lot; I have a great sense of accomplishment about it, but it was very painful.

Ironically, though she anticipated lack of support as a result of race, Leanita was surprised at the problems she incurred because of gender.

I [knew] that being black would always make a difference, but I certainly didn't think that being a female would make a difference.[15]

In an interview, Elizabeth McClain recalled her daughter, Leanita, saying as her career accelerated:

All this flack I'm getting is not because I'm black, it's because I'm a woman. They would resent any woman who can advance faster than they can . . . That comes from both sides. [It] comes from the white fellows and [it] comes from the black fellows . . .[16]

The impact of gender was implicit in Leanita's work, in the female-centered perspective in some of her editorials. When she wrote about "Gender's impact on [Chicago] elections," she noted the disparity between the current Mayor Jane Byrne's philosophy and praxis.

. . . for a woman who was elected with the help of female voters, [Mayor Jane Byrne] has not done very much to further the rights of women. She donned a white dress in the summer heat and marched for the ERA, but all of her closest advisers are men.[17]

Leanita was concerned not only with gender politics but with how a particular class of women were affected by the constraints of poverty and sexism, and in this editorial she suggested that the needs of "working-class and poor women concerned about the feminization of poverty" might be better met by Harold Washington's (a black man) "longtime liberalism and record on social programs."

Other editorials, such as the "High Cost Of Out-of-wedlock Births" and the "Tragedy Of Illegal Abortion," indicate Leanita's interest in issues that circumscribe black and other women's life. In a different editorial on the progress of black women, Leanita described the new "militancy and black women." It was a remarkable self-portrait, one that emphasized upwardly mobile coping strategies and cultural symbols.

The new militancy is not fist-waving or teeth-clenching or Swahili-speaking, though the Afro hairstyle is still prevalent. Rather it is business-suited, financially astute and well-spoken, but still with a heavy dose of the old-fashioned, emotional politics of "black is beautiful."[18]

As part of a cohort of professional women, Leanita also faced having to mediate personal relationships with career aspirations. Her divorce can be seen as part of a trend signifying the tensions professional women face. Moreover, in doing so, she confronted the frustrations middle-class black women have had establishing successful personal relationships with black men.[19] After seven years of what friends and family perceived as the ideal marriage (they were known as the "golden couple"), Leanita divorced her husband, black journalist, Clarence Page. Although some friends suggested that their "golden" relationship was, in reality, far from perfect, some family members argued that the security she garnered from the relationship should take precedent over Leanita's ideal notions about happiness and love, implying that she should conform to conventional female choices. Most importantly, Leanita herself was confused by the action. She wrote to a personal friend,

I left Clarence three weeks ago. Where can I begin to tell you why. I'm still trying to sort out the reasons myself . . . I hope I find the answer. . . . No one, particularly my family, understands. What's worse, I don't either . . . Friends tell me I'm just going through the "independent woman, 7-year itch, turning 30 crazies."[20]

It took Leanita a year and a half after her announcement to finalize the divorce; a few friends confirmed that she hid the impending separation from her parents, appearing at family gatherings accompanied by her ex-husband as if they were still a couple. For Clarence Page, Leanita's request was unanticipated and he too seems to have viewed her decision as a temporary digression. In 1983 she wrote to a different friend "he wants his wife to come back, to come to her senses, to get off the manic/depressive roller coaster." Despite the breach of their divorce, Leanita and Clarence Page remained good friends. And there is no doubt that she held a certain type of love for him. In fact, she often called upon him in moments of crisis both great and small—from suicide attempts to car breakdowns. Leanita's need for support, a need not so apparent when they were married, was something she could express only after separation.

Leanita's vacillation between independence from and dependence on her ex-husband is symptomatic of what psychotherapist Janis Sanchez-Hucles believes to be patterns conditioned by black women's history of

being strong while black men have traditionally been penalized for shows of strength and assertiveness. Many black women, therefore, are unable or unwilling to ask for help or to reveal areas of weakness to their mates. Conflicts about self-esteem and identity make these relationships even more complex.[21]

Leanita appears to have extended this pattern to all aspects of her life. She was stoic in public but experienced extreme self-doubt in private. These latter moments were only briefly exposed to a few close friends. Most of Leanita's interactions occurred within the corporate structure of the newspaper, which served for her as a kind of social laboratory. As a member of the board of a conservative paper that was sometimes hostile to blacks, she was in the position of having to explain, excuse, and justify the status-quo. From her colleagues' perspective, Leanita played the corporate game well. She presented to the public the image of an attractive, intelligent woman in full control, capable, and with the whole world before her. For this "image" and her achievements by the age of 30 as the first black and second woman on the *Tribune's* editorial board, Leanita was selected by *Glamour Magazine* as one of the "USA's Top Ten Working Women for '84." There were times, however, when she wrote publicly about the conflicts she confronted as a black woman, of having "a foot in each world." Central to her concern was the disparity between her life as a middle-class black and her poor origins. She enjoyed the privileges of her new world but understood the boundaries.

Through 10 years working my way to my present position at the *Tribune,* I have resided in a 'gentrified', predominantly white, North Side lakefront liberal neighborhood where high rents are the chief social measure. In neither place have I forgotten the understood but unspoken fact of my 'difference'—my blackness.[22]

This difference created boundaries that appeared to operate in three directions: the white community, the black community, and within Leanita herself. Though she did not see herself as an assimilated black American, her decision to reside in the white world and her status as a high-ranking professional pitted her, ironically, against the black community she hoped to serve. In these sets of social relations the unspoken difference was class.

We have forsaken the revolution, we are told, we have sold out. We are Oreos, they say, black on the outside, white within. The truth is, we have not forgotten; we would not dare. We are simply fighting on different fronts and are no less war weary, and possibly more heartbroken, for we know the black and white worlds can meld, that there can be a better world.

Leanita seemed caught between the values and memories of her childhood environment and the world of privilege she entered as an adult. The incongruities made her acutely aware of her situational difference from those with whom she grew up. She had survived where they could not.

It is impossible for me to forget where I came from as long as I am prey to the jive hustler who does not hesitate to exploit my childhood friendship. I am reminded, too, when I go back to the old neighborhood in fear—and have my purse snatched—and when I sit down to a business lunch and have an old classmate wait on my table. I recall the girl I played dolls with who now rears five children on welfare, the boy from church who is in prison for murder, the pal found dead of a drug overdose in the alley where we once played tag.

Her survival, this straddling of two worlds, was not without consequence. She suffered from a "survivor's complex," a mental reminder that despite her talents and skills she could be thrust back into the same environs.

In my heart, however, there is no safe distance from the wretched past of my ancestors or the purposeless present of some of my contemporaries; I fear such a fate can reclaim me.[23]

The above passage is evidence that Leanita viewed her own progress as a capricious and individual stroke of good fortune within a system determined to maintain blacks as a subordinate group. Despite specific historical events like the Civil Rights Movement, she acknowledged that there was little real structural change. There seemed to be just enough flexibility to allow access for a few individuals but insufficient to accommodate an entire group's mobility. Leanita was caught in a field defined by two opposite poles. She expected and achieved, to some degree, access to the pole marked "white middle-class community" while being pulled and pushed by the opposite one marked "black poor community."

I am burdened daily with showing whites that blacks are people. I am, in the old vernacular, a credit to my race. I am my brother's keeper, and my sister's, though many of them have abandoned me because they think that I have abandoned them.

Yet as a member of the black middle class she stood somewhere in between the two with considerable tension deriving from the fact that both sides accepted and rejected her simultaneously.

I run a gauntlet between two worlds, and I am cursed and blessed by both. I travel, observe, and take part in both; I can also be used by both. I am a rope in a tug of war. If I am a token in my downtown office, so am I at my cousin's church tea. I assuage white guilt. I disprove black inadequacy and prove to my parents' generation that their patience was indeed a virtue.

At the personal level, these constraints and ambiguities forced a painful cognition.

I have a foot in each world, but I cannot fool myself about either. I can see the transparent deceptions of some whites and the bitter hopelessness of some blacks. I know how tenuous my grip on one way of life is, and how strangling the grip of the other way of life can be.[24]

The events surrounding the 1983 Chicago mayoral election compelled Leanita to choose sides. With the death of Richard J. Daley in 1976, the political machine he'd built had started to erode. The decision of Harold Washington, a black Congressman, to enter the Democratic Mayoral Primary in 1983 signaled a change in the political history of Chicago. Blacks saw his presence as a clear sign that they might finally gain a leader who would be responsive to their needs. As Paul Kleppner states in *Chicago Divided: The Making of a Black Mayor*, "by registering and voting in unprecedented numbers, blacks shook the standing order and permanently changed the shape of the city's politics."[25] For many whites, Harold Washington was a threat to the tiered system that had maintained blacks and other minorities in the worst housing, inadequate schools, and the lowest paying jobs. The polarization of the City and the verbal abuse that characterized the election campaigns and media coverage were a consequence of the City's history of inequality.

In this context, many blacks, including Leanita, were forced to acknowledge the ambiguity and contradiction of their position as members of the middle class. Leanita wrote an essay published July, 1983 in *The Washington Post* entitled, "How Chicago Taught Me to Hate Whites." In it she delivered a personal, scathing, angry, yet clear analysis of race relations and critiques her own position as a fence straddler. The piece was a remarkable *tour de force*. It was not just an indictment of the other side but of her own past actions.

Chicago—I'd be a liar if I did not admit to my own hellish confusion. How has a purebred moderate like me—the first black editorial writer for the *Chicago Tribune*—turned into a hate-filled spewer of invective in such little time. . . . In one day my mind has sped from the naive thought that everything would be all right in the world if people would just intermarry, to the naive thought that we should establish a black homeland where we would never have to see a white face again.

Though her cultural identity was challenged, it was also reaffirmed in the same process.

. . . I am not one of those, despite a comfortable life, who have forgotten my origins. It is just that I had not been so rudely reminded of them in so long.

Leanita's reawakening from the illusion of acceptance to the shocking reality of her tenuous status in the sphere of middle-class life produced a crescent anger.

. . . I brought the madness from the streets into work with me. I dissected why some people had cultivated my friendship, why I was so quick to offer it unconditionally, straining as hard as they to prove a point—to say, see how easy it is if we all just smile and pretend?

The sense of inclusion was suddenly stripped away as Leanita deconstructed the precarious interracial loyalties of the class she had embraced.

I had put so much effort into belonging, and the whites in my professional and social circles had put so much effort into making me feel as if I belonged, that we all deceived ourselves. There is always joking about "it"—those matching of suntans against black skin, or the exchange of dialect or finding common ground on the evils of racism. But none of us had ever dealt with the deeper inhibitions, myths, and misperceptions that this society has force-fed us. The issue is there, no matter the social strata.[26]

Her own ambivalence combined with that shown her by both black and white communities; the result was that she had a foot in neither world. Without any support base, Leanita was vulnerable to the threats of physical violence and emotional harassment that accompanied the release of this essay. The *Tribune* received letters demanding her dismissal. Radio commentaries questioned her emotional state. The Chicago City Council passed a formal resolution demanding she apologize to the City. Paradoxically, as Leanita became more focused about who she was and where her alliances should be, she simultaneously acknowledged her own alienation from either community.

. . . Bitter am I? That is mild. This affair has cemented my journalist's acquired cynicism, robbing me of most of my innate black hope for true integration. It has made me sparkle as I reveled in the comradeship of blackness. It has banished me to nightmarish bouts of sullenness. It has put a face on the evil that no one wants to acknowledge is within them. *It has made me mistrust people, white and black. This battle has made me hate. And that hate does not discriminate.* (emphasis added)

Leanita was cautious about returning to her normal routines. She had been irreversibly changed by the racism that had emerged during the election. She could no longer claim innocence.

I have resumed lunching with some of the white colleagues I avoided for weeks, though the conversation will stay forever circumscribed. Some have fallen away, failures of my litmus test. New ones have been found. But no white will ever be trusted so readily again with the innermost me. It is difficult to have the same confidence in my judgment about whites that I used to have. It is difficult to say "friend."[27]

Almost as defense, Leanita constructed her own boundaries, delimiting the arena in which social intercourse between herself and whites would occur. In doing so she revealed a true consciousness, but one that was essentially contradictory.[28] Leanita concluded her editorial with what was both a plea to be released from the unbearable constraints that structured her social reality and what can also be read as a declaration of resistance.

. . . So here I am, blacker than I've ever been. But above all, human—a condition I share with everyone of every hue. I feel. I mistrust. I cry. And now I know that I can hate.[29]

The sentiments and emotions displayed in this, her last extended journalistic essay, demonstrate Leanita's understanding of the tensions between privilege and oppression in her own experience. What is most significant is that Leanita gained access to a public forum (a daily newspaper) and used it to expose and voice the anger and frustration felt by her and many others. Leanita's very presence at the *Chicago Tribune* was a contradiction. Yet her position there and the experiences that emerged as a result, pushed her toward a certain level of clarity. In her last editorial and in her suicide we see the culmination of a personal quest to articulate publicly the incongruities in herself and in society—even in the face of hostile and personal criticisms. In Leanita's life, we come to see how the personal and the political were intertwined and how individuals manipulate their social realities in order to contest the various domains that structure their oppression.

THE AMBIGUITY OF DEATH

It is from this particular viewpoint that I wish to offer one possible explanation of Leanita's suicide, fully cognizant of A. Alvarez's caveat that "no single theory will untangle an act as ambiguous and with such complex motives as suicide."[30] Yet it is precisely suicide's ambiguity coupled with

Leanita's deliberate and methodical execution of it that makes her death emblematic. Juxtaposed against her multiple identities as a board member of one of the most powerful newspapers in Chicago and the Midwest, a positive role model for the black community, and a professional with a career destined to propel her to national prominence, suicide becomes one more jarring contradiction in the vortex of her life.

In early April of 1984, after the furor had subsided over the election of Chicago's first black mayor (and her editorial), Leanita McClain began a personal pilgrimage. The trek took her from Chicago to San Francisco. She renewed old acquaintances and left behind a failing relationship with her lover as well as a nine-room house that seemed to consume her energy and money. For a while she put away the tranquilizers meant to help her sleep and established an equilibrium in what had become frequent emotional mood swings. She once scrawled on a torn piece of paper:

> I measure out my life in pills, Dalmane, Valium, Elavil
> Come and share in my delusion
> Revel in this mass confusion
> How has my life come to this?[31]

While in San Francisco, she momentarily discarded the numerous role identities that reflected the multiple, and sometimes conflicting, demands of her life. Leanita worked as a stagehand on a friend's play, and in a complete reversal of roles, was able to give comfort to an old journalism friend whose house had collapsed in the spring mudslides and who was now hospitalized. Toward the end of April and the beginning of May, she made phone calls to old teachers and long unseen friends to say hello, to chat about her career, and to reminisce. These brief moments of accord were her way of touching base, her way to recapture the joy of a past ruptured by the pain of the present. This pilgrimage was Leanita's way of saying goodbye.

One month after she completed this journey, Leanita McClain settled her affairs. Unlike the two or three previous attempts to take her life, she did not cry out to friends for help. For almost a year she had misled her doctor in an attempt to stockpile enough pills for an overdose. And so, with artistry and precision, Leanita McClain gathered together all the poems, essays, and stories she'd written since the age of seven in a scraggly red notebook prefaced by a typeset cover sheet stating "death notice page." In a peculiar, yet characteristic, attempt to record the world as she perceived it, Leanita wrote her parents' obituaries. Barbara Streisand, a long-time melancholic favorite played on the record player. On the nightstand beside her bed was a pencil sketch of Leanita at eight years old drawn by her eldest sister Leatrice. And on May 29, 1984, with great deliberateness, Leanita McClain cordoned herself from the world. She had written about the prospect of death since the age of twelve and pondered its impact throughout her life. Like her poetry, it was "an act . . . prepared within the silence of the heart, as is a great work of art."[32]

I choose to read Leanita's death not only as an act of self-criticism and anger, but also as her final attempt to exercise control over some aspect of her existence. By interpreting her action in this manner, we acknowledge that "suicide is, after all, the result of a choice. However impulsive the action and confused the motives, at the moment when a [woman] finally decides to take [her] own life [she] achieves a certain temporary clarity."[33] Yet, it is not Leanita's individual personality that I see as responsible for her demise, but rather a confluence of many factors—racism, sexism, conflicting class values, depression, failed personal relationships, and eroding support systems. These, coupled with Leanita's fragile sensibility and her vulnerability as an intellectually astute, politically insightful, aspiring black woman who was partly an innocent, configured in the development of despair so acute and hopelessness so great that she felt life was not worth living. And in choosing to act, she acquired, for perhaps the first time, some measure of control over her life.[34] One example of her attempt to exercise such control can be found in the contents of the six suicide notes she left;[35] it was as if Leanita wished to instruct us in the interpretation of her life. In a message entitled "Generic Suicide Note" she wrote:

Have you ever lived in a 9-room prison constructed of your own hopes?
It is not recommended.
Happiness is a private club that will not let me enter.
As my dreams will never come true, I choose to have them in perpetual sleep.[36]

In these lines, Leanita transformed the house, traditionally symbolic of security and love, into a jail. Her last line codified the severe disjuncture between her hopes and the reality of the world in which she lived. At the same time, it was also an affirmation of her effort to exercise control over some realm of her life. By characterizing suicide as sleep, she evoked a feeling of peace, security, and resolution. Thus, she seemed to exercise some personal control over what she experienced as an intolerable situation.

Leanita's private papers are filled with poems in which she anticipated her death and left messages that cautioned the reader against accepting easy explanations of her complex life. In one poem she wrote:

I should like to die in winter
When my blood upon the snow
Will leave a clue to those who pass
Of my brief, futile life.

The garnet stain like a Rorschaht [sic] test
Will lead each to his conclusion.
"Too much, too soon," one will say.
"Too little, too late," will say another.

And none will learn the truth of the matter.
My secret will melt with the snow.
But the spot will run red each winter hence.
Though I be rotted below.[37]

THE DIFFICULT MIRACLE OF BEING A BLACK WOMAN

I have taken Leanita's life and writings, and tried to interpret them in a way that is meaningful to her particular situation but which also places her within history.[38] Some may disagree over whether I have accurately discerned the "truth" of Leanita's life. To them I can only respond that in the dialogic process there is no single truth, but rather many voices, each telling only what they know.[39] Leanita's life extended "across the social class spectrum" and enables researchers and audiences to see "important distinctions" in the range of experiences that constitute black women's lives.[40] It is not so important that Leanita is not the typical black woman. What is central is that through her we can see the range of possibilities available to her and her access to resources and power. Her life story renders visible the forces that constrain individual potential and ultimately structure the way black women may live their lives in a variety of circumstances. We come to see the subtle and conflicting ways social categories interact to create domains of privilege and of oppression. Through Leanita's writings, we gain an appreciation of how incongruities form as individuals juggle identities of race, class, and gender. I believe that certain types of contradictions can enhance an individual's consciousness and broaden her understanding of her relationship to social structures. This is not the only way that individuals come to recognize and understand the conditions that shape and constrain their lives, but it is certainly the way in which Leanita's consciousness of self developed. By attending to her writing, her life, and the larger context, we can expand the analysis of the subjectivity of black women.

Leanita's life history exemplifies that certain kinds of contradictions are not only unjust at the social level but also may be unendurable at the personal level. Yet, the analysis of her life demonstrates that as these very forces give rise to anger and self-consciousness—of the kind seen in both her journalism and poetry—they also can become sources of creativity, achievement, and self-awareness. Unfortunately, for Leanita the constraints imposed on her by both her professional and private life appeared insurmountable. All of these, most likely, were major factors in this black woman's decision to commit suicide at the age of thirty-two on May 29, 1984. In response to the tragedy, one journalist wrote, "It is rare for a black woman to ascend to the professional heights that McClain attained . . . Understandably, then, the loss of [her] influence, power, and her ability to be a role model is perceived by some blacks as a group loss."[41] Truly this is an understatement. Leanita's loss is significant because she recognized and was able to write about the contradictions that formed her personal reality. In the text of her life, or at least in our interpretation of that text, the suicide resides as yet another discordant, incongruous facet of the complex social reality which each individual faces. Moreover, her writing demonstrates how she is caught in a discursive field defined by race, class, and gender that link her to the lives of other women in the United States and the world. If we are to develop more valuable tools for feminist research in particular, and social science research in general, our analysis must attend to how contradictions emerge and the subjective way in which they are experienced. This is one path by which we may travel toward greater understanding of the nature and intricacies of social inequalities as they are constructed, reproduced, and experienced.

NOTES

I am indebted to the Dabney, McClain, and Mowatt families for their support and permission to use Leanita's unpublished and private papers. I also wish to thank Dena Hurst Simmons, Clarence Page, Monroe Anderson, the teachers at Lucy Flower Vocational High School, and the many, many friends and colleagues of Leanita whom I cannot all name; they aided me through interviews, personal remembrances, and allowed me access to Leanita McClain's private papers. Some of the ethnographic data was collected under a 1985 University of Massachusetts at Amherst Faculty Research Grant. My gratitude to my mother, Bennie Wilson, and Yvonne McDowell Baham for their assistance, support, and friendship during the data collection. I especially wish to thank my editors Dr. Faye Ginsburg and Dr. Anna Tsing, the latter especially for her encouragement, critical comments, and continuing faith in me as a scholar. As well, I wish to acknowledge and thank my husband, Professor Ernest Allen, who shared with me his valuable research and insights on Afro-American identity and applied his editorial skills toward the shaping of this essay. Drs. Sylvia H. Forman, David Lewis, Betsy Oakes and Helan Page provided me with useful suggestions and comments on earlier drafts. A thank you is also in order to the Public Relations department of the Chicago Tribune which secured for me a complete set of Leanita's editorials, certain photographs, and pertinent clip files. This essay was completed under the support of a National Science Foundation (NSF) Minority Predoctoral Graduate Fellowship. However, any conclusions, opinions, or findings contained in this essay are completely my own and do not necessarily reflect the views of the NSF or other individuals and agencies mentioned.

The title of this work and some of the ethnographic data are taken from Incongruities: A Biography of Leanita McClain by Irma McClaurin-Allen (work-in-progress).

1. Patricia Hill Collins, "Learning From the Outsider Within: The Sociological Significance of Black Feminist Thought," Reprint from *Social Problems* 33, no. 6 (1986):S15.

2. Sandra Harding, *The Question of Feminism in Science* (Ithaca: Cornell University Press, 1986), 18. Harding provides a thoughtful and indepth discussion of "fractured identities."

3. Teresa de Lauretis, *Feminist Studies/Cultural Studies* (Bloomington: Indiana University Press, 1986), 9.

4. Bonnie Thornton Dill, "The Dialectics of Black Womanhood," in *Feminism & Methodology,* ed. Sandra Harding (Bloomington: Indiana University Press, 1987), 106.

5. James Clifford, "Introduction," in *Writing Culture,* eds. Clifford and Marcus (Berkeley: University of California Press, 1986), 15.

6. Leanita McClain Papers (undated).

7. Mike Royko, *Boss: Richard J. Daley of Chicago* (New York: Signet, 1971), 134.

8. Paul Kleppner, *Chicago Divided: The Making of a Black Mayor* (DeKalb: Northern Illinois University Press, 1985), 76.

9. Leanita McClain, "More of a home to me now . . . ," *Chicago Tribune,* 24 May 1981. Please note that in citing Leanita's editorials and essays in the body of this work, I have used the original publications date so that the reader may observe the chronological progression of her thoughts and feelings on issues. However, unless specifically stated otherwise, these works are available in full in Leanita McClain, *A Foot in Each World,* ed. Clarence Page (Evanston: Northwestern University Press, 1986).

10. Kevin Klose, "A Tormented Black Rising Star, Dead By Her Own Hand," *Washington Post,* 5 August 1984.

11. Quoted in Nancy Schulte, "Who, What, When, Where, Why of Race Relations at Chicago's Major Dailies; More Black Reporters in Newsrooms, But Editorial Influence Blurred," *The Chicago Reporter* 5, no. 9 (September 1976).

12. Leanita McClain, "The middle-class black's burden," *Newsweek* (October 13, 1980).

13. Leanita McClain. Interview with Cassiette Angela West. Chicago, Illinois, 23 April 1984, 1–15.

14. Mary Moore [pseud.]. Interview with author. San Francisco, California, 5 July 1985.

15. Ibid.

16. Mrs. Elizabeth McClain. Interview with author. Chicago, Illinois, 28 March 1985.

17. Leanita McClain, "Gender's impact on elections," *Chicago Tribune,* 12 January 1983.

18. Leanita McClain, "Militancy and black women," *Chicago Tribune,* 23 April 1983.

19. In a paper titled "Psychotherapy with Black Women: Strategies for Insight, Support and Change," Janis V. Sanchez-Hucles makes some useful observations about the difficulties black women must transcend. She writes, "Black women face double binds in setting and evaluating goals for work and achievement. If they strive for success and fail, is it because of their lack of ability, or racism or sexism? If they strive for success and achieve, is it because of their efforts and skills or affirmative action? If they are successful in their work, will it mean a better life or will it minimize their opportunities for marriage and a family? Another aspect of Sanchez-Hucles' argument is that "a central conflict for black women in male-female relationships is resolving independence-dependence issues." (See citation 21 below; 1–6.)

20. McClain to Hurst, October 1982.

21. Janis V. Sanchez-Hucles, "Psychotherapy with Black Women: Strategies for Insight, Support and Change," paper at the Annual Convention of the American Psychological Association, Los Angeles, 4 August 1985.

22. Leanita McClain, *Washington Post,* 23 July 1983.

23. McClain, *Newsweek.*

24. Ibid.

25. Kleppner, 135.

26. McClain, *Washington Post.*

27. Ibid.

28. I am grateful to Dr. Helan Page for her comments on this essay and for pointing out this aspect of Leanita's identity to me.

29. McClain, *Washington Post.*

30. A. Alvarez, *The Savage God: A Study of Suicide* (London: Weidenfeld and Nicolson, 1971), xii.

31. Leanita McClain Papers (undated).

32. Albert Camus, *The Myth of Sisyphus and Other Essays* (New York: Alfred A. Knopf, 1958), 4.

33. Alvarez, 75. I would also like to argue that such clarity symbolized the last year of Leanita's life. That as she not only saw but, reluctantly, acknowledged the world as it truly exists she became as Alvarez describes in *The Savage God* one of those "who take their own lives not in order to die but to escape confusion, to clear their head. They deliberately use suicide to create an unencumbered reality for themselves or to break through the patterns of obsession and necessity which they have unwittingly imposed on their lives." 114. I propose, as well, that the patterns of obsession or rather the contradictions Leanita faced were both internal and external. Thus I adhere to the hypothesis attributed to Emile Durkheim's research that "certain environments may (a) induce or (b) perpetuate or (c) aggravate suicide-potential." See Emile Durkheim, *Suicide* (New York: The Free Press, 1951), 26.

34. Alvarez suggests that "there may be some people who kill themselves like this: in order to achieve a calm and control they never find in life." Alvarez, 113.

35. Laura Washington and Cassiette A. West. "Gallant Voice for Justice Loses Battle Against Despair," *The Chicago Reporter* 13, no. 8 (August 1984).

36. McClain, *A Foot in Each World,* 5.

37. Leanita McClain Papers (undated). Also reprinted in McClain, *A Foot In Each World,* 5.

38. The title of this section is inspired by June Jordan's essay "The Difficult Miracle of Black Poetry in America or Something Like a Sonnet for Phillis Wheatley" in *On Call: Political Essays* (Boston: South End Press, 1985), 87.

39. See Clifford, 8 and 25.

40. Dill, 104.

41. Bebe Moore Campbell, "To Be Black, Gifted, and Alone," *Savvy* (December 1984): 68.

Notes on the Contributors

JOYCE CANAAN is writing a book based on her doctoral dissertation from which this paper comes. She received her Ph.D. in anthropology from the University of Chicago in 1990. She is teaching sociology at Liverpool University, has been an ethnographer on a research project on youth and the arts, and has co-authored the book *Common Culture* (Open University Press, 1990), with Paul Willis and others, based on research from this project.

SUZANNE C. CAROTHERS is Associate Professor of Elementary Education at The City College of The City University of New York. As Adult Literacy Program Director in the Office of the Mayor of New York, she coordinated the New York City Adult Literacy Initiative. She co-authored "Contrasting Sexual Harassment in Female and Male Dominated Occupations" in *My Troubles Are Going to Have Trouble With Me: Everyday Trials and Triumphs of Women Workers* (Rutgers University Press, 1984).

M. PATRICIA FERNÁNDEZ KELLY is a Research Scientist with The Johns Hopkins University Institute for Policy Studies and Associate Professor of Sociology at the same institution. She is author of *For We Are Sold: Women and Industry in Mexico's Frontier* (SUNY Press, 1983) and co-editor with June Nash of *Women, Men, and the International Division of Labor* (SUNY Press, 1983). With Lorraine Gray she co-produced the Emmy winning documentary "The Global Assembly Line," which focuses on the effects of economic internationalization on women in the U.S., the Philippines, and Mexico.

SUSAN ELIZABETH GERARD is a graduate student in sociology at the University of California at Davis. Her principal interests are feminist theory and sociology of gender. She has done research on temporary word processors and is currently designing a study of women, obesity, and appearance.

FAYE GINSBURG is an Assistant Professor of Anthropology in the Department of Anthropology at New York University, where she also directs the Graduate Program in Ethnographic Film and Video. She is author of

Contested Lives: The Abortion Debate in An American Community (University of California Press, 1989), and is currently writing on the impact of Operation Rescue on abortion politics.

SUSAN HARDING is Professor of Anthropology at the University of California, Santa Cruz. This essay is part of a larger project on narrative and politics in the Reverend Jerry Falwell's fundamentalist Baptist community in Lynchburg, Virginia.

ELLEN LEWIN has focused her research on motherhood since the early 1970s when she wrote her doctoral dissertation on maternal strategies among Latina immigrants in San Francisco. She has taught anthropology and women's studies at a number of universities, including UC San Francisco, Old Dominion University, and, currently, UC Berkeley. She is the co-editor of *Women, Health, and Healing: Toward a New Perspective* and is at work on a book on lesbian mothers.

EMILY MARTIN is Mary Garett Professor of Anthropology at The Johns Hopkins University. She is author of *The Cult of the Dead in a Chinese Village* (Stanford University Press, 1973), *Chinese Ritual and Politics* (Cambridge University Press, 1981), and *The Woman in the Body: A Cultural Analysis of Reproduction* (Beacon Press, 1987). She is currently working on a study of the cultural construction of the immune system.

IRMA MCCLAURIN-ALLEN is an Assistant Dean in the College of Arts and Sciences, an adjunct lecturer in Women's Studies, and a Ph.D. candidate in Anthropology at the University of Massachusetts at Amherst. Her writing has appeared in over 16 magazines and anthologies. Her latest works include *Pearl's Song* (Lotus Press, 1988) and an essay in *Black Writers Redefine the Struggle: A Tribute to James Baldwin* (University of Massachusetts Press, forthcoming).

SANDRA MORGEN is Assistant Professor of Women's Studies at the University of Massachusetts, Amherst. Her recent publications include *Women and the Politics of Empowerment*, edited with Ann Bookman (Temple University Press, 1988) and *Gender and Anthropology: Critical Reviews for Research and Teaching* (American Anthropological Association, 1989). She is currently writing a book on the women's health movement.

RIV-ELLEN PRELL is an anthropologist who is an Associate Professor in the American Studies Program at the University of Minnesota. She is author of *Prayer and Community: the Havurah in American Judaism* (Wayne State University Press, 1989) and a member of the Personal Narratives Group which edited *Interpreting Women's Lives: Theories of Per-*

sonal Narratives (Indiana University Press, 1989). She has also written about gender and Judaism in America and Europe.

RAYNA RAPP chairs the Department of Anthropology, New School for Social Research, helps to edit *Feminist Studies,* and has been active in the reproductive rights movement and the development of women's studies for twenty years. She is currently writing a book on the social impact and cultural meaning of prenatal diagnosis.

CYNTHIA SALTZMAN is writing a book on women and unions at Yale. She is also a post-doctoral fellow in Judaic Studies at Yale, beginning re-search on feminism and Judaism. She has been a Visiting Assistant Professor at Barnard College, Columbia University, and a Visiting Fellow at the In-stitute for Social and Policy Studies, Yale University. She received her Ph.D. in anthropology from Columbia University in January 1988.

JUDITH STACEY teaches sociology and women's studies at the Uni-versity of California, Davis. She is author of *Brave New Families: Stories of Domestic Upheaval in Late Twentieth-Century America* (Basic Books, 1990), *Patriarchy and Socialist Revolution in China* (University of California Press, 1983), and of various essays on feminist theory and politics.

CAROL STACK, Professor of Women's Studies and Education at the University of California, Berkeley, is author of *All Our Kin: Strategies for Survival in a Black Community* (Harper and Row, 1974) and *Holding on to the Land and the Lord: Essays on Kinship, Ritual, Land Tenure, and Social Policy,* edited with Robert L. Hall (University of Georgia Press, 1982). She is author of many articles on gender, family, and child policy and on race, culture, and consciousness in urban and rural communities. She is currently completing *The Call to Home: African Americans Reclaim the Rural South,* a book on the migration of urban Black families to rural homeplaces.

KATHLEEN STEWART is an Assistant Professor of Anthropology at the University of Texas at Austin. Her book, *Re-membering 'Appalachia': Narrative Poetics and Other Cultural Politics from An(Other) America* is forthcoming. She is currently working on a book on popular culture and nuclear politics in Las Vegas to trace polemical discourses of science, gov-ernment, country, and society as the Department of Energy attempts to site the first national nuclear waste repository at the Nevada Test Site.

SHARON THOMPSON is co-editor, with Ann Snitow and Christine Stansell, of *Powers of Desire: The Politics of Sexuality* (Monthly Review Press, 1983). Her articles and stories have appeared widely in feminist and other periodicals and anthologies. She is currently finishing a book on teen-age girls' narratives about sex, romance, and pregnancy (Pantheon, forth-coming), and she is a member of the Fiction Advisory Board of the *Village Voice Literary Supplement.*

ANNA LOWENHAUPT TSING teaches anthropology at the University of California, Santa Cruz, and is writing a book on gender, marginality, and state rule in the Meratus Mountains of Indonesia.

CAROLE S. VANCE, an anthropologist at the Columbia University School of Public Health, writes about sexuality, the body, and public policy. She edited *Pleasure and Danger: Exploring Female Sexuality* (Routledge & Kegan Paul, 1984), contributed to *Caught Looking: Feminism, Pornography, and Censorship* (Caught Looking Inc., 1986), and co-edited the special issue of the *Journal of Sex Research* 27, no. 1 (1990), "Feminist Perspectives on Sexuality." She has been active in many feminist groups, including the American Anthropological Association's Committee on the Status of Women, which she chaired.

KATH WESTON is an anthropologist who teaches at Arizona State University West. She is author of *Families We Choose: Lesbians, Gays, and Kinship* (Columbia University Press, forthcoming) and co-author of "Sexuality, Class, and Conflict in a Lesbian Workplace," in Estelle Freedman et al., *The Lesbian Issue: Essays from SIGNS* (University of Chicago Press, 1985).